PRODUIT DE FRANCE

Condrieu

APPELLATION CONDRIEU CONTRÔLÉE

Viognier

L. GURGAT

75 cl

Élevé et mis en bouteille

GRANDE CUVÉE
CHAMPAGNE

KRUG

REIMS

BRUT

PRODUCT OF FRANCE

75 cl e

BAXEVANS, JOHN   01/06/89
WINES OF CHAMPAGNE,\RN FRANCE
(5) 1987 WL 663.200944
1004 03 764086 01 4   (IC=2)

B100403764086014B

PRODUIT

Romanorum Villa in

CHATEAU DES ROQUES

MOULIN A VENT

Appellation Moulin à Vent contrôlée

MISE AU CHATEAU

Société Civile d'Exploitation de Romanèche-Thorins
Viticulteurs - Récoltants 71570 La Chapelle de Guinchay

Vaudien

F-DU-PAPE   75 cl

DU-PAPE CONTRÔLÉE

taire à F 84190

Propriétaire à Châteauneuf-du-Pape

LA RO

APPELLATION LA

RÉCOLTE

DE LA S.C.I. DU CHA

PROPRIÉTÉ DE LA FAMILL

ÉLEVÉ ET MIS EN B

BOUCHAR

NÉGOCIANT AU CHATEAU

PRODUI

VIN D'ALSACE

APPELLATION ALSACE CONTRÔLÉE

White Wine

ALSACE WILLM®

GEWURZTRAMINER   700 ml

ALSACE WILLM S.A. / BARR – FRANCE

PRODUIT DE FRANCE   PRODUCE OF FRANCE

Sonoma County

Wine Library

THE WINES OF CHAMPAGNE, BURGUNDY, EASTERN AND SOUTHERN FRANCE

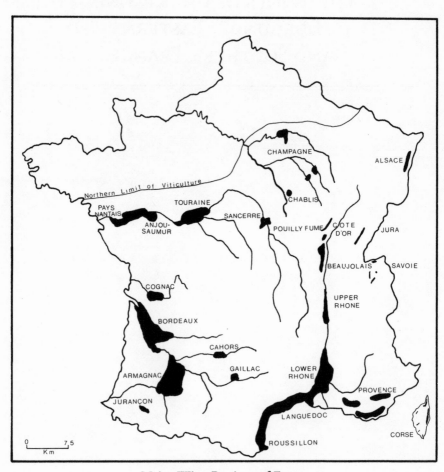

Major Wine Regions of France

THE WINES OF CHAMPAGNE, BURGUNDY, EASTERN AND SOUTHERN FRANCE

JOHN J. BAXEVANIS

ROWMAN & LITTLEFIELD
PUBLISHERS

ROWMAN & LITTLEFIELD

Published in the United States of America in 1987
by Rowman & Littlefield, Publishers
(a division of Littlefield, Adams & Company)
81 Adams Drive, Totowa, New Jersey 07512

Copyright © 1987 by Rowman & Littlefield

Library of Congress Cataloging-in-Publication Data

Baxevanis, John J.
   The wines of Champagne, Burgundy, eastern and southern France.

   Companion vol. to the author's The wines of Bordeaux
and western France.
   Includes index.
   1. Wine and wine making—France.   I. Title.
TP553.B35   1987   641.2'22'0944   87-13172
            ISBN 0-8476-7534-3

87   89   91   90   88
   1   3   5   4   2

Printed in the United States of America

TO DEAN

CONTENTS

ILLUSTRATIONS

Figures

Unless otherwise noted, illustrations were supplied by the domaines.

FOREWORD

THIS is the accompanying volume to *The Wines of Bordeaux and Western France*, inspired by the little known but highly insightful book, *A Wine Tour of France*, by Frederick S. Wildman, Jr. It is intended to familiarize and guide both the casual and experienced enophile through the labyrinth of French wines, describe each major AOC wine region, accent its more prominent features, and identify the more important producers.

This book surveys the viticultural regions of northern, eastern, and southern France and briefly outlines the main historical, economic, and geographic characteristics of one of the country's major agricultural activities. The seven major and three minor vineyards encompass 24 departments and collectively represent 632,100 hectares, or 64 percent of the national wine vine hectarage. Even more significant, the producing regions contain 57 percent of all national AOC, 91 percent of all VDQS, and 77 percent of all *vin de pays* hectarage. In addition, the various regions produce all the nation's Vin Doux Naturel and 80 percent of all rosé wines.

I should like to express my gratitude to the following persons, properties, cooperatives, and governmental offices who, over the years, have assisted my research for reliable documentation. I wish to thank the Office International de la Vigne et du Vin, the ministries of Agriculture and Commerce, l'Institut National Interprofessionnel des Vins de Table, Jerome Agostini of l'Institut National des Appellations d'Origine des Vins et Eaux-deVie, and La Direction de la Consommation et de la Repression des Fraudes, all in Paris for valuable statistical assistance.

I would like to express my appreciation to Charles Philipponat of Moët & Chandon, Roland de Calonne of Ruinart Père, Veuve Clicquot Ponsardin, Laurence de Billy of Pol Roger, and Remi Krug of Krug in Champagne. For pertinent information concerning Alsace and the Jura, I would like to extend my appreciation to R. T. Muré of Clos St.-Landelin, Dne. Zind-Humbrecht, Cave Vinicole Eguisheim, Hugel et Fils, Dne. Schlumberger, Dne. Klipfel, Pierre de Boissieu of Ch. Gréa, Michel Varigas of Henri Maire, and Christian Bourdy of Caves Jean Bourdy. Regarding Burgundy, I would like to acknowledge the assistance of K.

N. Ingleton of Dne. René Monnier, Pierre André of Chateau de Corton-André, Lycée Agricole et Viticole de Beaune, Claude Bouchard of Bouchard Père, P.-H. Gagey of Louis Jadot, Prince Florent de Mérode of Dne. de Serrigny, and Leguin-Roussot. In the Rhône, Provence and the Midi, I would like to take the opportunity to thank Max Chapoutier, Paul Jaboulet Ainé, Ch. du Vergel, Delas Frères, E. Guigal, Dne. Tempier, Moulin des Costes, Dne. Meyzonnier, Producteurs de Blanquette de limoux, Jean Pierre Ormières of Ch. Fabas, Ch. St.-Estéve, Dne. de la Renjarde, Ch. de Gourgazaud, and Domaines Viticoles des Salins du Midi.

I would like to take this opportunity to thank, in this country, Thierry Laloux, Commercial Attache of the French Embassy (Washington, D.C.), Alice Lubecon of Food & Wines of France, and Irving Kogen of the Champagne News Bureau, both in New York City. Special thanks for kind words and encouragement to professor Harm de Blij of Miami University and the National Geographic Society, Prof. Russell Emele for his company on numerous "wine expeditions," and to the East Stroudsburg University Research and Out-Service Training Fund. A special acknowledgment of gratitude to Mrs. B. Ash for her insightful comments, and the warmest of sincere thanks to Mrs. Cecile Daviduke for her ability to make sense of the French language; to Prof. Ian Ackroyd-Kelly for his sagacity, patience, and graphic skills; and to my wife, Magda, who endured more than I care to remember when "I was in the office". Finally, I wish to acknowledge the assistance and advice of Mr. Martyn Hitchcock, the proficient editing of Mrs. Janet Johnston, and the support and patience of Mr. Paul Lee, senior editor, all of Rowman & Littlefield.

THE WINES OF CHAMPAGNE, BURGUNDY, EASTERN AND SOUTHERN FRANCE

The Vineyards of Eastern and Southern France

WINE GRAPES PLANTED BY DEPARTMENT IN EASTERN
AND SOUTHERN FRANCE, IN HECTARES, 1979*

Department	Hectarage	Department	Hectarage
1 Aisne	1,532	17 Vaucluse	43,835
2 Aube	3,515	18 Haute-Corse	19,833
3 Marne	19,319	19 Corse du Sud	3,498
4 Bas-Rhin	4,577	20 Alpes-Maritimes	215
5 Haut-Rhin	7,176	21 Alpes-de-Haute-Provence	835
6 Jura	1,470	22 Var	41,496
7 Ain	815	23 Bouches-du-Rhône	17,742
8 Haute-Savoie	3,100	24 Gard	82,349
9 Isère	895	25 Hérault	143,011
10 Savoie	1,395	26 Aude	115,169
11 Yonne	2,583	27 Pryrenées-Orientales	55,835
12 Côte d'Or	8,038		
13 Saône-et-Loire	9,661	Total: Eastern and Southern France	636,230
14 Rhône	19,844		
15 Ardèche	12,966	Total: France	998,715
16 Drôme	15,526		

*Does not include wine grapes destined for distillation.

THE WINES OF CHAMPAGNE

CHAMPAGNE, the most famous sparkling wine region in the world, is a 27,000-hectare vineyard producing more than one million hectoliters of wine, nearly all of it white. Although it encompasses less than 3 percent of the entire French vineyard and produces a similar percentage of wine, its output represents more than 6 percent and 10 percent of all AOC wine in terms of production and value, respectively. It is one of the few wines with instant appeal and international awareness. In the entire country, Champagne is the largest producer of AOC sparkling wine made by the Champagne method; in 1984, Champagne's 84 percent of total production was followed by Blanquette de Limoux (5 percent), and Clairette de Die (3 percent) (Table 1.2).

The producing region encompasses five departments, of which Marne, with 75 percent of the total hectarage, is considered the most important.

Table 1.1   AOC Wine Production in Champagne, 1980

Appellation	Hectoliters	Percent of total
Champagne Rosé	2,417	.3
Champagne Blanc	848,137	99.7
Coteaux Champenois Rouge and Rosé	58	
Coteaux Champenois Blanc	111	
Rosé de Riceys	58	
Total Rouge and Rosé	2,533	.3
Total Blanc	848,248	99.7
Grand total	850,781	100.0

Source: French Ministry of Agriculture.

Table 1.2   AOC Sparkling Wine Production, 1984

Appellation	Hectoliters	Percent of total
Champagne Rouge	10,292	.6
Champagne Blanc	1,479,398	84.0
Blanquette de Limoux Blanc	80,447	5.0
Clairette de Die Blanc	52,605	3.0
Saumur Mousseux Rouge	1,511	negligible
Saumur Mousseux Blanc	41,455	2.4
Vouvray Mousseux Blanc	29,113	1.7
Crémant d'Alsace Rouge	916	negligible
Crémant d'Alsace Blanc	26,316	1.5
Bourgogne Mousseux Rouge	*	
Bourgogne Mousseux Blanc	*	
Crémant de Bourgogne Rouge	2,202	negligible
Crémant de Bourgogne Blanc	18,581	1.1
Crémant de Loir Rouge	288	negligible
Crémant de Loire Blanc	11,764	.7
Seyssel Mousseux Blanc	719	negligible
St.-Péray Blanc	1,000	negligible
Montlouis Mousseux Blanc	3,316	negligible
Bordeaux Mousseux Rouge	109	negligible
Bordeaux Mousseux Blanc	415	negligible
Total	1,760,447	100.0

*Asterisk indicates none reported in 1984.

Source: French Ministry of Agriculture.

Fifteen percent of the hectarage is in the Aube and 9 percent in Aisne, and the remaining 1 percent is shared by the departments of Seine-et-Marne and Haute Marne. Within the appellation boundaries, there are 157 vinegrowing communities in the department of Marne, 63 in the Aube, 27 in the Aisne, and 10 in Seine-et-Marne.

The Champagne region, located 70 kilometers northeast of Paris, forms an arc that gently curves southeast from the Ardennes forest on the Belgian border to the northeast border of Chablis. Lying between Picardy and the Paris Basin on the west and Lorraine on the east, it is roughly the same size as the state of Maryland. A widely diffuse region that lacks geographical unity, the northern portion is relatively flat and is the origin of the region's name, from the Latin *campus*, which means "plain." Although the highest elevation within the producing region of Reims and Epernay is but 280 meters above sea level, it contains numerous microclimates and topographic irregularities. In general, however, Champagne is divided into three distinct geographic regions: *Champagne Pouilleuse* ("Dry Champagne") is a wide, undulating chalk plain with little tree vegetation; *Champagne Humide* ("Wet Champagne") is a narrow curtain of clay-dominated country along the western portions of the district; and *Champagne Viticole Classique*, a raised section of chalk, is considered the finest in the production of quality wine. The Marne, Aube, and Aisne rivers flow through the region, one of the country's most affluent vinegrowing districts.

Of all the major quality-wine–producing regions of France, Champagne, the northernmost in latitude, has the lowest average annual temperature, the least number of degree-days above 10°C, the least number of sunshine hours from April to September, and the smallest amount of rainfall during the months of April through September. Because of the prevailing westerly winds, winters are quite mild and relatively humid. The area experiences significant snow accumulation, often interspersed with bouts of cold, clear weather. Although autumn is mild and relatively sunny, it is often cold enough to prevent proper berry maturation and, hence, the production of low sugar levels. Summers are warm and almost never hot. Autumn and spring, the two shortest seasons, are unpredictable, with the latter season the more precarious to the vigneron. March can be foggy, which interferes with the flowering, but the greatest danger is frost, with "black frosts" occurring every seven years, on the average. The most recent, in 1983, locally referred to as *gel du siècle* (the "frost of the century"), reduced production in the valley of the Marne by 51 percent, in the Montagne de Reims by 70 percent, and in the department of the Aube by 82 percent. Since the mean annual temperature of Champagne is 10°C, the culture of the vine is marginal at best, hence the production of white wine that necessitates appreciable amounts of chaptalization. To offset the unfavorable elements of latitude and low average temperatures, vineyards are located in highly circumscribed microclimates and soil locations.

Champagne soils are unique in that they contain a distinctive soft chalk. This material is a remnant of a former geologic sea whose abundant shellfish built up a remarkably thick layer of carbonate. Nowhere else on earth do we find such a high concentration of belemnite (an extinct cephalopod) fossils. The chalky soil, extending for 100 meters below the surface, is covered with a thin mantle of *limon* (a wind-blown material), retains water, stores solar radiation well, and is exceptionally friable. The iron-deficient chalk also induces chlorosis (a disease brought about by too much calcium), which is counterbalanced by the addition of *cendrés noirs*, a form of lignite that is rich in iron and other minerals.

History

Although there is evidence to support the thesis that wine was made in Champagne prior to the first century A.D., the Romans who arrived in A.D. 57, first actively pursued the cultivation of the vine. Following the fall of Rome, the viticultural fortunes of Champagne fell into the able hands of the Frankish king Clovis and the Merovingians, who did much to further the cause of viticulture by providing political tranquillity and economic prosperity. Viticulture continued to prosper under the Carolingians, who encouraged monastic orders to settle in the region. Ten Benedictine monasteries, several Cistercian, and the Knights Templars established vineyards in the Ludes and Epernay area during the crusading period. The most important of all religious endeavors was Hautvillers, where the legendary Dom Pérignon presumably first made white wine from black grapes, invented the bottle cork, blended together grapes and wines from different vineyards to create a homogeneous cuvée, and used sugar to induce a second fermentation. There is no denying the importance of the church in the viticultural history of the region: Saint Reims, the first archbishop of Reims in 530, bequeathed vineyards in his will; and for a thousand years during the medieval period in France, the church cultivated and extended the planted area. Pope Leo X owned a vineyard in Champagne, as did kings and princes. The fortunes of the church grew as the economic life of the region progressed, so that on the eve of the French Revolution, nearly half of the vineland of Champagne was owned by the church.

During the later Middle Ages, Champagne was one of the wealthiest and most powerful fiefs after a series of successful counts incorporated the region with the royal domain in 1314. During this time, Champagne became preeminent for its elaborate and important fairs, particularly in textiles. Its excellent transportation connections to all areas in northern France, its prosperous market position, and its significant wheat cultiva-

Plate 1.1 The Abbey of Hautvillers. Here the Rev. Dom Perignon, cellarer of the monastery, established the rules governing the making of champagne that is known as the *méthode champenoise*. The abbey is the property of Moët & Chandon.

tion assured the area's important strategic position. Reims became the place for most coronations; because of its proximity to Paris, the wines of Champagne became favorites.

In the 17th century, the wines of Champagne were popularized by Louis XIV and the "Order of the Coteaux," an exclusive club of discerning Champagne fanciers who drank nothing but Champagne and were instrumental in introducing the wine to England. It is important to note that although winemaking has had a long history, the production of sparkling wine dates only back to Dom Pérignon in the last quarter of the 17th century. The wine of that time, mostly red, rosé and "gris," bore no resemblance to contemporary libations, and only a small portion of total production was sparkling. Historical accounts reveal that in 1715, no more than 20,000 bottles of Champagne were made, and in 1789, only 400,000. It is clear, therefore, that production is the product of industrial growth, disposable income, and fashion, and not the product of ecclesiastical and medieval monarchial technology. With the rise of industrial Europe, primarily the United Kingdom, the Low Countries, Germany, and Switzerland, the production of Champagne grew from 6.6 million bottles in 1844 to 17 million in 1870, and to 27 million by 1900.

The post-revolutionary period in France was highlighted by a number of interesting developments, the first of which was the establishment of the large "houses." Of the twenty-five largest, eighteen were established between the years 1808 and 1868. In 1821 there were fifteen major houses in Reims, ten in Epernay, five in Avize, four in Ay-Mareuil, four in Cramant, Oger and Le Mesnil, and two in Chalons. Second, at least a quarter of the Grande Marques (large export-oriented firms) were houses founded by Germans, the most notable of which were Mumm, Piper, Roederer, Taittinger, Bollinger, Deutz, Geldermann, Kunkelmann, Delbeck, Heidseick, and Krug. Because Germany was the world's second-largest producer of sparkling wine and the principal importer of Champagne, it is not difficult to understand German interest in Champagne. Third, the *oïdium* and *phylloxera* epidemics had only a slight impact on production. Despite the fact that half of the original plantings were destroyed by the *phylloxera* aphid, replanting efforts kept pace with the destruction of vinifera vines. Thus, hectarage in the Marne declined only slightly from a high of 18,500 hectares in 1879, to 14,200 in 1884. Fourth, the "Belle Epoque" (1890–1914) is generally considered the golden age of Champagne, as it was a time of significant economic growth, continuous economic prosperity, exploding urban growth, and wildly extravagant social behavior. It was the time for fashion, elegance, exquisite cuisine, impressionism, and romanticism. During this time, the automobile came of age, aviation was born, and Champagne was *de rigueur* at all smart social functions. It became the socially preferred wine of royalty and industrial barons and the most popular wine on transatlantic cruise ships. The legendary Cora Pearl bathed in it (so did Marilyn

Monroe two generations later), and King Edward VII drank it from ballet slippers. It is the one wine that epitomizes abundance and luxury. One gourmand once said, "Champagne invented conspicuous consumption."

The frenzied growth of Champagne, like all commodities, came to an end early in the 20th century. Because the producing region was unable to meet demand, a number of scandals erupted that involved the fraudulent use of the name Champagne. The first major scandal in Munich in 1883 involved forged Deutz & Geldermann, and Veuve Clicquot-Ponsardin Champagne labels. Although a syndicate was formed in 1884 to protect the name and reputation of Champagne, the fraudulent use of non-Champagne wine as authentic Champagne continued until it reached crisis proportions during the period 1905–1911. The market, flooded with Champagne imitations from practically every viticultural area of France, precipitated a crash, and prices declined to such low levels that civil disorder arose. When the government was unable to stop the production and sale of fraudulent Champagne, the notorious Champagne riots erupted in 1910–1911, resulting in the destruction of shippers' facilities, wine, and vineyards. Eventually, this and other similar events led to the enactment of national appellation legislation—but not before hectarage in the department of Marne dropped from 15,000 to 4,500 between 1905 and 1910. Hectarage and production continued below "Belle Epoque" levels until the post–World War II period.

More recently, production has risen dramatically from an average of 50 million bottles in the 1950s to 219 million in 1970, and to 302 million in 1983. Equally important to the sudden and emphatic jump in production is the increase in hectarage. Between 1960 and 1980, the productive area almost doubled, from 11,900 to 23,900 hectares, and the number of bottles tripled. As production barely kept pace with demand, pressures began to build to further increase hectarage during the decade of the 1980s by 5,000 hectares, a large percentage growth for a conservative viticultural region. Because potential vineland was expected to increase 50-fold in price once official authorization was granted, small growers, cooperatives, and other people owning land in the expansion areas formed a formidable pressure group. As a consequence, land prices per hectare have risen to $125,000 for vineland rated approximately 85 percent, and much higher for plots rated above that level. The Grande Marques, an equally formidable pressure group, maintain that any expansion of the planted area will mean a decline in wine quality. They contend that since 1945 Champagne has witnessed a monumental augmentation that has gone far enough, and that during the past 40 years, sales have increased 641 percent. Nevertheless, the Comité Interprofessionel du Vin de Champagne authorized the expansion of 5,000 hectares, with the possibility for additional plantings in the 1990s. As of this writing, close to 27,000 hectares are currently planted, out of the 34,000 hectares that are officially delimited but as yet not approved for production. Large houses, who own about 20 percent of all vineland, will not be allocated "new" hectarage, and priority will be given to those growers owning less than 2.5 hectares. Although all areas are expected to receive some portion of the expanded total hectarage, the main beneficiary region is the Aube and the lower Marne valley near Château Thiery. The rationale for the expansion is not hard to find: increased international and domestic demand, which by 1995 is expected to exceed 400 million bottles.

The Producing Regions

The first delineation of the Champagne vineyard in 1908 included only the departments of Marne and Aisne. In 1911, the producing area was expanded to include portions of the departments of Aube, Seine-et-Marne and Haute Marne as secondary zones. This latter status created such a furor that in 1927 it was eliminated, and today the Champagne vineyard consists of four major districts:

1. Montagne de Reims. This is a small 300-meter plateau that is completely covered by thick forest and encircled by vineyards, almost all of which face north, northeast, and east. The most important communes in the production of quality wine are Ambonnay, Bouzy, Louvois, Beaumont-sur-Vesle, Mailly, Sillery, Verzenay, Tauxières, and Verzy. Other important villages include Ludes, Chigny-les-Roses, Trépail, Vaudemanges, Rilly-la-Montagne, Villers-Allerand, and Villers-Marmery. All the above lie south of Reims, except for a small producing region that is located north of the Vesle River, northwest of the city. Southwest of Reims is "la Petite Montagne," a secondary zone in which the commune of Ville Dommange enjoys a good reputation. Because vineyards in both areas face north and east, they are susceptible to frost, hence the area is known for the cultivation of black grapes and the production of full-bodied, vigorous, firm, and flavorful wines.

2. Vallée de la Marne. The Marne valley is the south-facing portion of the Montagne de Reims that stretches from Vincelles to Mareuil-sur-Ay along both banks of the Marne River. The principal communes, all located in the eastern portion (and north bank) of the river valley, include Ay, Dizy, Mareuil-sur-Ay, and the slightly lesser growths of Mutigny, Avenay, Bisseuil, Champillon, Hautvillers, and Cumières. Although black grapes still dominate, Chardonnay hectarage has been increasing, and the wines, although fresh, clean, and fragrant, are less vinous and firm than those of the Montagne de Reims region.

3. Côte de Blancs is a narrow, north-south stretch of vineyards that lies in a ribbon from Cuis to Vertus. The slope, sheltered by forest on the west, faces east and southeast, and the gray-yellow soils favor the Chardonnay that produces the finest Blanc de Blancs wines. The principal communes are Cramant, Mesnil-sur-Oger (said to make the fullest Chardonnay), Avize, Cuis, Oger, and Vertus.

4. Aube, located southeast of the main producing vineyards, refers to a discontinuous arc of vineyards between the Aube and Seine rivers. This

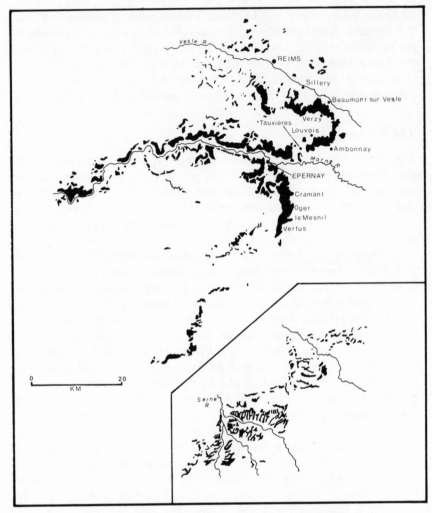

Figure 1.1   The Vineyards of Champagne
(insert: productive vine hectarage in the Aube)

small but rapidly expanding area contains no first-class vineyards due to the high incidence of frost and the presence of Kimmeridgian limestone.

Champagne vine hectarage is officially divided into four quality categories by commune: Grand Cru, Premier Cru, Deuxième Cru, and Troisième Cru. Every plot containing vines is classified, and each grower is paid proportional to its category, with 100 percent of the contracted price going to Grand Cru growths, all thirteen of which are located in the Montagne de Reims, Vallée de la Marne, and Côte de Blancs. Premier Cru vineyards are rated between 90 and 99 percent, and Deuxième and Troisième Cru hectarage, most of which is located in the peripheral areas of the three main quality regions and the Aube, is rated between 77 and 89 percent of the contracted price.

The most important elements determining grape quality are the nature of the chalky subsoil, aspect, exposure, and altitude above the valley floor. The finest sites are nearly all located on loose, gravelly surface material, preferably with *limon* accumulations. The soil must also be dry and have a well-fractured, chalky subsoil. Southerly to southeasterly in aspect, Grand Cru sites are located between 150 and 200 meters above the valley floor to take full advantage of air currents and avoid temperature inversions. Finally, it is desirable to have an open exposure with thick forest occupying upslope positions. All of the preceding indicate that: (a) the Champagne vineyard is not homogeneous, but rather a patchwork of highly fragmented microclimates; (b) a good portion of the Montagne de Reims is more prone to frost, and its grapes ripen at least one week later than those of the Côte de Blancs; (c) the Marne enjoys higher-than-normal temperatures and is a good heat trap; and (d) the Côte de Blancs is well protected, has warm soils, and an excellent aspect.

The official classification of Grand and Premier Cru vineyards is as follows:

1. *Montagne de Reims*

Beaumont-sur-Vesle		Tours-sur-Marne	100% black grapes
	100% black grapes	Verzy	99% black grapes
Mailly	100% black grapes	Trépail	95% white grapes
Puisieux	100% black grapes	Villers-Marmery	95% white grapes
Sillery	100% black grapes	Chigny-les-Roses	94% black grapes
Verzenay	100% black grapes	Ludes	94% black grapes
Ambonnay	100% black grapes	Montbré	94% black grapes
Bouzy	100% black grapes	Rilly-la-Montagne	94% black grapes
Louvois	100% black grapes	Villers-Allerand	90% white grapes
Tauxières	100% black grapes	Tours-sur-Marne	90% white grapes

2. *Vallée de la Marne*

Ay	100% black grapes	Champillon	93% black grapes
Mareuil-sur-Ay	100% black grapes	Mutigny	93% black grapes
Dizy	95% black grapes	Cumières	90% black grapes
Avenay	93% black grapes	Hautvillers	90% black grapes
Bisseuil	93% black grapes		

3. *Côte des Blancs*

Cramant	100% white grapes	Grauves	95% white grapes
Avize	100% white grapes	Vertus	95% black grapes
Le Mesnil-sur-Oger		Bergères-les-Vertus	
	99% white grapes		95% white grapes
Oger	99% white grapes	Bergères-les-Vertus	
Oiry	99% white grapes		90% black grapes
Cuis	95% black grapes	Grauves	90% black grapes

4. *Others*

Chouilly	95% white grapes	Pierry	90% black grapes
Chouilly	95% black grapes		

The Grapes and Wines of Champagne

Champagne is produced from only three grape varieties: Chardonnay, Pinot Noir, and Pinot Meunier. Several other varieties contribute about 5 percent of the regional hectarage, although they are officially used not for the production of AOC Champagne but for local consumption. They include Pinot Blanc Vrai, an obscure grape variety that, while having a neutral aroma, tends to be somewhat higher in alcohol and has more body than Chardonnay; Arbanne, a very fragrant grape that ripens early and covered as much as 10 percent of the total planted area as recently as 1935; and Petit Meslier, the most widely planted grape variety after the *phylloxera* epidemic. This vine is difficult to grow, however, has low yields, matures late, and has a tart flavor. Producing firm, highly alcoholic wines it grows mainly in the Aube and Epernay regions. The Gamay à Jus Blanc, covering fewer than 50 hectares, is mainly cultivated for local consumption.

Among the three principal "Champagne" grapes, Pinot Meunier, with 44 percent of the planted area, is the most widely planted. The Pinot Meunier is an inferior relative of Pinot Noir but easier to cultivate. Hardier than both Pinot Noir and Chardonnay, it grows in less desirable areas and produces a wine with a muted bouquet and higher acid levels. While it is more rustic and less elegant and refined than the other two, it seems to blend well, ages faster, and has a lower flavor intensity than either Chardonnay or Pinot Noir. Whether growers want to admit it or not, it forms, except for prestige and special cuvée bottles, the *cépage de base* for all except Blanc de Blancs Champagne.

The second most-important black grape variety is Pinot Noir, known locally as Pineau and Franc Pineau. It constitutes about 24 percent of the total planted area, a figure that has steadily fallen as the demand for lighter, fresher, less assertive wine has become more fashionable. Planted mainly in the Montagne de Reims, Pinot Noir is the dominant grape in the production of old-fashioned, full-bodied, flavorful wines intended for long keeping. It imparts strength, fullness, vinosity, body, tannin, and depth of flavor. For vintage wine intended for long cellaring, Pinot Noir maintains the longest flavor intensity, Chardonnay the lowest, with Pinot Meunier in a middle position. For length and intensity of aftertaste, there is no substitute for Pinot Noir.

Chardonnay, increasing in importance, occupies approximately 31 percent of the planted area. Imparting freshness, elegance, lightness, delicacy, aroma, and acidity to all blends, it is the basis for all Blanc de Blancs wine. Historically, Chardonnay was known as the "Fromenteau" because its bright gold-colored berry resembled wheat. Although it is currently the "in" grape, more than 90 clones have been identified in the region, and its quality differs markedly throughout the producing area. As it is more predictable in its yield and sugar production, it has become the preferred grape of the small vigneron who wishes to minimize the risk of reduced income due to vintage variability. Equally important is the fact that because it is more delicate in flavor and aroma, it is ideally suited to the American market, which has become the largest importer in recent years.

Recently, two specific concerns have been brought before the public: the high density of the vines per hectare, and increased harvest yields per hectare. The average vine density (10,000 plants per hectare) is the highest in France and has increased slightly in recent years. Concerned voices maintain that root competition dwarfs the vines and makes them prematurely old, thus diluting the quality of the must. Equally significant is that over the past 20 years, yields have tripled from 5,000 kilos to the hectare in 1960 to 15,000 kilos to the hectare in 1984, the latter figure representing the second-highest AOC yield in the country.

More than 97 percent of all wine is white, sparkling, and made in four basic quality levels: non-vintage, vintage, luxury or prestige, and tête de cuvée (special bottlings to commemorate a special event). Most Champagne is a non-vintage wine made by blending the wine of two or more vintages to produce a consistent house style that varies as little as possible from year to year. It is for most large firms the staple wine and, in some instances, the basis for the accumulation of a significant fortune. The object of a producer is to make consistent wine of a uniform quality that does not reflect the ups and downs of individual vintage years. It should be noted that each Champagne house produces its own style of wine by varying grape varieties, fermentation, and aging characteristics to suit its stated objectives. Therefore, some produce darker, fuller, more tannin-rich wines, while others prefer lighter, more delicate, and fresher styles.

The color of good Champagne should range from pale straw to light gold. Vintage wine is usually darker, and in both cases the color deepens with age. The mousse should be light, delicate, small in size, abundant, and persistent; the bouquet should be fresh, clean, and multilayered; the flavor should be vinous, pleasant, and distinctive in both fruit and yeast; the aftertaste should be long and lingering, and under no circumstances should it be overly sour, flat, stale, have a weak carbonation, and lack bouquet. Non-vintage Champagne, normally aged for only one year, matures fully in the bottle between the second and third years, and usually deteriorates by the fourth.

Vintage Champagne is made from grapes harvested of a given year, and because the wine is not back-blended, it tends to be more distinctive, ages better, is more expensive, and should be a better bottle than blended, non-vintage wine. Vintage Champagne is a peculiar combination of

Table 1.3 How Champagne Is Made: Méthode Champenoise

Harvest lasts from two to three weeks. Grapes are selected and sorted in the vineyard and placed in large wicker baskets called "mannequins." About 1.5 kilos of grapes produce a bottle of Champagne.

Pressing is done in a wide, shallow press to prevent skins from staining the juice (white Champagne is made predominantly from black grapes). By law, 4,000 kilos of grapes may produce a maximum of 2,666 liters of wine. Three pressings are made: (a) the "cuvée" contains 2,050 liters of must, (b) the "première taille" contains 410 liters, and (c) the "deuxième taille" contains 205 liters. The finest houses use only cuvée as the sole or dominant element in luxury and vintage wines.

First fermentation occurs in wooden casks or in stainless steel and produces a dry, still wine. It is stored and blended into a cuvée (blend), usually in the spring following the vintage. From 10 to 30 cuvées may be created. For the finest bottles, "reserve wine" (the best cuvées of former vintages) may be added to form a style unique to the producer.

Second fermentation: The wine, bottled with yeast and sugar (*liqueur de tirage*) undergoes a long, slow fermentation. The yeast culture converts the sugar into alcohol and carbonic gas, the bubbles in the wine. The carbonic gas is dissolved and the wine is now legally "Champagne." The lower the temperature and the longer the fermentation, the finer the carbonation. Non-vintage wine ages for one year; vintage wine ages for three years.

Remuage: During fermentation, dead yeast cells collect on the sides of the bottle. The bottle is racked neck downward and given a one-eighth turn daily by the "remuers," who gradually (over two to three months) raise the bottle to vertical so the sediment slides down into the neck. This "riddling" process is done automatically in all but the more prestigious and traditional firms.

Dégorgement: The bottle is frozen in a brine solution. The temporary seal is broken, and the frozen pellet containing the sediment deposit is removed. The *liqueur de dosage*, or liqueur d'expedition (cane sugar and wine) is added to produce the desired degree of dryness or sweetness.

Labeling occurs after aging from three months to several years is completed. Unlike other wines, Champagne is ready for drinking when it is purchased.

The high cost of champagne is caused by the complicated, labor-intensive and capital-intensive process, the cost of promotion, expensive bottles and corks, the high cost of the grapes, and the cost of maintaining stocks for an average of three years. Stock inventory is directly related to the size of the harvest and the demand schedule for the wine.

harvest conditions and house style, hence its distinctiveness and appeal. The proportion of grapes, for example, will vary with the character of the vintage, both of which will determine the course of vinification, blending, and the amount of aging given to the wine. Moreover, there is no formula as to what constitutes a vintage year; in addition to a host of subjective judgments, it is not merely a question of ripe or unripe grapes, but stock availability, prices, and market conditions. In general, vintage Champagne is usually aged for a minimum of three years in the bottle and is (or should be) fuller and more complex, with a more pronounced yeasty flavor and bouquet, than a non-vintage wine. It usually matures within five or ten years depending on the vintage and the house style. Only a few bottles continue to improve after fifteen, and only a precious few after twenty years. Old Champagne is very fragile and sensitive to poor storage

Table 1.4   The Language of Champagne

Blanc de Blancs: made entirely from Chardonnay grapes. The style is usually lighter and more delicate than Pinot-dominated wines.

Blanc de Noirs: a white wine made entirely from Pinot grapes. This style is usually fuller and more robust on the palate.

Crémant: a wine having about half the pressure (three instead of six atmospheres) of regular Champagne.

Tête de Cuvée: a champagne from a superior blend of rare, costly wines that sells between three and five times the price of regular vintage wine.

Late disgorged: a wine with a pronounced flavor due to prolonged contact with dead yeast cells.

Au Naturel: a term indentical to "Brut Sauvage" or "Brut Zero," all meaning natural, with no dosage added. The wine is absolutely dry and tart.

Brut: a "dry" Champagne whose usual percentage of sugar varies between .5 and 1.5 percent.

Extra Dry: contains between 1.5 and 2.5 percent sugar.

Sec: slightly sweet; contains between 2 and 4 percent sugar.

Demi-Sec: sweet; contains between 4 and 6 percent sugar.

Doux: very sweet; contains more than 6 percent sugar. The six expressions listed above vary from house to house, are not completely standardized, and are subject to contemporary tastes. In western Europe and Anglo-America, the prevailing fashion is for Brut Champagne, while Latin America, overseas French possessions, and African nations demand sweeter wines.

and handling conditions. Vintage Champagne usually sells at a 25 percent premium (sometimes more) over non-vintage and may, or may not, offer value over its more humble stable mate.

Prestige or luxury cuvées are wines designed for those who prefer greater luxuries than simple vintage wines. These cuvées are usually non-vintage blends of superior (meaning older) cuvēes, but are not necessarily better than vintage wine. It is a rare instance when their quality is proportional to their asking price (usually they are twice the cost of good vintage), and they hardly ever offer good value. "Super deluxe" bottlings (to commemorate special events) are placed on the market only at infrequent intervals and in limited quantities. The most expensive of all Champagne, they are usually offered in special, very fancy bottles and eye-appealing, expensive boxes. It is important to note that the exotic wines do not sell quickly, and therefore may be too old or even damaged by improper handling and storage. If such wine is purchased, it should be bought only from retailers with a high turnover who specialize in such wine.

Crémant is a mousseux with about half the carbonation of conventional Champagne. Historically less expensive than regular Champagne, it was considered a lesser wine, but during the last twenty years it has experienced a resurgence in popularity. As of 1975, the term "Crémant" (creamy) has been redefined to include only those wines made by the Champagne method and reserved only for those wines subject to appellation status. The best Crémant is the refreshing "Crémant de Cramant," named for the commune of Cramant in the Côte de Blancs.

Rosé Champagne is usually the most expensive in every style category. Its output, which depends upon the prevailing fashion of the times, varies between 1 and 5 percent of total Champagne production. Although rosé ("pink") Champagne originated in the second half of the 19th century, its popularity swings radically with each generation. It was the rage during the "Belle Epoque," but did not sell well during the 1930–1975 period. Judged by rising sales figures over the past ten years, however, it appears to be gaining in popularity once again. In 1975, in New York at least, it would have been difficult to find more than a mere handful of rosé Champagne on retailers' shelves. Today, one can easily find a dozen or more vintage rosé with prices ranging from a modest $20 for the most humble up to $100 for a deluxe version. Imports to the United States have risen from 48,000 bottles in 1981 to 185,000 bottles in 1984, a figure that represents approximately 2 percent of all imported Champagne.

Although it has frequently been promoted for women, rosé Champagne has rougher edges, is longer lived, and has more tannin, body, and flavor than white Champagne. It is also expected to exhibit more fruit, more acid, and more fragrance, but unfortunately it rarely does. The style varies enormously from house to house: from dark pink to a faint salmon color, from full-bodied to light, and from a fruity aroma and yeasty bouquet to none at all. The mystique of "pink" Champagne is manipulated by the trade to stimulate sales and interest. Rosé Champagne, usually advertised heavily during the month of February because of Valentine's Day, is usually known as the wine of lovers, a "naughty" and

---

Table 1.5 CHAMPAGNE VINTAGES

1985	Small harvest provided a good vintage, with only small amounts of vintage-quality wine.
1984	Non-vintage quality. Late flowering, wet September, and considerable rot produced low alcohol levels. 196 million bottles.
1983	Vintage quality although not considered above average; a number of houses have decided not to produce any. 300 million bottles.
1982	Vintage quality with higher-than-normal alcohol levels. 295 million bottles.
1981	Vintage quality limited by a small harvest. 76 million bottles.
1980	Non-vintage. 91 million bottles.
1979	Vintage quality. 181 million bottles.
1978	Vintage quality, but a small harvest limited supply to 68 million bottles.
1977	Non-vintage; small harvest.
1976	Vintage quality excellent; early picking produced rich, ripe grapes.
1975	Vintage quality excellent; classic, full-bodied, well-flavored wines.

"party" wine, and the pink color is usually associated with decadence, frivolity, and the "good times."

There are three ways to make rosé Champagne. The first is by leaving red-skinned grapes in contact with the must to stain the juice; the second, by adding a little red still wine to white Champagne; and third, by adding red still wine with the dosage. It is interesting to note that the first two methods are equally good: prevailing opinion, at least by the major houses, is that each one, if done correctly, will give satisfactory results. A related but critical issue deals with the preferred or ideal grape variety (or varieties) used. Some large houses use 100 percent Pinot Noir, others blend with Pinot Meunier, while still others vary these two with Chardonnay. The problem is that the wine's true color and overall character will not be known until some bottle-aging has occurred. Both methods, simple in principle, are somewhat technical and require considerable skill in order to achieve the desired results, which are clarity and consistency. Above-average rosé, therefore, is difficult to make, and significantly more expensive than white Champagne, the best of which is produced by Bollinger, Deutz, Krug, Taittinger, Moët & Chandon, Gosset, Laurent-Perrier, Paul Roger, Veuve Clicquot-Ponsardin, Pommery, Billecart-Salmon, Secondé-Prévoteau, Alfred Gratien, Oudinot, Piper-Heidsieck, and Ruinart.

The still red, rosé, and white wines of Champagne until 1952 were known as *vin ordinaire*, later as *vin nature de la Champagne*; as of 1974, the name was changed again to *Coteaux Champenois*. Production varies drastically each year because still wine can be made only from the overproduction of grapes after satisfying Champagne requirements. Since 1950, production of all types has fluctuated from fewer than 300,000 bottles to more than 4.2 million. The Coteaux Champenois Blanc is a full, robust wine that, although good and unusual, is always overpriced. The best Coteaux Champenois Rouge comes from the commune of Bouzy, and although technically sound, it too lacks value. The best rosé comes from the Aube and has its own appellation—Rosé des Riceys, a charming wine from the village of the same name.

Structure of the Industry

Of the 17,000 growers in 1980, approximately 52 percent owned less than 1 hectare, 38 percent owned between 1 and 7 hectares, and 10 percent owned more than 8 hectares. Yet, despite the high degree of fragmentation, the number of individuals who made wine commercially grew from 2,458 in 1970 to more than 5,000 in 1984.

Champagne is marketed by four types of licensed firms: négociant-manipulant, récoltant-manipulant, coopérative-manipulant, and marque d'acheteur. By far the most important group, the négociant-manipulants (120 in number) produce and sell Champagne, and vary significantly in size, type of operation, and reputation. For example, some, but not all, own vineyards, lease vineland, and have long-term contracts with vignerons for grapes, must, or wine. Practically all make a complete line consisting of non-vintage, vintage, rosé, prestige, and super deluxe quality wines. Close to thirty large, medium, and small firms dominate exports and the production of quality wine, especially prestige labels. Over the past 100 years, these firms have heavily promoted the wine and its region as no other group has, thus becoming the backbone of the industry in terms of production and the development of overseas markets. Since 1960, their share of total Champagne production has declined from 75 percent to slightly less than 50 percent, and although they still dominate the lucrative overseas market, they are competing feverishly for available grapes. Since they carry a significant inventory and maintain the largest cellars, they are heavily capitalized.

Récoltant-manipulants are small growers who grow grapes, make and sell still wine to the large négociants, and also Champagne under their own labels. From a historical point of view, they are a new breed of Champagne maker running a cottage industry. They cultivate grapes, then ferment, age, bottle, and sell directly from their doorsteps, and personally load the wine into the car of the client who drives to the winery. This is very chic, and the savings, should the wine be of comparable Grande Marque quality, are sizable since there are no elaborate promotional expenses. The amount of récoltant-manipulant–produced Champagne has increased from 10 percent of total production in 1955, to 15 percent in 1970, to 25 percent in 1985, and there is every indication that it will continue to rise in the near future. Récoltant-manipulants supply the domestic market, principally Paris, and the ever-present tourist from any of the neighboring countries, but because of few overseas commercial contacts, little brand recognition, and limited quantities, exports by individual houses are limited. Lacking large quantities of blending stock, the recoltant-manipulant is also restricted in his ability to regulate quality from year to year. In 1984, récoltants sold 56 million bottles in France but exported only 3 million.

Coopérative-manipulants, like récoltants, are major suppliers of grape must and wine to négociant houses. The number of cooperatives grew from zero in the early 1930s to 122 in 1981, with 10,800 members controlling 11,000 hectares of vineland. Of the 122 cooperatives, 108 are nothing more than cooperative press houses and primary fermenters. Although only 14 make Champagne, they produce nearly one-third of all wine sold, usually bulk. Recently, cooperatives have grouped together into unions, selling wine to négociant houses, bottling more wine under their own label, and establishing overseas markets.

A marque d'acheteur is a firm that buys récoltant and coopérative Champagne and sells it under its own label. Commonly referred to as BOB, or "buyers own brand," the label is usually peculiar to a particular chain of retail outlets in specific markets. BOB wine is more common than one realizes and a formidable element in the distribution of Champagne.

Exports

Responsible for 10 percent of the volume and 16 percent of the value of all wine exports, Champagne plays an important role in the nation's wine industry. Until 1955 when the domestic market became larger than the foreign, Champagne was the premier luxury wine whose sales were directly related to international economic conditions. In recent years, however, exports have fluctuated between 30 percent and 45 percent of total production. It is estimated that the ten largest négociant firms are responsible for more than 75 percent of all exports.

From an international perspective, Champagne accounts for approximately 12 percent to 15 percent of the world's sparkling wine production, a figure that has declined as other countries have increased their output in recent years. Germany now produces close to 300 million bottles of Sekt; Italy has increased production from 50 million to 165 million bottles over the past twenty years; Spain increased production from less than 30 million bottles in 1955 to 124 million in 1985; and the U.S.S.R., during the past twenty-five years, has increased sparkling wine production from 70 million to 204 million bottles. Less dramatic in growth and output are Australia, with 41 million bottles, and the United States, with 106 million bottles. Needless to say, France is beginning to experience serious competition in the international arena, particularly from Spain. It is also important to note that the price gap between Champagne and domestic sparkling wine has widened, as new technologies produce a large number of less expensive alternatives to traditional Champagne.

Although Champagne began to be exported in 1820, significant quantities have crossed international boundaries only recently. Exports grew from 13 million bottles in 1950 to 19 million bottles in 1968, 30 million in 1974, 55 million in 1980, and 63 million bottles in 1984. More Champagne was shipped to the United States in 1984 than in any other previous year. Shipments amounted to 12.8 million bottles, a 32 percent rise over 1983. This is the largest quantity ever shipped to the United States, and the largest amount of Champagne ever shipped to any foreign market. The United Kingdom, historically the largest export market, is now second, Germany third, Belgium forth, and Italy fifth. The overseas market, however, changes continuously. In 1980, Italy was the largest importing country with 8.6 million bottles, followed by the United Kingdom, the United States, Belgium, West Germany, Switzerland, and Venezuela. In 1973, the United Kingdom was the largest importing country with 10.9 million bottles, but in 1974, it imported only 4.6 million bottles. Because Champagne is an expensive, nonessential commodity, its import is strongly tied to the economically affluent areas of central and northern Europe, the United States, fashionable international resort regions, and major international capitals.

The Geographic Production of Champagne

While Champagne is made in at least forty different settlements throughout the producing region, Reims, Epernay, Ay, Avize, and Chalons-sur-Marne are collectively responsible for more than 90 percent of total output. Of the five major areas of production, the single most-important site is Reims. A very affluent city and the largest (pop. 160,000) in the appellation, it has admirably managed to blend 2,000 years of history into one neat package. In addition to being the historic site of royal coronations, Reims is the center of the Champagne industry. It is home to more négociant houses than any other city, and produces more than 40 percent of all Champagne. Among the largest houses are the following:

Veuve Clicquot-Ponsardin (1772), one of the oldest, largest, and most revered of the "old guard" houses, makes a full line of wines. With 275 hectares of vineland (rated 98 percent), supplying 25 percent of requirements, it is also one of the largest property owners. Two-thirds of the grapes are Pinot Noir and one-third Chardonnay. The firm historically was known for well-knit, full-bodied wines that were capable of extended aging, but it now makes wines in a more popular style—less dry, more

Plate 1.2   Harvest at Veuve Clicquot-Ponsardin

supple and fruity. The very best are often refined, big, complex, firm, rich, very satisfying, and quite reliable. The non-vintage Brut is one of the finest values, the Rosé is superb, and the La Grande Dame, the luxury label, is absolutely marvelous. Recently it has acquired *Canard-Duchêne*, several shippers, and Givenchy perfumes. The firm exports more than 75 percent of production.

Krug (1843) is a superb, medium-sized house that makes only extraordinary luxury wines. This quality house, part of Rémy Martin, is known for full, robust, well-flavored wines. Recently the wines have been made slightly lighter and cleaner, but remain first class and well above the average for the industry. The firm ferments only in oak vats, and the must used is from the first pressing only. The wines are by no means "delicate" but are huge monsters that are dry, "yeasty," and well scented. They are

Plate 1.3   Racking wine at Krug,
one of the most traditional houses in Champagne

aged longer than usual, with the best cuvées aged longer than six years. The house makes a limited line consisting of special bottlings, Grande Cuvée, vintage, and rosé. The special bottling, Krug Clos du Mesnil, comes from grapes grown in a walled vineyard in the Côte des Blancs. Made from 100 percent-rated Chardonnay, it has a fine mousse, an exquisite and refined character, and is very expensive. The vintage wine, made with 75 percent red grapes, is a heavy, robust, "meaty" wine. Grande Cuvée, made with a small proportion of red grapes, is decidedly lighter in body, livelier, and fresher on the palate. The rosé is characterized by fullness, a grapey aroma, and persistent carbonation. The wines of *Krug* should not to be missed by the serious Champagne lover.

Taittinger (1734), one of the largest of the prestigious houses, owns 250 hectares of vineland in excellent locations, which supply about half of the firm's requirements. The house also owns Bouvet-Ladoubey, a house that specializes in Chardonnay-based Champagne. Taittinger, emphasizing suppleness, delicacy and lightness, manages to produce wines in the middle range of the sweetness spectrum and attempts to avoid wines that are overly dry and austere on the palate. *Louis Roederer* (1776) is a superb house that makes traditional, outstanding, oak-aged wines. The firm owns 180 hectares, of which 75 are located in the Côte des Blancs, 55 in the Montagne de Reims, and 50 in various locations in the Marne valley. With vineyards supplying more than 85 percent of its needs, Roederer is one of the most self-sufficient of the Grandes Marques. The house is known for Cristal, a vintaged wine with impeccable credentials that is full and smooth, with an excellent mousse and outstanding depth of flavor. All the wines are flavorful, well scented, supple and very expensive.

Ruinart Père et Fils (1729) is considered the oldest Champagne house. Its impressive cellars house a complete line of wines, most of which are known for their smoothness, fine mousse, delicate flavor, and outstanding

---

Table 1.6   The Wines of Louis Roederer, a Grande Marque

Carte Blanche: a sweet Champagne with 6 percent residual sugar, made from 66 percent Pinot Noir and 34 percent Chardonnay.

Grande Vin Sec: identical to Carte Blanche, but with 4 percent residual sugar.

Brut (non-vintage): a wine with 1.25 percent residual sugar, made from 66 percent Pinot Noir and 34 percent Chardonnay.

Brut (vintage). a wine with 1.25 percent residual sugar, made from 66 percent Pinot Noir and 34 percent Chardonnay.

Brut Blanc de Blancs: the lightest and driest of all wines made entirely from Chardonnay; contains only 60 percent of the normal amount carbon dioxide.

Brut Rosé: more full bodied than any other wine, made from 80 percent Pinot Noir and 20 percent Chardonnay. Contains a high percentage of reserve wine and is not vintaged.

Cristal Brut: with 25 percent of the firm's total output, this is a vintage wine from the best cuvées, representing the finest wine. It is full bodied yet light on the palate, fruity, elegant, and has a marvelous yeasty flavor and bouquet.

bouquet. All the wines are medium bodied, flawless, and offer good value. The firm is now part of the Moët-Hennessy group. *Besserat de Bellefon* (1843), owned by the Pernod-Ricard company, is a large, quality-oriented house that maintains an excellent reputation for rich, stylish, round, delicate, and elegant wines. The modestly priced wines offer excellent value and include, like most other négociant houses, a complete line. *Piper-Heidsieck* (1785) is a large, family owned, and technologically oriented firm with a line of wines typical of a major house. *Henriot* (1808), a large, dynamic firm, has established a reputation for modern, stylish, clean, soft, but uninspiring wines. It makes a wide assortment of BOB wines, and since its amalgamation with Rémy Martin in 1985, it concentrates on Chardonnay-based wines. The firm owns 110 hectares located in Cramant, Oger, Vize, and Vertus. *Charles Heidsieck* (1851), the larger and better firm of the two Heidsiecks, makes a more traditional, fuller, richer wine. The house makes a complete line, but the vintage wines appear to be better. *Lanson Père* (1760) is a large, dynamic, highly innovative firm that owns 226 hectares of vineland mainly in Bouzy, Ambonnay, Dizy, Cramant, Avize, and Oger. The wines, principally non-vintaged, light, and made to be consumed when released, are made for the popular-priced segment of the market. While the number of wines made staggers the imagination, the mainstay is the firm's famous vintage and non-vintage Black Label.

G. H. *Mumm* (1827), owned by Seagram, is a large, 9-million-bottle house with 220 hectares of vineland. The second-largest producer of Champagne (along with two subsidiaries—Perrier-Jouët and Heidsieck & Co. Monopole), it is one of the oldest firms with a long and varied history. It produces a full line of vintage and non-vintage wines of various shades of sweetness, the most popular being Cordon Rouge. *Pommery & Greno* (1836) is a quality-oriented house that makes a limited line of essentially creamy, light to medium-bodied dry wines that offer excellent value. Overall quality has improved markedly since 1980 when the company was purchased by a large holding company. With its impressive cellars and 300 hectares, the firm is the second-largest vineland owner in the appellation. *Heidsieck & Co. Monopole* (1785) is one of the oldest houses producing medium- to full-bodied, robust, dry, rather austere wines. This large house owns 110 hectares of vineland in Bouzy, Ambonnay, Mailly, and Verzenay. Other producers include *Abel Lepitre* (1924, part of a larger group of companies, known for light, fresh, inconsistent wines); *George Goulet* (1834, well regarded in the production of fragrant, full-bodied, firm wines); *Palmer*, (1948, a small, little-known house, making superb, distinctive, well-flavored wines); *Abele* (1757, known for fresh, lively, well-flavored wines); *Montaudun* (1919, specializing in full-bodied, crisp, yeasty, well-flavored, old-fashioned wines with a dominant Pinot Noir character); *Massé* (1853, owned by Lanson, one of the few firms marketing full-bodied, robust, dry wines only for the French market); *Marie Stuart* (1867, making a complete line of average-to-excellent-quality wines); *Bruno Paillard* (a small firm marketing above-average wines); *Jacquart* (an aggressive cooperative, making average to above-average wines).

Epernay is a small, affluent, stylish and immaculately kept city located on the northern edge of the Côte des Blancs. It contains the largest Champagne firm and no fewer than ten negociant firms, of which six rank among the finest in the entire appellation. *Moët & Chandon* (1743), part of the Chandon-Hennessy group of companies, is the largest Champagne house in the appellation. It produces at least 10 percent of all Champagne and perhaps as much as 15 percent when its subsidiaries, Mercier, Ruinart, and De Cazanove, are considered. The firm, with 850 hectares (1,133 hectares including subsidiary holdings), is the largest vineyard owner. (It also makes sparkling wine in California, Brazil, and Argentina.) With cellars exceeding 51 kilometers of tunnels, the group employs 1,664 full-time workers, stocks 94 million bottles, and accommodates more than 300,000 tourists annually.

Moët & Chandon, the leading brand in and out of France, exports between 20 percent and 25 percent of all appellation Champagne made in the region. The firm expanded rapidly when it absorbed Ruinart in 1963, acquired a 50 percent interest in Parfums Christian Dior in 1968, and Mercier in 1970. In 1971 it became the majority shareholder in Parfums Christian Dior and merged with Hennessy to form the holding company of Moët-Hennessy. In 1973, it purchased 520 hectares in the Napa Valley, in 1974 it purchased 125 hectares in Brazil, and in 1977 acquired a majority holding interest in Rozes Limitada in Portugal and France. Over the next nine years it acquired a genetic engineering firm, a biotech company, horticultural nurseries, and a large importing firm in New York City. Despite large size and recent acquisitions, it has maintained quality Champagne production and makes a complete line of wines that consistently offer value to the overseas consumer. In addition, it has recently constructed a winery in Landiras (Graves) for the production of low-alcohol wine for the "under 30 year-old market." *Pol Roger* (1849) is a small, reliable firm with an outstanding reputation for old-fashioned, classic, full-bodied, fragrant, well-structured wines that exhibit finesse and elegance. The firm owns 75 hectares, mainly in the Côtes des Blancs, which supply 40 percent of company requirements. It exports more than 60 percent of output, mainly to the United Kingdom where it has a loyal following.

De Castellane (1895) is a large, quality house that still vinifies in oak and ages its wine for an extended period of time. This is a traditional house with an emphasis on heavy, solid, well-structured wines with a bias toward red grapes. *Alfred Gratien* (1864) is a superb house that ranks among the upper tier of quality Champagne houses. The expertly made wines with a distinct Pinot Noir character, are full-bodied, rich, and delicate. Fermentation still occurs in oak, and all wines maintain an excellent reputation for consistency. *Perrier-Jouët* (1811), now part of the Mumm group of companies, is a large house that enjoys a good reputation for light to medium-bodied, fruity wines. *Ch. de Boursault*, a small house with a good reputation, makes full-bodied but delicate wines that offer good value. *A. Charbaut* (1948) is a large house in partnership with De Courcy Père. The wines are rarely seen in the United States and most foreign markets, as they are sold under a number of private labels. *Mercier*, a large house now part of Moët-Hennessy, is one of the few firms that concentrates on the French market. The wines are moderately priced, light-bodied, easy to drink, and mainly non-vintaged. Other producers include *Delahaye, Bauget-Jouette, Oudinot* (1899), *De Cazanove* (1811), *Leclerc-Briant, De Courcy, Marne & Champagne* (1934), *Giesler* (1837), *Trouillard* (1919), *De Venoge* (1837), *Boizel* (1834); *A. Desmoulins; Lang-Biemont; Nicolas Feuillate; Jules Pierlot; Sacotte; Gaston Chiquet; José Michel; Pertois-Lebrun; R. Renaudin; Louis Kremer; Pierre Gimonnet; Claude Mandois; Sugot-Feneuil; Vollereaux; R. and L. Legras;* and *P. Gobillard.*

Ay, the third most-important Champagne town, stands in the center of vine-clad hills that are reputed to have supplied Pope Leo X, as well as most French kings, with wine. The town is the site of three above-average Champagne houses and an interesting museum. *Bollinger* (1829), founded by a native of Würtemburg, owns 52 hectares of 100 percent–rated vineyards in Ay, Bouzy, Louvois, and Verzenay, as well as 32 additional hectares widely scattered in other communes. This is a first-rate house that makes classic, rich, old-fashioned wines that are full-bodied, firm, powerful, and multidimensional in terms of depth of flavor and aroma. The wines, austere, dry, dark in color and dominated by Pinot Noir in flavor, aroma, and body, are fermented in wood and receive extended aging. All wines are made with substance, depth, balance, and complexity. *Gosset* (1948) is a small, quality oriented firm that makes full-bodied, well-structured, firm yet rich wines that rank close to the upper echelon of fine Champagne. It is curious that the Gosset family, which has been in the wine business since 1584, did not make Champagne until 1948. The house is a major stockholder in Philipponnat. The Pinot Noir–dominated wines almost always offer excellent value. *Champagne Deutz* (1838), recently merged with Delas Frères, is a medium-sized house that owns 37 hectares of vineland, most of which are located in Ay. Above average in quality, the wines, emphasizing higher than normal percentages of Pinot Noir and Pinot Meunier, are known for their fullness, distinctiveness, and well-flavored character. *Ayala* (1860) is a well-known, medium-sized firm that makes fresh, stylish, fruity, and crisp vintage wines only. They are not very well known in the United States, but appear to be very popular in France and neighboring countries. In general they are less dry on the sweetness spectrum and usually offer good value. Other producers include

Edouard Brun (1898), *René Brun* (1941), *Emile Hamm* (1930), *Roland Fliniaux* (1900), *Ivernel* (1880), *Henri Goutorbe, Collery* (1895), *Gérard Autréu, Raoul Collet,* and *Robert Driant.*

In addition to the high degree of concentration of Champagne houses in Reims, Epernay, and Ay, a small number of quality houses are found in several smaller communes. One of the most important is the house of *Joseph Perrier* (1825, Chalons-sur-Marne), a small house with 20 hectares and an established reputation for full-bodied, chewy, fruity wines that offer outstanding value. All wines are impeccably made, very reliable, and age magnificently. The house of *Laurent Perrier* (1812, Tours-sur-Marne), in near-ruin after World War II, was reorganized and staged a remarkable recovery from the sale of 80,000 bottles in 1949 to more than 9 million in 1985. It is now the third-largest Champagne house and makes a number of special wines for foreign markets. All wines are expertly made, above average in quality, reliable and mainly non-vintage. The large, quality oriented house of *Canard-Duchêne* (1868, Ludes) has an established reputation for light, elegant, and fruity wines. A dynamic firm, it has increased production considerably over the past 30 years due to its production techniques and modest pricing policy. In the village of Avize, the principal Champagne houses are *Union Champagne, Bricout & Koch* (1820), *Jacques Selosse, Sanger, F. Bonville,* and *Michel Gonet.*

In the village of Mesnil-sur-Oger, the principal Champagne house is *Salon* (1914), followed by *Julien Tarin, Delamotte* (1786), *Dominique Pertois, François Gonet,* and *Launois.* Adjoining Ay to the east, the village of Mareuil-sur-Ay contains two above-average houses: *Philipponat* and *Billecart-Salmon.* The former house has a well-established reputation for a limited line of semi-dry and semi-sweet wines that are well made and exhibit a good dosé of refinement. *Billecart-Salmon* (1818), a small and little-known firm, while not in the same class as Bollinger or Krug, is above average in quality, with a fanatical following. The distinctive wines, emphasizing Pinot Noir, are rich, full-bodied, dry, zesty, fresh, and highly individualistic. Other houses include *Alexander Bonnet* (1932, Riceys), *Société de Producteurs* (1929, Mailly), *F. Bonnet* (1922, Oger), *Barancourt* (1969, Bouzy), *Jacquesson & Fils* (1798, Dizy), *H. Germain & Fils* (1898, Rilly-la-Montagne), *Duval-Leroy* (Vertus), and *Lechère* (Avize).

2

THE WINES OF ALSACE

IN a remote corner of northeastern France, between the low, rounded,
green Vosges Mountains and the Rhine River, lies Alsace. Probably
the least known of the major quality wine regions of the country, it is
situated on the western side of the Rhine *graben*, one of the most unusual
"geologic troughs" in the world. On the north it is bounded by the Saar
River, and by the Jura Mountains in the south. It is a region of wooded
upland slopes, hop fields, tobacco, dairy farms, orchards, and vineyards.

The Alsatian vineyard, encompassing a total area of 13,500 hectares,
extends almost without interruption in a long, narrow ribbon from the
western outskirts of Strassbourg in the north to Mulhouse in the south.
The producing region, rising from the edge of the Alsatian plain to
altitudes of about 425 meters, is approximately 100 kilometers in length,
but hardly more than 3 kilometers in width. The entire viticultural
expanse involves more than 400 parishes and 8,400 vinegrowing families.

Wine production since 1980 has averaged more than 800,000 hectoliters per annum, or about 2 liters for every man, woman, and child in
France. Alsace contributes about 2 percent of national wine production,
1.4 percent of vine hectarage, and 6 percent of all wine exports. While it
produces 5 percent of all AOC red and 12 percent of all AOC white wine,
close to one-quarter of all white AOC wine consumed in France originates
from this vineyard. Twenty percent of production is exported, and
viticulture in Alsace contributed one-quarter of the regional agricultural
product—a very unusual feature because, despite its international reputation for the production of quality white wines, the Alsatian economy is
overwhelmingly oriented toward tertiary and industrial pursuits, with
less than 8 percent of the total population engaged in agriculture.

There are five AOC appellations in Alsace, of which dry white table

wine dominates production with 94 percent of total output (see Table
2.1). This is followed by red and rosé, and then by the increasingly
popular Crémant d'Alsace, of which the white is most prominent. AOC
production as percent of total regional production is higher here than in
any other French vineyard. Standards are extremely high, and the
consistency of the quality is well maintained and properly balanced with
asking prices. With more than 30 different varieties (from quince to
blueberry), Alsace is also the nation's largest producer of eau-de-vie.

As a frontier region between Gaul and Teuton, Alsace is the "odd man
out" as a wine-producing region in continental France. Part French, part
German, the Alsatians are not only bilingual, but have their own "patois"
language strongly influenced by German. It is a country where wurst
becomes saucisson; sauerkraut, choucroute (there is even a "route du
choucroute"); and where white wines, named after the dominant grape,
are bone dry and highly fragrant. In comparison with the rest of the
country, the grape varieties, bottle shape, language, music, art, architecture, place names, and cuisine are distinctly more Germanic than French.

The kaleidoscope of contrasting French and German cultures has
produced (although there are some who might take exception) the most
charming, idyllic cultural landscape, as well as a bewitching and absorb-
ing viticultural scenograph. No other region of France has such a high
frequency of medieval villages, public fountains, and gabled and old half-
timbered buildings, all of which are nothing less than fairy-tale, picture-
postcard quality. It is an area of fortified churches, dozens of castles,
countless monasteries, Gothic and Renaissance architecture, unique private homes, numerous national parks, quaint medieval streets named after
grape varieties, and a population that has developed its passion for flower-
decked windows and balconies into an art form. While the obsession runs
deep throughout the region, it is most pronounced in Molsheim, Andlau,
Itterswiller, Dambach-la-Ville, Sélestat, Ebersmunster, Diebolsheim,
and Obemheim. No wonder the fastidious Hallgarten described Alsace as

Table 2.1   AOC Wine Production in Alsace, 1980

Appellation	Hectoliters	Percent of total
Alsace Blanc	557,268	93.0
Alsace Rouge and Rosé	26,931	4.5
Crémant d'Alsace Blanc	14,478	2.4
Crémant d'Alsace Rosé	627	.1
Total Rouge and Rosé	27,558	4.6
Total Blanc	571,746	95.4
Grand total	599,304	100.0

Source: French Ministry of Agriculture.

a region of "vineyards and garden." Finally, unlike the Loire with its regal atmosphere and the Gironde with its many magnificent châteaux and large estates, Alsace is a vineyard where both the grower and the winemaker live in villages.

History

It is often said that the historic business of Alsace was war and wine. Primarily because of its position in the center of western Europe, it was the source of conflict between Celts, Romans, and Germanic tribes. The area was invaded repeatedly throughout history because it straddled the major north-south Rhine route and commanded two significant east-west routes: at Strassbourg in the north and at the Belfort Gap in the south, between the Vosges and the Jura mountains. Missing no opportunity to command these strategic routes, the Romans founded all the major settlements in existence today, including the two most important— Strassbourg and Mulhouse. The former, referring to the "castle commanding the roads," is located in the northern terminus of the Vosges Mountains, a vantage point it has maintained for nearly 2000 years. Uniquely situated north of Basel, and midway between the industrial giants of Nancy and Stuttgart, Strassbourg is a major metropolis on the Rhine and the seat of the Council of Europe. Mulhouse, much smaller and less industrialized, commands the Belfort Gap.

Although seed and plant fossils of *Vitis silvestris* have been discovered and dated to 3000 B.C. in Alsace, the origins of winemaking began with the arrival of the Romans. The industry grew slowly; Pliny the Elder recorded isolated instances of winemaking in the second half of the first century. As the military power of Rome began to diminish, the weak and outnumbered Celts could not effectively prevent the expansionist pressures of the northern Germanic, non-vinegrowing tribes. By the middle of the 5th century all of the Rhine-facing portion of Alsace was overrun and permanently settled by Germanic tribes. Without overflowing into the Lorraine or west-facing portions of the Vosges Mountains, the delimited frontier region has endured for fifteen centuries. On the French Lorraine side of the Vosges, farmsteads are scattered, while on the Alsatian side they are grouped in villages; in Lorraine, settlements are generally located on hilltops, while in Alsace they are nestled in valleys or at the foot of the Vosges; in Lorraine place names are hyphenated and Latin in origin, while in Alsace they end with the suffixes *wihr* and *heim*. While *wihr* is thought to derive from the Roman "villa" and/or "a source of water," its more-probable origin is from *wehr*, referring to a defensive site. Alsace formed the nucleus of Charlemagne's Holy Roman Empire, and for the next 1500 years sovereignty constantly shifted between the French and Germans.

Effective and sustained viticultural activity emerged only after King Clovis subjugated all of Alsace and encouraged Frankish settlement. By 870, when Alsace was given to "Louis the German," viticulture was thriving and Alsace's wines were sold as far north as the Baltic. As a result of the benevolent policies of the Merovingian and Carolingian dynasties, a steady expansion of vine hectarage made its imprint felt over the next three centuries. Benedictines, as the most important group, established vineyards in Guebwiller and Murbach, among others. The Abbey of Murbach, founded in 727, became in time the largest single owner of vineyards in Alsace during the 9th and 10th centuries. Carthusians established vineyards south of Strassbourg and in Molsheim, while the Knights Hospitaller of St. John created commanderies in Bergheim and other places. The Abbey of Ebermunster, the Alspach convent, the Abbey Munster and the Cathedral of Strassbourg were also instrumental in furthering the course of Alsatian viticulture. Until the French Revolution, more than 80 percent of the vineland was owned by the church, nobility, and often foreign aristocracy, particularly the house of Württenberg.

Although politically divided, the area prospered during the period 700 to 1600 because of its position at the crossroads of several international trade routes. Cities became rich and the regional population grew during the late medieval period. Alsatian wine became a common article of commerce along the Rhine and was exported to England during the reign of Edward III in the 14th century. More than 170 parishes produced wine in the late 16th century, but economic prosperity came to an abrupt halt during the Thirty Years War (1618–1648). Alsace was repeatedly attacked, occupied, and plundered by a succession of German, Swedish, Spanish, French, and Swiss armies. At the war's conclusion, Alsace was a devastated region with its population reduced by two-thirds, and economic life assumed subsistence characteristics. Its economic fortunes improved immediately when Louis XIV, in 1648, incorporated a good portion of Alsace with France. While Strassbourg and the northern portion remained independent until 1681, French Catholic settlement and viticulture was encouraged in the southern sections of the region. Vinegrowing expanded rapidly from fewer than 500 hectares in 1648 to more than 7,000 in 1789. The best sites, as well as the bulk of vineland, were owned by the church and nobility. In one swift and bold move, the Revolution secularized religious property and broke up aristocratic holdings with predictable results—quality and production both declined from previously high levels. During the period when the French monarchy was restored, however, there was a marked improvement in vineyard expansion. In 1808 there were a reported 23,000 hectares of vineland, and by 1828, hectarage had increased to 30,000. By 1850, the Bas-Rhin was a formidable vinegarden with more hectares planted in vines than the

Haut-Rhin, most of it located on fertile but marginal vineland along the Rhine River. The Bas-Rhin produced more than 400,000 hectoliters of wine, or nearly one-third more than the Haut-Rhin, and exported more than one-sixth of its output.

Although hectarage and production continued to grow at more modest levels after 1828, the second half of the century produced obstacles: increased Algerian production, railroad construction that helped bring cheaper Midi wine to northern France, and *oïdium* and *phylloxera* (which reduced output from 336,000 in 1851 to less than 90,000 hectoliters in 1880), all disrupted normal and historic trading patterns. Most important, France lost the Franco-Prussian War and had to cede Alsace to Germany until 1918. During the 48-year occupation, Alsatian traditions were degraded by the Germans, and an official policy to "Germanize" the population was instituted. To prevent Alsatian wines from competing with those of Germany, Alsatian growers were forced to plant inferior-quality but high-yielding vines for the production of large quantities of inexpensive wine, shipped in bulk and used for blending. Riesling and Gewürztraminer, two grapes targeted for uprooting, were replaced with the more common Chasselas and Elbling. Hectarage increased along the rich bottomland of the Rhine River, the average yield for the entire vineyard doubled, and a number of hybrid grapes were introduced.

In 1918 Alsace emerged from the war reunited with France, but with reduced hectarage, poor-quality vines, a tarnished reputation, and no markets. Competition from other French vineyards and consumer prejudice were formidable obstacles to an effective and sustained recovery. To overcome these impediments, a number of négociants and growers decided to name their wines after grape varieties, to restrict yields, to abandon rich bottomland, to vinify dry, and to increase quality standards in an attempt to improve the poor "Germanic" image and offer the French consumer wine totally different from that produced in other vineyards. Because of expensive replanting, a world depression, and low wine prices, the Alsatian vineyard declined from a high of 25,000 hectares in 1903 to fewer than 9,500 in 1948. World War II was particularly hard since Alsace was one of the major battlegrounds. Half of the vineyards experienced some type of damage, and at least six towns were totally destroyed.

Post–World War II economic development schemes, a rise in tourism, and a restructuring of the wine industry have done much to foster a bright economic future. Vine hectarage has increased, wine quality has improved tremendously, hybrid grapes have virtually been eliminated, and AOC status was granted in 1962. All of the following highlight recent significant achievements: the value of wine exports increased from less than 20 million to more than 300 million Francs for the period 1970 to 1982; wine exports increased from 50,000 to more than 200,000 hectoliters; and since 1951 non–AOC hectarage declined from 4,000 to 500 hectares, while AOC hectarage increased from 6,500 to more than 12,000 hectares.

The Physical Geography of Alsace

The Rhine River between Karlsruhe and Mulhouse flows through a *graben*, a flat 35-kilometer plain bordered by fault lines with rather steep cliffs—the Vosges in Alsace and the Black Forest in Germany. The area comprises three distinct geographic regions: the plain of Alsace, the foothills of the Vosges, and the Vosges Mountains. The plain of Alsace is a long (170 by 35 kilometers) narrow corridor, lying between the Rhine River and the foothills of the Vosges. It is drained by tributaries of the Rhine, of which the Ill, Fecht, and the Bruche are the most prominent. The flat area, very fertile in alluvial and *limon* deposits, is principally planted in hops, wheat, tobacco, barley, corn, and sugarbeets. It is the most productive portion of the region, with large mechanized farms exhibiting a prosperous ambiance. It contains few vineyards and none with AOC status. The Vosges foothills are a series of terraces and ledges that are composed of a wide assortment of soils derived from sand, limestone, granite, and schist rock. The best vineyard sites are located along a narrow, north-south ribbon. The area is dotted with small, picturesque villages; while fruit trees line roads and frame isolated farmsteads and towns, viticulture dominates all aspects of agriculture. The Vosges Mountains, 150 kilometers in length and one-quarter as broad, form a range of hills covered with magnificent dense fir and beech forests. They reach a maximum altitude of 1,500 meters in the south and slope toward the north in the department of Bas-Rhin, north of Sélestat. The peaks are rounded and forested, and nowhere is the altitude sufficiently high to establish a treeline. While gradual on the west, slopes are steeper and broken, with numerous terraces facing the Rhine in the east. The major rivers flow westward toward the Mosel, eastward toward the Rhine, and southward toward the Saône. More than 70 percent of the entire area is forested, with practically no vineland along the west-facing exposures.

The climate is decidedly continental, with large annual fluctuations in temperature and rainfall. Winters are cold but summers are hot, and late-spring frost and hail in summer are common. Sunshine in September and October is very persistent, while humidity and temperatures are very favorable for ideal grape maturation. When compared with other wine-producing regions, Alsace has the same average annual temperature (11° C) as Chablis and Tours, one degree more than Reims, and four degrees less than Montpellier. Very significant is the fact that the number of days with temperatures above 10°C and total number of degree-days is more than at Reims, Chablis, Macon, Dijon, or Tours. With a few isolated examples in the Midi, Alsace, with fewer than 550 mm. of precipitation, is the driest of all the major AOC vineyards.

Climate is influenced by the gradual slopes of the west-facing Vosges and the relative steepness of the lee exposure. Maritime influences bathe west-facing slopes, producing dense forest, rain, and foggy conditions, while the east-facing terraces along the Rhine get the full benefit of direct

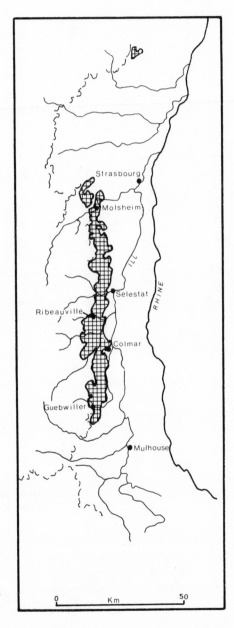

Figure 2.1   The Vineyards
of Alsace

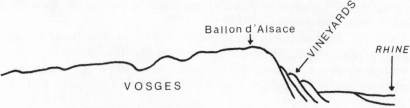

Figure 2.2   Alsace: Cross Section of the
Vosges Mountains
Showing the Location of Vineland

sunlight and are markedly drier. In the west, where the weather is humid, the stone and closed-shuttered houses are bleak in appearance, while on the east they are half-timbered and decked with geraniums. When it is raining in Lorraine, a gentle, drier, and warmer wind blows in Colmar, an important wine town that has the same number of sun hours during the growing season as the Côte-Rôtie.

Vineyards, oriented in an easterly and southeasterly aspect, are discontinuous and found in a thin north-south ribbon almost always protected by the higher, forested elevations in the west. The best producing areas are never found on the heavy loam soils of the Rhine nor in exposed upland locations, but generally at elevations that vary between 200 and 400 meters above sea level. The finest vineyard sites are in the southern portion of the producing district between Bergheim and Rouffach, along a hot thermic belt where temperatures are higher by 1.5°C than in neighboring areas, with ideal wind-flow movement and excellent diurnal temperature fluctuations. Throughout the entire vineyard, the long, cold winter allows only an abbreviated, cool spring to emerge, thus delaying the growth of the vine and promoting a slow but steady maturation throughout the growing season, which adds plenty of fruit to the wine. Vines are therefore pruned and oriented with three objectives in mind: to reduce the harmful effects of frost, to channel the flow of air, and to provide maximum exposure to sunlight. As a consequence, the best sites are located on the edge of escarpments, terraces, or palisades. Vines stand tall, in wide rows, with the "gobelet" method of training prohibited.

The matching of specific grape varieties with soil is a refined art, and rarely are errors made in growing the wrong variety on unsuitable soil. The actual sites are a function of protected exposures with a favorable aspect and well-drained soils, all of which form unique micro vineyard sites. Individual vineyard sites are arranged on terraces and exert a special influence on the growth, yield, and quality of wine produced. It is generally acknowledged that the finest growths come from vineyards situated on limestone, granitic sands, schist, and sandstone rock. The largest concentration of quality sites is in the Haut-Rhin, an area where granite dominates, whereas the Bas-Rhin is subjected to sandstone and

limestone soils. Colluvial material is ubiquitous, and *limon*, found everywhere, varies in intensity. Within these broad generalizations, soils vary
widely within a 50-meter expanse, and the wine from a specific grape
variety varies dramatically with the nature of the soil.

In the Kaysersberg–Kientzheim region are three vineyards within one
kilometer of each other, all with southerly aspects, that give three
different types of Gewürztraminer wine. The alluvial deposits of the
Weiss valley contain soils that are slightly to very slightly acidic and have
excellent water-retaining characteristics. The wines are early maturing,
fruity, and light. The granitic soils along the flank of Mt. Schlossberg
contain colluvial material, are shallow, of moderate fertility, highly
mineralized, do not retain water well, and are somewhat less acidic than
those found in the Weiss valley. Here the Gewürztraminer matures late
and produces average quality, and often coarse wine. Located on the north
side of Kientzheim, the limestone region of Sigolsheim, with its more
alkaline soils, produces intensely flavored, long-lived wine with excellent
acid balance. It should be noted that in less favorable, colder, and more
humid years, the granitic soils of Schlossberg, due to their greater
permeability, often produce the better wine.

The Grapes and Wines of Alsace

Of the eight major grape varieties, Riesling, Gewürztraminer, Sylvaner,
and Pinot Blanc account for 80 percent of the total planted area. In recent
years, Riesling, Pinot Blanc, and Pinot Noir have exhibited the most
significant increases in hectarage—from 22 percent in 1965 to more than
45 percent in 1984. Gewürztraminer, Pinot Gris, and Muscat are
maintaining hectarage share, Sylvaner has declined from 27 percent to 19
percent, and Chasselas and *cépages en mélanges* slipped precipitously from
26 percent to 6 percent for the same period. These figures appear more
spectacular when compared with 1939, when Sylvaner, Chasselas, and
cépages en mélanges accounted for more than two-thirds of the total planted
area (see Figs. 2.4 and 2.5).

Gewürztraminer, with 2,600 hectares or 21 percent of the entire
vineyard, constitutes the most widely planted vine in Alsace. While it has
many synonyms, it differs significantly from the plain Traminer, and can
only be named as "Gewürztraminer" on the label. The plain Traminer, a
much inferior grape for the production of wine, was forced upon the
Alsatian growers after 1870, and as of 1973 it was officially banned in
Alsace. The present "pink" Gewürztraminer clone contains larger leaves,
oval pinkish berries, and a large grape cluster that is loose and conical in
shape; whereas the plain Traminer is rounder, lighter in color, with
cylindrical grape clusters that hang compactly. Gewürztraminer is
thought to have originated in the Palatinate region just north of Alsace.
Gewürztraminer is a late-ripening grape with variable acid levels that

Table 2.2 Alsatian Grape Varieties, 1939, 1965, 1980 and 1984

Grape variety	1939 (percent of total)	1965 (percent of total)	1980 Hectares	1980 Percent of total	1984 Hectares	1984 Percent of total
Gewürztraminer	9	18.9	2,397	21.0	2,652	20.7
Riesling	7	10.6	2,048	17.8	2,567	20.0
Sylvaner	26	26.5	2,576	22.4	2,441	19.2
Pinot Blanc	9	9.7	1,916	16.7	2,476	19.3
Pinot Noir	.5	1.1	517	4.5	783	6.1
Tokay d'Alsace	3.8	3.9	521	4.5	618	4.8
Muscat d'Alsace	3.5	3.0	428	3.7	519	4.1
Chasselas	21	12.8	487	4.2	338	2.6
"Cépages Mélanges"[a]	20.2	13.5	594	5.2	409	3.2
Total	100.0	100.0	11,484	100.0	12,803	100.0

[a] "Cépages Mélanges" refers to a wide assortment of "non-noble" varieties that produce large quantities of inexpensive wine.

Source: French Ministry of Agriculture.

tolerates a wide variety of soils and is susceptible to gray rot. Although uniquely distributed in France, it grows best on heavy clay soils and not on granite, particularly in Barr, Rorschwihr, Bergheim, Mittelwihr, Sigolsheim, Kientzheim, Kaysersberg, Ammerschwihr, Ingersheim, Turckheim, Wintzenheim, Eguisheim, Westhalten, Orschwihr, and Guebwiller. The finest individual vineyard sites are those of Hengst, Kitterlé, Rangen, Kaefferkopf, Mamburg, Sporen, Zisser, and Eichberg.

Depending upon the nature of the soil, aspect, and altitude of the vineyard, the aroma, flavor, and overall character and ability to age vary enormously. In this respect, Gewürztraminer is much like California Zinfandel—it can be made into many different styles and thus defies easy generalizations. Because of its pronounced spicy flavor, pungent aroma, and bouquet, it is easily recognized and hard to forget. As a result, most Americans have trouble drinking it with a meal, despite the fact that it is most versatile as an aperitif with almonds, rich sauces, chicken, ham, and even choucroute. It is absolutely magnificent with smoked salmon, strong

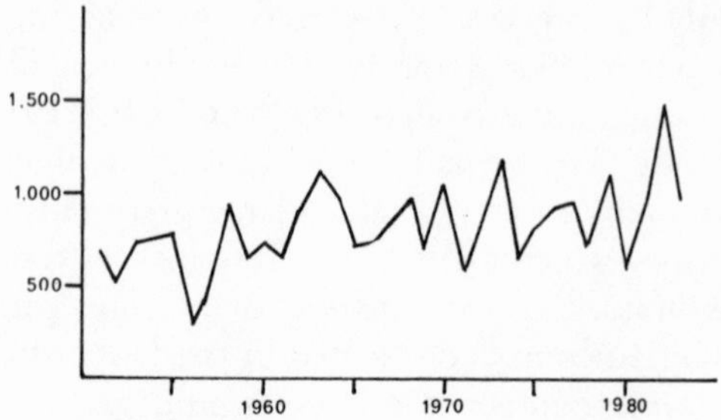

Figure 2.3 Alsace: Wine Production, 1951–1983 (in thousands of hectares)

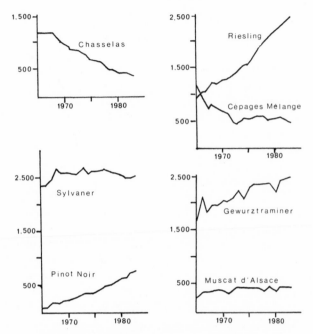

Figure 2.4   Alsace: Hectarage Evolution of
Principal Grape Varieties and *Cépages
Mélanges,* 1965–1983

cheese, and quiche. The finest Gewürztraminer is full-bodied, balanced, spicy in flavor, and with an aroma reminiscent of nutmeg. It makes a superb Vendage Tardive that is capable of considerable bottle-aging. As good as it is, however, it seems to lack the delicacy, elegance, fruity and honeyed taste of an outstanding Riesling; at its worse it is marred by an austere taste and a "hollow," bitter aftertaste.

During the German occupation of 1870 to 1918, Germany did not allow extensive plantings of Riesling. Therefore Riesling's fame is quite recent, and hectarage has increased from fewer than 500 in 1930 to more than 2,500 by 1984. Today, it is considered the *grand vin cépage* of Alsace, not only the finest in the appellation but the most extraordinary in the Haut-Rhin department, especially in the region between Ribeauvillé and Ammerschwihr. First introduced in Alsace in the 15th century, it had long remained in obscurity due to its low yield, high acid levels, and late-ripening culture. Although it resists disease well, it is very sensitive to wind burn, and hence demands well-sheltered sites that have well-drained soils and plenty of sunshine. As a consequence, it occupies the finest sites of both the Bas- and Haut-Rhin. In hot, dry summers, the wine is incomparable—full-bodied, highly scented, with multiple layers of fruit. The wine varies with type of soil, exposure, and altitude. In general, sandy soils produce early maturing wine, while those with some limestone spawn true *vin de garde* libations. The best communes for the production of Riesling are Wolxheim, Dambach-la-Ville, Scherwiller, Ribeauvillé, Hunawihr, Mittelwihr, Kaysersberg, Riquewihr, Zellenberg, Ammersch-wihr, Husseren-les-Château, Orschwihr, Thann, and Mittelbergheim. The finest individual vineyards are Clos Ste.-Hune, Schlossberg, Sporen, Mandelberg, Brandluft, Rangen, Kastelberg, and Schoenenbourg.

The Sylvaner is a highly underrated vine first introduced to Alsace by the Germans in 1870 for the production of high-volume, inexpensive wine. At one time it accounted for nearly one-third of the entire vineyard. The Sylvaner matures late, gives predictable high yields, resists mildew and other diseases, and tolerates frost reasonably well. It is the most common grape in the Bas-Rhin and the main carafe and blending wine. Its wine, commonly referred to as the "Beaujolais of Alsace," is fresh, acidic, and zesty, often with *gout d'terroir*. Although not very complex, it is clean on the palate, has a beautiful pale yellow-green color, and often acquires the taste of raspberries, a most unusual flavor for a white wine. It is always pleasant, light, racy, often petillant, and unceasingly quaffable. Its main disadvantages are a lack of depth of flavor and high acidity—features that many find objectionable—and therefore it is not considered in the same league as other "noble" vines. Yet the better sites in good years are able to produce wine that is equal in quality to Riesling and Gewürztraminer in flavor, concentration, and overall appeal. Sylvaner is concentrated in the Bas-Rhin, especially in Barr, Mittelbergheim, Epfig, and Dambach-la-Ville. The only other major area of cultivation occurs in Rouffach in the Haut-Rhin, and the finest single vineyard for quality production is Zotzenberg in the commune of Mittelbergheim.

Pinot Blanc is planted in approximately one-fifth of the Alsatian vineyard, and over the past forty years it has doubled its hectarage share at the expense of the Chasselas. It resists disease and frost well, attains high yields, and can be planted in rich soil close to the Alsatian plain on relatively flat land. The appeal of Pinot Blanc is further accentuated by its ability to grow well in cool, exposed sites where it produces a wine used as the base for all Crémant; with its neutral flavor and low acid content, it is ideally suited for blending purposes. Although it lacks the concentration of Gewürztraminer, Riesling, and Sylvaner, and the fruitiness and dis-tinctive taste of Tokay and Muscat, Pinot Blanc is not considered a *vin de garde*, but a simple, nonaristocratic vine, commonly made into early maturing wine. It is described as "square" and not "round" because of its muted nose, neutral flavor, and inability to improve with bottle age. The best producing areas are in the Bas-Rhin, and in particular the communes of Beblenheim, Wintzenheim, Pfaffenheim and Cléebourg.

The Pinot Noir grape is the current "darling" of Alsace. Hectarage has increased from fewer than 50 hectares in the 1930s to 198 in 1969, 515 in 1980, and 783 in 1984, making it the fastest-growing vine in the appellation. Among the better producing areas are Cléebourg, Marlenheim, Ottrot, St.-Hippolyte, Turckheim, and Rodern, the latter being the most important. Red and rosé wines, made totally dry, have a pronounced fragrance and are fresh and flavorful. The rosé, a novelty twenty-five years ago, has now suddenly become a "serious" wine and is considered as one with a "future." Although the rosé is light, fragrant, pleasant, easily drunk, and the better of the two, it ranks well below other French rosé in terms of concentration, balance, flavor, and bouquet. The red, a minor element that offers poor value even in the producing region, is the focus of a major attempt to make it more full-bodied and flavorful.

Pinot Gris or Tokay d'Alsace, with 600 hectares, represents approximately 5 percent of the Alsatian vineyard, a figure that has remained relatively stable over the past 60 years. There are three specific types: Le Petit Grain, producing excellent wine from limestone and sandy soils; Le Moyen Grain, doing best on poor, well-drained, sandy soils; and Le Grand Moyen, the least desirable, slowly being phased out of production as it produces coarse, common wine. Although it appears to be a very adaptable vine, yields are much lower than most other varieties, and the vine is difficult to grow due to its susceptibility to *coulure*. The best sites are Cléebourg, Obernai, Beblenheim, Mittelwihr, and Kientzheim.

Tokay d'Alsace produces strong, austere, often coarse, high-acid wines. They are strongly flavored, have a long, penetrating bouquet, and are ideal with rich, creamy foie gras, flavorful roasts, smoked fish, spiced meat, and quiche. At its best, it is fresh and full-bodied, with a long, lingering finish and a good, clean taste. As of 1986, the wine will officially be known as Pinot Gris.

Muscat d'Alsace has been cultivated in Alsace ever since the 16th century and, with 500 hectares, occupies about 4 percent of the entire vineyard. There are two variants—Muscat à Petit Grains and Muscat Ottonel; the latter, early maturing, is the preferred vine and the better of the two in the production of flavorful, light, fruity and highly aromatic wine. Because of frost sensitivity, low and unpredictable yields, both are expected to decline in the coming decades. The best producing communes are said to be located in Guebwiller, Ribeauvillé, Riquewihr, Voegtlin-shoffen, Mittelwihr, Wettolsheim, and Gueberschwihr, all of which are located in Haut-Rhin. The wine, characterized by the distinct pungent odor and flavor of the Muscat grape, is full on the palate, usually bone dry, and considered the preferred aperitif. It is absolutely delicious with crackers and cheese, magnificent with fruit tarts, and makes a fabulous sorbet as well as an excellent cooking wine. At its best, the Muscat d'Alsace is perfectly balanced with a distinguished flavor and odor that set it apart from similar wines from the Midi; at its worse, it is overly austere because of its dryness, and hence, bitter on the palate. The very finest bottles can be expensive but worth the financial investment.

With 300 hectares, Chasselas, or "Flambeau d'Alsace," has declined over the past 45 years from more than 21 percent of total hectarage to less than 3 percent. Although more important in southern and western Switzerland, the Chasselas in Alsace retains a lowly position and is considered the historic workhorse of the carafe trade. Maturing before any other variety, it is a very prolific vine known for light, undistinguished, acidic wine that is second-rate at best.

Historically, *cépages en mélanges* referred to a mixture of "non-noble" varieties is used to produce "Zwicker" or blended wines of common quality. They included a long list of grapes, of which the Gentile Blanc and Rouge, Knipperlé, Auxerrois Blanc, Trollinger, Goldriesling, Pinot Meunier, Müller-Thurgau, Elbling, and Chasselas were the most prevalent. Between 1945 and 1973, laws were passed forbidding the establishment of any new vineyards, and since 1973 the production of "Zwicker" wine has been banned. Historically, the different varieties were actually planted together in a common vineyard called "parcelles en mélanges." Hectarage declined from 20 percent in 1939 to 3 percent in 1984, with further declines expected in the future.

Alsace produces twelve different AOC wines: seven varietals (Pinot Noir, Pinot Blanc, Riesling, Gewürztraminer, Sylvaner, Muscat, and Pinot Gris); Edelzwicker (a blended wine from the above varieties); Rouge and Rosé (from Pinot Noir only); Crémant; and Primeur. Minute and infrequently made *vin de paille* also occurs, but cannot carry the Alsace AOC designation.

Nearly all white Alsatian wines are distinguished by their firmness, brilliant appearance, and fragrance, and except for those labeled by qualitative expressions, are very dry. They are unbelievably fruity, delicate, eminently drinkable, and highlighted by a balance between acidity, extract, and fruity grape aroma. The very best are nearly always named after the grape from which they are made and not after the place of production, as is common in all other areas of France. Since 1919, the wines have shown a marked improvement, and the numerous legislative acts have not debased the appellations' reputation. As a consequence, Alsatian white wines are the most individualistic of any region in the nation. Historically, the wine was racked every three to four months in the first year, thus "browning" the wine—but no more. Stainless steel and no air contact is the rule, with only a handful of producers using wood either to ferment or to age.

Unlike Germans to the north who sweeten wine with sussreserve after fermentation, Alsatians add sugar beforehand and vinify until no sugar remains. The wines, therefore much higher in alcohol than the German, are clean, crisp, and have a distinctive *goût de terroir* taste mixed with bitterness, features that are not necessarily unpleasant. Unlike in other French white regions, Alsatian wines are rarely flat, and because of their high acid level, they resist oxidation.

Wine Classification

Vin ordinaire is wine from any one or a combination of several "ordinary" grapes, such as Chasselas, Müller Thurgau, Auxerrois Blanc, Knipperlé, all of which cannot be named on the label. It also refers to wine made from grapes grown on unsuitable soil and terrain. It constitutes the most common wine—light in body, acidic, often "biting," and "nervous" in constitution—and rarely does it attain alcohol levels above 10.5 percent.

Edelzwicker, on the other hand, is made from *cépages en mélanges* and is entitled to the "Vin Fin d'Alsace" designation. It should be noted that despite the prefix *edel* (meaning "finest"), these are common-to-average blended wines and are not the equal of varietals. Quality varies enormously by producer, yield, types of grapes used, producing area, and other factors. It is now considered the official carafe wine of the region, and only minute quantities are exported, mostly as a curiosity.

Varietal table wine (made only from Riesling, Gewürztraminer, Pinot Noir, Pinot Gris, Muscat, Pinot Blanc, and Sylvaner) is considered the finest in the appellation. It must contain a minimum alcohol content of 10 percent for Riesling and Muscat, and 11 percent for Gewürztraminer and Pinot Gris. Historically the wines were made dry, but increasingly the trend is for larger houses and premium producers to make "German types," which is to say, with some element of sweetness. Therefore, in addition to the regular bottlings of dry varietal wine, there is a steady progression of increased extract, sugar, and concentration for wine labeled with additional qualifications. When the expression "Grand Cru" appears on the label, the wine can be made only from Gewürztraminer, Riesling, Muscat, or Pinot Gris, from sites yielding less than 70 hectoliters to the hectare. When this expression is identified with a specific vineyard, 100 percent of the wine must originate from the stated site. Simple qualifying expressions, such as "reserve sélection," are not regulated by law and do not necessarily imply origin from superior growths. On the other hand, the name Gewürztraminer, Riesling, Muscat, or Pinot Gris, followed by "Cuvée" or any other similar expression, indicates origin from a superior growth.

Vendage Tardive and *Sélection des Grains Nobles* are two regulated expressions referring to "late-harvest" wines whose grape sugar may or may not be entirely fermented out. The only grapes allowed for their production are Riesling, Gewürztraminer, Pinot Gris, and Muscat. Historically these wines were made only in exceptional years and in small quantities, but the trend recently has been to increase their production in an attempt to imitate German equivalents. There is no mention of *botrytis* on the label, and there are few other regulating aspects other than *oechsle* readings.* Vendage Tardive is the product of grapes with a must density of 95 oechsle

---

*Oechsle measures the specific gravity, or the quantity of sugar in the must prior to fermentation.

for Riesling and Muscat, and 105 for Gewürztraminer and Pinot Gris. Requirements are slightly higher for Sélection des Grains Nobles, because not only are the grapes *edelreife*, but picking is by individual berry. The oechsle must reading is at least 110 (often much higher), and the alcohol content may exceed 15 percent. For both Vendage Tardive and Sélection des Grains Nobles, chaptalization is not permitted, and the yield is restricted to 65 hectoliters to the hectare. Needless to say, they are exceptional wines (especially when there is perfect balance between acid and sugar) that appear to have unlimited aging potential. Considered the finest wines of Alsace, they certainly are the most expensive.

Crémant d'Alsace is a new appellation first granted AOC status in 1976 for mousseux made by the Champagne method. The wine is expensive but a good value and an interesting alternative to Champagne in the middle to lower price range. It was first made in large commercial quantities by Dopff & Irion, but now the Eguisheim cooperative is the largest producer. Production increased from minute quantities in the late 1960s to more than 7 million bottles in 1984. Made primarily from Pinot Blanc, Riesling, Pinot Gris, and Pinot Noir, with standard levels of pressure just as in Champagne, it should not be confused with the Crémant wines of the Loire. The wine is fresh, fragrant, light in color, but highly variable in quality and style. More than 80 percent of production comes from the cooperatives of Beblenheim, Eguisheim, Pfaffenheim, and Traenheim. The principal private producers for quality Crémant are Dopff & Irion, Kuentz-Bas, and Alsace Willm.

Red and *rosé* wines are the product of Pinot Noir. Historically insignificant, production has recently risen to 5 percent of regional output and is increasing in importance. Both wines offer considerable appeal to German and Swiss tourists who wish to sustain a meal with a more "traditional" wine. The red is pale in color, lacks harmony, and offers little value. Considered the better value, the rosé is more fragrant, has an excellent color and refreshing taste, and compliments food much better.

First made by the energetic Laugel firm in 1984, *Alsace Primeur* is the latest innovation in the region. Made from Pinot Blanc in the style of Beaujolais by the carbonic maceration technique, the wine is light in alcohol, fresh, but thin and unsubstantial by Alsatian standards. Apparently it is a hit with tourists, as demand outstrips production. Primeur production from Pinot Noir is not far behind.

The Grand Cru Vineyards

Unlike Burgundy, where climate and commune names play a prominent role in the nomenclature of wine, Alsatian wines are usually named after the grape variety. Here, as in Burgundy and other similar areas, the reputation of the producer and/or shipper is very important in separating the bad, indifferent, and superior bottles. Within the past twenty-five years, however, a broad movement has emerged with the intent of introducing Grand Cru designations to specific vineyards. Although the movement is wrought with threats of factional warfare, the concept has accelerated in both appeal and incipient official recognition of the concept.

The Grand Cru legislation passed in 1983 identifies 25 *lieu-dits*, or specific soil and microclimatic sites whose dimensions vary from 2 to 80 hectares. Whenever the expression "Grand Cru" is mentioned on the label, the wine is restricted to the minimum requirements mentioned above. The problem lies not with the tendency to break with tradition or begin the practice of placing vineyard names on the label, but in the delineation and ranking of both vineyard sites and communes, and the selection of authorized grape varieties. A tentative agreement was reached in 1984, and as of 1985 the designation "Grand Cru" is in effect, although the final, official demarcation of all contested sites has not been resolved. The prevailing opinion is that the number of sites will grow from the present modest list, and that it will take another ten years before the controversy is resolved. The present picture is very much confused, since a number of famous vineyards, such as Sporen, Mambourg, and Mandelberg, are not considered "Grand Cru" because "less desirable" grapes such as Sylvaner, Pinot Noir, and Pinot Blanc are cultivated there. The accompanying table (2.3) shows the primary vineyards, the imbroglio notwithstanding, in both the Bas- and Haut-Rhin, with the latest "official" Grand Cru vineyard sites underlined.

The Industry Structure

Alsace is an area of small, part-time growers and tiny, highly fragmented vineyard plots. Of the 8,400 growers in 1983, 80 percent cultivated less than 1 hectare. In 1945 Alsace had 160,000 individual registered vineyard plots; this had shrunk to 118,000 in 1980, and it is expected that by A.D. 2000, the figure will be further reduced to fewer than 50,000. As the consolidation efforts have progressed, the number of growers has also steadily declined from 34,000 in 1900 to 12,000 in 1972, to 9,200 in 1980, and to 8,400 in 1983. In terms of number of growers and vine hectarage controlled, the industry is fragmented into the following broad groups:

1. *Manipulants Totaux* are individual growers who grow grapes, ferment, age, and bottle wine exclusively from their own estate. Their number is growing rapidly, although in 1983 they still represented less than 1 percent of all growers and held approximately 3 percent of all vineland. Another 5 percent, controlling 16 percent of all vineland, performs all of the above operations, but does not produce estate wine.

Table 2.3   Major Alsatian Vineyards in Haut- and Bas-Rhin, 1983

Haut-Rhin

Commune	Name of Vineyard	Commune	Name of Vineyard
Ammerschwihr	Kaefferkopf, Meiwihr	Pfaffenheim	Schneckenberg, Berweingarten,
Beblenheim	Sonnenglanz (32.8)[a]		Rossgarten,
Bennwihr	Rebgarten		Hartweg, Steinert
Bergheim	Altenberg (35),	Ribeauville	Geisberg (8.5),
	Burlenberg,		Kirchberg (11.4),
	Kantzlerberg (3.2),		Osterberg,
	Rothenberg,		Trottacker,
	Blosenberg		Zahnacker,
Cernay	Huben		Hagel
Colmar	Hardt	Riquewihr	Schoenenbourg,
Eguisheim	Pfersigberg,		Sporen
	Eichberg (57.6)	Rodern	Gloeckelberg (23.4)
Gueberschwihr	Goldert (45.3),	Rouffach	Clos de St.-Landolin,
	Weingarten,		Isenbourg,
	Haulen,		Litzeltal
	Pflanzer	Saint-Hippolyte	Gloeckelberg
Guebwiller	Kessler (28.5),	Sigolsheim	Mambourg,
	Saering (26.7),		Vogelgarten,
	Kitterlé, (25.8),		Altenberg,
	Spiegel (18.2),		Sigolsheimer,
	Heissenstein,		Hügel
	Wanne,	Soultzmatt	Zinnkoepfle,
	Gans,		Burgweg,
	Schimberg		Weingarten,
Hattstatt	Hatschbourg (47.3),		Breitenberg
	Elsbourg	Thann	Rangen (18.8)
Herrlisheim-près-Colmar	Elsbourg	Turckheim	Brand (60),
			Schneckelsburg,
Hunawihr	Rosacker (26.1),		Eichberg,
	Muhlforst,		Steinglitz,
	Ste.-Hune,		Kirchthal,
	Heitzloch		Weingarten
Ingersheim	Florimont,	Voegtlingshoffen	Hatschbourg,
	Letzenberg		Hagelberg
Katzenthal	Sommerberg (28.3)	Walbach	Cotes du Val St.-Gregoire
Kaysersberg	Schlossberg (30),	Westhalten	Zinnkoepfle,
	Geisburg		Sulzaberg,
Kientzheim	Schlossberg (30),		Strangenberg,
	Furstentum,		Steinstuck,
	Koehrenburg,		Schlopberg,
	Clos des Capucins Altenberg		Clos de St.-Landolin
Mittelwihr	Mandelberg	Wettolsheim	Steingrubler
Niedermorschwihr	Sommerberg	Wintzenheim	Hengst (75.7),
Orschwihr	Lippelsberg,		Wartstein
	Bollenberg,	Wuenheim	Ollwiller (35.8)
	Affenberg,	Zellenberg	Hagenschlauf,
	Pfingstberg		Schlossreben,
			Mantelkragen

Table 2.3 Continued

Bas-Rhin

Commune	Name of Vineyard	Commune	Name of Vineyard
Andlau	Kastelberg (5.8), Wiebelsberg (12.5), Moenchberg (11.8), Brandhof	Eichhoffen	Moenchberg (11.8)
		Epfig	Fronholz, Pflänzer
		Itterswiller	Kirchberg
		Kintzheim	Hahnenberg
Avolsheim	Finkenberg	Mittelbergheim	Zotzenberg, Stein, Brandluft, Pfoeller
Barr	Kirchberg (40.6), Freiberg, Krug, Pfloeck, Gaensbroennel, Zisser, Ritteney		
		Molsheim	Bruderthal, Finkenberg, Hahnenberg Stierkopf
		Mutzig	
Bergbieten	Altenberg (29)	Nothalten	Munchberg
Bernardville	Eichelberg	Orschwiller	Hahnenberg, Praelatenberg
Châtenois	Hahnenberg		
Dahlenheim	Engelberg	Scherwiller	Rittersberg
Dambach-la-Ville	Bernstein, Birschberg, Frankstein, Frauenberg, Plettig, St.-Sebastian	Wolxheim	Altenberg, Horn

aGrand Cru vineyards are underlined. Figures in parentheses indicate hectarage. Total Gand Cru hectarage is approximately 5 percent of the regional total.

2. *Manipulants Partiels* are growers who make wine, but bottle only a small portion of their production; they represent 33 percent of all growers and control approximately 37 percent of all vineland.

3. *Vendeurs en vrac* are growers who vinify, but who do not store and bottle wine. They represent 5 percent of all growers and control a similar percentage of vineland.

4. *Vendeurs Raisins* are growers who sell grapes to négociants and coopératives; they represent 20 percent of all growers and control 10 percent of all vineland.

5. *Coopératives* and their members represent 35 percent of all growers and control 32 percent of all vineland.

6. *Négociants* represent less than 1 percent of all growers but control 7 percent of all vineland.

In terms of wine production, 40 percent of all wine is made and/or distributed by grower-négociants who make wine from their own grapes; purchase additional grapes, must, and wine; and ferment, age, bottle, and distribute wine. Collectively, they handle about 50 percent of all Alsatian wine. Forty-five percent of all wine is made and/or marketed by cooperatives, and the remaining 15 percent is made by owner-growers. Coopératives, relatively new to the region, increased rapidly in number after 1945. Although there were nine in 1954, they did little except act as warehouses in the regulation of stocks. With time, they began to supply négociants with wine, and after 1955 they expanded operations to bottling and distribution as well. By 1984 their number increased to eighteen, with many having several branches. Of the total, four are responsible for nearly three-quarters of production. They offer a cheaper bottle price, but rarely can they compete with the big private houses and specialty producers in the production of fine wines. They have improved standards, provide valuable technical assistance to growers, and have helped stabilize the market. For total wine production in Alsace, see Figure 2.5.

The manipulants viticulteurs are rapidly increasing in importance. Small as they are, their reputation rests on quality, and they sell directly to a fanatical lot who take pride in discovering their "own" special kind of winemaker. To counteract the competitive edge of coopératives and manipulants, the big négociants are increasing their share of available vineland by purchasing quality vineyards, leaving a good portion of the less expensive line of wines to coopératives, and concentrating in the

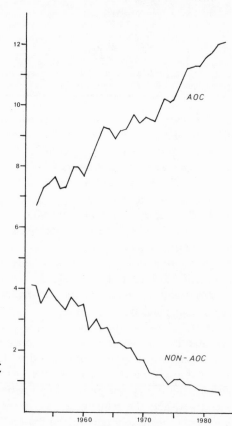

Figure 2.5   Alsace: AOC
and non-AOC Hectarage,
1950–1983
(in thousands of hectares)

production of quality wines. Hugel, Trimbach, Dopff "Au Moulin," Dopff & Irion, Willm, and Laugel dominate the négociant trade.

Wine exports over the past thirty years have shown a spectacular increase from 11,000 hectoliters in 1954 to 255,000 in 1983, with the value in FF increasing from 6 million to more than 310 million for the same period. The country with the largest share, as well as the most rapid growth, is West Germany, followed by four neighboring countries who collectively account for more than 88 percent of total 1983 exports (see Figs. 2.6 and 2.7). Wine exports are important because one-quarter to one-third of total output is exported each year and perhaps even more if we consider the significant quantities of wine purchased by tourists. For some négociant firms, exports account for more than 50 percent of total production and/or sales.

THE PRODUCING REGIONS OF ALSACE

The Bas-Rhin

The producing regions of Alsace are divided into two large vineyards: north of St.-Hippolyte is the Bas-Rhin, an area of less than 3,800 hectares of vines, or 28 percent of the entire Alsatian hectarage; south of St.-Hippolyte, extending to the northern suburbs of Mulhouse, is the Haut-Rhin, with 9,600 hectares, the larger and more important quality-producing section. The Bas-Rhin, colder than the Haut-Rhin, is much lower in elevation and composed of sandstone and alluvial soil material. It produces short-lived, acidic wines mainly from Sylvaner and *cépages en mélanges*, the former being widely considered the most important variety in the region. For both regions, the primary producing communes and their major producers are presented below in a rough north-south order.

The Bas-Rhin is divided into two sections: a minor vineyard in the extreme north, and the more important area between Nordheim and Sélestat, in the south. The entire district is drained by the Mossig, Brunche, Andlau, Giessen, Lipvrette, and Ill rivers, all of which, with

Figure 2.6 Alsace: Value of Wine Exports, 1958–1984 (in millions of French Francs)

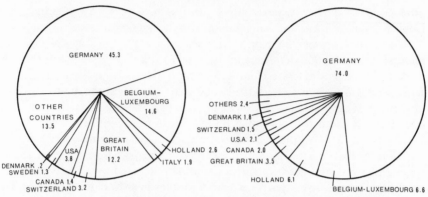

Figure 2.7   Alsace: Destination of Exports by Principal Country
(*left*, 1960; *right*, 1980) (in percent)

the exception of the Ill, are really oversized streams. In the extreme
northern section, lying next to the southern extremities of the Rheinp-
falz, is the Cléebourg vineyard, a minor 125-hectare district consisting of
the communities of Rott, Oberhoffen, Steinseltz, and Cléebourg. Its basis
for existence is the presence of extensive outcroppings of Muschelkalk,
Keuper, and limestone soils, similar to those of Luxembourg. It is an area
of 200 small, part-time growers who belong to the local cooperative in
Cléebourg. The area, producing no Muscat and little Riesling, is known
mainly for the production of Pinot Noir, Pinot Gris, Pinot Blanc, and
Sylvaner. Historically it was more important in terms of hectarage and
production, especially for the production of inexpensive, bulk Müller-
Thurgau and Auxerrois-based wines. The region is dominated by the
medieval town of Cléebourg, a strassendorf (street city) where more than
half of the houses predate the year 1700. The wines of note are a rosé made
from Pinot Noir, and Pinot Gris.

    South of the Mossig valley and extending to Sélestat lie the vineyards of
the true Bas-Rhin, an area of twenty-two major communes and hamlets
for the production of what is generally described as carafe wine. Viticulture here does not compete well with industrial, urban, and dairyland
uses, and over the past 100 years, total vine hectarage has been reduced by
84 percent; it is expected to decline still further. Despite the high number
of small and part-time growers, land consolidation is proceeding at a
rapid pace, with more than half the entire vineyard using mechanical
pickers, the highest such figure in Alsace. Approximately 65 percent of
all wine is made by the region's six cooperatives located in Cléebourg,
Andlau, Dambach-la-Ville, Obernai, Traenheim, and Orschwiller. The
most important grape is Sylvaner, of which Avolsheim has the highest
concentration. Soils, comprised of sandstone and occasional outcroppings
of limestone, are more homogeneous than the Haut-Rhin. Barr, Bliensch-

willer, Nothalten, Epfig, Itterswiller, Andlau, Mittelbergheim, Dorlisheim, Wolxheim, Westhoffen, Heiligenstein, and Dambach-la-Ville are the main communes responsible for 85 percent of total hectarage and production.

With approximately 505 hectares under vine, Dambach-la-Ville is the largest wine commune in the Bas-Rhin. This undisturbed, medieval strassendorf town of fortified towers with beautiful gateways, moss-covered roofs, and gabled houses is totally surrounded by vineyards and dominated by a 700-meter mountain. In August it hosts one of the larger and better wine festivals. Bernstein and Plettig are two average but well-known vineyard sites, followed by Frauenberg, St.-Sebastian, Birschberg, and Frankstein. The biggest négociant and grower, *Willy Gisselbrecht*, is known for stylish and very popular Pinot Blanc and Gewürztraminer. The slightly smaller house of *Louis Gisselbrecht* makes soft Riesling and Sylvaner. The wines of both houses are of average quality but subject to inconsistency. *Louis Hauller*, a smaller but more reliable house, makes light, easy drinking wines of which Sylvaner, Riesling, Pinot Noir, and Gewürztraminer have established reputations. *François Meyer* (Riesling), *Pierre Kirschner* (Riesling, Sylvaner), *Michel Martz* (Riesling), *Genevieve Schwartz* (Riesling), and *Paul Beck* (Pinot Blanc, Sylvaner, and Gewürztraminer), all make above-average wines. The largest producer in the commune, *Cave Vinicole Dambach-la-Ville*, makes many wines and is widely known for outstanding Riesling.

Located south of Barr, Mittelbergheim, one of the largest communes with 180 hectares of vines, is known for four vineyards with above-average reputations: Zotzenberg, Stein, Brandluft, and Pfoeller. Zotzenberg and Stein have established a reputation for exquisite Sylvaner, and Brandluft for Riesling. Primarily because the soil is porous and contains oolitic conglomerate material, the commune as a whole is known for the finest Sylvaner in the Bas-Rhin. The three prominent producers in the commune are *E. Boeckel, Albert Seltz* and *Jean Beyer*. The first is known for above average, delicate Sylvaner and Gewürztraminer, zesty Sylvaner from the Zotzenberg vineyard, and distinctive Rieslings from the Brandluft and Wiebelsberg vineyards. *Albert Seltz* makes good Sylvaner, Pinot Blanc, and Riesling; and *Jean Beyer* is known for Sylvaner from the Epfig vineyard. Other above-average producers include *Pierre Riestch, Alfred Wantz, Armand Gilg,* and *Bernard Haegi.*

Andlau, a medieval town founded in the 9th century and surrounded by many old, refurbished castles, is located in the center of the producing region between Dambach-la-Ville and Barr. Its vineyards were owned by numerous abbeys and monasteries, and for five centuries, beginning in the 13th, the archbishop of Strassbourg and the abbey of Landlau were the commune's largest vineland owners. The wines of Andlau have a distinctive flavor and aroma due in part to the presence of schist rock in the subsoil. The best vines are Riesling, growing in sandy soil, and Sylvaner and Gewürztraminer in heavier, clay soils. There are four vineyards of note: Moenchberg, Kastelberg, Brandhof, and Wiebelsberg. Three firms with a regional reputation are *J.-P. Klein* (excellent, rich, full-bodied wines, particularly Sylvaner); *Dne. Fernand Gresser*, (a small grower making distinctive wines, especially Riesling from Kastelberg); and *André Gresser* (a small but growing negociant house with a reputation for Riesling from Moenchberg and Wiebelsberg). *Coopérative Vinicole d'Andlau* enjoys an excellent reputation for Sylvaner.

Heiligenstein-Barr and the three satellite communities of Goxwiller, Bourgheim, and Gertwiller account for 450 hectares of producing vineyards. Heiligenstein is known for Pinot Blanc and a rare Savagnin rosé, the best of which is made by *Willm* and sold as "Klevner de Heiligenstein," the commune's most famous vineyard. Although much smaller than Heiligenstein, Barr is the site of seven important vineyards: Krug, Ritteney, Pfloeck, Zisser, Freiberg, Kirchberg, and Gaensbroennel. Nearly three-quarters of the commune's 94 hectares either sit upon or skirt the Kirchberg and Freiberg hillsides. As the most common soils are clay and limestone, Gewürztraminer accounts for one-third, Sylvaner 20 percent, and Riesling 19 percent of total hectarage. The two houses with established reputations are *Dne. Klipfel* and *Alsace Willm*. Klipfel, part of the André Lorentz négociant business, is one of the few remaining houses that still uses oak and occasionally makes outstanding wines sold in smart restaurants. The Clos Zisser Gewürztraminer is reliable and absolutely superb, as is the Gewürztraminer from Kirchberg. Alsace Willm is a small, old house with a good reputation for full-bodied, well balanced wines capable of extended aging. It is best known for Riesling from Kirchberg, Gewürztraminer from Clos Gaensbroennel, and Grand Reserve Exceptionnelle Riesling. Four other, less prominent producers are *Charles Wantz* (Pinot Noir and Gewürztraminer), *Antoine Klingenfus* (Gewürztraminer), *Zeyssolff* (Sylvaner and Riesling), and *Pierre Hering* (Riesling from Kirchberg, and Gewürztraminer from Gaensbronnel).

Between Dambach-la-Ville and the western borders of Sélestat are three towns with a combined area of 334 hectares that make average to above-average wines. Dieffenthal is known for good, reliable, soft Pinot Noir; Scherwiller for Riesling; and Châtenois, from a portion of the Hahnenberg vineyard, excellent Riesling, Gewürztraminer, and Pinot Gris. Restored and occupied by Kaiser Wilhelm II, the marvelously preserved castle of Haut-Koenigsbourg towers over the towns of Kintzheim and Orschwiller, two small villages lying on the border between the Haut- and Bas-Rhin. They are located southwest of Sélestat and enjoy outstanding reputations. The best-known site is Praelatenberg and a small portion of Hahnenberg. The only other major commune in the Bas-Rhin is Marlenheim (located in the northern portion of the district), known for above-average Pinot Noir (called Vorlauf), a large cooperative, and the firm of *Maison Michel Laugel*, an old 17th-century firm, now either the largest or second-largest producer in Alsace, making huge quantities of Edelzwicker and Crémant, both of which are made soft, smooth and priced to sell. *Mosbach*, in Marlenheim, makes distinctive Gewürztraminer, Pinot Gris, and Pinot Noir. *Roman Fritsch*, a small grower, makes excellent Riesling.

Other communes and wine houses include, in the Obernai region, *J. Paul Seilly* (a small but growing négociant), *Union Vinicole Divinal* (Riesling, Muscat, and Gewürztraminer), *J.-P. Bechtold* (Pinot Blanc, Riesling), and *Soc. Vinicole St.-Odile* (superb Riesling). The commune of Wolxheim, located on the Mossig River, contains two of the best but rarely encountered vineyards, Altenberg and Horn, both of which are good for Riesling, the latter particularly good from *François Muhlberger*. In Molsheim, a small town overlooking the Broune River, winemaking is dominated by *Lucien Neumeyer*, a small but growing négociant house. Sélestat, located between the Ill and Geisser rivers, is known for Charlemagne's residence, narrow crooked streets, and two growers with good reputations—*Alphonse Zimmerman* and *Claude Bleger*. In Epfig are two producers with a good reputation—*Dne. Ostertag* (Sylvaner and Riesling) and *Roger and Roland Geyer* (Riesling); in Traenheim, *Frederick Mochel* (Gewürztraminer) and *Cave Vinicole de Traenheim* (Riesling and Pinot Gris); and in Orschwiller, the southernmost village in the Bas-Rhin, three excellent producers—*Raymond Engel* (Sylvaner and Riesling), *A. Zimmermann* (Riesling), and *Louis Siffert* (Gewürztraminer).

The Haut-Rhin

The Haut-Rhin officially begins with St.-Hippolyte, a small town lying almost entirely within its medieval walls. It is known for the Gloeckelberg vineyard and two small houses: *G.A.E.C. St.-Fulrade*, a 10-hectare estate making good rosé and Pinot Blanc, and *Fernand Engel*, enjoying a local reputation for Muscat. Within a stone's throw, nestled in the foothills of the Vosges along the Eckenbach stream, is Rodern, a hamlet with a reputation for fine Pinot Noir, especially that which emanates from the Rouge de Rodern vineyard. Rorschwihr, located on the northern outskirts of Bergheim, is known for Gewürztraminer and two above-average growers: *Louis Gassman* and *Willy Rolli-Edel*, the former making outstanding Vendage Tardive Réserve Gewürztraminer, and the latter enjoying a good reputation for above-average Riesling and excellent Gewürztraminer. Bergheim, less than 2 kilometers northeast of Ribeauvillé, is the first of the quality communes of the Haut-Rhin, with four excellent vineyards—Altenberg, Kantzlerberg, Burlenberg and Rothenberg—of which the first two are absolutely first-rate. The best sites ring the 300-meter Kantzlerberg hill that overlooks the town. Composed of clay and limestone, they are excellent for the production of Gewürztraminer and Riesling. Of the more than ten producers, *Marcel*

Deiss makes outstanding Gewürztraminer and Riesling; the firms of *Gustave and Jerome Lorentz* collectively rank as one of the larger houses and are best known for good Gewürztraminer and Riesling; and *Louis Freyburger* maintains a good reputation for Pinot Gris, Pinot Noir, Muscat, and outstanding Altenberg Gewürztraminer.

A classic strassendorf city with fortified bastions at either end, Ribeauvillé, located at the end of a small valley drained by the Stengbach stream, has a fair-sized population of 5,000 inhabitants. It produces exquisite Riesling, outstanding Gewürztraminer, and above-average Pinot Gris. Its viticultural acclaim is the result of a unique combination of soil and microclimate. One of the best soils for Riesling is Muschelkalk ("kalk" referring to fossil shells in the calcareous rock), which runs in a thin and discontinuous belt from Sigolsheim to Ribeauvillé through Zellenberg and Hunawihr. In addition to the excellent, deep and friable soil, Ribeauvillé's microclimate is peculiar: air streams are regularly chaneled downward, constantly churning the air, reducing the incidence of spring frost, and mitigating the otherwise low winter temperature. No fewer than six major vineyards are found within the commune boundaries: Kirchberg, Osterberg, Trottacker, Hagel, Zahnacker, and Geisberg.

The largest négociant firm on the outskirts of Ribeauvillé is the 17th-century (1626) *Trimbach* firm. It owns or leases more than 100 hectares, mostly in superior sites located in Ribeauvillé and neighboring communes. The flagship and one of the best vineyards, Clos Ste.-Hune, is entirely owned by this house. The expertly made wines receive no or little wood-aging and are known for their high acid levels and their propensity to age gracefully. This large house makes a large number of wines that are reasonably priced and offer excellent value. Other smaller producers include *Robert Faller* (for superb Riesling from the Geisberg vineyard); *A. Kientzler* (Geisberg Riesling and Muscat); *Jean Sipp* (fresh Riesling from the Kirchberg and Schlossberg vineyards); *Bott Frères* (Muscat and Riesling); and *Paul Schwach*.

Just to the south and across the valley from Ribeauvillé is the important hamlet of Hunawihr. It was badly damaged in 1945 and has an interesting fortified church. Known for the superb vineyards of Rosacker, Muhlforst, Clos Ste.-Hune, and Heitzloch, it is important in the production of above-average Gewürztraminer, Riesling, and Pinot Gris. While most of the soils are heavily impregnated with clay and planted in Gewürztraminer, the finest sites contain limestone and produce outstanding Riesling and Pinot Gris. In addition to the fine Rosacker vineyard, the most famous site, Clos Ste.-Hune, makes one of the most celebrated Rieslings. The two producers of note are the local coopérative (outstanding Riesling) and the firm of *Mittnacht*, a small, average-quality producer. South of Hunawihr is the 189-hectare hamlet of Zellenberg, whose population numbers about 300 residents. Because its soils contain less limestone than those of Hunawihr, there is only one vineyard of note—

Mantelkragen. This former ecclesiastical settlement produces mainly Gewürztraminer and Riesling, has twenty growers, and has three producers with a reputation: *J. Becker* (an old 17th-century house with 12 hectares in the Rimelsberg, Hagenschlauf, and Froen vineyards, makes excellent Riesling, Muscat, Gewürztraminer, and Pinot Blanc); *Marcel Rentz* (Riesling, Pinot Blanc, and an unusual white wine from Pinot Noir); and *David Ermel*.

Riquewihr remains the unchallenged jewel and the nation's most delightful wine town. Built in 1291, more than 70 percent of the town predates 1600. It is totally surrounded by vineyards on three sides, cuddled by the Vosges, and irrigated by the charming Sembach stream. The town reflects a significant historical past, with half-timbered houses, narrow crooked streets, countless cul-de-sacs, public water troughs, a large medieval museum, and spotlessly clean houses. Miraculously, it escaped destruction during the closing days of World War II. In addition to its medieval charm, Riquewihr is known for two outstanding vineyards: Schoenenbourg, the most famous, located north of the village and planted almost exclusively in Riesling; and Sporen, equally good but less well known, located southeast of the town on rolling terrain and growing a much larger variety of grapes. The soils of Schoenenbourg, containing marl-keuper limestone in addition to sand and pebble, are very rich in minerals and retain water well. The vineyard is located at an altitude of 350 meters, has an excellent aspect, and is said to be the finest site for the production of Riesling and Muscat. The Sporen vineyard, oriented toward Mittelwihr, is at 250 meters, and because its soils contain heavy accumulations of iron oxide, they are outstanding for Gewürztraminer.

Of all the major "old" négociant firms, the house of *Hugel* (in existence since 1639) is most widely known. Unlike the other, often larger, firms, it owns little vine hectarage, preferring instead to purchase grapes from nearly 300 growers. It does, however, produce excellent Gewürztraminer, Pinot Gris, and Riesling from 24 widely scattered holdings, of which the Sporen and Schoenenbourg vineyards are considered the best. While it makes an enormous range of wines, its reputation rests on the production of spectacular Vendage Tardive, Sélection des Grains Nobles, and Réserve bottlings, all of which are rich, opulent, and long lived; with concentrated bouquet and flavor. *Dopff & Irion*, a house merging two old wine-related families under a new banner, is the largest firm in Riquewihr and the fourth-largest Alsatian property owner. Cultivating more than 120 hectares, it makes and distributes a full line of wines. While the "Diamond" label represents the least expensive, fine estate wines are marketed under the "Dne. du Château de Riquewihr" label. More than half of production is exported, and it is a major force in the production of Pinot Noir. *Dopff "Au Moulin"*, a large grower/négociant basking in the glory of a 400-year-old history, owns 80 hectares and makes a wide assortment of wines. Containing considerable acidity, the wines, usually

Plate 2.1   The house of Hugel, "since 1639" one of
the more traditional houses in Alsace

characterized by hard, steely, and austere features, are longer lived than
most. The firm is the largest private producer of Crémant, and its
Riesling, Muscat, and Gewürztraminer are above average. Other producers include *Jean Preiss-Zimmer* (Riesling), *J.-J. Baumann* Gewürztraminer, Riesling, and Pinot Gris), *René Schmidt* (Schoenenbourg
Riesling), *Raymond Berschy* (fresh, zesty wines), *Roger Jung* (Riesling, and
Gewürztraminer), *Mittnacht-Klack* (Riesling), and *M. Wiedderhirn*.

Beblenheim, along with Mittelwihr and Riquewihr, serves as a good
example of a medieval walled town. The village lies on the foot of the
Sonnenglanz and is known for the production of exceptional Riesling,
Sylvaner, Muscat, Pinot Gris, and Gewürztraminer. Composed of Muschelkalk, the Sonnenglanz ("sunshine hill") site produces superb Riesling
from gravelly slopes and exceptional Gewürztraminer from flatter sites

containing more clay. Within the past 50 years hectarage has doubled, and there are about 200 growers. The coopérative makes a wide range of above-average to excellent clean, fruity wines, of which Riesling and Pinot Gris are particularly good. *Bott-Geyl*, a small shipper, has a good reputation for Riesling, Muscat, Pinot Gris, and Gewürztraminer. Mittelwihr, like Bennwihr, Sigolsheim, and Ammerschwihr, was totally destroyed in 1945 and has since rebuilt; but unlike the other villages, it is unusual because it lacks its former medieval ambiance. It contains nearly 300 producing hectares, has one excellent vineyard (Mandelberg), produces two wines of note (Gewürztraminer and Riesling), and is the site of a peculiar microclimate. Because it is surrounded by high cliffs on three sides, the warming effects of the sun and the constant downdrafts reduce the incidence of spring frosts and lengthen the growing season. *Preiss-Henny*, with 32 hectares, is the largest grower/négociant and a good, reliable, export-minded firm making above-average Muscat, Riesling, and Gewürztraminer. Other producers include *Edgard Schaller* (Muscat and Riesling), *Philippe Gocker, J.-P. Mauller, J.-B. Specht, Fernand Siegler-Kuster, Pierre Wurtz, Ernest Horcher,* and *Greiner-Schlerot.*

Slightly to the east of Mittelwihr is the large 273-hectare commune of Bennwihr, the site of one of the largest cooperatives specializing in Gewürztraminer and Riesling. The historic village of Wettolsheim, known as the birthplace of Alsatian viticulture, is the second-largest wine commune after Ammerschwihr in the Haut-Rhin. The soil is a collage of limestone, gravel, granite, and sandstone, and the best site is the Steingrubler vineyard. The wines exhibit fresh, acidic, full flavors and plenty of essence. The grape with "the" reputation is the Muscat, which produces full-bodied, flavorful wines. The energetic firm of *Anton Gaschy–F. Brucker* has become the region's largest producer-exporter, generating a reputation for good value despite the inconsistency of its wines. *Munsch and Mann*, a well-run small house, makes wines that are sought after because of their crisp, subtle flavor. With 328 hectares of vineland, Sigolsheim, the third-largest wine commune in the Haut-Rhin, was totally destroyed in 1945 but has since been rebuilt. It is famous for the location of five important vineyards: Mambourg, Vogelgarten, Altenberg, Hügel, and Sigolsheimer, of which the first three are the finest. Planted mainly in Gewürztraminer, they are all located on good southern and southeastern exposures containing a considerable amount of limestone and clay. Mambourg, the most famous site, contains more limestone than all the others and has developed a reputation for good-to-excellent Gewürztraminer. Altenberg, with more clay and impaired drainage, is not as good. The biggest producer is the local coopérative, the second-largest in Alsace. The most celebrated of the several négociants is *Pierre Sparr*, a firm with a good reputation for single vineyard wines. It is a large 18th-century house that owns 35 hectares of widely dispersed vineyards in excellent locations.

Lying half a kilometer west of Sigolsheim, the tiny village of Kientzheim is known for full-bodied Gewürztraminer, Pinot Gris, and Riesling. Along the Kaysersberg–Kientzheim–Sigolsheim slope is the largest concentration of Gewürztraminer—responsible for 17 percent of all that is planted in the Haut-Rhin. Nearly the entire planted area is composed of four famous vineyards: Koehrenburg, Furstentum, Schlossberg, and Clos des Capucins (as well as a small portion of Altenberg). The most famous vineyard in the region, Schlossberg, was the first to be granted Grand Cru status. It contains 30 hectares, and since its soils are nearly 100 percent granitic in origin, it is an ideal site for the production of Riesling.

Kaysersberg, along with Kientzheim and Sigolsheim, lies in the deepest and highest portion of the Weiss valley. Once an important Roman city, it is today a small, isolated, 58-hectare vinegrowing commune. The vine-clad hill overlooking the town was historically known as "Mons Caesaris"; however, the town's contemporary circular form and structure, with its formidable walls, numerous squares, and 800-year-old houses, betrays a more medieval history. Kayserberg, known as the birthplace of Albert Schweitzer, contains two first-class vineyards and growers. Since it is situated in the center of the best portion of the Alsatian vineyard, it is considered one of the top four communes in the production of quality wine. The two principal vineyards of note are Schlossberg and Geisburg, the former being the better of the two. The house with "the" reputation is *Faller Frères*, owner of the former 25-hectare ecclesiastical vineyard of Clos des Capucins. It is a firm with impeccable credentials, easily ranking as one of the top four in the production of quality wine, all of which are made to age. The finest wines carry the Dne. Weinbach label and are very expensive, but because of their superb and consistent high quality, offer considerable value. Wines from this house are close to perfection and should not be missed, particularly the Riesling and Gewürztraminer. *Marcel Blanck* is a grower with a reputation for unusual Edelzwicker, Pinot Gris, Sylvaner, Pinot Blanc, and Riesling.

Ammerschwihr, a town destroyed in 1945, is the second-largest wine commune in Alsace after Dambach-la-Ville, and the largest in the Haut-Rhin. Located along the south bank of the Weiss River, it is known for two above-average vineyards: Kaefferkopf and Meiwihr. The former, one of the most celebrated, lies on a hillside south of Ammerschwihr. Its granitic soil is planted mainly in Riesling, Pinot Gris, Pinot Blanc, and Gewürztraminer. The Meiwihr site, although somewhat less celebrated, is planted in similar grapes. The main producers are *R. Sick–P. Dreyer* (refined Crémant, elegant Rieslings, and full, spicy, *vin de garde* Gewürztraminers), *Vins d'Alsace Kuehn* (Riesling, Pinot Blanc, Gewürztraminer, and Sylvaner), *Les Caves J.-B. Adam* (outstanding Sylvaner and Pinot Gris), *Jerome Geschickt* (Riesling), *Jean Schaetzel* (superb Gewürztraminer and Riesling), *Maurice Schoecht* (Riesling), *René Schneider, Henri Ehrhardt,* and *H. & J. Heitzmann.*

Two kilometers south of Ammerschwihr, huddled against the wooded Vosges, are the well-regarded wine towns of Katzenthal and Niedermorschwihr. The 168-hectare Katzenthal vineyard, which was nearly destroyed in 1945, has a reputation for Gewürztraminer and quality wine production from a small portion of the Schlossberg vineyard. The growers of note are *J.-P. Eckle* and *Bernard Frères.* The former house makes above-average and reliable Muscat, Pinot Gris, Riesling, and Gewürztraminer; and the latter produces a sprightly Riesling. The neighboring 100-hectare town of Niedermorschwihr was formerly owned by the Knights Hospitaller of St. John and contains one vineyard, the Sommerberg, which is above average in the production of quality Riesling. The growers with a good reputation are *Marcel Mullenbach* (intense wines), and *Albert Boxler* (Riesling). Located upriver from Ingerheim on the north bank of the Fecht is Turckheim, the site of substantial Pinot Noir plantings. The fortified town is triangular in shape and contains a number of medieval gateways, intimate squares, 500-year-old walls, and an imposing town hall. The surrounding vineyards lie on granitic soils and produce above-average Pinot Gris, Muscat, and Pinot Noir. The most important vineyard is Brand, a medium-sized plot of 30 hectares producing outstanding wine. Other less well-known vineyards include Steinglitz, Kirchthal, Weingarten, Lerchenberg, Berg, Straeng, Schliff and Molsheimergasse. The producing region also includes the three minor hamlets of Zimmerbach, Walbach, and Wihr-au-Val. The Turckheim coopeative, the largest producer in the commune, makes a complete line of above-average wines, especially Gewürztraminer, Riesling, and Pinot Noir. The house with a superlative reputation is *Charles Schleret,* a small but highly conscientious producer of Pinot Noir, Gewürztraminer, and Muscat.

Ingersheim, located on the northwestern border of Colmar on the Fecht River, is a 211-hectare vineyard of small growers, practically all of whom belong to the local cooperative. The town, like many others in the vicinity, was heavily damaged in the closing months of World War II. It is known for one average vineyard, Florimont, located on limestone soil, with a fair reputation for Sylvaner and Gewürztraminer. The wines are darker than in neighboring communes, full-bodied, and contain low acid levels. Located in the center of the Haut-Rhin between the shallow Lauch and Fecht rivers is the charming 15th-century town of Colmar, the historical center for regional trade. It has a winsome medieval section of narrow, irregular streets and half-timbered houses. The name is derived from the Roman *Villa Columbaria,* which for a short time served as one of Charlemagne's many residences. Colmar boasts of Auguste Bartholdi, the native son who created the Statue of Liberty, a superlative wine museum, and the "Musee Unterlinden," after the Louvre, the second-most-popular museum in France. Although not the largest wine town, it is the largest city between Mulhouse and Strassbourg, the home of the Viticultural Institute, and the center of the wine trade. The surrounding area is known for its light, gravelly soils and a microclimate that is considered one of the driest in all France. The above-average wines are heavily impregnated with spice and *goût d'terroir*. The *Union of Colmar Vignerons* stores and bottles the output of several cooperatives. *SYNVA*, a large syndicate of shippers-growers with medium quality and value wines, is a formidable factor in the domestic market. *Charles Jux-Jacobert*, one of the largest property owners in Colmar, is known for above-average Crémant.

To the south of Turckheim is the small village of Wintzenheim, flanked by two famous vineyards—Hengst and Wartstein. The soils are mainly limestone with considerable infusions of sandstone, and hence are radically different from the dark granitic soils of the north. Hengst, the best vineyard, is a site with plenty of limestone, planted in Gewürztraminer and Pinot Blanc, while Riesling dominates gravelly sections. *Joseph Meyer* and *Dne. Zind-Humbrecht*, two of the largest and most prestigious wine firms, make their headquarters in Wintzenheim. The former is a good-sized firm known for outstanding Pinot Blanc, Gewürztraminer, and Riesling, wines that are consistently fresh, classy, full-bodied, and well made. The Hengst vineyard Rieslings are legendary, and the Vendage Tardive Gewürztraminer superb. Leonard Humbrecht, owner of Dne. Zind-Humbrecht, manages the affairs of a firm that has been in existence since 1620. He owns nearly 30 hectares of vineland in the Rangen, Hengst, Brand, and Herrenweg vineyards. Among the many wines made, Pinot Gris from Rangen, the Herrenweg Gewürztraminer, and the

Plate 2.2   Harvest at Zind-Humbrecht

Rangen Rieslings are all absolutely magnificent. *Bernard Staehle* is a small house known for above-average Riesling.

Eguisheim, one of the most beautiful towns of the Haut-Rhin, is the birthplace of Pope Leo IX and the site of a former Roman watchtower. It is the home of the fine and reliable firm of *Léon Beyer* and marks the southern border of the fine wine region (only Guebwiller and Thann, two isolated pockets of above-average wine production, are found farther south). The town, surrounded by three fortified towers called "Châteaux de Eguisheim," has a unique circular form. The best sites are Pfersigberg, Eichberg, and Côtes d'Eguisheim, the first two being the most important and known for Riesling and Gewürztraminer, respectively. The deep and permeable soils are a potpourri of chalk, *limon*, limestone, and sand. In addition to Riesling and Gewürztraminer, above-average Pinot Gris and Sylvaner are also made, the latter being far better than that from Dambach-la-Ville. The largest producer in the commune, and the biggest cooperative in Alsace, is *Cave Vinicole d'Eguisheim*, which is responsible for more than 800,000 cases. It has more than 540 members, controls nearly 680 hectares, and is the largest producer of Crémant. Nearly one-fifth of production is sold through retail outlets, and a similar percentage is exported; all wines are excellent and offer outstanding value. The reliable 400-year-old firm of *Léon Beyer* ranks among the top five quality producers of Alsace. The wines are clean, flavorful, lighter in body than most, and offer considerable refinement and individuality. Although the firm produces a wide range of wines, the special cuvées, réserve, Vendage Tardive, and individual vineyard wines are excellent. Other producers include *Antoine Stoffel* (Riesling and Muscat), *Joseph Freudenreich* (Gewürztraminer), *Paul Ginglinger* (superb Riesling), and *Bruno Hertz* (Rangen Gewürztraminer).

Husseren-les-Châteaux, lying upslope from Eguisheim with a magnificent view of the Alsatian plain, is the highest village in Alsace. Viticulture began only after the Thirty Years War, and its vineyards were secularized only after the French Revolution. The soil, heavy in limestone, degrades into heavy clay in places; as a result the commune lacks the presence of a famous vineyard and is planted mainly in Gewürztraminer, Riesling, and Pinot Blanc. Although the village lacks the prestige of a major growth, it does serve as the headquarters of one of the most prestigious houses in Alsace. The wines of *Kuentz-Bas* are meticulously made, substantial yet delicate on the palate, very rare, and outstanding in every way. Voegtlinshoffen, a town located at the foot of the Vosges, was owned until 1887 by the city of Basel, Switzerland. Located on high ground, the vineyards are not generally subjected to spring frost. Soils are mainly clay and sand, and the preferred vines, Pinot Blanc, Muscat, and Gewürztraminer, produce mild, soft, eminently quaffable wines. Of the three vines, the one that receives meticulous care and commands the highest prices is the Muscat. The village has two vineyards with above-average reputations: Hagelberg and Hatschbourg, the latter considered superior. The two producers with reputations are *Théo Cattin* (outstanding Muscat and Gewürztraminer), and *X. Stemplel*.

While the wines of Voegtlinshoffen are considered of fair quality, the minor plantings of the neighboring village of Obermorschwihr produce common, undistinguished wines. The same can also be said for Herrlisheim and Hattstatt farther south. To the southwest, with 190 hectares of vineland, is Gueberschwihr, a commune with a better reputation largely due to the presence of two above-average vineyards—Goldert and Weingarten. For the most part, the Gewürztraminer, Pinot Blanc, Muscat, and Sylvaner output eventually find their way into innocuous regional blends. The villages of Soultzmatt and Westhalten lie along the north slope of the Soultzmatt valley next to the minor l'Ohmbach stream. The hectarage surrounding both is devoted almost exclusively to vinegrowing, with only the Zinnkoepfle vineyard separating the two. The vineyards, with magnificent southern aspects, are underlain by limestone and are rather steep, often reaching elevations of 400 meters. Although nearly half the planted area is composed of Sylvaner, the vine of note is the Muscat, which produces fresh and flavorful wine. The most famous vineyard is Zinnkoepfle, followed by Strangenberg and Sulzaberg, the first producing excellent Gewürztraminer, and the other Pinot Blanc and Pinot Noir. Confined to Sylvaner and Riesling, the vineyards and wine of Soultzmatt are less distinguished. The main producers are *A. Heim* (outstanding Gewürztraminer, Riesling, and Pinot Blanc), *Coopérative de Westhalten, Jules Zimmermann,* and *Léon Boesch.*

The vineyards of note in Pfaffenheim are the Schneckenberg (called "snails hill"), Bergweingarten, Steinert, Hartweg, and Rossgarten, all of which are good for Pinot Planc, with only the first considered of Grand Cru quality. Among the many producers with above-average reputations is the local cooperative, which makes an interesting Pinot Blanc and excellent Riesling and Muscat. *Joseph Rieflé*, a small house, makes excellent Pinot Gris and a good, flavorful Riesling. Equally good and often better, *René Schaefle* makes excellent Pinot Blanc and outstanding Riesling and Gewürztraminer. On higher ground farther south are the vineyards of Rouffach, a small rustic town surrounded by oak and poplar where time appears to have stood still. Virtually every square inch of vineland was owned by the church prior to secularization after the French Revolution. The best sites are Clos de St.-Landolin, Isenbourg, and Litzeltal. What Rouffach lacks in modernity it more than makes up for with its major and highly successful grower, *A. O. Muré*, a 16-hectare domaine that dates back to 1630, and the owner of the most famous vineyard in the area— Clos de St.-Landolin. The firm makes solid, highly concentrated, wellstructured, old-fashioned wines intended for long keeping. The Riesling, Gewürztraminer, and Muscat are carefully made and highlighted by distinctive elegance and finesse. The Clos St.-Landolin vineyard, sheltered by the highest point of the Vosges Mountains, is as a consequence the driest of all vineyards, receiving less than 450 mm of rain annually. The soil, mainly oolitic rock, produces intensely flavored wines. Clos de St.-Landolin Réserve Gewürztraminer is consistently well made, and like all other wines made by Muré, underrated and an outstanding value. Despite the historic importance of *Ch. d'Isenbourg*, its wines are only average in quality.

Located in a small narrow valley between Soultzmatt and Guebwiller, the twin villages of Orschwihr and Bergholtz Zell are the largest of the southern communes. Because the soils contain a fair mixture of limestone and sand and a good dose of *limon*, the preferred vines are Riesling and Gewürztraminer. The four best vineyards are the Bollenberg (a limestone hill), Lippelsberg, Affenberg, and Pfingstberg, the first two being considered superior. Historically the town of Orschwihr and its vineyards were owned by the Hapsburgs and the archbishop of Strassbourg. In addition to Gewürztraminer and Riesling, Muscat, Pinot Noir, and Sylvaner are also planted; the latter, considered the finest, is more full-bodied and more distinctive than any other Alsatian Sylvaner, with a capacity to age well. The principal producers are *Lucien Albrecht* (Riesling), *Paul Reinhart* (Riesling and Gewürztraminer), and *J.-P. Dirler* (Spiegel Riesling).

Guebwiller, with its 142 hectares of vineland, lies in full view of the Ballon de Guebwiller, the highest mountain in the Vosges. The town, with its 500-year-old town hall, is pressed against the hill overlooking the tranquil little valley of the Lauch. Its vineyards were established by the monks of the Abbey of Murbach, located nearby. While a good portion of the hectarage on this part of the Vosges foothills produces common, undistinguished wine, deep accumulations of *limon* have given rise to no fewer than eight important vineyards—Kitterlé, Wanne, Kessler, Gans, Saering, Heissenstein, Speigel, and Schimberg—all of which are above average in the production of Gewürztraminer and, to a lesser extent, Riesling. The Gewürztraminer-Riesling wines of Kitterlé (a steep vineyard that is well exposed to the south-southeast) are outstanding and very expensive. *Dne. Viticole Schlumberger*, the largest domaine in Alsace with 148 hectares of producing vineyards, ranks in the top five in the production of premium wine. Although the firm's flagship vineyard is the 12-hectare plot in Kitterlé, it also owns a portion of all the others. The wines are impeccably made, aged in wood, distinctive in taste, very fat, rich, refined, never austere, and not overly dry. Thann, west of Mulhouse in the extreme southern portion of the Haut-Rhin, is a former fortified town lying next to the Thur River. The vineyards comprise fewer than 55 hectares and are the product of unusual soil and climatic elements. All sites face south, are situated on a series of terraces, and are higher in elevation than any other in Alsace. The soils are mainly volcanic in origin, high in silica, and brown in color—unique features for Alsace.

Plate 2.3   The Kitterlé vineyard (courtesy Dne. Viticole Schlumberger)

As a consequence, the wines have a pronounced *goût de terroir*, are high in alcohol, particularly flavorful, and very distinctive. The finest vineyard, and one of the most famous, is Rangen, followed by Staufen. The wines with a reputation for flavor, dark color, and distinctive bouquet are Gewürztraminer and Riesling. *Ch. Ollwiller* is a very impressive estate in the region but makes disappointing wines.

THE WINES OF THE JURA

THE Jura wine-producing district is a small, compact, 1,500-hectare AOC vineyard located in eastern France between the Ain and Doubs rivers. More than 40 percent of the entire area is forested and sparsely settled, dominated by summer and winter tourist attractions, dairying, and clock manufacturing.

The Jura consists of several parallel ranges separated by valleys and small, irregular tablelands between Burgundy and Switzerland, extending from the Saône northeastward to the Rhine north of Basel, Switzerland. The hills, consisting of beds of limestone, are folded into a series of larger folds in which the valleys are narrow and the hilltops low, round, green, and uneven. Th entire region is one of pine-studded valleys, upland meadows, and woodlands. It is crescent-shaped, measuring 210 kilometers long by 42 kilometers wide, and its various summits, although higher than those of the Vosges to the north, do not exceed 1,800 meters. Throughout, the valleys (regionally called *vaux*), exhibit the erosive force of glaciers with moranic deposits dominating surface soils everywhere.

The climate is described by one prominent geographer as "eight months of snow, two months of wind, but the rest of the year is fine." It is most definitely continental in character, with seasonal extremes exaggerated by relief and location. Spring is a season of high frost expectation; summer is warm and dry; fall, which is particularly long, warm, and dry, facilitates the production of high sugar levels; winter is long, cold, and windy, with high snow accumulations.

All viticultural sites are determined by two specific features—an *adret* exposure and the existence of chalky and/or gravelly soils. The vineyards are, in fact, found at 200 to 500 meters in elevation—100 meters below the flange (or cirques) of cliffs that overlook the irregular glacial valleys below, thus sheltering the vines from cold northerly and prevailing westerly winds. The best sites are located on marl and limestone soil rich in fossils. Individual vineyard sites are small, fragmented, and act as a significant part-time cash crop to dairy farmers, restauranteurs, and hotel keepers. Few vignerons are solely dependent upon viticulture for their livelihood.

Vineyards, found in the Jura and Doubs departments, form the frontier with western Switzerland north of Lake Léman (Geneva) and were part of the medieval province of Franche Compté. Of the two, the Jura department is the most important, and although the vineyards are found in 11 of the 32 cantons, the largest single concentration occurs along two prominent hills bordering the Bresse valley. This area, dominated by Arbois, measures less than 9 kilometers in length and contains the important communes of Arlay, Pupillin, Les Arsures, Poligny, and Villette. Vinegrowing continues southward for another 25 kilometers to St.-Amour, but the intensity and quality of wine production are secondary to other activities. Although total hectarage amounts to less than .001 of the entire national total, a curious feature of this marginal viticultural area is that both hectarage and wine production are expanding rapidly. There are about 450 individual exploitations, one-fifth of which make wine.

Although the vines were first planted by Romans, two post-medieval events influenced the future viticultural history of the region. The first was the introduction of "Commandaria-type" (also called Cyprus Mana) wine from Cyprus in the 14th century, and the second was the Spanish occupation in the 16th century that introduced the technique of "yellow vinification" or "Sherry-type" wine production. Hectarage and wine production grew steadily after the region was incorporated with France in 1668, so that by the middle of the 19th century there were more than 16,487 hectares with an output of 308,657 hectoliters of wine, a good portion of which found an outlet in Switzerland. Hectarage increased to the all-time high of 20,000 in 1890, only to fall to 4,000 by 1930, and to fewer than 600 in 1960 (see Fig. 3.1). During the past fifteen years, renewed interest in the Jura has been reflected by new plantings occurring at a rate of 15 hectares a year. With 1,500 hectares in 1980, approximately one-half of the entire hectarage is AOC, producing approximately 30,000 hectoliters annually (Table 3.1).

Of the 29,816 hectoliters of AOC wine produced in 1980, nearly three-quarters were white, of which 90 percent or more were dry. Of the six AOC appellations, Arbois Rouge, Rosé, and Blanc account for more than 53 percent of the regional total. Forty percent is produced by the regional wines of Côte du Jura Blanc, Rouge, and Rosé; the remainder is composed of two small appellations—Château-Chalon, known for excellent, well-aged wines, and Etoile Blanc, of which a good portion is "star" or mousseux wine.

Figure 3.1   Jura: Vine Hectarage, 1860–1985
(in thousands of hectares)

Despite the fact that the wines are little known outside the region and are treated as curiosities by most gourmands, they are all expertly made and consistently good. While a good proportion can be described as delightful and charming, at least one-third of production and nearly all AOC wines are "serious" by any measurement, ranging from above average to superb in quality. They are known for distinctive taste, aroma, longevity, and fair-to-excellent value. In the final analysis, the wines are known for their complexity and an earthy, as opposed to fruity, taste. During the 17th and 18th centuries the wines of the Jura were Versailles favorites and widely known, but now less than 10 percent are consumed outside the region.

The most important quality white grape is the Savagnin. Because of its peculiar growing habits (it matures late, is subject to *coulure*, is thick-skinned, has a pronounced aroma similar to musk, and is subject to periodic bouts of *botrytis*), it demands, and gets, rich limestone and marl soils, heat traps, and the sunniest exposures. As a result the best sites are protected from cold winds, located well below the treeline between 270 and 450 meters in elevation, and always positioned in amphitheatre-like aspects. The yield is limited to 40 hectoliters to the hectare, but in reality the figure is closer to 30, and for Château-Chalon, it is closer to 25. Other white grape varieties include Chardonnay, Gamay Blanc, and Pinot Blanc. Chardonnay produces an excellent dry wine in Arbois, but when blended with other varieties, particularly the Poulsard, the resulting product is less good. The important red vines are Poulsard, Trousseau, Gamay, Pinot Noir, Pinot Gris, and Mondeuse. The most important in terms of hectarage is the Poulsard, used for red and rosé, which produces pleasant to thin, watery, pale and extremely acidic wines. Trousseau is usually mixed with Pinot Noir or Pinot Gris to give a fuller, more consistent wine, which in good years can be particularly good.

Table 3.1   AOC Wine Production in the Jura, 1980

Appellation	Hectoliters	Percent of total
Arbois Rouge and Rosé	9,177	30.8
Arbois Blanc	6,790	22.8
Château Chalon[a]		
Etoile Blanc	1,424	4.8
Côte du Jura Rouge and Rosé	1,881	6.3
Côte du Jura Blanc	10,544	35.3
Total Rouge and Rosé	11,058	37.0
Total Blanc	18,758	63.0
Total	29,816	100.0

[a]Château Chalon produced no wine in 1980; its production is highly irregular, usually less than 350 hectoliters
per year.

Source: French Ministry of Agriculture.

The Jura Wine Specialties

Vin Jaune, made exclusively from the Savagnin grape and believed to have
been first made by Benedictine monks in the 16th century, is one of the
finest and most distinctive wines of France. Although the origin is
obscured in history, the wine is made by first drying the grapes for several
months prior to crushing in January or February. The grapes are grown
only on limestone and marl soils, picked as late as possible and fermented
very slowly. When picked after the first snow, the wine is called *vin de
gelée*, and it is very similar to *Eiswine*. After the wine is made, it is stored
in wooden barrels (and not topped) where it acquires a local "flor" yeast
similar to Sherry. After an aging period of six to ten years, the wine turns
bright yellow (hence the name), and only then is it bottled. The wine is
maderized and can thus appeal to Sherry aficionados.

Vin Jaune has a harsh and bitter taste when young, but with aging these
characteristics disappear, the wine becomes· softer, acquires its golden-
amber color, and develops an extraordinary nut-like bouquet and a most
satisfying sensation on the palate. It is dry with some residual sweetness
lurking in the background, has 14 percent to 16 percent alcohol,
improves with age for more than twenty years, and is usually served at
room temperature or slightly chilled. Its biggest attractions are a powerful scent and an indescribable flavor. It is produced only in exceptional
years, the most recent being 1959, 1964, 1969, 1973, and 1979. The
wine, bottled in 65 centiliter stump-shouldered *clavelins*, develops as it
ages into an unusual blend of chalk, spice, and honey. The finest comes
from Château-Chalon and Arbois. The yellow wines of the Côtes de Jura
appellation, or those from L'Etoile, are not the same, but poor imitations.

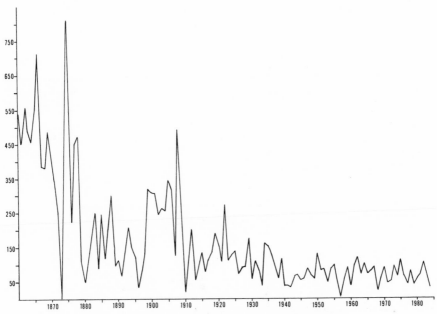

Figure 3.2   Jura: Wine Production, 1860–1984
(in thousands of hectoliters)

Vin de Paille (or "hay wine") is made from dried grapes (historically on straw mats, hence the name) that undergo a very cold and long (as long as four years) fermentation. The resulting wines are sweet and can attain as much as 18 percent alcohol. They age for a minimum of two years in wood and bottle before they are considered ready for consumption, but are able to age gracefully for decades thereafter. The Jura is the largest viticultural region of France that still produces commercial quantities of *vin de paille*. Like *vin jaune*, *vin de paille* is the product of above-average vintages and is much better than its reputation suggests. The wine has a golden-amber color, a high glycerine content, a concentrated flavor that is complex, satisfying, and distinctive, thus offering an outstanding value. The best producing region is the commune Voiteur. The largest and one of the finest producers of both *vin jaune* and *vin de paille* is *Henri Maire*, followed by *Désiré Petit, Lucien Aviet, Ch. Gréa,* and *Grand Frères*.

THE JURA APPELLATIONS

Arbois

Arbois produces between 14,000 and 25,000 hectoliters of wine a year (white, red, rosé, *vin jaune, vin de paille,* and mousseux) of which red and rosé wines constitute more than 50 percent of appellation share and more than one-quarter of regional AOC wine production. White wine production is about one-third that of the red and rosé output. Along with Château-Chalon, Arbois is the most famous vineyard within the Jura appellation. It is the center of a thriving tourist industry and home to one of the nation's most celebrated native sons, Louis Pasteur. The center of the wine-producing region is the graceful and charming little town of Arbois and one dozen small settlements, all of which are surrounded by glacial cirques and meandering rivers. The finest of the satellite communes in the Arbois region are Pupillin, Montigny-les-Arsures, Mesnay, and Les Arsures, all of which are good enough to have their names placed on labels.

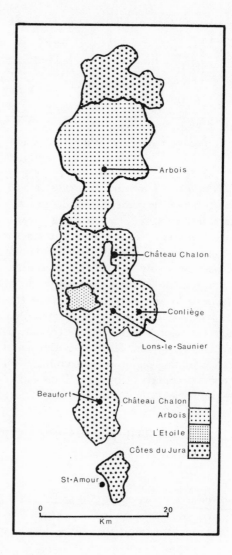

Figure 3.3   Jura: Major Appellations

The wine of repute is the Rosé d'Arbois, a little-known, obscure, underrated, but above-average wine—in fact, one of the best in France. It is very lively, tasty, fruity, and dark, turning slightly topaz with age. Red Arbois is significantly inferior, although popular. It is of medium body, warm, satisfying, low in alcohol, and lightly scented. The second most important wine is a still white made from numerous varieties, the best of which, from Arbois and Pupillin, has an unusual nutty flavor, is perfectly dry, well balanced, and ages well for three years. Above-average to excellent *vin de paille* and *vin jaune* are also made, the latter being considered the equal to Château-Chalon, particularly in Poligny, Arbois, and Pupillin. Small amounts of mousseux are made but are not considered the equal of L'Etoile.

The principal driving force in the viticultural fortunes of the Jura is the firm of *Henri Maire* located in Arbois. With 300 hectares, it owns one-eighth of the planted area of the Jura, has a storage capacity of 85,000 hectoliters, and makes more than 20,000 hectoliters of wine annually, or 60 percent of regional total. The firm has four principal properties: *Dne. de Monfort, Dne. de Grange Grillard, Dne. du Sorbie,* and *Dne. de la Croix d'Argis.* In addition, the firm makes absolutely superb Château-Chalon, *vin de paille, vin jaune,* mousseux (called "vin fou"), and at least a dozen more. The finest wines are hard to find outside the region, as most are sold to fine restaurants and private clients. After Henri Maire, the next largest

Plate 3.1   Harvest at Dne. de Montfort

producer is the modest cooperative of Arbois, then *Fruitière Vinicole d'Arbois, Jean Bourdy, Lucien Aviet, Daniel Dugois, Jacques Forêt, Roger Lornet, Rolet Pére, Abbaye de St.-Laurent,* and *La Maison du Vigneron.*

Château-Chalon

Château-Chalon takes its name from a pretty medieval village perched on a cliff overlooking the Seille valley. The appellation is confined solely to the production of *vin jaune,* the finest wine of the Jura and the most expensive. In addition to Château-Chalon, the wine can also be made in Ménétru, Nevy-sur-Seille, and Domblans, which are collectively responsible for 85 percent of all *vin jaune* made. The peculiarity of its geographic concentration is directly related to the location of a blue, chalky soil, the highest proportion of which is found in Château-Chalon and to a smaller extent in Arbois and Pupillin. Yields are extremely low, and the annual harvest rarely exceeds 325 hectoliters. Out of a possible 65 hectares, less than 40 hectares are in production in Château-Chalon, an easy explanation as to why the wine is so rare and expensive.

The wine is richly concentrated in substance, flavor, and fragrance and acquires, as it ages, a magnificent amber color. The final product lies somewhere between a Tokay and a well-aged Sherry. Local experts refer to its *goût de jaune* (taste of yellow). It is served cold as an aperitif or at room temperature after dinner. It is a primary ingredient in a number of local dishes and is incomparable with cheese, nuts, and chicken. Located in Arlay just north of L'Etoile, the négociant firm of *Jean Bourdy* is known for fresh and zesty white wines, strong and sharp red wines, outstanding Château-Chalon, fragrant *vin jaune,* and a particularly good mousseux, among others.

L'Etoile

L'Etoile, located south of Château Chalon, is strictly a white wine region (table wine, *vin jaune, vin de paille,* and mousseux) known for its fine, distinctive, light, refreshing wines, most of which are made into mousseux. The mousseux is considered the best that this small commune has to offer. A delicate libation of pale color, it is highlighted by a refined bouquet and a long-lingering finish. Quintigny, a neighboring hamlet, also has the right to market its mousseux as L'Etoile. The still wine is flavorful and light in body, with a faint, bitter aftertaste and, like the mousseux, made only from Savagnin and Chardonnay grapes. Small amounts of *vin jaune* and *vin de paille* are also made from the same grapes, but do not compare with the better growth of Château-Chalon and Arbois. Principal producers are *Dne. de Montbourgeau, Ch. l'Etoile,* and *Ch. Joly.* Just south of L'Etoile, in the small village of Rotalier near Beaufort, is the small 7-hectare, 17th-century property of *Ch. Gréa.* This well-managed vineyard, planted in Trousseau, Poulsard, Savagnin, and Chardonnay grapes, makes 3,000 cases of first-class wine worthy of any cellar. "Sur la Roche" is a full-bodied, fresh rosé from Trousseau and Poulsard; "Le Clos" is a robust Chardonnay with considerable body and fragrance; "Le Chanet" is a spicy white wine from Chardonnay and Savagnin; and "En Cury" is a marvelous *vin jaune*, rarely made and only in small quantities.

Côtes-de-Jura

Producing the same type of wines as Arbois, this regional appellation includes all the intermediate quality sites along the entire length of the producing region—from Mt. Begon, north of Arbois, south to Lons-le Saunier. The largest single appellation, it produces more white wine than any other. Although well-flavored, they appear to be very assertive yet "hollow" in terms of character and refinement, hence their consumption as "carafe wines." The rosé is robust and heady, but not the equal of Arbois. The red, the least important, is poorly balanced, light in color, and often very acidic.

4

THE WINES OF SAVOIE

THE vinegrowing region of Savoie lies south of the Jura within the departments of Savoie, Ain, and Haute-Savoie. It contains 3,200 hectares, of which 1,400, officially classified as AOC, produce between 50,000 and 80,000 hectoliters of wine annually. In terms of area and production it is twice the size of Jura, the vineyards are more dispersed, and it contains six AOC and three VDQS appellations. The producing region is not topographically homogeneous because it straddles the pre- and high-Alps; the former, much lower, stretch from Lake Léman south to Durance, while the high-Alps are situated next to Switzerland and Italy. The producing regions are drained by the Rhône and Isère rivers and a multitude of tributaries, all swift-flowing alpine streams. The entire region is highly mountainous and dominated by Mont Blanc, Europe's highest peak.

The continental climate is reinforced by alpine influences characterized by brutally cold winters, a high incidence of temperature inversions, and spring frosts. To take full advantage of air flow and maximize solar insolation, vines are staked in all areas except on the flatter and more undulating areas along Lake Léman. Unlike the Jura, however, the valleys of Savoie are deeper, more sheltered, and as a consequence, hotter and drier. These climatic conditions are maintained because the more humid portion of the Alps are the windward margins of the pre-Alps, and not the high-Alps that are arranged close to the Swiss and Italian borders. The valleys of Savoie, therefore, receive less than 550 mm. of rainfall a year (very similar to Valais in southern Switzerland), which makes this area one of the driest in all France, while mountain peaks 2 kilometers away remain snow-covered throughout the year. Autumn is particularly favorable to grape maturation due to the presence of mild, Foehn-type winds.

Viticulture in an alpine (Savoie) or sub-alpine environment (like the

Table 4.1 AOC Wine Production in Savoie, 1980

Appellation	Hectoliters	Percent of total
Vin de Savoie	17,811	30.4
Vin de Savoie Blanc	34,310	59.0
Roussette de Savoie Blanc	2,311	3.9
Crépy Blanc	2,240	3.8
Seyssel Blanc	1,420	2.4
Seyssel Mousseux Blanc	544	.5
Total Rouge	17,811	30.0
Total Blanc	40,825	70.0
Total	58,636	100.0

Source: French Ministry of Agriculture.

Jura) is a precarious activity in which weather and climate are influenced by the forces of altitude, prevailing winds, and exposure. Altitude, for example, influences air pressure, air composition, air temperature, insolation, soil temperatures, evaporation, humidity levels, incidence of cloudiness, precipitation, and snowfall. Exposure, by contrast, exaggerates or modifies the quantity of the altitudinal elements in terms of *ubec* (shady) versus *adret* (sunny) positions, wet and dry positions, or windy and protected positions, respectively. The advantages of *adret* slopes, which are usually drier and more protected, are evident and of paramount importance. *Adret* aspects receive much higher levels of direct sunlight, which produces higher soil and plant temperatures. Therefore, the higher-than-normal altitude of the vines is not coincidental with a decrease in biotic possibilities.

After thousands of years of alpine acclimatization, man has discovered that his settlements and agricultural activities are best stratified by altitude on both *adret* and *ubec* exposures. Highland areas up to the snowline are devoted to pasture along the *adret* aspects, while *ubec* aspects above 400 meters are usually forested. In fact, more than three-quarters of all forest and more than 90 percent of all coniferous forest is located on *ubec* exposures. Vineyards lie between 200 and 500 meters along sheltered, maximum insolation sites—mostly along the *adret* and solar-reflected sites of Lake Léman and Lake Bourget (the largest in France), and along the upper banks of the Ain, Leysse, Arc, and Isère rivers.

Savoie, historically known as *Sapaudia,* gained its importance from its position commanding the Mont Cenis and the Little St.-Bernard Pass between France and Italy. Throughout recorded history, Ligurians, Celts, Romans, Burgundians, and Franks settled and developed similar, but separate, cultural entities, each with its own history. In the 11th century, the area came under the influence of the Holy Roman Empire, while in the following century it came under the domination of the House of Savoy. Despite the spread of Italian culture, the entire region managed to preserve its predominant French language and cultural institutions. The region, politically vacilating between France and Italy, was made a permanent part of France only in 1860.

Seventy-five percent of the wines of Savoie are white, of which 15 percent are sparkling. They are known for their pronounced taste, bouquet, high acidity, refreshing character, and reliability. Red and rosé wines, both of which are thin and unappealing, account for 25 percent of the total production.

While the vineyards of Savoie were first developed by Romans (and were favorably mentioned by Columellus), their extent was small and the industry always minute until the religious orders began to take interest during the Dark Ages. A curious footnote to the history of viticulture in this region concerns the area's most celebrated vine, the Altesse. It is reported that when Louis, Duc de Savoie, married Anne de Lusignan in 1432, she brought the Altesse vine from Cyprus, along with the method of making "Mana," a wine similar to the vins de paille of the Jura. The Altesse vine is now called Roussette, primarily in Morastel, Monthoux, Seyssel, and Frangy. The most important white grape, however, is the Jacquère, a low-alcohol grape, made still and petillant and always consumed within the first year. The largest concentration lies between Aix-les-Bains and Montmelian. Chasselas makes Fendant-type wines along the south shore of Lake Léman. The Savagnin (related to the Traminer), Cacaboué, and Molette (used only in the production of mousseux) are all obscure, indigenous varieties that are slowly disappearing. On the other hand, Chardonnay and Aligoté are increasing their hectarage. The Roussanne, a very difficult grape to grow, is considered the equal of Roussette in the production of quality wine. Among red grapes, the most important in terms of hectarage are the indigenous Mondeuse (it also makes minor quantities of white wine), the obscure Joubertin and Persan, and the more important, but difficult-to-grow, Pinot Noir and Gamay.

Vine hectarage and wine production have recently expanded with the increase of winter and summer tourists, to whom the wines of Savoie, despite their high price, appear to be very popular (Table 4.1). Seventy percent are produced by cooperatives, and more than 90 percent are consumed within the region; only minute quantities are exported, primarily to Switzerland.

THE WINE-PRODUCING APPELLATIONS

Vin de Savoie

White wines are mostly colorless, dry, fresh, light, agreeable, well-made, and very appealing, the very best made with a high proportion of Jacquère and Roussette grapes (lesser wines contain more Chasselas). The wine is often kept on its lees, to become petillant, and is consumed very young. The best sites for white wine are Montmélian, Apremont, Abymes, Marginan, and Chautagne. Commune names important in the production of a specific wine considered above average in quality are traditionally mentioned on the label. Red wine made from Mondeuse is light in color, very fragrant, and appears to improve after two years of bottle confinement. Montmélian, Chignin, Cruet, Bergeran, Arbin, and St.-Jean-de-la-Porte are considered the best sites. Red and rosé from Gamay have a deep color and a much more pronounced aroma, but lack finesse, balance, and delicacy. The best site for both is Chautagne. While *Dne. des Granger Longes* enjoys an excellent reputation for a wide range of wines, *Yves Ollivier, M. Simiand, Marcel Tardy,* and *Dne. des Rocailles* and the *Coopérative Le Vigneron Savoyard* all produce outstanding Apremont,

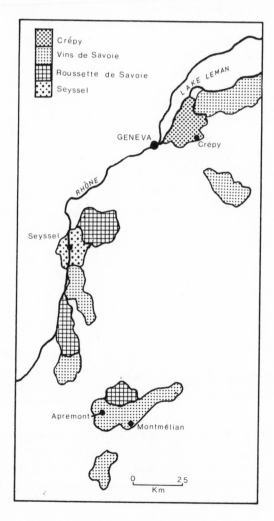

Figure 4.1 Savoie: Major Appellations

one of the better white wine-producing communes. *Cave Coopérative des Vins Fins Cruet in Arbin, Ch. Monterminod, Edmund Jacquin,* and *André Quenard* are all known for above-average-quality red wine. The small city of Chamberry is the center of a small, but thriving, vermouth industry.

Specialties within the Savoie appellation include the following: Roussette de Savoie-Frangy, an appealing, full white wine that comes from a small area north of Seyssel. Eleven additional communes produce a white made from Roussette and a red made from Mondeuse, each of which has the right to put its name on the label. The wines of Vin de Savoie–Ayse originate from vineyards that extend over three communes, Ayse, Marignier, and Bonneville, along the upper banks of the Arve River. Made from Savagnin, Roussette, and a maximum of 30 percent other varieties, this is a full-bodied wine with considerable character and one of the few wines offering substantial value. Vin de Savoie-Ripaille is made mainly in the commune of Thonon-les-Bains on Lake Léman. It is a dry wine from the Chasselas grape with attributes that are similar to fendant. A similar wine, Vins de Savoie-Marignan, comes from the commune of Sciez on the banks of Lake Léman between Massogny and Thonon-les-Bains. The largest producers of Savoie wines are the cooperatives of Abymes, Apremont, Cruet, Montmélian, and Chautagne. Among the many "smaller" producers are *Michel Rousseau* in Monthoux; *Jean Neyroud* in Frangy; *Marcel Fert* in Ayse; *Louis Magnin* in Montelion; and *Ch. de Monterminod* in Challes-les-Eaux.

Roussette de Savoie Blanc

With about 4 percent of AOC production, Roussette de Savoie Blanc is a vineyard comparable in size to Crépy. The wine is pale yellow, highly fragrant and delicate, with a unique taste. The finest wine comes from the following five sites: Frangy, Marestel, Monthoux, Monterminod, and Ayse. Major producers include the cooperative of Cruet, *Ch. Monterminod, Edmund Jacquin, Daniel Fustinoni,* and *Masson Frères*.

Crépy

Crépy production fluctuates between 2,000 and 5,000 hectoliters annually, and despite is rather high prices, it remains one of the most popular wines of Savoie. The wine is very dry, fresh, and often distinguished with a touch of finesse. It is low in alcohol, has a pale green-yellow color, the scent of violets, and the taste of hazelnuts. The vineyards in the communes and hamlets of Crépy, Loisin, Douvaine, and Ballaison are all planted on chalky soil with a southwesterly aspect along the south shore of Lake Léman. The wines have the reputation of being able to age for five years without losing their fragrance. Vines growing on less desirable sites in Sciez, Massongy, and portions of Loisin, Ballaison, and Douvaine have their wines marketed as "Vins de Petit-Crépy," an unofficial label designation. While 20 percent of total production is made petillant, small amounts of mousseux from Ayse, south of Crépy, enjoy a good reputation. *Ch. Ripaille* and *Goy Frères* are two very popular and reliable producers.

Seyssel Blanc and Mousseux

The smallest of the AOC appellations is Seyssel, a wine (made entirely from Chasselas) with a considerable following and high prices to compliment its popularity. The Seyssel appellation is known for dry, full, supple, still white wine and mousseux, the former outproducing the latter by a significant margin. With a combined production of 4,000 hectoliters, Seyssel produces but 3 percent of the total output of Savoie. The production region involves nearly 500 hectares, found north and south of Seyssel, in the departments of Ain, Savoie, and Haute-Savoie, the former being the most important and the latter the least. Approximately 100 hectares are used for the production of mousseux, a rapidly growing appellation.

Although historical references are found to wine production in the second century around the charming town of Seyssel (divided by the swift-flowing Rhône), hectarage and production of wine as early as A.D. 900 were small and monopolized by the numerous monasteries and abbeys that surrounded the influential episcopal seat in Seyssel. Each site was carefully selected and given a name, and so important did the individual vineyards become that eventually they became attached to the Chartreuse of Arvières. Until the middle of the 1840s the dominant activity was the raising of iris roots for the extraction of fragrance, and vineyard real estate stood at 100 hectares, producing less than 1,150 hectoliters of wine annually. Viticulture grew rapidly after the iris industry declined, with production reaching the all-time high of 6,800 hectoliters on the eve of the *phylloxera* epidemic. Since the 1870s the industry has declined steadily to present levels, but there are now indications that the deterioration has been stabilized.

Distributed over eleven communes, approximately 400 hectares are devoted to the production of still, dry Seyssel. The tiny, fragmented and widely scattered plots are mainly along the left bank of the Rhône between Seyssel and Corbonod. Vines are grown either on sand/gravel/limestone, or gravel/sand outcroppings mixed with clay. The most improtant growths bear the names of Corbonod, Seyssel (Ain) and Seyssel (Savoie), the latter located on the right bank and considered less good.

Seyssel, little known, underrated by most, and scorned by Burgundians, is as a consequence a fine value within the producing region. It rarely attains alcohol levels beyond 11 percent, is dry, "tender," pale yellow in color, and known for its pleasant bouquet of violets. The wine is extremely delicate and ready to drink by March following the vintage.

Despite the small quantities produced each year, it is suprising to find three dozen producers in Corbonod, two dozen in Seyssel (Ain), and about a dozen on the right bank portion of the town. Seyssel Mousseux differs from still wine in a number of significant ways. In addition to Chasselas, and Roussette, Molette can also be added and the yield increased to 40 from 35 hectoliters to the hectare. The final product is small in quantity, although it rises to 600 hectoliters in a superb vintage. It is an outstanding mousseux—light in body, refreshing on the palate, and blessed with a long, penetrating bouquet. The largest, and one of the best, producers is *Varichon & Clerc,* located in Seyssel. The Le Duc Blanc de Blanc, with assertive carbonation, delicate flavor, and penetrating fragrance, offers outstanding value. The non–AOC mousseux, less refined and more robust, has a more pronounced flavor and yeasty nose. In addition to Varichon, *J. Perrier, Dne. de la Tacommière,* and *Clos de la Peclette* all enjoy excellent reputations for good, reliable Seyssel.

The Bugey VDQS Appellation

The three VDQS appellations are Bugey Blanc, Bugey Rouge, and Roussette de Bugey. The latter produces less than 400 hectoliters, while the former two produce nearly 10,000 hectoliters, with Blanc being slightly more important. The producing district, lying midway between Savoie and Beaujolais, is better known as the birthplace of Brillat-Savarin than for its wines.

The red wines, made form Gamay, Pinot Noir, Pinot Gris, Mondeuse, and Poulsard, are light and refreshing but with little character. White wines, made from the Mondeuse Blanc, Chardonnay, Roussette, and Aligoté, are slightly better. The Roussette de Bugey, made from a blend of Roussette and Chardonnay, is fuller and more satisfying than most.

THE WINES OF BURGUNDY

THE vineyards and cellars of Burgundy are the most hallowed ground of all French vineyards. It has been said that it is the "viticultural soul" of the nation, without peer, and matchless throughout the world in the production of incomparable red and dry white wines. Yet while it may be the best known of all the major wine regions of the country, it remains the least understood. With 3.9 percent of the nation's vine hectarage, Burgundy produces 4.2 percent of all wine, and as a quality wine region it ranks third, with 14.4 percent of all AOC wine production (after the Gironde, with 22.4 percent, and the Côtes du Rhône, with 18.6 percent). Approximately three-quarters of its nearly 3 million hectoliters of wine produced annually is officially classified as AOC.

Located in east-central France, the old province of Burgundy, mainly confined within the four departments of Yonne, Côte d'Or, Saône-et-Loire, and Rhône, has ill-defined borders. The area is geographically diverse, united only by the historic and now-obscure political boundaries of the province. The entire region takes its name from the ravenous Teutonic tribe, the Burgundi, who invaded the region the 5th century. It is bounded by the Massif Central on the west, the Alps and the Saône River on the east, the granitic hills of Beaujolais on the south, and the hilly uplands of the Yonne on the north. The Saône, the dominant river of Burgundy, along with the Rhône, form the southern extension of the Rhine graben and separate the Massif Central from the Jura and the French Alps.

Burgundy is divided into six specific viticultural regions. From north to south they are as follows: *Chablis,* located in the department of Yonne 105 kilometers north-west of Dijon, is a white wine region responsible for

Table 5.1 Burgundy AOC Wine Production, 1980

Appellation	Hectoliters	Percent of total
Burgundy, Regional Appellations	219,304	11.8
Chablis	82,930	4.4
Côte de Nuits	51,800	2.8
Grands Crus de la Côte de Nuits	7,252	.3
Côte de Beaune	143,437	7.7
Grands Crus de la Côte de Beaune	5,224	.2
Côte Chalonnais	38,513	2.0
Mâconnais	199,805	10.8
Beaujolais	1,108,741	60.0
Total	1,857,006	100.0
Total Rouge and Rosé	1,521,881	82.0
Total Blanc	335,125	18.0
Total	1,857,006	100.0

Source: French Ministry of Agriculture.

about 5 percent of total production (Table 5.1); the *Côte d'Or,* beginning just south of Dijon and extending to the Chalonnais, is considered the premium red and white wine region of France. It produces 15 percent of total output, with the southern portion, the Côte de Beaune, being three times larger than the northern section, the Côte de Nuits; the *Chalonnais* produces both white and red wines, and with 3 percent of total production, is the second-smallest of the regional appellations; the *Mâconnais,* lying farther to the south, produces between 10 and 15 percent of regional production and is considered the largest single area for the production of white wine; *Beaujolais* produces red wine and is responsible for about 60 percent of total regional output; *Coteaux du Lyonnais* is a small, 9,000-hectoliter appellation adjoining Beaujolais and extending southward to the outskirts of Lyon. The viticultural region known as Burgundy, therefore, is a fairly long, essentially narrow strip extending from Chablis to Lyon for roughly 250 kilometers (see Fig. 5.1).

The evolution of wine production and vine hectarage in the four departments is presented in the accompanying tables and graphs, all of which indicate a number of interesting developments. First, the fall of the two largest vineyards, Yonne and the Saône-et-Loire, and the rise of the Rhône as Burgundy's biggest producer, are impressive. Second, all four departments peaked in terms of production on the eve of the *phylloxera* epidemic, then showed precipitous declines until the 1950s, when stability was achieved. Third, the relative stability of the Côte d'Or in the past 150 years, in contrast to the momentous changes of the other three departments, is remarkable. The above fluctuations in vineland and wine production did not occur in isolation, but are expressions of regional and national economic development forces.

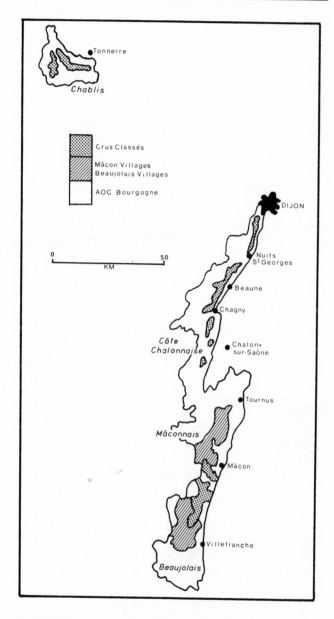

Figure 5.1
The Vineyards
of Burgundy

Burgundy, a large, heterogenous geographic region is located in the east-central portion of the country on the crossroads to Switzerland, Italy, and the Midi. It lies between the industrialized areas of the north and the tourist-rich Mediterranean, between the Alps and the sparsely populated Massif Central. Although its name conjures up a picture of plenty and visions of the good life, Burgundy is poor country; the landscape lacks the fat "land of plenty" ambiance of the middle Loire, Alsace, and Cham-

pagne. The area lacks fossil fuels, other minerals, and large tracks of
fertile agricultural resources capable of competing with the more affluent
areas of the nation. There are two cities of note, and both are peripheral to
the 40,000-hectare vine region. Lyon, the largest city of eastern France, is
the economic and cultural capital of a much wider region than just
Burgundy. Dijon, much smaller and although historically much more
important as the center of the powerful dukes of Valois, is today nothing
more than a provincial capital unable to absorb the bulk of rural migrants.
Between these two urban centers, Beaune, with 21,000 inhabitants, is
the largest city within the producing region. The rest of the several
hundred settlements are small, ordinary villages which project neither
charm, color, nor interest.

For the past 150 years the only unifying theme for the four departments was economic depression. The agricultural population declined
fivefold, arable land declined fourfold, pasture and forestland uses more
than tripled, and nonagricultural land uses increased by more than 1,000
percent. Although agriculture employs 12 percent of the entire population, stock rearing is the most important activity in terms of land use and
total financial earnings. This is followed by viticulture, which occupies
less than 1.4 percent of all arable land but contributes nearly one-eighth
of the total agricultural product. It is obvious, therefore, that although
present vine hectarage is less than one-quarter of what it was 100 years
ago, it is the region's most profitable agricultural activity in terms of
earnings per hectare.

History

Burgundy lies along an ancient tin road, and because it is adjacent to
major geological troughs leading to the Rhine and the Alps, it attracted
Roman legionaires who were the first to introduce the vine and organize
its commercial cultivation. In short order, new varieties were introduced
and production began to compete with Rome. This prompted Emperor
Domitian to order the systematic destruction of Burgundian vineyards in
A.D. 89, a proclamation that remained in force for two centuries until it
was rescinded by Probus. During the early Middle Ages viticulture was
encouraged by the Merovingians and later by their successors, the
Carolingians. The legendary Charlemagne, one of the prime movers, did
much to expand vinegrowing, and after his death in 814 the region was
divided, eventually leading to the creation of Burgundy as an important
duchy.

Due to the influence of religious orders in Burgundy, the dukes grew in
power and began a long process of bequeathing land to the various
ecclesiastical groups. After Cluny was established in the 10th century,
Clos de Vougeot was founded in 1089 and the Abbey of Clairvaux in
1112, and in 1141 the Cistercian nuns established Clos du Tart. By this

time, wine quality and sophistication in the industry had progressed sufficiently for discriminating tastes to distinguish various quality grapes. In 1395, Philip the Bold banned the Gamay from the region, and subsequent edicts forbade the importation of wine from other areas. So dedicated were the dukes to the production of quality wine that they eventually became known as the "Lords of the best wines in Christendom." Burgundy was permanently incorporated with France in the latter half of the 15th century, and due to its political unification efforts and homogeneous population, its history during the time of religious friction was more serene than that of the southwestern and northeastern portions of the country.

Understanding ecclesiastical influence in the history of Burgundian viticulture is absolutely indispensable to understanding the enological history of the region. The Merovingians and Carolingians were not only ardent Catholics, but practiced what they preached by furthering the cause of Christianity in western Europe. It was the Carolingians who converted the Saxons and Wends to Christianity and Charlemagne who "retained" the Moors, restored Leo III to the papacy, and was eventually crowned Emperor in Rome on Christmas day, paving the way for the establishment of the Holy Roman Empire. Throughout the Middle Ages Burgundy was staunchly Catholic and also fertile ground for the establishment of numerous religious orders.

The bequeathing of vineland to the church began in 587 when King Gontran gave choice vineland to the Abbey of Bèze; in 775 Charlemagne relinquished his vineyards at Aloxe to the monastery of Saulieu; and Charles the Bold presented vineland to the Abbot of St.-Martins. By the 14th century, about twenty religious houses were located in Beaune: the Abbey of St.-Viviant was, for a time, the major vineland owner in Vosne, and the Abbey of Cluny, considered the intellectual center of France, had become the largest landowner in Burgundy. For nearly eight centuries, the largest concentration of religiously owned and dominated vineland in France was found in Burgundy, particularly in the Côte d'Or. Monasteries, abbeys, convents, churches, and religious orders prospered as land was bequeathed to them. The most important religious groups were the Benedictines, Cistercians (who originated in Burgundy), Carthusians, and the Knights Hospitaller of St. John.

The largest and most important, the Benedictines, called the "black monks," had a monopoly on western monasticism until the 12th century. They reached their greatest numbers in France and for a time controlled more than one-fifth of all prime vineland in Burgundy. They were found in Avallon, Dijon, Couchey, Gevrey, Fixin, Flagey, Pommard, Aloxe, Savigny, Beaune, Santenay, Givry, the Mâconnais, and Juliénas in the Beaujolais. Originating in Citaux, the Cistercians, referred to as the "white monks," established vineyards in Aloxe, Brochon, Fixin, Musigny, Morey, Meursault, Clos de Vougeot, Beaune, Savigny, Chalon, and

Pontigny. While the Carthusians were largely restricted to Brochon and Beaune, the Hospitallers and others were more widespread in Chassagne, Pommard, Savigny, Volnay, Dijon, and Beaune. As a consequence, religious expression was felt throughout Burgundy but particularly in the Côte d'Or, where more than fifty vineyards contain "Clos" in their name, and another forty boast a religous name.

By the 12th century monastic orders owned about one-third of all vineland, and by the eve of the French Revolution more than two-thirds of the finer sites were under ecclesiastical control. The anticlerical ideology of the later 18th century, expressed in the radical and successful French Revolution, changed the viticultural landscape of Burgundy forever. Fragmentation took place during the years 1781 to 1825, when the policy of *le bien national* ("for the national good") was implemented. Ecclesiastical and noble properties were seized and secularized among the masses, with inevitable consequences. Of the 40,000 individual exploitations, 35,000, the second-highest such figure in all of France, are now less than 2 hectares. In the whole of the Côte d'Or, fewer than twenty-five growers own more than 20 hectares.

While tiny plots of ground, each forming a separate vineyard, are common throughout the country, Burgundian vineyards are characterized by excessive "Balkanizaion" in terms of ownership. Here, a separate vineyard of 25 hectares may have twice as many owners, of which three-quarters own less than half a hectare. While there may be slight variations in topographic peculiarities, in theory 50 different wines result because the small growers sell their grapes to different shippers or larger growers. The multiplicity of ownership and fragmentation of vineland means a low level of capitalization and standardization, with a profusion of appellations and labels and a hierarchy of quality levels that is absolutely unbelievable. Some growers of Grand Cru climats, for example, own as few as 100 vines—in one row. With few exceptions, all major vineyards are under multiple ownership: the 50-hectare Clos de Vougeot climat alone has 78 owners, the 11-hectare Bonnes Mares, 23 owners, and the 15-hectare climat of Clos de la Roche, 22 owners.

The Burgundy Appellation System

With more than 90 different appellations, Burgundy has more AOC appellations than any other wine-producing region in France. The system, which can only be described as "Byzantine" in its conception, implementation and comprehension, consists of four different and distinct tiers: (a) *Generic* or regional (11 percent of production); (b) *Subregional* (67 percent of production); (c) *Communal* or village (20 percent of production); and (d) *Climat,* classed growth or vineyard (less than 2 percent of production). For each of the above, alcohol content and yield per hectare are crucial to the system. For example, Grand Cru wine must attain a potential natural

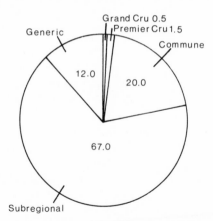

Figure 5.2 Burgundian Wine Production by General Appellation (in percent)

alcohol content of 11.5 percent; Premier Cru, 11 percent; Communal wines, 10.5 percent; and all others, a minimum of 9 percent. The yield per hectare is lowest for individual classed growths at 35 hectoliters to the hectare; for communal, 40 to 45 hectoliters; subregional, 40 to 55 hectoliters; and for regional, the maximum yield varies between 50 and 60 hectoliters.

The major wine appellations within the generic group are:

1. *Bourgogne Grand Ordinaire.* Among the generic appellations, Bourgogne Grand Ordinaire Rouge, Rosé, and Blanc are wines whose grapes originate anywhere within the region and may include any of the following varieties with no stated percentages: Pinot Noir, Gamay, Tressot, and César for red wine; Chardonnay, Pinot Gris, Pinot Blanc, Aligoté, Melon, and Sacy for white wine. With very little being bottled or sold with a vintage date, these wines comprise 5 to 10 percent of generic production.

2. *Bourgogne Passetoutgrains.* This appellation produces about one-quarter of all generic Burgundy. It is a red or rosé blended wine made from two-thirds Gamay and one-third Pinot Noir, with a minimum alcohol strength of 9.5 percent. It is widely distributed within the region but hardly ever exported. Although it is meant to be consumed young, it is better in its second year, and only under exceptional conditions does it offer any value.

3. *Bourgogne Aligoté and Bourgogne Aligoté Bouzeron.* These two appellations account for 15 percent of generic production. The Bourgogne Aligoté is made from grapes grown throughout Burgundy, while the latter, and much the better wine, comes from the Bouzeron region in the northern section of the Chalonnais. While the Bourgogne Aligoté may contain Chardonnay, Pinot Blanc, Pinot Gris, and other varieties, the one from Bouzeron is nearly 100 percent Aligoté. Varying greatly with the vintage, the wines in general are acidic and not well balanced, but can be appealing in good years.

4. *Bourgogne.* Bourgogne Rouge, Rosé, and Blanc, accounting for 50 percent of all generic wine, refers to wines that are subject to place and varietal restrictions. White wine is made only from Chardonnay and Pinot Blanc without any Aligoté. Red and rosé are made from Pinot Noir, César, and Tressot (in Yonne), and Gamay may originate only within the confines of the nine Beaujolais growths. In theory at least, this is the best of the generic appellations. Minimum alcohol strength for red and rosé is 10 percent, and for white 10.5 percent.

5. *Bourgogne Irancy.* This is a minor red wine appellation that produces 1 percent of all generic wine from a combination of grapes grown in Yonne. The wine exhibits individuality and character and offers by far, along with Bourgogne Aligoté Bouzeron, the best value of all generic wines.

6. *Crémant de Bourgogne.* Made red, rosé, and white, Crémant de Bourgogne (formerly known as Bourgogne Mousseux) constitutes 6 percent of total generic production. While 30 percent of the grape composition must be Pinot Noir and Chardonnay, the Gamay grape is restricted to 20 percent. The remainder is a widely varying mixture of Pinot Gris, Aligoté, César, Tressot, and other grapes. While all is made by the Champagne method, the white outproduces the rosé and red by a wide margin. Aged for nine months, the wine has a mild fruity aroma and is moderately active in its carbonation. Its popularity is increasing, and although the wine is heavily advertised as an alternative to Champagne, sparkling Saumur, and Vouvray, it is not inexpensive.

The next tier on the quality ladder are the subregional wines consisting of (a) Bourgogne Hautes-Côtes de Nuits, (b) Bourgogne Hautes-Côtes de Beaune, (c) Côtes de Beaune-Villages, (d) Mâcon Rouge, (e) Mâcon Supérieur, (f) Mâcon-Villages, (g) Beaujolais, (h) Beaujolais Supérieur, and (i) Beaujolais-Villages.

Communal or village appellations refer to wines made from grapes grown within the confines of village boundaries. It is important to note, however, that a large number of exceptions are made, as wine produced in one village may to be sold under the name of a neighboring commune. Another problem is the curious and confusing custom of hyphenating village and famous vineyard names. Beginning in middle of the 19th century, several villages obtained permission to append the name of the most celebrated vineyard to that of the commune. The chief culprits were Gevrey, Chambolle, Flagey, Vosne, Nuits, and Aloxe. Beaune, Volnay, and Pommard have not followed suit. It is also imperative to remember that Gevrey-Chambertin is not a vineyard but a blended communal wine that is not likely to contain a single drop of the more famous Chambertin vineyard.

Vineyard growths are divided into Grand and Premier Cru, the former being superior to the latter, with each individual vineyard entitled to its own separate appellation. In general, they command the highest prices and enjoy international recognition. The Grand Cru vineyards are located on the best possible sites—the upper or middle portions of southeast-facing slopes—never in the uppermost sections or on rich bottomland. As proof of their majestic and above-average position, they need not mention the name of the village on the label, and their names appear in bold lettering. Premier Cru vineyards are more numerous in number and cheaper in price.

The Grape Varieties of Burgundy

The wines of Burgundy are essentially varietal: the finest red solely from Pinot Noir, the finest white only from Chardonnay, and Beaujolais only from Gamay. Within the four departments, the following additional grapes are allowed to be made into AOC wines: Pinot Gris, Aligoté, Pinot Blanc, Melon, Tressot, César, and Sacy, the last three being confined to the Yonne department. The following can be used in the production of non-AOC wines: Ravat-6, Kuhlmann 188-2, Maréchal Foch, Pinot Meunier, Gamay Teinturier, Landott 244, Oberlin 595, Seibel 5455 and 8337, Sauvignon Blanc, Baco Noir, and several more. Tables 5.6 and 5.11 indicate the general distribution of the principal grape varieties in the departments of Côte d'Or and Saône-et-Loire, and their percent share of national hectarage for each grape variety in selected years.

Of the nearly 17,000 hectares planted in Pinot Noir in France, approximately 49 percent of the total is located in the three departments of Yonne, Saône-et-Loire and the Côte d'Or, the latter being most important with 33 percent. About 43 percent is planted in Champagne, and the remaining 8 percent is widely scattered in the Loire valley and Alsace. The Pinot Noir is the premium grape in the production of the finest Burgundies from the Côte d'Or, Mercurey and Givry. Indigenous to Burgundy, the Pinot Noir is precocious in its growing habits: it suffers from frost but is resistant to winter cold. It is a medium yielder of about 40 hectoliters to the hectare, although this can be, and usually is, stretched. It demands exposures that face east and southeast, with well-drained, iron-rich soils that are not overly acidic. Although the berries are thick skinned, they are very sensitive to heat and have a tendency to sunburn and overipen quickly, thus imparting an alcoholic and raisinlike taste that spoils the balance and harmony of the wine. Higher temperatures also reduce color intensity. The Pinot Noir is susceptible to virus infections, rot, and produces little leaf during the growing season.

Of the more than 150 Pinot Noir clones in Burgundy, only a dozen will yield above-average wine. Many are named after villages, flowers, or personalities. Pinot Fin, Pinot Classique, and Pinot Tordu are among the finest. Their yield is comparatively low, and their wine is far superior to Pinot Droit, a vine that is notorious for its large berries. Pinot Fin, one of the finest clones, has a small, dark blue berry that produces more glycerine than Pinot Droit. It makes a wine with excellent color, a complex aroma, bouquet, and flavor, and with age its flowery and fruity fragrance changes to multiple layers of elusive flavors too difficult to describe. The wine is full-bodied, silky, soft on the palate, and free of astringency. To be at its best, yields must be kept low, fermentation should be slow and at room temperature, overripe berries must be discarded, and wood-aging is imperative. When compared with Gamay, the Pinot Noir produces higher alcohol levels, significantly more extract, higher fixed acidity, but lower volatile and total acid levels.

The second-most-important red grape is Gamay à Jus Blanc, which is grown mainly for the production of Beaujolais in the southernmost area of Burgundy. A very unpretentious, common, and coarse grape everywhere else in Burgundy, it rises to great heights on the granitic hills of Beaujolais and is responsible for one of the most popular wines in the world. It is absolutely worthless as a wine grape when cultivated on rich, alluvial soils, and attains levels of mediocrity in those containing lime-stone. The very productive Gamay is usually trained *en gobelet*. It is a vine with large black berries yielding four times the weight of Pinot Noir under most conditions. The wine that is produced in the Beaujolais is absolutely first rate, very aromatic, and very appealing—widely imitated but unmatched anywhere else.

Like Pinot Noir, the Gamay has many clones, of which a Jus Blanc is considered superior to the various *teinturiers* (dyers). The Gamay à Jus Blanc, though widely distributed in central France and the Loire valley, has 58 percent of its total plantings, a high degree of concentration, in the department of Rhône. Over the past thirty years, hectarage in the department has increased by one-third, and it is expected to continue growing in the future. The Gamay Teinturier, mainly confined to the department of Saône-et-Loire, is declining in importance.

The principal white grape of Burgundy is the Chardonnay, one of the finest vines in the production of still and sparkling white wine. In 1979, nearly 44 percent of total national hectarage was found in Burgundy, more than half of which was in the department of Saône-et-Loire. The largest single concentration of Chardonnay, however, is in the Marne department; the Jura and the Aube, with less than 3 percent of all hectarage, are minor regions. Of the 40,000 vine hectares in Burgundy, only 5,700 are planted in Chardonnay.

Chardonnay was supposedly named after a village of the same name in Burgundy. It is not related to the Pinot family of grapes and should not be confused with Pinot Blanc. It is highly restricted to the stony and limestone soils of Chablis, Côte de Beaune, Champagne, Rully, Pouilly-Fuissé, Montagny, and the Jura. The vine, not vigorous or resistant to mildew, is very susceptible to *millerandage,* a physiological condition in which the size of the bunch and the individual berry are much smaller than usual. As the grapes contain more flavor, sugar, and extract, this condition, depending on the grower and the character of the vintage, is not necessarily bad. The smaller yield, however, discourages the planting of certain clones that are more susceptible to *millerandage*.

In all the premium white wine regions of Burgundy, Chardonnay produces dry, steely, crisp, fruity, and refreshing wine. While color varies from pale yellow to golden with green highlights, the flavor ranges from austere to buttery, its aroma and bouquet from simple to complex, and overall character from sharp to round, full, and satisfying. At its worse, Chardonnay tastes flat, dull, is overly sulfured, oxidized, and often very acidic. In the final analysis, Chardonnay can be called a classy grape producing the finest white table wine in the world. The trick in making classic Chardonnay is to capture the "ripe" and not the "green" acids of the grape, to allow the wine to lie on its lees, and to age in wood. When compared with Aligoté, Chardonnay has significantly higher alcohol and fixed and total acid levels.

Although quality wine by reputable producers continues to be made, overall quality levels, over the past thirty years, have dropped. The apparent decline in quality Chardonnay is attributed mainly to the use of less desirable clones and to overcropping. At the turn of the century, yields of scarcely more than 20 hectoliters to the hectare (yields have since quadrupled) produced bigger, more flavorful, and far more concentrated wines. Equally important is the fact that the number of Chardonnay clones increased to more than two dozen, all sharing subtle but significant differences in growing habits, yield, and wine character. It should also be emphasized that excessive fertilization is now quite common. The most popular types planted are Fin, Moyen, Droit, Jura, Côte Chalonnais and Champagne.

The second-most-important white grape is the Aligoté, a very prolific vine known for relatively high yields, high acid levels, and hard, steely wines. Of the nearly 1,200 hectares planted in this variety, three-quarters are found in the Côte d'Or, with the remainder in the Saône-et-Loire department. Reputedly, the best sites for its production are Rully, St.-Aubin, Bouzeron, and Pernand-Vergelesses. Although solidly Burgundian in origin and character, Aligoté is relegated a secondary position in the hierarchy of white winemaking, and is found on sites not considered ideal for Pinot Noir and Chardonnay. Further, it is not allowed to carry the commune name of the appellation, but must be sold as Bourgogne Aligoté and Aligoté Bouzeron as its highest possible appellations. In optimal years, however, it makes passable acidic wine of medium body with a sharp edge, but in cloudy, cool years it is a poor, almost undrinkable wine. Because of its neutral taste and high acid levels, a good deal is used to "improve" the less acidic Chardonnay (there is more Aligoté in the Côte d'Or for this purpose than some would like to admit). Perhaps its greatest achievement is its use in the making of Kir, a Cassis—

white wine aperitif popularized and named after a celebrated World War I hero, Felix Kir.

Three other lesser white wines are Pinot Gris, Pinot Blanc, and Melon. The first is the more important of the three throughout the four departments, while the second, no longer encouraged or given official sanction for future plantings, is slowly dispapearing. The Melon, an inferior grape, is used officially only for the production of Borgogne, as it

---

Table 5.2 BURGUNDY VINTAGES

Because the Côte d'Or has nearly 75 different appellations and a highly variable physical character, it is impossible to describe specific vintages with easy generalizations. Local factors such as the age of the vines, vineyard practices, vinification, harvest completions, etc., affect the vintages; so also do micro-climatic conditions.

1986 10–16*	An above-average harvest characterized by widespread rot. The finest white are round and balanced; the reds are soft, fruity, and highly variable.
1985 14–19	Widespread frost reduced output, especially in Chablis. The very best red wines are well colored, big, concentrated, and rich; the finest white are round, fruity, and well scented.
1984 4–10	Below-average harvest; wet summer, rot widely present; wines thin, poorly structured, and unappealing.
1983 13–19	Below-average harvest; best vintage since 1978 but not better than 1976, some wines approach the power and classic character of the 1964s. Wines dark, well structured, austere, and capable of aging. Widespread variability, but the very best are firm and powerful.
1982 11–13	Huge harvest; very similar to 1979, with low acid levels and early maturation. Whites better than reds.
1981 8–11	Below-average harvest; frost, hail, and rain reduced harvest size; widespread rot and uneven quality. Wines very expensive and over-capitalized.
1980 7–9	Average harvest, uneven vintage, low acid and early maturing wines. Whites better than the reds. Slightly below 1981 in quality, with some barely palatable. Overpriced and offer little value.
1979 8–10	Above-average crop, light and early maturing wines. Whites better and more balanced; both vary widely and lack structure; not for laying down.
1978 16–18	Below-average harvest; excellent red and white wines, both better than the 1976s, especially the whites. Very expensive.
1977 5–11	Above-average harvest; high in acid, with the whites somewhat better than the reds. Highly variable throughout the Côte de Nuits, with a lot of feeble and poorly structured wines.
1976 15–17	Below-average harvest; above-average wines at best. Despite the success of the vintage, quality highly variable and prices high. Acid levels, in general, are low but wines will not last as long as the high vintage rating suggests. Reds better than whites.
1975 4–10	Below-average harvest; vintage characterized by light-bodied and feeble wines. Côte de Nuits more successful, but, in general, poor overall qualities. Whites better than reds.

*In ratings following year, 20 = best, 0 = worst.

gives high yields, matures rapidly, is coarse on the palate, and has low alcohol levels.

THE WINES OF YONNE

The Yonne department, which lies north of the Massif Central and west of the Morvan plateau, is an underdeveloped agricultural region of scattered forest, wheat growing, and extensive pastures. More than 50 percent of the 250,000 inhabitants are engaged in agriculture, making this area one of the most rural and poorest in all of France. Highlighting the status of underdevelopment, the population declined by more than 100,000 in the past 100 years, while the five surrounding departments all grew in number. Although the famed vineyards of Chablis loom majestically in the vocabulary of most wine aficionados, vineland within Yonne comprises less than .1 percent of total arable land, a sharp contrast to the more respectable 1.4 percent found in the Côte d'Or. The entire department produces about 275,000 hectoliters of wine annually from 3,500 hectares, of which 40 percent is AOC wine.

Yonne contains little industry, just one medium-sized city, and a few grand chateaux, as in the Loire and Médoc; its uneventful history is obscured by its more illustrious neighbors to the north and south. Once, however, economic conditions were significantly better. Due to its proximity to Paris, which is less than 100 kilometers away, the region produced large quantities of table wine. In the latter half of the 19th century more than 43,000 hectares were planted, and by 1880 hectarage had increased to nearly 50,000. Except for Chablis and surrounding communities, the wines were mostly red and made from Pinot Noir, Gamay, César, and Tressot grapes. With the *oïdium* and *phylloxera* outbreaks, viticulture suffered a serious and irreversible setback. As the pace of French industry accelerated during the second half of the 19th century, Yonne became more isolated. Rail facilities bypassed this once-thriving viticultural center, which benefited Burgundy and undercut Yonne's ability to compete effectively. More important, outmigration of young, energetic hands changed the demographic and agricultural landscape from one of youthful, intensive agriculture to more extensive features. During the first half of the century, Yonne offered little hope and opportunity to its youth. Depressed wine prices during the first decade, the post–World War I period, the depression of the 1930s, and low wine prices during 1952, 1957, 1963, and 1965 did little to encourage and foster the prospect of a better tomorrow. By 1945 economic underdevelopment was a permanent condition, and vine hectarage had shrunk to fewer than 4,000 hectares for the Yonne department and 471 for Chablis. In the final analysis, the chronic labor shortages, the persistent low yields of aging vines, and the dominance of Burgundy made Yonnne one of the most neglected viticultural regions of central France despite its proximity to the capital region.

It is ironic that after 1950, the negative conditions that had proved so devastating to the local economy began to look financially attractive to negociants and businessmen. The combination of low real estate prices and the strong international demand for dry white wine provided the necessary stimuli for new vine plantings. As the price of quality wine rose to unprecedented levels, interest in rejuvenating a good portion of the Chablis vineyard was renewed. More significant, technological improvements in combating frost were successfully introduced; as a result, vine hectarage more than tripled during the 1950 to 1980 period. As production rose from less than 20,000 hectoliters in 1970 to more than 118,000 in 1982, Chablis's percentage of total AOC Burgundy rose from less than 1.7 in 1967 to more than 5.5 in 1982. Today, Chablis is responsible for more than 70 percent of all AOC white wine produced in areas north of the famed Montrachet vineyards in the Côte d'Or. Average vineyard size has quadrupled, modern machinery has become the norm, and the number of part-time farmers has declined by two-thirds.

Climate and Soils

Located in the northcentral portion of the country, Yonne is not directly affected by the moderating influence of the North Atlantic. As a result, the climate is continental, with cold, dry winters and hot summers—weather conditions aggravated by an exposed windswept location. Of all the major viticultural regions of France, this area exhibits the most seasonal temperature variations and the fewest number of days (178) with temperatures above 10°C. In fact, the most significant environmental hazard, frost, is more severe in Chablis than elsewhere in Burgundy. When it occurs in spring, it has the capacity not only to reduce yields, but to kill the plant outright. These deadly frosts are locally known as *gelée noire,* or black freeze. During the 1950s, the only vintages above average in yield were those of 1952, 1955, and 1959; in the past forty years, more than sixteen severe and moderate bouts with frosts have resulted in some degree of financial distress among growers.

The four common explanations why the Chablis region is prone to frost are (a) the physical layout of the land; (b) the significant altitude of the upper hilly portions; (c) the exposure to cold air, and (d) the topography of the Serein valley, which traps and prolongs temperature inversions, often for days. As a consequence, the valley floor is devoid of vines. The Petit Chablis and Chablis appellation vineyards are found along the valley margins, and only sites higher than 100 meters are reserved for Grand and Premier Cru vineyards. The same generalization holds true in the rest of the department, except that unlike Chablis, which mandates that only Chardonnay be grown on AOC land, more frost-resistant vines like the hybrids Sacy, Tressot, and César are found. As recently as 1920, half the hectarage in Yonne consisted of Pinot Blanc and Sacy grapes.

The soils of Yonne are highly variable, and vineyards are limited to protected sites containing limestone, gravel, and as little clay as possible. The Chablis vineyard contains Kimmerdgian limestone, a hard rock that fractures easily and facilitates the vertical percolation of water on hilly slopes. The limestone beds alternate with layers of clay, and the subsoil contains heavy accumulations of calcium carbonate. The best sites are located along steep slopes where the clay layer is thin or where the limestone outcrops. Along lower margins, the limestone decomposes into fertile clay that is good for cereal production but poor for vines due to its poor drainage and proclivity for frost concentration. The best growths, therefore, are found not only on steep hillsides but also along south and southwesterly aspects.

Chablis

The vineyards of the Yonne department are separated into two virtually exclusive districts by the Yonne and Serein rivers. The latter, no more than a stream, is the center of the famous Chablis appellation. The home of one of the world's most famous white wines is the lethargic, almost somnolent town of Chablis, which is nestled next to the Serein. The wine assumes its name from the town, which is derived from the Celtic words for "habitation near the woods." Because it is the most northern of all Burgundian appellations, Chablis is commonly referred to as the "Golden Gate of Burgundy."

Unlike the touristy, historic, and ecclesiastically rich Côte d'Or, Chablis, with fewer than 4,000 people, boasts no grand restaurant, no jewels the likes of Bâtard, La Tâche, or Richebourg, no memorable hotels, and no significant historical tales. It is an unspoiled tourist backwater, slow and deliberate in its ways and almost medieval in its ambiance. And yet, despite its lack of charisma, its wine is one of the most prestigious and sought-after in the world. Judging by the large number of Bulgarian Chablis, pink Chablis from California, and New York State Chablis found everywhere in the United States, this is one of the most imitated wines known to man.

Although winemaking dates back to the Romans, significant growth did not occur until the Serein valley became the home of the monks of Saint Martin and the Cistercians. The latter came from the south, bringing with them the famous Chardonnay grape, locally referred to as "Beaunnois." While the surrounding areas and the Yonne River dominated production, the Chablis district, because of its susceptibility to frost, remained small and insignificant. In 1895, after the full brunt of the *phylloxera* epidemic was over, Chablis had scarcely more than 367 hectares of producing vineyards. Today, more than 2,000 hectares support approximately 440 growers, of whom 60 percent cultivate fewer than 1 hectare. This type of fragmentation encourages few "château" or "estate"

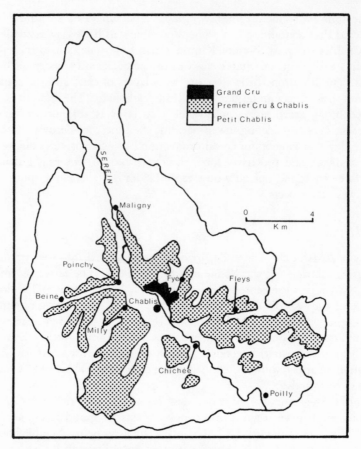

Figure 5.3   The Chablis Vineyard

bottlings, hence, Chablis negociants account for about 45 percent of sales, while the remainder is distributed by Côte d'Or and Bordeaux negociants. Nearly all the wine is consumed outside the Yonne department.

Lying midway between the frontiers of Champagne and the Côte d'Or, Chablis's output has more affinity with that of Champagne than of Burgundy. The wine is white and dry; almost all of it is good, with the very best being described as superlative; because of its consistency, it offers better value than the more expensive wines of the Côte de Beaune. Genuine Chablis is an extraordinary wine—crisp, tart, golden yellow with greenish highlights, full-bodied, flavorful, refreshing, and blessed with a fruity bouquet. Although often earthy (*goût de pierre à fusil,* or "having the taste of gun metal") acidic, and austere in taste, good vintages produce wine that is complete and elegant, with big round flavors and a pronounced long finish. All the foregoing attributes make the wine an excellent accompaniment to fish, fowl, and cheese.

Made entirely from Chardonnay, the wine's flavor has changed dramati-

Plate 5.1   Chablis and its vineyards (JJB)

cally over the past twenty-five years to suit contemporary tastes. Almost all receives little or no wood-aging; its flavor components derive from the maturity of the Chardonnay grape and the nature of the fermentation process. Most of it, therefore, is less acidic, less steely, and much softer and fruitier than it used to be, which explain its appeal to the average consumer. For a variety of reasons, wine quality varies dramatically throughout the appellation. Rootstocks, for example, differ in terms of their adaptation to the lime-saturated soil and in their ability to mature properly. The intensity and type of fertilizer vary with the grower, and although stainless steel fermentation is the norm, its temperature and length are not subject to strict formula. Usually the vintage begins in October and lasts for another three to four weeks, with Grand Cru grapes picked last. Those wines fermented and aged in wood prior to bottling are the deepest colored and longest lived, as well as the most expensive.

The Chablis Appellations

Since 1938 the Chablis vineyards have been classified into four officially delimited areas, each with minimum yields and alcohol strength. At the pinnacle of quality is Chablis Grand Cru, a collection of seven vineyards with a combined total of 145 hectares. The wine must contain a minimum of 11 percent alcohol and its yield be limited to 35 hectoliters to the hectare. Production over the past fifteen years has risen steadily and now exceeds, in good years, more than 6,000 hectoliters. In addition to the appellation, the vineyard name is included on the label: Vaudésir, les Preuses, les Clos, Grenouilles, Bourgos, Valmur, or Blanchots. All are contiguous and located north of the town of Chablis, with a southern and southwesterly aspect along some of the steepest terrain.

Grand Cru wines are distinguished by depth of color, intensity of flavor, and pronounced bouquet. When compared with Premier Cru they are loaded with extract, more full-bodied, multidimensional, rounder, and capable of aging longer. The *créme de la créme* are the three climats of les Preuses, les Clos, and Grenouilles. The first has a distinctive dark color, spicy bouquet, a pronounced flavor, and is long lived. By contrast, les Clos is softer, better balanced and, in good years, one of the most harmonious Chablis available. Grenouilles is a medium-bodied and well-balanced wine, but not as big as les Preuses. Of the remaining less distinguished, Vaudésir exhibits a reputation for refinement and elegance; Valmur is known for its suppleness and distinct finish; Blanchots is known for its pronounced nose, mellow and well-balanced flavor; and Bourgos can be full-bodied and rich, but often is marred by excessive acidity. Lying between Vaudésir and les Preuses is a small climat, la Moutonne, that used to be a brand name but is now considered the equal of the other seven and is included within the Grand Cru appellation.

The second quality tier, Chablis Premier Cru, forms a collection of fourteen vineyards with approximately 665 hectares. The wine must contain a minimum of 10.5 percent alcohol, and its yield per hectare is limited to 40 hectoliters. Within the past ten years, hectarage has increased by one-third and production has more than doubled. Less than twenty years ago, twenty-nine individual climats were identified and given the right to the Premier Cru appellation; but in 1967, the list was consolidated to twelve, most of which lie adjacent to Grand Cru sites on the north side of the Serein River. Under the new regulations, specific climats can still be vinified and sold separately, but the tendency is to combine and sell the finished wine under the umbrella name. As of 1983, a new Premier Cru has been identified, Vaudevey, located in the commune of Beines with approximately 37 hectares. The complete list of Premier Cru vineyards, along with their individual climat names, which may or may not be placed on the label, are listed in Table 5.3. Although there are dissenting opinions, the following are considered the best of the 14: Montée de Tonnerre, for its spicy flavor, bouquet and certain *goût de terroir;* Fourchaume, for its fuller taste and pleasing color; and Mont de Melieu, for its subtle bouquet, soft and supple taste, and touch of elegance.

The Chablis appellation, with 1,407 hectares, represents more than 57 percent of hectarage and more than 60 percent of total wine production. Produced from no more than 40 hectoliters per hectare, the wine must attain a minimum alcohol level of 10 percent. The main areas of production are Chapelle-Vaupelteigne, Lignorelles, Maligny, Poinchy, Milly, Fyé, Courgis, Fleys, Beines, and Béru. Although it is not customary to place individual climat designations on Chablis appellation wines, Montaigus, Chalevaux, and Epinottes are frequently seen and considered above average in quality.

Table 5.3 Grand and Premier Cru Vineyards of Chablis

Grand Cru

Blanchots   les Clos   Valmur   Vaudésir   les Preuses   Bourgos   Grenouilles

Premier Cru

Mont de Milieu (Vallée de Chigot)

Montée de Tonnerre (Chapelots, Pieds d'Aloue, Sous Pieds d'Aloue, Côte de Brechain)

Fourchaume (la Fourchaume, Vaupulan, les Vaupulans, Côte de Fontenay, la Grande Côte, les Quatre Chemins, Vaulorent, l'Homme Mort, l'Ardillier, Bois Seguin, Germe Couverte, Dine-Chien, les Couvertes)

Montmains (les Forêts, le Bout des Buttaux, le Milieu des Buttaux, Vaux Miolot, les Ecueillis, Vaugerlains)

Vaucopins (Adroit de Vaucopins)

Vosgros (Adroit de Vosgros, Vaugiraut)

Les Beauregards (Vallée de Cuissy, Côte de Cuissy, Haut des Chambres du Roi, Bec d'Oiseau, les Corvées)

Côte de Léchet (le Château)

Vau Ligneau (la Forêt, Sur la Forêt, Vau Girault, Vau de Longue)

Beauroy (Côte de Troesmes, Sous Boroy, Benfer, Vallée des Vaux, Adroit de Vau Renard, le Cotat Château, le Verger, Frouquelin, Côte de Savant)

Vaillons (Sur les Vaillons, Châtain, les Châtains, Séchet, les Lys, les Beugnons, les Grandes Chaumes, Champlain, les Minots, les Roncières, les Epinottes)

Vau de Vey (Vignes des Vaux Ragons, la Grande Chaume)

Les Fourneaux (Morein, Côte des Pres Girots, la Côte, Sur la Côte)

Vauderey

Petit Chablis, the last of the appellations, contains but 246 hectares. With a minimum alcohol level of 9.5 percent, it is early maturing, pale in color, and the lightest in body of all Chablis. Its vineyards are on the outskirts of the region, on the poorest soils and on the most exposed sites.

The "Kimmerdgian" Controversy

The first legal delimitation of Chablis as a specific geographical region occurred in 1919. Modifications were made in 1927 and 1928, with provisional national delineation as a district appellation in 1929. Final INAO approval, given in 1938, encompassed an area of twenty settlements, most of which had a subsoil of Kimmerdgian limestone. The location of all Grand and Premier Cru vineyards, and a good portion of plain Chablis, were thus situated within the confines of this geologic formation. Yet the majority of vineyards classified as Petit Chablis were planted in Portlandian limestone, a type of rock chemically and structurally similar to Kimmerdgian, but that degrades into heavy clay. Approxi-

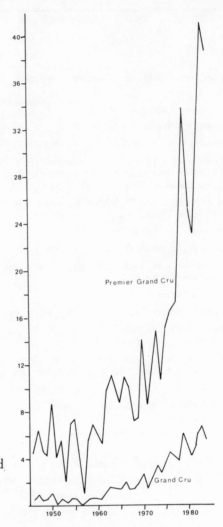

40—
36—
32—
28—
24—
20—

Premier Grand Cru

16—
12—
8—

Figure 5.4   Chablis: Grand and
Premier Cru Production,
1946–1985
(in thousands of hectoliters)

4—

Grand Cru

1950   1960   1970   1980

mately one-third of all vineyards entitled to the Chablis appellation were
not located on Kimmerdgian rock, and hence, the source of a serious
dispute.

In the early 1970s, a movement arose to expand the limits of Chablis to
areas not possessing Kimmerdgian limestone. This did, in effect, increase
the potential hectarage of the appellation fourfold. The protagonists of
this movement were Le Syndicat de la Defense de l'Appellation de Chablis
and La Federation des Viticulteurs Chablisiens. The latter was organized
by the owner of Dne. de l'Eglantière, who was in favor of enlarging the
Chablis AOC boundaries beyond their pre–1919 limits. As justification,
the proponents for change argued that a more equitable delineation was

long overdue—that the original decision in 1929 excluded from the Chablis appellation five communes located below Chablis in the Serein valley. It was maintained that these five communes consistently produced above-average wine, even though they rested not on the more valuable Kimmerdgian but on Portlandian limestone. Most significant, the proponents maintained that it is not the type of rock that is important in this area, but the quality of the drainage that effects overall wine quality. The case was finally brought before the INAO. After some years and a number of delays, the INAO in 1976 took the position that Kimmerdgian formations need not be the sole criterion in the delination of vineyards, but that aspect, microclimate, soil structure, and topography "perfectly suited to the production of Chablis" must also be included in future demarcations.

Moreover, to confuse the picture, as so often occurs in the French appellation system, certian Kimmerdgian soils would be excluded from the Chablis designation because of their poor drainage. The INAO also drew up a list of certain soils to be included while excluding others just as suitable. In the final analysis, the drainage features of surface soils were given a greater importance than subsoil. Just as significant, the decision to disregard and downplay the "Kimmeridgian" qualification had the effect of upgrading a good deal of Petit Chablis to the more expensive Chablis category. Beginning with the 1978 vintage, the amount of wine entitled to carry the "Chablis" appellation name increased fivefold, while the number of potential hectares increased sixfold, from 1,100 to nearly 7,000. The appellation that most benefited from the 1976 "revision" is Chablis, which increased its share of production from 50 to 60 percent from 1975 to 1983, while Petit Chablis declined from 16 to 6 percent. Should the demand for Chablis continue, and should the standards of quality be maintained, hectarage and production will increase significantly in the coming decades.

Some of the more prominent négociants are as follows: *Joseph Drouhin,*

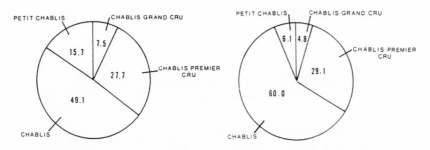

Figure 5.5   Chablis: Wine Production, by Appellation, 1974 *(left)* and 1984

Figure 5.6   Chablis: Wine
Production, All Appellations,
1946–1985
(in thousands of hectoliters)

known for stylish, well-polished, almost always technically flawless and expensive wines, has recently expanded vineland to 36 hectares and seems poised for a significant share of the Chablis market. *J. Moreau* is known for fresh and lively wines meant to be consumed young. The firm is a major property holder, exports 80 percent of production, and successfully markets branded wine under the "Moreau Blanc" label. *Bichot,* a large house with more than 80 hectares, markets wine under a large number of *sous marque* labels, nearly all containing light, early drinking wine for mass appeal. *A. Regnard,* a large firm, makes average to above-average Fourchaume but is otherwise inconsistent. *Lamblin* distributes a broad range of average, thin, early maturing wines that are often marred by inconsistency. *Simmonet-Fèbvre,* a negociant and property owner, makes clean, fresh, early maturing wines under a variety of labels, and is the only firm making mousseux. *Partrick de Ladoucette* specializes in wines that have individuality and character. *Bacheroy-Josselin* is known for good, early maturing wines that offer good value. *Chanson* ships large quantities of Chablis to the United Sates, most of which is of average quality. *Cave Coopérative "La Chablisienne,"* the largest cooperative in the Yonne department with 190 members, is responsible for at least 20 percent of all Chablis. Although it makes good, clean wines, mostly Chablis and Petit Chablis, more than 70 percent of production is destined for sale to large Burgundian negociants.

The principal private producers are *William Fèvre* (said to make the largest quantity of Grand Cru wines in Chablis; the wines, subjected to wood-aging, are full-bodied, well scented, and merit extended cellaring); *Dne. Auffray* (the hard to find les Clos, les Preuses, and Vaudesirs are stunning); *Robert Vocoret* (a small producer with a superlative reputation, one of the few firms that still uses wooden vats for fermentation, producing wines that are full-bodied, with a beautiful dark golden color, and multidimensional in flavor); *René Dauvissat* (making superlative Grand Cru and Premier Cru wines); *Louis Michel* (a small house that owns 20 hectares of mostly Grand and Premier Cru properties, making full-bodied, old-fashioned wines); *J.-M. Reveneau* (full-bodied, wood-aged wines that are profusely flavored and capable of extended bottle-aging); *Paul Droin* (a small house with impeccable credentials, making superb Vaudesir, Valmur, and les Clos); *Jean Durup* (one of the largest producers in Chablis, making early drinking, somewhat flat-tasting, technically correct but undistinguished wines; best known for a crisp Fourchaume and for Dne. de l'Eglantière); *Dne. A. Long Depaquit* (known for skillfully made but inconsistent Chablis); *Dne. Jean Defaix* (known for dry, austere, powerful wines); *Louis Pinson* (a traditional grower makes rich, full-bodied, highly flavorful wines); *Jean Collet* (fermenting in wood and producing full-bodied, old-fashioned wines that age gracefully); *Phillippe Testut* (known for distinctive, full-bodied, flavorful wines, particularly Genouilles); and *Marcel Duplessis* (a small grower with old-fashioned ideas of what good Chablis should be, producing full-bodied, highly individualistic wines).

OTHER YONNE VINEYARDS

Sauvignon de St.-Bris

One of the most important non-Chablis vineyards of the Yonne is the small VDQS appellation of Sauvignon St.-Bris. Official VDQS status was awarded in 1974 to an irregular area encompassing the communes of Vincelottes, St.-Bris-le-Vineaux, Chitry, and Irancy, all located south of Auxerre. The Sauvignon Blanc grape, along with minor amounts of Pinot Blanc and other vines, produce fewer than 3,500 hectoliters of white wine annually. The wine, light in color when young, is acidic, and although often unbalanced, appears to be better than most other wines. It has recently enjoyed a burst of popularity primarily because the producing districts lie close to the tourist traffic visiting Auxerre and the Cistercian Abbey at Pontigny. *J.-P. Tabit, Philippe Defrance,* and *Claude Seguin* are three important producers.

Auxerre, Tonnerre, Avallon, and Joigny

The only other vineyards of note in Yonne are those of Auxerre, Tonnerre, Avallon, and Joigny, with the first two considered the better of the four. Collectively, the four make about 40,000 hectoliters of wine–small amounts of rosé, slightly more red, and the majority white. Over the past 100 years vine hectarage has been reduced by 90 percent, but there are signs that a revival is about to take place.

The best sites of Tonnerre are situated on slopes near the Armançon River. The non-appellation wines are acidic, fairly high in alcohol, light in color, and lack finesse and suppleness. The finest wine is red—very robust, often coarse, slow to mature, and known for its bitter aftertaste.

In iron-rich soils, the best growths are found within the village confines of
Dannemoine, Tonnerre, and Epineuil. Among white wines, the best is
made from Chardonnay. Approximately twenty-six specific growths have
been identified, but few have achieved any measure of distinction.

The Auxerre vineyard is located west of Chablis along the right bank of

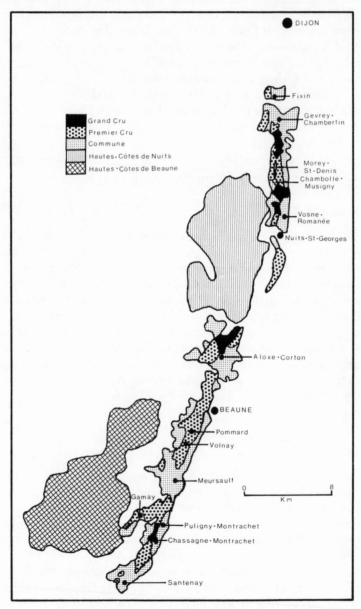

Figure 5.7   The Vineyards of the Côte d'Or

the Yonne River and is known for the AOC red and rosé wines of Irancy. The wine of note is a fresh, yeasty, flavorful, and early maturing red wine that does not travel well. Of the two remaining vinegrowing districts— Avallon and Joigny—the former is better known for its white wine made from Chardonnay.

THE WINES OF THE CÔTE D'OR

The Côte d'Or, the most valuable vineyard in the entire world, is the smallest of the "grand" wine regions of France. Beaujolais to the south produces five times more wine, Champagne more than three times, while the combined output of Pomerol, St.-Emilion, the Médoc, Graves, and Sauternes is six times larger. For the department as a whole, non-agricultural land use increased from 4,000 hectares to more than 50,000 between 1846 and 1985, while uncultivated agricultural land increased nearly fourfold. Forestland increased by two-thirds, pastureland tripled, and arable land declined by half for the same period. For the years 1846 to 1985, vineland as percent of total cultivated area declined from 5.6 to 1.4 percent, and total vine hectarage declined by more than 28,000 hectares from the peak of 36,914 hectares in 1878. For the four principal departments, hectarage and wine output for selected years are presented in Tables 5.4 and 5.5. Total wine production is shown in Figure 5.8.

Burgundy is a viticultural region of small growers. In 1984, 3,400 vinegrowers' average holding was roughly two-thirds of a hectare. It is estimated that more than half of all growers cultivate part time, that at least 29 percent of all hectarage is leased to larger growers and negociants, and that another one-third is cultivated under the *métayage* system.

Table 5.4   Vine Hectarage in the Côte d'Or, Saône-et-Loire, Rhône, and Yonne, 1816, 1875, 1929, and 1979

	Côte 'd'Or	Saône-et-Loire	Rhône	Yonne	Total
1816					
hectares	24,000	27,700	29,800	35,000	116,500
percent	(20.6)	(23.8)	(25.6)	(30.0)	(100)
1875					
hectares	33,745	43,612	46,665	37,485	161,507
percent	(21.0)	(27.0)	(29.0)	(23.0)	(100)
1929					
hectares	12,122	23,376	20,296	6,781	62,565
percent	(37.4)	(37.4)	(32.4)	(10.8)	(100)
1979					
hectares	8,046	9,688	19,870	2,585	40,189
percent	(20.0)	(24.1)	(49.5)	(6.4)	(100)

Source: French Ministry of Agriculture.

Divided into the Côte de Nuits and the Côte de Beaune, the Côte d'Or extends from Marsannay south to Dijon, to the northern margins of the Chalonnais—a distance of 40 kilometers. Lying between Dijon and Aloxe, the Côte de Nuits, mainly a red wine region, contains the bulk of Grand Cru climats that produce the fullest and most enduring of all red Burgundies. The Côte de Beaune, beginning at Aloxe and continuing south to Santenay, contains the largest concentration of fine white wine and light, early maturing, but more delicate red wines than its more famous neighbor to the north.

The Climate and Soils of the Côte d'Or

The hillsides that slope down to the Saône are known as the Côte d'Or. They form a long, narrow ribbon of vineyards located between the plateau to the west and the Saône floodplain to the east. The Morvan, the northern extension of the Massif Central, is a massive, granite, and metamorphic block whose elevations are sufficiently high to shield the vineyards from inclement westerly weather. Along its upland margins, elevations rising to 1,400 meters attract rain, thus producing pasture and thick beech and oak forests. Along the eastern margins that overlook the Saône, the Morvan changes in character to a series of lower ridges (rarely more than 750 meters high) composed of limestone, marl, granite, and schist rock. Along this east-facing aspect of the Morvan the famous vineyards are concentrated in a long, sinewy ribbon for nearly 40 kilometers.

Because Burgundy is located inland and north of Bordeaux, the climate is decidedly continental, with greater seasonal variations in temperature and rainfall. Rainfall is a moderate 700 to 750 mm per year; the driest

Table 5.5   Wine Production in the Côte d'Or, Saône-et-Loire, Rhône, and Yonne Departments, 1816, 1875, 1929, and 1979

	Côte d'Or	Saône-et-Loire	Rhône	Yonne	Total
1816					
hectoliters	564,000	762,000	723,500	882,000	2,931,500
percent	(19.2)	(26.0)	(24.7)	(30.1)	(100)
1875					
hectoliters	2,088,814	2,220,872	1,291,883	2,244,328	7,845,897
percent	(26.6)	(28.3)	(16.5)	(28.6)	(100)
1929					
hectoliters	429,508	971,637	800,743	275,927	2,477,815
percent	(17.3)	(39.2)	(32.3)	(11.2)	(100)
1979					
hectoliters	281,314	446,833	1,063,233	91,600	1,882,980
percent	(14.8)	(24.0)	(56.4)	(4.8)	(100)

Source: French Ministry of Agriculture.

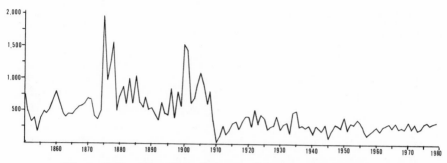

Figure 5.8   Côte d'Or: Wine Production, 1850–1980
(in thousands of hectoliters)

months are February and March, the wettest May and June. More than half of all precipitation falls April through September, giving the Côte d'Or a wet growing season and a rather high incidence of *coulure* (most pronounced under cool and wet conditions) and *oïdium* (under warm and wet conditions). Adding to harvest uncertainties is the significant fact that precipitation in August, September, and October is highly irregular in volume and unpredictable in duration. The prevailing westerly winds bring rain and humidity, while *la Bise* winds from the north deliver dry and cold weather. The southern Mediterranean influences do not penetrate the Yonne department or the northern fringes of the Côte d'Or.

Temperatures for the region as a whole average between 10° and 11°C (January is the coldest month and July the hottest), but can range between -20°C to 38°C under abnormal circumstances. While the mean temperature for Dijon is 10.6°C, that of the entire growing season is 16.5°C, a low figure compared to other major wine-producing areas. Exceptional vintage years tend to have more than 35 days of 25°C temperatures, low relative humidity, and a longer-than-average growing season. Practically all above-average vintages occur when the growing season exceeds 160 days. Hours of sunlight vary enormously from 2,500, as a maximum, to fewer than 1,700 hours during cold and damp vintage years.

Because the Côte d'Or is located away from any significant body of water, grapes suffer from low temperatures, early and late frosts, and an inconsistent growing season, all of which combine to produce insufficient sugar levels. The biggest climatic hazards are spring frost, a poor flowering due to increased humidity and precipitation, hail in June and July, and the uncertainty of rain during the final month of maturity. Hail, in particular, is worrisome to growers, not because it reduces the size of the crop but because it facilitates the spread of mildew.

Within the region, microclimatic variations occur. While the upland areas receive more rain, the Côte d'Or receives less rain than the Côte de Beaune and is more susceptible to the beneficial effects of the drying northerly *la Bise* wind. The finest sites, lying midway up the lee slopes facing due east or southeast, are sheltered from the rain-bearing westerly winds and positioned away from valleys and slopes that attract frost.

The hillsides of the Côte d'Or are a complex series of geologic formations that have been eroded as part of the Saône–Rhône drainage system. The soil is a highly variable mixture of oolitic calcareous material, limestone, marl, schist, and silica. The hilltops are either exposed rock, brushland, or forest, while the Saône valley contains alluvial material heavily impregnated with clay. Grand Cru climats rest on oolite limestone sites containing abnormal amounts of potassium, phosphorus, and iron elements, which give the soil a reddish color. Those vineyards fortunate enough to lie on such land produce true *vin de garde* wine—classic in structure, flavor, and aroma. Examples are the Grand Cru sites of Chambertin, Musigny, Vosne, and Morey. Farther south, the Côte de Beaune is flatter and much broader than the Côte de Nuits. Here the iron-phosphorus-potassium elements are weaker, the amount of silica is reduced, and the proportion of clay is higher. Thus the Côte de Beaune red wines are less full and weaker in constitution. The premium sites for the production of white wine are small, isolated areas containing marl and limestone, such as Corton, Meursault, Puligny, and Chassagne. In portions of Puligny and Chassagne, for example, more than one-third of the soil consists of silica, one-quarter of clay, and the remainder of marl. The variegated nature of soil, aspect, and climate are described as follows: (a) preferred sites consist of well-drained, east-facing slopes whose soils warm easily and retain heat throughout the day and night; (b) where silica dominates, red wines are light in body, early maturing, and often coarse; (c) where clay dominates and the subsoil is well drained, the wines are full-bodied, tannin-rich, and alcoholic; (d) limestone and marl soils are planted in Chardonnay, producing wine that is alcoholic with an expansive bouquet; (e) soils containing iron oxide, potash, and phosphoric acid produce well-colored, highly fragrant, *vin de garde* wine; (f) the best soils are moderately alkaline, not acidic; (g) the poorest soils for the production of quality wine are those located on flat land with clay and silt. The principal grape varieties of the Côte d'Or are presented in Table 5.6.

The Wines

Historically, red Côte d'Or Burgundy was a light wine, consumed young, with little extract or tannin. But by the first quarter of the 19th century, the demand had shifted to darker, fuller, and more concentrated wine that was capable of aging and competing with Bordeaux. The very best had an enormous sweet bouquet, an aroma of ripe fruit, and a long, lingering flavor. Becoming the preferred wine of kings, millionaires, and the finest restaurants, Burgundy enjoyed an immense exposure and gathered a loyal following. Despite difficulties in purchasing due to the multitude of

Table 5.6   Major Grape Varieties in the Côte d'Or, 1968 and 1979

Grape variety	1968 Hectares	1968 Percent[a]	1979 Hectares	1979 Percent[a]	As percent of national total
Pinot Noir	4,500	30.6	5,700	62.0	33.1
Chardonnay	800	5.5	1,000	10.9	77.0
Aligoté	900	6.1	600	6.5	60.0
Gamay Noir	700	4.8	500	5.4	15.1
Plantet	400	2.7	100	1.1	
Oberlin	400	2.7	100	1.1	
Baco Noir	300	2.0	50	.5	
Others	6,700	45.6	1,150	12.5	
Total	14,700	100.0	9,200	100.0	

[a]Percent of departmental total.

Source: French Ministry of Agriculture.

names and producers, it was always easy to sell, not because it was expensive but because of its inherent quality and the element of fashion.

As it was given time in wood, good Burgundy went through specific maturation phases: it was fruity and acidic in youth, awkward and dull at middle age, but when fully mature developed into an eminently satisfying, smooth, complex libation—features that enabled its price to appreciate and the wine to be considered a secure investment, much in the manner of first-growth Médoc. This type of Burgundy continued until the *phylloxera* epidemic changed the character of the dominant vines, rootstocks, and vineyard practices. Eventually the number of new clones, the increased use of sugar, and the economics of wine production, particularly in the past two generations, changed the essence of Burgundy from what it was a century ago. Now we have two types of winemaking philosophies—the *méthode ancienne* and the *méthode nouvelle*—the latter the favored method in the production of both white and red wines.

Burgundy at its best—subtle, supple, complex, and with a sweet nose—should be reserved for the finest entrée. It should always have flesh, flavor, and fullness on the palate, and never be overpowered by alcohol or by excessive color. Unfortunately a good percentage of all available red Burgundy is pale, with tasteless flavor and flimsy structure. Its name and reputation have been severely tarnished by debasement and scandal over the past forty years, so that Burgundy today is but a former shell of its illustrious predecessor and offers little value. As a consequence, for most of the world, "Burgundy" has become a generic name (Californian Burgundy, Chilean Burgundy, New York State Burgundy) and is no longer thought of as a regional name with above-average attributes. Even in France, Burgundy is associated with central France and not with the

Côte d'Or. Although exports of "Burgundy" continue to grow, the figures portray a misleading picture. Nearly 85 percent of all Burgundy entering the United States is generic in nature, mostly "branded" wine from the lowest end of the quality spectrum. Authentic Burgundy from the Côte d'Or is hard to come by unless one rises to the $50 per bottle and up price range.

White Burgundy does not fare much better. Not only is overcropping a standard feature, but the density of vines per hectare exceeds 10,000, one of the highest figures in France. To "stretch" the vintage, vineyards are often heavily fertilized with nitrogen and potassium. Fermentation occuring with commercial yeasts reduces the individuality of the wine, and the whole of production is processed in stainless steel, with a good portion of the wine being subjected to both chaptalization and acidification, thus producing unbalanced wine. The custom of *batonnage* (the stirring of the lees to improve aroma and freshness and prevent oxidation) has largely been abandoned, while the heavy use of filtration and pasteurization have become routine practices throughout the producing region. In the final analysis the *méthode ancienne* produced darker, fuller, more flavorful wines capable of extended aging. The practice of long, slow, fermentation with a measureable amount of stalk, which produces long-lasting, tannin-rich wines, has been abandoned in the effort to "move" wine faster and to extend profit margins.

Buying Burgundy

No other French wine region presents such a bewildering and complex market as Burgundy. Even a general knowledge of the negociant, grower, and vintage is not sufficient to guide the consumer properly to an educated selection. Unlike Bordeaux, where Ch. Latour of the 1975 vintage is consistent no matter where, the 1975 Clos de Vougeot varies from grower to grower and negociant to negociant. To say that Burgundy is "variable" is to understate the nature of the confusion. A particularly complicated affair, the choice of a good bottle is usually called "Burgundy roulette." In the absence of market reliability, it is imperative to understand the following axioms:

1. *Good Burgundy is very expensive.* As a region Burgundy produces the world's most expensive wine due to a combination of elements, of which the following are the most important: (a) a combination of insatiable demand, stable production, and a marginal climate produce high prices, but not necessarily high quality; (b) the price of good Burgundy is inelastic, and the very wealthy consumers continue to buy whatever the asking price; (c) the exclusivity of the product in conjunction with limited supplies acts as an inertia in maintaining high prices; (d) false propaganda concerning the quality of the vintages maintains interest, demand, and

sales; (e) direct selling by the grower in Burgundy reduces the amount of wine entering normal distribution channels.

2. *High prices are no guarantee of quality.* Good (not necessarily excellent or outstanding) Burgundy is very expensive, and bad wine is not necessarily cheaper than average-to-above-average wine.

3. *Burgundy disappoints more often than it pleases.* When good it can be memorable, but more often it is dreadful and flippantly bad.

4. *Burgundy offers little or no value.* Burgundy offers one of the lowest quality to price ratios. For everyday drinking, the best white wine value lies in Montagny and Rully; for red, Beaujolais, Givry, and Mercurey. Discriminating eyes and palates can unearth a few values among the ranks of Grand and Premier Cru, but not many and only rarely. These expensive libations should be purchased by the bottle for tasting, and then by case only if they merit the asking price.

5. *So-called "declassified" wines should be avoided.* Although the system of "declassification" is officially discontinued, the practice continues. Recent regulations have allowed growers an extra 20 percent over the appellation's normal maximum yield. If the grower wants full appellation status for his wine, it must be presented for a tasting with a pass-fail grade only—which is to say that if the wine does not make the grade for the higher appellation, all would be declassified to plain Burgundy. The problem is the regulating authorities, who routinely approve nearly all the wine submitted.

6. *Burgundian labels are misleading.* (a) "Monopole" refers to an exclusive right to a product or to the exclusive privilege to produce and sell the wine regardless of property ownership. Not a term regulated by the EEC, it has been subjected to much abuse. By imitating the label of a more famous climat and name, the winemaker misleads the consumer into believing he is purchasing the original or an exceptional wine. (b) "Mise au Domaine" refers to wines made and bottled at the property and is identical to the expression "Mise en Bouteilles au Domaine." But if the property is small, the wine is usually bottled from a portable truck bottling facility. This designation is still more meaningful than "Mise en Bouteilles Dans Nos Caves" and "Mise en Bouteilles au Château," two expressions referring to the fact that the wine was bottled in *someone's* cellars or property, but not necessarily the owner's. (c) "Vigneron" is another confusing expression, because under the *métayage* system, the share-cropper shares the yield with the property owner, both of whom make wine from the same grapes, marketed under two separate names. (d) "Mise à la Propriété" alludes to the fact that the wine was bottled either on the property of the grower or the bottler—but which one? The following expressions do not signify estate-bottled wines: "Mise en Bouteilles en France," "Mise en Bouteilles Dans Nos Chais," "Mise en Bouteilles Par le Propriétaire," and "Mise en Bouteilles Dans la Region de Production."

7. *Negociants are characterized by unreliable reputations, changing functions, and highly variable wines.* Because Burgundian holdings are too small to warrant conventional operations, a large number of growers (perhaps as many as 55 percent), especially in the Côte d'Or, sell their grapes and/or wine to larger growers or negociants. As recently as 1970, more than half of all single-vineyard wine was blended and marketed by negociants. Negociants are of three types: (a) those who buy, blend, age, bottle, and distribute wine; (b) those who buy grapes as well as wine and go through the above processes; and (c) those who lease and/or own vineland, as well as process (b). There are countless variations on the above three themes, including a few negociants who will not age wine. The Comité Interprofessional de la Côte d'Or et de L'Yonne lists 189 negociants in the two departments, with an additional 303 in the Saône-et-Loire and Rhône. Negociants are historically referred to as "éleveurs et propriétaires"—an expression that defines the functions of aging, distributing, and shipping wine.

The Burgundian negociant, family owned and racked with nepotism, has experienced difficulties on a number of fronts. Some growers have expanded their hectarage, which enables them to capitalize their estates more effectively, bottle their own wine, and sell directly to the public, hotels, and restaurants. Some growers have also engaged in the profitable disposal of a good deal of stock through "futures" offerings, thus bypassing the historical role and function of the negociant. Another major assault on the economic viability of the traditional shipper is the rise of large, multinational importing and/or distributing firms that bypass the negociant functions of brokering, storage, and shipping. Over the past thirty years, the total volume of wine handled by negociants has declined by at least 20 percent, forcing many negociants to diversify their traditional functions and activities. One of the more recent innovations toward survival has been their expansion of vine hectarage in Grand and Premier Cru climats. But to improve the wine is another, more difficult chore.

The issue of wine reliability is a multifaceted problem: the misrepresentation of the negociant's address and label; the use of *sous marques;* and the fraudulent production and distribution of wine. Negociants have long misled the public by shipping less expensive wine from a prestigious postal address in the Côte d'Or. Second, although negociants maintain that *sous marques* (multiple labels for the same wine) are absolutely essential, the author maintains that the practice is questionable, even though it is legal. *Sous marques* have become a convenient way to sell fraudulent wine as authentic in many unsuspecting foreign markets. Moreover, the quality, type, and character of the wine vary significantly to cater to the wishes of that market. For example, to satisfy the American market for brilliant color and an absence of sediment, wines are heavily filtered and fined. Whatever the merits of the *sous marque* imbroglio, few discerning consumers are aware that in the United Kingdom the wines of Faiveley are known as Jules Regnier and that Bichot is a holding company for Charles Drapier, a major shipper in the Pacific.

THE WINES OF THE CÔTE DE NUITS

Beginning south of Dijon and continuing for 21 kilometers to Congoloin, the Côte de Nuits is a thin strip of prime viticultural land that produces about three-quarters of the finest red Burgundy from the Côte d'Or. Not only is the wine one of the most expensive in the entire world, but its 1,300 vine-clad hectares constitute the most valuable agricultural land in France. The red wines of the Côte de Nuits are considered superior to those of Beaune in terms of aroma, bouquet, body, intensity of color, and longevity. Small quantities of average to above-average white wine is made in Chambolle-Musigny, Vougeot, and Nuits St.-Georges, but it is a minor element in regional output.

The Côte de Nuits contains six major village appellations, three regional appellations, 23 Grand Cru, and more than 120 Premier Cru vineyards. The Côte de Nuits–Villages, Bourgogne-Hautes Côte de Nuits, and Bourgogne-Marsannay-la-Côte are the three district or regional appellations collectively accounting for one-quarter to one-third of

Table 5.7 AOC Wine Production in the Côte de Nuits, 1980

Appellation	Hectoliters	Percent of total
Chambolle-Musigny Rouge	4,412	8.5
Côte de Nuits–Villages Rouge	7,499	14.5
Côte de Nuits–Villages Blanc	6	
Fixin Rouge	1,098	2.1
Gevrey-Chambertin Rouge	14,383	28.0
Morey-St.-Denis Rouge	2,196	4.2
Morey-St.-Denis Blanc	16	
Nuits-St.-Georges Rouge	8,884	17.2
Nuits-St.-Georges Blanc	19	
Vougeot Rouge	432	1.0
Vougeot Blanc	70	
Vosne-Romanée Rouge	4,884	9.4
Bourgogne-Marsannay–La Côte Rosé and Rouge	1,191	2.3
Bourgogne-Marsannay–La Côte Blanc		
Bourgogne Hautes–Côtes de Nuits Rouge	6,469	12.5
Bourgogne Hautes–Côtes de Nuits Blanc	241	.3
Total Rouge	51,448	99.3
Total Blanc	352	.7
Total general	51,800	100.0

Note: Table does not include Grands Crus production.

Source: French Ministry of Agriculture.

total production. The reputation of the Côte de Nuits rests with the 23 Grand Cru vineyards (shown in Table 5.8) that collectively produce between 5 and 10 percent of total regional output. Premier Cru vineyards encompass approximately 460 hectares and produce about one-quarter of total output.

Côte de Nuits-Villages

This appellation's blended wines, historically known as Vins Fins de la Côte de Nuits, originate from any of the communes of Fixin, Brochon, Prissey, Comblanchien, or Corgoloin. Production is variable because, of the 315 hectares subject to this appellation status, Fixin contains 126 and, depending on the nature of the vintage and market conditions, a significant portion of output may be marketed under the communal or the villages banner. Nearly the whole of production is red and must contain a minimum of 10.5 percent alcohol. The wine, highly variable in quality, is coarse and not the equal of plain Fixin or other communal wine.

Bourgogne-Marsannay-la-Côte

Bourgogne-Marsannay-la-Côte is a regional appellation despite the fact that the majority of grapes are harvested in the communes of Marsannay-la-Côte and Couchey-en-Côte d'Or. Under no circumstances should one assume this wine to be the product of a commune, despite its reference to Marsannay. Most of the wine is red, although white and rosé are also produced, the latter being considered the best of the three. The principal producer is the local cooperative, but the reputation for quality rosé rests

Table 5.8   Grand Cru Wine Production in the Côte de Nuits, 1980

Appellation	Hectoliters	Appellation	Hectoliters
Bonnes Mares Rouge	347	la Tâche Rouge	107
Chambertin Rouge	509	Latricières-Chambertin Rouge	250
Chambertin Clos de		Mazis-Chambertin Rouge	218
Bèze Rouge	480	Mazoyères-Chambertin Rouge	–
Chapelle-Chambertin Rouge	187	Musigny Rouge	191
Charmes-Chambertin Rouge	998	Musigny Blanc	8
Clos des Lambrays Rouge	131	Richebourg Rouge	102
Close de la Roche Rouge	484	la Romanée Rouge	28
Clos St.-Denis Rouge	156	Romanée-Conti Rouge	33
Clos de Tart	181	Romanée-St.-Vivant Rouge	169
Clos de Vougeot Rouge	1,387	Ruchottes-Chambertin Rouge	74
Echézeaux Rouge	966	Total Rouge	7,275
Grand Echézeaux Rouge	218	Total Blanc	8
Griotte-Chambertin			
Rouge	59	Grand total	7,283

Source: French Ministry of Agriculture.

with *Clair-Daü, Dne. Fougeray, René Bouvier, André Bart,* and *Bruno Clair.* Overlapping this appellation is the semi-official Côte Dijon region, a 600-hectare appellation located south and west of Dijon that produces a wide array of red, rosé, and white wines from Gamay, Pinot Noir, Aligoté, and Chardonnay, and a good number of hybrids. The region is associated with St.-Bernard, founder of 68 abbeys and a formidable element in the Cistercian monastic order. The vineyards closest to Dijon are located in Chenové, a neglected village that makes small quantities of below-average wine.

Bourgogne Hautes-Côtes de Nuits

Hautes-Côtes de Nuits is a 10,000-hectoliter regional appellation that encompasses at least fourteen villages making red, rosé, and white wines. The entire producing area, west of Chambolle and north of Pernand-Vergelesses and located on hilly terrain, involves the three important and rapidly expanding villages of Villars-Fontaine, Villers-la-Faye, and Marey-les-Fussey. Over the past twenty years hectarage has expanded rapidly, and the quality of the wine (more than 95 percent red) has improved markedly, especially the white.

Fixin

With six Premier Cru climats (les Meix-Bas, les Hervelets, les Arvelets, Clos Napoléon, la Perrière, and Clos du Chapitre), Fixin is the northernmost of the major communes of the Côte de Nuits. Of the six, Clos du Chapitre, with good color, fragrance, and body enjoys the best reputation, followed by la Perrière. The producing region contains a unique microclimate in which the incidence of hail and frost is lower than in any other Nuits commune, thus assuring bigger, more predictable harvests. The town contains fewer than 800 inhabitants and 135 hectares of vineland, which produce 2,000 hectoliters of wine annually. Fixin was the summer residence of the dukes of Burgundy, and prior to the *phylloxera* epidemic viticulture was more prominent. Today there is renewed interest in the appellation and hectarage is growing.

The wines, all red, dark, and full-bodied, contain more *sève* than any other in the Côte de Nuits. Although they lack the elegance of Chambertin, they are high in alcohol, contain plenty of extract and tannin, and require at least ten years to round out. They offer one of the best values of all Burgundies, especially in good vintages. Among the handful of producers, *Dne. Pierre Gelin,* the largest property owner of Fixin, is known for Clos Napoléon and Clos du Chapitre. The quality producer of Fixin is *Dne. Bertheaut,* a small but highly reliable grower who makes above-average les Arvelets, as well as minuscule quantities of Gevrey-Chambertin, among others. The wines in no way resemble the light-colored and thin-tasting libations of the Côte de Beaune, but are old-fashioned, *vin de garde* wines that require time to soften. Other growers include *Dne. de la Perrière, Bruno Clair, J.-P. Guyard, Dne. Dr. Marion,* and *André Bart.*

Between Fixin and Gevrey is the commune of Brochon, a 150-hectare vineyard producing nothing but Bourgogne-quality wine. The wines were originally labeled "Vins de la Côte de Nuits," but no longer—their anonymity is protected since they are blended into innocuous libations of varying quality. In general, they resemble those of Fixin but seem to lack the grace, smoothness, body, and fragrance of the better neighboring growths.

Gevrey-Chambertin

The 3,000-resident commune of Gevrey became an overnight success, as did most things in France associated with Napoleon, when the Great Emperor declared that Chambertin was his favorite wine. The name was hyphenated by imperial decree in 1847, thus debasing the name ever since. With nearly 400 hectares of vines producing more than 16,000 hectoliters, Gevrey-Chambertin is the largest commune in the Côte de Nuits, responsible for more than one-quarter of total output. There are nine Grand Cru climats and 23 Premier Cru. The former are huddled together on the middle slope of the Montagne de la Combe Gri, and Except for Chambertin and Clos de Bèze, the remaining seven have appended their name to Chambertin. Located west of the town, the bulk of the Premier Cru climats lie on steeper slopes.

Approximately half the commune's hectarage, mainly that portion lying east of N74, lies on flat rich soil and produces wine unworthy of the name Chambertin. Not only is the topography unsuitable for first-class wine, but the soils lack the perfect balance of limestone and iron-impregnated elements so essential to the maintenance of the commune's reputation. It is, therefore, very difficult to find authentic, quality commune Gevrey-Chambertin at reasonable prices. Moreover, a significant amount of vineland in Brochon is allowed to sell its wine under the Gevrey-Chambertin banner. Communal Gevrey-Chambertin, therefore, varies from thin, acidic libations to memorable delights. Careful selection is necessary in view of the fact that value is not readily available. Among the more than 100 growers and negociants who distribute communal Gevrey-Chambertin, the following are widely available: *Dne. Rebourseau* (reliable); *Pierre Amiot* (good but inconsistent); *Pierre Bourée* (above-average to outstanding); *Georges Brycszek* (average wines that offer value); *Dne. Pernot-Fourrier* (exceptional, full-bodied, well-flavored wines offering outstanding value); *Henri Richard* (big, masculine wines); *Dne. Louis Trapet* (above average); *Dne. Drouhin-Laroze* (well flavored but early maturing); *Georges Vachet* (little known but consistent); *Pierre Bernollin* (reliable, fruity wines); *Alain Burguet* (reliable wines that offer complexity and solid value); *Yvon Burguet* (average); *Faiveley* (good but highly variable); *Philippe Leclerc* (reliable, average to above-average, offering excellent value); *Moillard* (below-average to average, and overpriced); *Dne. des Varoilles* (variable and expensive); *Dne. Armand Rousseau* (average, well structured, offering good value); *Dne. Tortochot* (unreliable and expensive); and *Pierre Rossignol* (reliable, offering good value).

The most famous vineyard of Gevrey is the 28-hectare, 7th-century site of Chambertin owned at one time by the Abbey of Bèze. "The wine of Napoleon" has incomparable color, fragrance, elegance, and body. It requires, even by today's *méthode nouvelle* efforts, time to mature fully. Among the nearly two dozen growers, the most important in the production of average to above-average wine are *Clair-Daü* (big, firm, powerful wines requiring time to mature); *Bouchard Père* (consistently well-made wines, usually offering excellent value); *Dne. Armand Rousseau* (above-average, long-lived, but expensive wines); *Louis Rémy; Dne. Hubert Camus; Dne. Louis Trapet; Joseph Drouhin; Dne. Dujac; Faiveley; Pierre Gelin; Tortochot;* and *Dne. de Varoilles.* The smaller, 15-hectare Benedictine site of Clos de Bèze, lying next to Chambertin, produces wine that can be sold as Chambertin (but not vice versa) and is considered by many to be its superior. It tends to be more delicate and early maturing, and usually is more expensive since production is normally lmited to 7,000 cases a year. Among the handful of producers the following are to be noted: *Drouhin-Laroze* (above average to excellent); *Dne. Dr. Marion* (refined and elegant wines); *Dne. Drouhin-Laroze* (big, well-structured, and *vin de garde);* *Faiveley* (well polished and expensive); *Robert Groffier* (soft, fruity, and excellent); and *Charles Rousseau* (above average).

The 30-hectare Charmes-Chambertin climat, the largest in Gevrey-Chambertin and the second-largest in the Côte de Nuits, produces about 11,000 cases, a good deal of it outstanding and the equal of both Chambertin and Clos de Bèze. It should be noted that it also includes the 19-hectare Mazoyères-Chambertin vineyard, the latter having the legal right to market its wines under the more famous names of Charmes. Among the many producers are *Pierre Bourée* (excellent, full-bodied); *Dupont-Tisserandot* (rich, fleshy, well scented and flavored); *Jean Rachet* (outstanding and refined); *Henri Richard* (full-bodied and mouth-filling); *Dne. Taupenot-Merme* (soft and early maturing); *Dne. Rebourseau* (fruity and supple); *Charlopin-Parizot* (well made and fruity); *Joseph Drouhin* (reliable); *Dne. Dujac* (inconsistent); *Moillard* (below average and overpriced); *Dne. Armand Rousseau* (inconsistent, but often exceptional); *Dne. Camus* (above average but inconsistent). In the extreme southern portion of the commune lies the 7-hectare Latricières-Chambertin climat, a site that has less iron in the soil but more silica, hence produces thinner, less concentrated wine. Nevertheless, considered by many to be the near-equal of Clos de Bèze and Chambertin, it is hard to find and frightfully expensive. Among the principal producers are *Dne. Louis Trapet,* and *Bernard Maume.*

Chapelle-Chambertin, a 5-hectare climat first developed by the monks of Bèze in the 12th century, is known for the production of smooth, velvety, light-colored wines. Mazis-Chambertin, a 12-hectare site, produces about 3,000 cases of light, early maturing wine that is firm yet silky on the palate. The most prominent producers are *Dne. Pierre Gelin, Dne. Rebourseau, Bernard Maume, Dne. Tortochot, Dne. Camus,* and *Vachet-Rousseau.* The 7-hectare Ruchottes-Chambertin climat is somewhat over-rated, despite the fact that its history dates back to 895. It produces fewer than 1,000 cases of wine annually, most of it undistinguished and overpriced. The wine of *G. Mugneret* is well made, full-bodied, spicy, and usually offering good value. The 13-hectare Griotte-Chambertin output, rarely seen in the United States, is known for rather bland, often dull wine. The bulk of the finest Premier Cru climats are located on rather steep limestone and stony slopes northwest of Gevrey. Of the nearly 84 hectares devoted to this second-tier classification, the following enjoy good reputations: Clos St.-Jacques (a stylish, expensive wine with a wide following); Lavaut (a single-dimensional, supple wine); les Varoilles; Estournelles; Cazetiers; Combes-aux-Moines; and Aux Combottes.

Morey-St.-Denis

Morey, a much smaller town than Gevrey, has been in continuous grape production since the 10th century. As its name suggests, religious affiliation has been pervasive (St.-Denis became a walled "Clos" during the Middle Ages, Clos de Tart and Clos des Lambrays were founded by nuns, and six additional vineyards were developed by the Cistercian order) with a large number of religious orders owning all the choice climats until the French Revolution. Soils consist of clay, marl, and chalk, and form a contiguous alignment with the Grand Cru climats of Gevrey and Chambolle. Despite contemporary prominence, its claim to fame is rather recent because the wines, prior to 1927 (the year Morey was appended to St.-Denis) were sold either as Gevrey-Chambertin or Chambolle-Musigny. Since the name remains unfamiliar to most buyers, communal St.-Denis wine is less expensive than Gevrey-Chambertin or Vosne-Romanée, and offers above-average value since quality is equal to its more famous competitors. Although the wines share a marked resemblance to those of Gevrey-Chambertin in terms of constitution (big, rich, and capable of extended cellaring), they are more succulent, fruitier, and satisfying. At their best, they are complex, never hard, and devoid of rough edges, excess acidity, and tannin; at their worse, they have a tendency toward dullness and lack scent. The commune contains fewer than 110 hectares of vineland, producing between 2,000 and 3,000 hectoliters.

Despite its modest production, the commune is known for five exceptional Grand Cru climats whose combined planted area is less than 31 hectares. Bonnes-Mares, smallest of the five with less than 2 hectares (the bulk is located in the neighboring commune of Chambolle), is considered slightly less good than the other four. More reliable, under-rated, and offering good value, Clos de la Roche, the largest climat with nearly 15.5 hectares, is the fullest of all and very fragrant. An ecclesiastical property for 600 years, Clos St.-Denis, containing but 6.5 hectares, is the most celebrated vineyard in the commune, although quality seems to be second to another former religious retreat—Clos de Tart (7 hectares and one of the few properties whose physical dimensions have remained the same since 1250). Originally known as Climat de la Forge, it was sold in 1141 to the nuns of Notre Dame de Tart (a Bernadine order), who owned the vineyard until 1793. Today it is a monopole of the Mommessin negociant firm, and although its owner does not make full use of the potassium and magnesium-rich soils in the production of dark, full, long-lived, and wood-aged wines, the climat has the potential to rival the very best of the Côte de Nuits. The last remaining Grand Cru, Clos des Lambrays, historically one of the most celebrated, has not made first-class wine recently. The vineyard was a monopole of the Cosson family for nearly a century until it was sold to a syndicate in 1979. In addition to the five above-average Grand Cru climats, the commune contains nineteen Premier Cru vineyards, of which Monts-Luisants is exceptional though expensive (it also produces a rare and excellent white wine), followed by Clos de la Bussière, le Clos des Ormes, and les Ruchots.

Above-average producers include the following: *Dne. Arlaud Père* (*vin de garde,* muscular wines of impeccable quality, of which Clos de la Roche is one of the best); *Mommessin* (for Clos de Tart); *Bouchard Père* (for ouststanding Clos de la Roche); *Bernard Serveou* (for excellent les Sorbés); *Dne. Dujac* (owning 11 hectares in ten different appellations, making above-average but inconsistent-quality wines at high prices); *Pierre Amiot* (for soft, elegant wines); *Louis Jadot* (stylish Bonnes-Mares); *Robert Groffier* (firm wines, especially Bonnes-Mares and Musigny); *Georges Bryczek; Dne. Louis Rémy Rameau Vadey; Dne. Armand Rousseau; Henri Mauffré; Dne. Taupenot-Merme;* and *Jean-Paul Magnien.*

Chambolle-Musigny

Chambolle-Musigny, a 5,000-hectoliter vineyard whose hectarage has grown by 20 percent in the past forty years, lies mostly on hilly terrain to the east of its small village. It produces mostly red wine, with minor amounts of outstanding but scarce white wine. The soil in the middle portion contains more limestone and less clay than similar areas immediately north and south. Its wines have been described as "bottled velvet" because they are considered the most feminine of all red wines of the Côte de Nuits—very "tender," delicate, with a pronounced aroma and a subtleness that is most appealing.

Two Grand Cru climats are outstanding: les Musigny (10 hectares) and Bonnes-Mares (13.7 hectares). The most prestigious of the two is Musigny, whose soil contains more limestone than any other climat in the appellation and, with the iron oxide in the subsoil, produces wine of extraordinary quality, beautiful color, devastatingly complex flavor, aroma, and bouquet. Somewhat spicy in flavor and always full of sweet fruit, this wine is sublime, refined, and satisfying. It is one of the oldest climats, dating back to 1110 when a religious order of monks began large-scale production. Although fragmented into small plots after the French Revolution, nine proprietors are in business today, of whom Dne. Comte Georges de Vogüé is the most important, followed by Faiveley, Dne. Jacques Prieur, Joseph Drouhin, Dne. Roumier, Dne. Clair-Daü, Maison Leroy, and Alain Hudelot-Noellat. Bonnes-Mares, a wine known for its longevity but less fine than Musigny, produces fewer than 6,000 cases. There are nineteen Premier Cru climats, of which les Amoureuses (as good as Bonnes-Mares), les Charmes, les Cras, les Combottes, and Aux Combotes are above average. All others rarely appear under their own climat name, but usually as Chambolle-Musigny Premier Cru. Their wine, soft and of variable quality, is rarely as abrasive as Gevrey-Chambertin or Fixin.

Dne. Comte de Vogüé, although not the largest property owner in the Côte d'Or, remains the most important domaine in Chambolle in terms of reputation. It controls more than two-thirds of Musigny and a good portion of Bonnes-Mares, les Amoureuses, and other climats in the appellation. The wines are inconsistent and not always up to top standards. The reputation rests with Musigny, but its variable quality and high prices offer little value. Musigny Cuvée Vieilles Vignes, the finest wine produced, is made from the oldest vines. Above average producers include *Gaston Barthod* (les Charmes is excellent); *Dne. des Varoilles* (stylish, well-flavored, and scented); *Daniel Funes* (fruity, supple, refined); *Robert Sirugue* (firm, well-structured); *Dne. Pernot-Fourrier* (outstanding hard-to-find wines); *Dne. Servelle-Tachot* (fruity, early maturing); *Dne. Hudelot* (for Bonnes-Mares and les Charmes); *Dne. Roumier* (excellent Chambolle-Musigny, Musigny, and Clos de la Bussière); *Robert Groffier* (excellent Amoureuses); *Bouchard Père* (excellent Bonnes-Mares and others); *Drouhin-Laroze* (above-average Bonnes-Mares); *Faiveley* (for Musigny); *Dne. Taupenot-Merme* (elegant wines); *Raoul Clerget* (excellent, fleshy, chewy, substantial wines); *Joseph Drouhin* (stylish Amoureuses, Musigny, and others); *Jean Grivot;* and *Dne. Dujac.*

Vougeot

Clos de Vougeot, with 50 hectares (80 percent of the commune's total), is the largest single climat in the Côte d'Or. Originally known as Gilly-les-Vougeot (after the Vougeot stream), it was developed by Cistercians into a walled vineyard and has been in continuous production since 1089. Construction of the Château started early in the 12th century but was not completed until 1551. Today its hectarage is fragmented among 77 owners (38 of whom own less than one-third of a hectare, with the largest possessing slightly more than 5). The Ministry of Transportation owns two acres and uses them to store utility poles.

Although Clos de Vougeot ranks as a national monument, its current quality is shamelessly overrated. Needless to say, considerable variation in quality exists among its many owners, because not every plot is capable of producing quality wine worthy of fame. The best grapes come from the uppermost sections that contain a reddish-brown soil with appreciable amounts of limestone. Vineyards located at the lower third of the climat, however, are planted on poorly drained soil that contains more clay, hence, the wine produced is coarse and not the equal of Grand Cru status. Furthermore, because there are so many owners, a not-inconsiderable amount of authentic Clos de Vougeot wine grapes are mixed with others of lesser pedigree to amplify pitifully low production levels relative to demand. As a result, Clos de Vougeot represents the worst value of any Grand Cru in Burgundy. The wine at its best is of beautiful color, with an enormous bouquet and a long, lingering aftertaste. Unfortunately these libations are hard to find, and most bottles should be viewed with suspicion. A small portion of the vineyard, named La Vigne Blanche du Clos de Vougeot, produces fewer than 1,000 cases of rather ordinary but interesting white wine. In addition to Clos de Vougeot, there are four Premier Cru vineyards (le Clos Blanc, les Petits-Vougeots, les Cras, and le Clos de la Perrière) whose quality is marginal at best. Since the names rarely appear on labels, their wine is probably sold as Clos de Vougeot. The following are known for above-average quality wine: *Dne. Drouhin-Laroze, Dne. Charles Noëllat, Dne. Engel,* and *Dne. Rebourseau.*

Vosne-Romanée

The small, unpretentious medieval village of Vosne, 1 kilometer south of Clos de Vougeot, contains what many consider the finest viticultural site in the world. From 174 hectares, the commune produces between 5,000 and 6,000 hectoliters of red wine, nearly all of average to outstanding in quality. Indeed, it is often said that there are no ordinary wines here, only great and near great, including communal blends.

Viticulture in Vosne-Romanée, as the name suggests, dates back to Roman days (Romanée-Conti, for example, is named after a Roman military outpost). During the Middle Ages, nearly the entire commune was controlled by the Priory of St.-Vivant. Between Vosne-Romanée and Clos de Vougeot lies Flagey, a hamlet hyphenated with its famous climat of Echézeaux in 1886. The wider appellation of Vosne-Romanée and Flagey-Echézeaux gets its reputation from seven Grand Cru sites, all of which are world-famous and command high prices. La Tâche is a 6-hectare site producing 2,000 cases of full-bodied but delicate wine. The climat, entirely owned by the Dne. de Romanée-Conti, is now much bigger than its historic boundaries, as it has absorbed les Gaudichots, a neighboring Premier Cru. Romanée-Conti, a 1.8-hectare climat, produces 700 cases of full-bodied, velvety, well-balanced wine considered the finest in France. It is also entirely owned by the Dne. de Romanée-Conti. Richebourg, an 8-hectare site, produces 2,500 cases of wine that ranks just below Romanée-Conti in quality. Romanée St.-Vivant, with nearly 10 hectares and 3,000 cases, offers excellent value. Romanée, a tiny four-fifths of a hectare climat, produces less than 300 cases of very rare and expensive wine. Grands-Echézeaux, approximately 9 hectares in size, produces about 3,000 cases of absolutely superb, underrated wine offering excellent value. Echézeaux, with 30 hectares and an output of 12,000 cases, is the largest and is considered to fall short of Grand Cru quality standards. In addition to the above vineyards, the commune contains ten Premier Cru climats, of which Aux Malconsorts, les Suchots, la Grande Rue, Aux Brûlées, and les Chaumes are considered outstanding.

The vineyards of Vosne-Romanée are located on well-protected sites with ample underground water, a high proportion of fragmented lime-stone, and one of the highest concentrations of iron oxide in the soil. The wines are not only fragrant, but light in color, smooth, and supple. They range from among the most expensive wines in the world to modestly priced communal libations that offer exceptional value. Making some of the most expensive wines in the world is the most famous grower of the commune and the Côte d'Or–Dne. de la Romanée-Conti, a 25-hectare property whose qualilty rarely befits its image or asking price. In addition to la Tâche and Romanée-Conti, the domaine owns portions of Montra-chet, Grands-Echézeaux, Richebourg, and Romanée St.-Vivant. The vineyards until 1945 were planted in pre-*phylloxera* stock, but are now grafted on American stock. Although all the wines are made to last, inconsistency and high prices remain the major obstacles to a rejuvenated reputation. *Louis Gouroux,* a much smaller but meticulous grower, makes exceptional Echézeaux and Grands-Echézeaux. Above-average wines are also made by the following: *Dne. René Engel* (for Vosne-Romanée, Grands-Echézeaux, Echézeaux, and les Brûlées); *Dne. Mongeard-Mugneret* (out-standing, *vin de garde,* wood-aged Echézeaux, Grands-Echézeaux, les Suchots, and Vosne-Romanée); *Gérard Mugneret* (outstanding, full-bod-ied, well-flavored wines); *Dne. Marey-Monge* (superb, dark, full, Grand Cru wines); *Henri Jayer* (for Brûlées, Clos Parantoux, and les Beaumonts); *Jean Grivot* for les Beaumonts and Vosne-Romanée); *Henri Noëllat* (sought-after wines, especially les Suchots); *Charles Noëllat* (for St.-Vivant and Richebourg); *Jacques Cacheux* (supple, fruity, and early maturing wines); *Dne. Henry Lamarche* (for Vosne-Romanée, le Grande Rue Monopole, Grands-Echézeaux, and Echézeaux); *Robert Arnoux* (for les Suchots); and *Jean Gros* (for Clos de Réas).

Nuits St.-Georges

Straddling the Muezin River, the good-sized, circular, medieval town of Nuits St.-Georges is the largest in the Côtes de Nuits. It contains 270 hectares and produces 9,000 hectoliters of wine. The town is also a leading producer of Crème de Cassis, other distilled beverages, and sparkling wine, and is a focal point for a good number of negociants.

Making only 1,000 cases of white wine, Nuits St.-Georges is a village of red wine whose quality ranges from common to excellent. The appellation does not have a Grand Cru, and as such the wines are sometimes underrated hence a rare opportunity for good value through careful selection. There are thirty-eight Premier Cru, and an additional ten climats from the neighboring village of Prémeaux which has the right to label its wines Nuits St.-Georges. Les St.-Georges, the most prestigious climat in the village, has the reputation for *vin de garde* qualities, while the second-best, les Vaucrains, is known for elegance and breeding. All other vineyards are variable, and their quality rests solely on the reputation of the producer. The very best wines exhibit elements of fat, richness, and smoothness, punctuated by alcohol and extract. At their worst, the wines are dull, lacking in direction, and unbalanced. Few communal wines ever rise above the description "innocuous" and should be avoided. The problem of selection is compounded by the existence of a large number of *sous-marques* and "phantom" negociants. The neighboring small village of Prémeaux, located on the foot of the Bois de la Montagne south of Nuits, contains about 62 hectares of vineland which produce average to above-average wines. They are usually better balanced than neighboring Chambolle, softer than Gevrey-Chambertin, and often the equal of or better than Nuits St.-Georges. The climats with established reputations are Clos des Corvées, Clos de Forêts, les Didiers, and Clos de la Maréchale.

The grower with "the" reputation in Nuits St.-Georges is the 11-hectare domaine of *Henri Gouges,* whose wines have a non-oaky style (earthy, elegant, and loaded with fruit), are well flavored, and are consistently highlighted by intensity and concentration. He is the best known for les St.-Georges and les Vaucrains, both of which appear to be the equal of Grand Cru status. Les Porrets, a monopole wine, is absolutely sensational, as is les Pruliers. The *Hospice de Nuits-St.-Georges* owns 10 hectares of Premier Cru vineland and usually makes above-average Didiers St.-Georges from a 2-hectare monopole climat. Its wines are all expensive but less well known than the Hospices de Beaune. Other producers include the following: *Dne. Lupé-Cholet* (owned by two sisters who produce 10,000 cases of Ch. de Viviers [Chablis] and equal amounts under the Ch. Gris, Clos de Lupé, and Lupé-Cholet labels; *Robert Chevillon* (makes several plummy, fruity, and generous wines, of which les

St.-Georges, les Pruliers and les Cailles are excellent); *Michel Dupasquier* (well-structured, full-bodied wines); *Roger Dupasquier* (elegant, fruity, well-flavored wines); *Alain Pelletier* (spicy and firm wines); *Machard de Gramont* (a 30-hectare domaine that makes a number of wines, of which les Haut-Pruliers is one of the finest); *D. Rion* (one of the better growers, known for rich, opulent, highly distinctive wines); *P. Misserey* (a small, conscientious house known for smooth, supple les St.-Georges and les Vaucrains); *Jean Grivot* (makes an excellent and rarely seen les Boudots); *Alain Michelot* (for exceptional Nuits-St.-Georges and Aux Chaignots); and *Lionel T. Bruck* (a small house known for dark, well-flavored and robust wines). In Prémeaux two notable growers are *Jules Belin* and *Dne. Jean Confuron*. Belin is known for above-average-quality wine from Clos de Arlot and other Premier Cru climats, and Confuron enjoys and above-average reputation in the production and distribution of wines to NATO, the United Nations, and other national and international agencies and governments.

The Premier Cru vineyard of Clos de la Maréchale is the last major classified growth in the Côte de Nuits. Between it and the northern area of Ladoix, dominated by the three sleepy communes of Prissey, Comblanchien, and Corgoloin, is a 3-kilometer stretch of vineland producing nothing more than ordinary wine. The approximately 5,000 hectoliters of wine is sold under the Côte de Nuits–Village label. Here there are two producers of consequence—*Trapet-Lalle* and *Dne. de la Poulette,* the former known for full-bodied, strapping wines and the latter for softer, more refined libations, particularly for les Vaucrains. Dne. de la Poulette owns 15 hectares, nearly all in excellent Premier Cru locations.

THE WINES OF THE CÔTE DE BEAUNE

Forty kilometers long and somewhat wider than the Côte de Nuits, the Côte de Beaune contains 3,000 hectares' of AOC–classified vineland, nearly three times the number of its more illustrious neighbor to the north. While there are twenty village appellations, the district appellations are limited to three: Bourgogne Hautes-Côtes de Beaune, Côte de Beaune–Villages, and Côte de Beaune, the three collectively producing 15 percent of all Côte de Beaune wine made. Varying between 5,000 and 6,000 hectoliters, of which slightly more than half is red, Grand Cru production, is limited to seven specific sites in the extreme northern and southern portions. Premiers encompass more than 700 hectares, or about 20 percent of the Côte de Beaune vineyard. Unlike the Côte de Nuits, which is mainly a red wine region, one-quarter of total wine production in the Côte de Beaune is white. Red wines, in general, are weaker in constitution, early maturing, and somewhat more delicate and fragile than those emnating from the Côte de Nuits. White wines, however, vary from average to extraordinary, with the very best restricted to the four communes of Corton, Meursault, Puligny, and Chassagne.

Bourgogne Hautes-Côtes de Beaune

Located on rolling hills, this geographically wide appellation begins at Mavilly-Mandelot west of Beaune and stretches south to Nolay. While vineyards are widely scattered among two dozen parishes, vineland now exceeds 1,500 hectares and is growing in spite of the astronomical cost of vineland along the "Côte." Making white, rosé, and red wines, this appellation accounts for nearly 10 percent of the entire AOC wine output of the Côte de Beaune. Of the three colors, the red is the most important in terms of volume and quality. Small quantities of rosé from Gamay are made in the village of Orches, southwest of Auxey-Duresses.

Côte de Beaune–Villages

Excluding those from Aloxe, Pommard, Volnay, and Beaune, the wines from sixteen communes can be blended and sold as Côte de Beaune–Villages. This is a very confusing appellation, since the wines of the former four communes are not declassified downward to the Côte de Beaune–Villages appellation but to simple Bourgogne. The appellation was created to market the wines of poor to indifferent years, which explains the widely fluctuating annual output. In theory the wines should be better than plain Côte de Beaune or Bourgogne, but not necessarily. The wine, with a minimum of 10.5 percent alcohol, offers very little value. The appellation *Côte de Beaune* is now rarely used to define nondescript wine originating on the hillsides west of Beaune.

Ladoix-Serrigny

Officially, the Côte de Beaune begins at Ladoix-Serrigny (two hamlets along the famous N74), whose only claim to fame is that out of the 119 hectares of vineland, 22 are located west of the road and are entitled to be sold as Corton Premier Cru or Aloxe-Corton. They are all located on rich, dark, red-brown soil, most of which contains at least 50 percent lime-stone. The wines are full-bodied, rich, and resemble their more famous neighbors that skirt the upper and middle portion of the Bois de Corton. The Premier Cru climats are les Basses Mourettes, les Grandes Lolières, les Petites Lolières, la Toppe-au-Vert, la Coutière, and la Maréchaude, the latter considered the finest vineyard in the commune. The remaining 97 hectares lie on communal flatland, are inferior in quality and, depending on the nature of the vintage, the wines are marketed under various appellations, of which the Côte de Beaune–Villages tends to be the most important. Production varies between 2,000 and 4,000 hectoliters, of

Table 5.9   AOC Wine Production in the Côte de Beaune, 1980

Appellation	Hectoliters	Percent of total
Aloxe-Corton Rouge	4,709	3.3
Aloxe-Corton Blanc	15	
Auxey-Duresses Rouge	4,322	3.0
Auxey-Duresses Blanc	1,283	.9
Beaune Rouge	11,682	8.1
Beaune Blanc	480	.3
Blagny Rouge	259	.2
Chassagne-Montrachet Rouge	7,749	5.4
Chassagne-Montrachet Blanc	6,224	4.3
Cheilly-les-Maranges Rouge	754	.5
Dezize-les-Maranges Rouge		
Chorey-les-Beaune Rouge	5,167	3.6
Chorey-les-Beaune Blanc	12	
Côte de Beaune Blanc	135	.1
Côte de Beaune–Villages Rouge	9,097	6.3
Ladoix Rouge	2,470	1.7
Ladoix Blanc	126	.1
Meursault Rouge	807	.6
Meursault Blanc	13,701	9.6
Monthélie Rouge	3,608	2.5
Monthélie Blanc	69	
Pernand-Vergelesses Rouge	2,525	1.8
Pernand-Vergelesses Blanc	511	.4
Pommard Rouge	9,716	6.8
Puligny-Montrachet Rouge	427	.3
Puligny-Montrachet Blanc	9,379	6.5
St.-Aubin Rouge	2,841	2.0
St.-Aubin Blanc	1,228	.9
St.-Romain Rouge	1,569	1.1
St.-Romain Blanc	1,269	.9
Sampigny-les-Maranges Rouge	94	
Santenay Rouge	12,448	8.7
Santenay Blanc	182	.1
Savigny Rouge	10,403	7.3
Savigny Blanc	298	.2
Volnay Rouge	6,975	4.9
Bourgogne Hautes–Côtes de Beaune Rouge	10,762	7.5
Bourgogne Hautes–Côtes de Beaune Blanc	141	.1
Total Rouge	108,384	76.0
Total Blanc	35,053	24.0
Total general	143,437	100.0

Note: Table does not include Grands Crus production.

Source: French Ministry of Agriculture.

which more than 99 percent is red; the remainder is undistinguished white wine usually sold under a regional banner.

The principal producers are *Prince de Mérode* (of Dne. de Serrigny, a small but well-regarded house with 11 hectares and a reputation for Corton, Aloxe-Corton, and Clos du Roi); *Chevalier-Dubois* (a reliable

Plate 5.2   Part of the cellars of Dne. Prince Florent de Mérode,
Ladoix-Serrigny

producer of full-bodied, traditionally made Corton and Aloxe-Corton);
Capitan-Gagnerot (a reliable house making outstanding wines that offer
exceptional value), owns vineland in la Maréchaude, Aloxe-Corton,
Renardes, les Petites Lolières, and is the largest owner of les Moutottes);
Christian Gros (known for robust, spicy wines); *Les Terres Vineuses* (makes
medium-bodied, early maturing wines); *Pierre Ravaut; André Nudat, Dne.
Cachat-Ocquidant;* and *Dne. Rougeot.*

Pernand-Vergelesses

Located along steep slopes on the west side of the Bois de Corton is
Pernand-Vergelesses, a small village with a rising reputation. With 150
hectares of vineyards it is one of the few communes in the Côte de Beaune
that has increased its hectarage over the past twenty-five years. It contains
portions of Corton and Corton-Charlemagne, along with five Premier Cru
climats: Caradeaux, Creaux de la Net, les Fichots, les Basses-Vergelesses,
and Ile des Vergelesses, the latter considered a supergrowth equal to
Grand Cru status.

Pernand-Vergelesses makes both red and white wines, with Pinot Noir
planted on reddish soil and Chardonnay on limestone. Although similar
to the wines of Aloxe-Corton, red wines are much bigger, more robust,
and better than most wines from Beaune, which are early maturing and
highly variable. White wine is coarse and not the equal of the better

Corton's, yet more than three-quarters of total output is sold under the more prestigious name of Aloxe-Corton. The commune is one of the few north of Bouzeron in the Chalonnais to have established a reputation for Aligoté. The principal producers are *Dne. Bonneau du Martray, Dubreuil-Fontaine, Dne. de Baron Thénard, Dne. Rapet, Dne. Laleure-Pilot, Marious Delarche Père, Denis Père,* and *Rollin Père.*

Aloxe-Corton

The small village of Aloxe, located at the foot of the south-facing Bois de Corton, a 1,200-meter high, forested, oblong hill, stands as the symbol of the finest red wine of the Côte de Beaune. Production, nearly all of it red, varies between 4,000 and 6,000 hectoliters, and it is outrageously expensive. The village name was hyphenated with Corton, the most prestigious climat, in 1862. The wines, favorites of Charlemagne, the dukes of Burgundy, and French kings, are also associated with Voltaire, who did much to popularize them. Red wines have a reputation for brilliant color, longevity, flavor, delicacy, and a penetrating, lasting bouquet. Unlike most Beaunes, the wines of Aloxe-Corton are "firmer" and characterized by a particular *goût de terroir*. The minuscule quantities of white wine are outstanding—fruity, big, powerful, and blessed with a touch of elegance. Communal wines are a poor choice: they originate from the poorest sites, are overpriced, offer little value, and include liberal quantities of wine originating in Ladoix, Serrigny, and Pernand-Verge-lesses. Seldom above average in quality, they are often harsh and lack balance, flavor, and bouquet. The best wines are from Grand and Premier Cru sites, but because of their high prices, they offer little value.

Grand Cru climats include Corton-Charlemagne, and le Corton (les Renardes, le Clos du Roi, les Bressandes, les Perrières, la Vigne au Saint, les Grèves, les Languettes, les Fiètres, les Meix, les Chaume, les Pougets). All lie along steep and gentle slopes with an east and southeast aspect on excellent, well-drained soil that is heavy in iron oxide and limestone. There are also eight little-known Premier Cru sites (in addition to thirteen additional sites in neighboring communes), of which les Guérets, les Fournières, and la Maréchaude are the most important. Of the 228 hectares in Aloxe-Corton, Grand and Premier Cru account for more than 140, the largest such contiguous expanse in the Côte de Beaune. Because they encompass territory in Ladoix-Serrigny, Pernand-Vergelesses, and Aloxe, differences in topography, soil character, and microclimate pro-duce different types of wine. Dating back to the 15th century when Charles the Fearless cleared the land and planted Pinot Noir vines, Corton and Clos du Roi are considered the finest among Grand Cru sites, producing slow maturing wine, the near-equal of similar growths in the Côtes de Nuits. Clos du Roi dates from 1477 when the dukes of Burgundy began large-scale production; eventually it passed to Louis XI

Table 5.10   Grand Cru Wine Production in the Côte de Beaune, 1980

Vineyard	Hectoliters	Percent of total
Corton Rouge	2,714	52.0
Corton Blanc	36	.6
Corton-Charlemagne Blanc	1,308	25.0
Charlemagne		
Bâtard-Montrachet Blanc	485	9.3
Bienvenue-Bâtard-Montrachet Blanc	135	2.6
Criots-Bâtard-Montrachet	71	1.4
Chevalier-Montrachet Blanc	194	3.7
Montrachet Blanc	281	5.4
Total Rouge	2,714	52.0
Total Blanc	2,510	48.0
Grand total	5,224	100.0

Source: French Ministry of Agriculture.

and acquired the royal designation. Situated on high ground with an excellent southern exposure, Corton-Charlemagne, the most celebrated white wine vineyard, is considered by many as the equal to Montrachet. It is dreadfully expensive, since fewer than 14,000 cases are produced each year.

The principal negociant houses are as follows: *Louis Latour* owns more than 15 hectares of Grand Cru property as well as a similar amount scattered among various Premier Cru sites. The flagship, Château Corton-Grancey, a branded name whose white wine originates in a large number of classified vineyards, is considered by many to be one of the finest wines in all of France, although it rarely compares with the finest Montrachet. Also made are Aloxe-Corton, Clos de la Vigne au Saint, and Corton-Charlemagne. *Pierre André,* one of the largest negociants and growers, distributes wine from all major appellations in Burgundy and the Rhône. The wines, from Aloxe-Corton, le Corton, Clos du Roi, and les Theurons, are all very reliable, above average in quality, classy, expensive, and distributed mainly to fine restaurants or sold to private clients. Also *Bouchard Père* (wines are always consistent and above average to outstanding); *Louis Jadot* (makes and distributes average to excellent wines, of which les Pougets, Corton-Charlemagne, and les Bressandes are considered the most consistent); *Moillard* (makes a respectable Clos du Roi); *Reine Pédauque* (known for Dne. Les Terres Vineuses); and *Daniel Senard* (for light-bodied wines). The principal growers with a good reputation are *Bubreuil Fontaine* (for Clos du Roi and les Bressandes, both of which are rich, balanced, and well-scented); *Charles Viénot* (for le Corton); *Dne. Louis Chapuis* (for les Languettes and les Perrières); *Michel Voarick* (for Clos du Roi); *Dne. Cachat-Ocquidant* (superb, full-bodied wines); and *Capitan-Gagnerot.*

Plate 5.3   Château Corton-Grancey (courtesy Louis Latour)

Savigny-les-Beaune

Savigny-les-Beaune, with 400 hectares and more than 11,000 hectoliters, is the third-most-important wine commune in the Côte de Beaune. The village is located in a valley between Aloxe-Corton and Beaune with the Rhoin stream dividing the vineyards into two distinct sections. The slopes against the north bank extending to Pernand-Vergelesses produce darker, fuller, and more alcoholic wines than those vineyards located along the south bank, which yield more common, less interesting wine. The commune contains twenty-three Premier Cru climats, much of which is shared with neighboring villages. Les Vergelesses, les Marconnets, and les Jarrons, from the upper slopes, are widely considered the best sites and known for fruity, flavorful wines. In general, the wines are overshadowed by the reputation of Aloxe-Corton and Beaune, offer only relative value as most of the wine is nondescript and often dull. Minute quantities of white Aligoté-based wine are also made. The principal producers are *M. Doudet-Naudin* (for distinctive, full-bodied, dark, plummy wines, especially le Corton, Pernand-Vergelesses, Savigny, Aloxe-Corton, and an exceptional Aux Guettes); *Pavelot-Glantenay; Dne. Simon Bize; Valentin Bouchotte, M. & J. Giboulot, M. Girard-Vollot; Pierre Guillemot; J.-M. Maurice; Henri Villamont; Pierre Petitjean; Albert Lacroix;* and *Laurent Gauthier.*

Half the size of Savigny, the neighboring commune of Chorey-les-Beaune lies to the right of N74 and makes undistinguished red wine that

Plate 5.4   Part of the cellars of Louis Latour

is usually sold as Côte de Beaune, Côte de Beaune–Villages, or Chorey-les-Beaune, the latter an obscure, semi-official appellation. Nearly all of the planted area is located on flat, rich ground producing wine that bears little resemblance to fine Burgundy. The area contains a little more than 100 hectares and produces 6,000 hectoliters of wine. The commune's principal grower, *Tollot-Beaut,* a small house with a superlative reputation, makes supple, yet firm, well-structured les Grèves, les Bresandes, and Clos du Roi. *Dne. Germain* is a reputable and highly consistent firm known for big, fleshy wines, particularly les Teurons and Cent Vignes.

Beaune

South of Savigny-les-Beaune lies the medieval, circular, fortified town of Beaune (replete with ramparts and bastions) that serves as the nucleus of the Burgundian wine industry. Once the seat of the Burgundian parliament and the residence of Burgundian dukes, Beaune, due to its nodal location, has long been the largest city between Dijon and Lyon and is the only city that has shown signs of growth in recent years. Throughout history it was the site of many military and political squabbles, and peace did not arrive until the 16th century. With a population of 21,000 residents, Beaune is the home of at least six dozen shippers, most of whom store their wines under the city in vast subterranean cellars. It is also the site of an interesting wine museum, a viticultural school, and the Hospices de Beaune.

Beaune produces more than 14,000 hectoliters of wine under the various Beaune appellations from more than 500 hectares of vineland, of which 200 are considered above average in quality. The wines at their best are known for their delicacy, finesse, and long, lingering bouquet. Value, unfortunately, is found only in selected climats; blended commune wines are most definitely below average, dull, lifeless, and often without character. The commune is not only the biggest producer in the Côte de Beaune but boasts the largest single, unbroken stretch of vineland in the Côte d'Or. It is ironic that Beaune lacks the presence of a single Grand Cru, but it does contain twenty-eight Premier Cru climats and seven additional sites shared with other villages. The finest are les Bressandes, les Marconnets, les Grèves, Clos des Mouches, les Perrières, and les Fèves. They are the thoroughbreds of fine Beaune—soft, delicate, of moderate alcohol, smooth, and very satisfying.

The main negociants with a good reputation: *Joseph Drouhin* (founded in 1880, one of the leading grower/negociants in Beaune with more than 60 hectares of vineland distributed in Chablis, Clos des Mouches, Corton-Charlemagne, Bâtard-Montrachet, Chambertin, Musigny, and others. The domaine wines, and those of the Marquis de Laguiche, are all expertly made, stylish, light-bodied, elegant, and very expensive); *Bouchard Père* (founded in 1731, owns 92 hectares of vineland, of which 71 are Grand or Premier Cru sites. All wines are expertly made, above average to outstanding in quality, and very reliable. In addition, the firm markets "Valbon" in the United States and vinifies more than 1 million liters annually); the house of *Louis Latour* (one of the largest negociants of the entire Côte d'Or, known principally for average-to-excellent white wines. Founded in the 19th century, this firm owns more than 53 hectares of vineland in Aloxe-Corton and at least six other communes. While the reputation of the house rests on a small number of prestigious vineyard and commune wines, more than 90 percent of sales are regional and communal blends); *Louis Jadot* (owns 27 hectares of vineland in various communes and concentrates in the production of white wine, particularly from Aloxe-Corton and red wines from Beaune, of which le Corton, les Pougets, and les Theurons are particularly good); *Jaffelin* (an old 19th-century negociant house now part of Joseph Drouhin, considered one of the top houses of Burgundy and, although not a major property owner, distributes a wide array of wines, most of which are expensive and highly variable); *Patriache Père* (dating back to 1780, one of the largest Premier Cru vineland owners and producer of Kriter sparkling wines); *Chanson Père* (46-hectare domaine founded in 1750, a prime distributer of Beaune Premier Cru wines, as well as estate wine from Clos des Fèves, les Teurons, and les Bressandes. The house style is for lightly wood-aged, soft, elegant wines, whose quality ranges from below to above average); *La Reine Pédauque* (a large house very popular in the United States); *Dne.*

Antonin Guyon (a large 48-hectare house with major holdings in the Hautes-Côtes de Nuits); *Bichot* (since 1831, with a large number of *sous marques,* now considered the largest exporter of Burgundian wine, most of which is communal and regional blends that offer little value); *Moillard* (very popular in the United because of sensible prices); *Jaboulet-Vercherre* (a Côte du Rhône firm, distributes a wide variety of wines in many export markets); and *P. de Marcilly.*

Among the list of small but above-average growers and negociants are *Pierre Ponnelle* (a 19th-century house maintaining high standards in the production of les Bonnes-Mares, Musigny, and Clos du Roi); *Dne. Besançenot-Mathouillet* (makes outstanding wines, particularly les Cents Vignes and les Theurons, both of which offer extraordinary value); *Jean-Marc Morey* (known for a fruity, soft, almost rich les Grèves); *Dne. Albert Morot* (for les Cent Vignes, les Bressandes, and les Marconnets); *Remoissenet Père; Champy Père; Dne. Bernard Delagange; Dne. Parent; Robert Ampeau; Jacques Germain;* and *Leonce Bocquet.* Finally, the Lycée *Agricole et Viticole,* an agricultural school founded in 1884, owns nearly 9 hectares of ordinary to excellent vineland. The school makes wines that are technically flawless, often among the best, but difficult to locate.

One of the most venerable institutions of Beaune is the Hospices de Beaune. Nicolas Rolin, as chancellor to the dukes of Burgundy, dedicated this structure in 1443 and endowed the hospital with vineyards. Over the years, shippers and growers have bequeathed additional vineland that now totals about 40 hectares. The accumulated individual parcels are widely scattered and vary in size from .12 to 2 hectares, and quality fluctuates dramatically despite the fact that all parcels are Premier Cru sites. The wines are expensive, often sloppily made, and nearly always a poor value. Their distinguishing feature lies in the interesting bottle labels (the cuvée is identified, the name of the benefactor, and sometimes other curious items are noted) and not the contents. Annual sales now exceed 25 million FF, but unless the consumer is an expert on the nature of the individual cuvée, it is best to seek other wines.

Pommard

Taking its name from Pomona, the Roman goddess for fruit and gardens, the 360-hectare, 10,000-hectoliter Pommard vineyard is one of the best known of all Burgundian communes. Continuously planted in vines since 1005, it is one of the oldest viticultural areas of France. Slightly less than half the hectarage lies east of the town on rather flat land where soil is productive and, hence, yields are consistently high, but wines are significantly below quality standards. It has twenty-six Premier Cru climats, of which les Rugiens-Bas, les Rugiens-Hauts, les Epenots, and Clos de la Commaraine are considered the finest, followed by les Arvelets, les Jarollières, les Chaponnières, and les Pézerolles.

Darker than most Beaunes, Pommard is fruity and supple, with only a faint aroma and bouquet. The very best can be alcoholic and, hence, able to improve in the bottle past its fifth birthday. Although darker and fuller than Volnay, its primary competitor immediately to the south, it is lower in tannin, earlier maturing, and lacks balance and roundness. The wine is almost always overrated, overpriced, often adulterated and/or carelessly imitated. A commune Pommard is nearly always a poor value, not only because its authenticity is in doubt but because its character exhibits excessive variation. In general, the wines are heavily filtered and fined, and in the final analysis, more than 95 percent of all Pommard is average or worse, despite its historic notoriety. Individual climats also demonstrate wide fluctuation in quality: les Argillières, very light in color and body, is rather common due to a high concentration of clay in the soil; both Rugiens are full and firm; the Epenots have an unusual finesse and breeding unknown in any other growths; Clos de la Commaraine is delicate, supple, and elegant; les Chanlins Bas is soft and rather tasteless; and Clos Micot is coarse and unappealing.

The principal producers: *Ch. de Pommard* (the largest contiguous vineyard belonging to a single owner, a rare event in Burgundy, lies mostly on flat land of marginal quality; the wines, although stylish, delicate, and of fine color, are very expensive. The soil, however, contains a high iron oxide accumulation, and because the grapes are vinified in oak the wines are particularly long-lived and well scented); Clos de la Commaraine, by *Jaboulet-Vercherre* (above average and one of the finest in the appellation); *Dne. Lahaye Père* (known for mouth-filling wines with beautiful color and an expansive bouquet): *Comte Armand* (for Clos des Epeneaux); *Herbert de Montille* (for les Pézerolles and les Rugiens Bas, both of which are superb, robust, and long lived); *Joseph Voillet* (for les Pézerolles); *Michel Gaunox* (for excellent les Rugiens Bas and les Epenots); *Machard de Gramont* (for les Clos Blanc); *Marquis d'Angerville* (for stylish, scarce wines known for their dark color, powerful bouquet, and lingering finish); *Felix* and *Roger Clerget* (for les Rugiens, les Arvelets, and les Pézerolles); *Pothier-Rieusset* (rare *vin de garde* wines); *Dne. Goud de Beaupuis* (one of the few growers to make exceptional *vin de garde* Epenots); *Dne. Billard-Gonnet,* (makes rich, concentrated les Rugiens); *Jean Garaudet* (known for well-structured wines); *Jean Tartois; René Virely-Arcelain; Dne. Parent; Henri Boillot; Jean Michelot; Dne. du Clos des Epeneaux; Bernard Caillet;* and *Bidot-Bourgogne.*

Volnay

Located south of Pommard, the 8,000-hectoliter quality vineyard of Volnay is known for twenty-six Premier Cru climats, of which les Caillerets, les Champans, les Chevret, les Angles, and les Fremiets are considered above average to the point of approaching Grand Cru status. Three types of soil account for the unusual quality of Volnay wine: the highest elevations contain as much as 50 percent limestone; a middle strip, just below the town, has a high iron oxide content with the calcareous rock and gravel proportions reduced to 25 percent; and a lower portion, with less stone but richer in organic material, produces less fine wine. The best sites of Volnay all lie north, south, and immediately east of the village of Volnay.

The reputation of the commune is based on a handful of Premier Cru sites whose wines are known for fragrance, finesse, and a silky texture. The finest are light to medium bodied and appear lighter than they actually are next to Chambertin, but are far more delicate and supple with an extraordinary aroma of violet and the flavor of ripe fruit. By Côte de Nuits standards, Volnay is an early maturing wine, but one of the very best that the Côte de Beaune has to offer. They were favorites of Louis XI and XIV, as well as of Thomas Jefferson. The commune along its southern margins also produces small quantities of white wine, nearly all of which is sold as Meursault. The largest property owner in Volnay is the *Marquis d'Angerville,* a prestigious producer of fine Volnay, particularly Volnay des Ducs, a nonclassified monopole vineyard known for delicacy and structure. One of the most prestigious properties is *Dne. de la Pousse d'Or,* maker of stylish wines that are well placed in fine restaurants, especially Clos de la Bousse d'Or and Caillerets-60 Ouvrées. Other consistent producers include *Bouchard Père, Hubert de Montille, Comte de Moucheron, Robert Ampeau, Dne. Clerget, Dne. Glantenay; Henri Boillot; Joseph Voillot;* and *Comte de Lafon.*

Monthélie

At the foot of a steep hill southwest of Volnay lies Monthélie, a small hamlet with only a handful of recognized climat sites. Although the 103-hectare vineyard (producing 4,000 hectoliters) is well situated and admirably protected from wind, the soil contains less limestone and iron and thus yields more robust, weakly scented, and alcoholic wines. The best vineyards are les Duresses, les Champs-Fulliot, and Sur Lavelle. Nearby, the obscure Côte de Beaune commune of Auxey-le-Graud produces red wine usually marketed under the Monthélie appellation. The main producers are *Ch. de Monthélie* (for above-average-quality wine offering considerable value; *Xavier Bouzerand; Jean Changarnier; Maurice Pinquier; André Ropiteau; Louis Deschamps; and René Thévenin-Monthélie.*

Auxey-Duresses

Upslope from Meursault along the bend of a minor stream is the little-known commune of Auxey-Duresses, which is responsible for 6,000 hectoliters of wine, three-quarters of which is red. Because it has difficulty selling its produce under its legal appellation name, most of it has historically been distributed in bulk to be blended under regional names such as Côte de Beaune–Villages. The red wines lack finesse, smoothness, harmony, and when compared with Monthélie and Volnay to the north, they appear unbalanced and clumsily made. Althougth the potential for improvement appears to be present, the white, likewise, appears heavy, lacks structure, and is early maturing. The Premier Cru climats in order of importance are les Duresses, Bas-de-Duresses, Reugne, la Chapelle, and Climat du Val. The principal producers are *Michel Prunier* (the standard for strong, assertive, highly flavorful and aggressive libations); *Robert Ampeau* (for supple, early maturing wines that are very unusual for the appellation); *Leroy* (one of the most exclusive negociant/grower firms, making and distributing overpriced *vin de garde* wines); *Dne. du Duc de Magenta; Henri Latour;* and *F. Lafouge-Clerc.*

St.-Romain

St.-Romain, a small but thoroughly charming village with a superb view of Auxey-Duresses and Meursault, is located in the high country west of the famed white wine vineyards. It received its AOC status in 1967 and produces between 3,000 and 5,000 hectoliters of wine from 120 hectares. Although the appellation has more than ten recognized climats, none has received recognition. But Clos des Ducs, les Sous le Château, Clos de la Braniere, les Corvées, and la Combe-Bazon, located on hillsides with excellent aspects, are all considered above average. More than 70 percent of production is red wine, mostly robust, often thin, weak, and more often than not unreliable. The white, much the better wine, is locally described as "zesty," fresh, and can be very appealing in good vintages. The standard for above-average St.-Romain white wines are *Fernand Bazenet* and *Henri Buisson,* both of whom make full-bodied, well-balanced wines. *Roland Thévenin,* one of the largest negociants, distributes a large number of estate wines, some of which offer considerable value. The white wines of *René Thévenin-Monthélie* are well balanced, fruity, and supple.

Blagny

The 150-hectare amphitheater-shaped Blagny vineyard lies near an ancient Roman road on a protected hill overlooking the magnificent Puligny-Montrachet vineyards below. Blagny makes both red and white wines of similar style, but significantly weaker and less elegant than its more famous neighbors. Production (between 500 and 1,000 hectoliters) varies significantly with the vintage because a good portion of the wine is entitled to be sold under the more prestigious appellations of Meursault and Puligny-Montrachet. Blagny has six Premiers Cru climats, of which la Jennelotte, la Pièce-Sous-le-Bois, and Sous le Dos d'Ane have the right to be sold as Meursault.

Meursault

South of Auxey-Duresses are the three white wine regions of Meursault, Puligny-Montrachet, and Chassagne-Montrachet (the first and last slightly larger in size than Puligny), which collectively produce between 25 to 40 percent of all white wine in the Côte de Beaune. The wines, all dry and the most expensive in France, are widely recognized as the finest in the world. Made solely from Chardonnay and cultivated on soils with high limestone accumulations, they are full-bodied, round, alcoholic, flavorful, and complex.

Of the three, Meursault is described as the most feminine, which refers to its suppleness, early maturing features, and less complex character. Puligny-Montrachet is more masculine, less rich, but more intense in flavor and aroma. The wines of Chassagne-Montrachet are firm, more flowery, richer in flavor, and elegant with exceptional balance. At its best, the wine from all three areas is at its optimum between two and six years, depending on the vintage, when the flavor is full, dry, and rich on the palate.

Lying between Monthélie and Puligny-Montrachet at the base of a small, narrow valley, Meursault, with more than 500 hectares of vineland and an output of 15,000 hectoliters, is the most important of the three white wine villages. Its name is derived from the Latin *muris saltus* ("leap of the rat"). The vineyards are divided into two main sections: immediately to the north and contiguous with the Premier Cru climats of Volnay are the sites of les Plures, les Cras, and les Santenots Blancs. South of Meursault is the largest expanse of Premier Cru growths—les Bouchères, la Gouttes d'Or, le Poruzot, le Poruzot Dessus, les Genevrières Dessus, les Charmes Dessus, and les Perrières, of which the last three are considered the finest. In all, the sixteen white wine Premier Cru climats, encompassing more than 100 hectares, represent less than one-tenth of communal vineland. This is a very important consideration in the purchase of fine white wine because the bulk of the hectarage lies on flat to gently rolling terrain that is decidedly inferior in the production of Meursault. Ordinary wine is sold as Côte de Beaune–Villages, but due to the high prices for even inferior Meursault, it is tempting for growers not to declassify and to take advantage of the lenient regulations. As dull and lifeless as the bulk of production tends to be, it is difficult not to like the output of first-rate Meursault. Due to its high glycerine content, it is smooth, fruity, and very appealing. Although known for its white wine, Meursault also produces some very good red wine in the northern section, where most of it is sold as Volnay.

Notable among the many producers, *Bernard Michelot* and *Dne. Ampeau* are known for excellent old-fashioned les Perrières and les Genevrières; *Comte Lafon* for above-average Meursault; *Dne. Joseph Matrot* for outstanding Meursault-Charmes; Dne. René Mannier makes first-class Clos des

Chênes, les Charmes, and les Chevalières; *Ch. de Meursault;* and *Guy Roulet* for Clos de Mon Plaisir, les Tessons, and les Charmes. Other quality-oriented firms include *François Gaunoux, Gabriel Fournier, Hubert Bouzereau-Gruere, Jean Germain, Dne. Buisson-Battault,* and *André Brunet.*

Puligny-Meursault

Of the three white wine communes of the Côte de Beaune, Puligny is the smallest in hectarage (300) and production (10,000 hectoliters). It not only makes incomparable white wine today, but at one time was the black currant capital of France. Both Puligny and Chassagne are important in the world of white wine because le Montrachet, the most prestigious vineyard, lies along their borders, and both wish to be identified with the most glorious wine in the world—the greatest of the great white Burgundies. The commune is known for four supreme Grand Cru climats: le Montrachet, Bâtard-Montrachet, Chevalier-Montrachet, and Bienvenues-Montrachet. Their combined hectarage is about 10.5 hectares, producing fewer than 5,000 cases. The best climats are le Montrachet and Bâtard, but the quality differences in comparison with the other two are minuscule and often exaggerated. All produce wine of pluperfect quality—big, powerful, with incredible depth, and a long, lingering bouquet and aftertaste. Of the eleven Premier Cru, le Cailleret, les Combettes, and les Pucelles are considered above average. Curiously, small amounts of good red wine is sold as Blagny.

The main producers are *Dne. Etienne Sauzet* (for les Combettes, les Referts, and Bâtard-Montrachet), *Marquis de Laguiche* (outstanding le Montrachet), *Chartron & Trébuchet* (excellent, fresh, clean and flavorful wines), *Dne. du Baron Thénard* (superb wines), *Bouchard Père, Dne. Jacques Prieur, Dne. de al Romanée-Conti, Joseph Drouhin, Robert Carillon, Dne. Ramonet-Prudhorn, Dne. Lefaive, Dne. Lequin-Roussot, P. Bouzereau,* and *Dne. Delagrange-Bachelet.*

Chassagne-Montrachet

The large 14,000-hectoliter vineyard of Chassagne-Montrachet is the southernmost of the three white wine communes. Although its reputation rests on the production of white wine, the appellation makes 20 percent more red than white, a good portion of which is above average in quality and highly underrated. It is surprisingly full-bodied, darker, more flavorful, and more durable than most wine from the Côte de Beaune. The commune has three Grand Cru climats; le Montrachet, Bâtard-Montrachet and les Criots-Bâtard-Montrachet. The three collectively contain less than 11 hectares, with Montrachet alone producing less than 2,000 cases. While all exhibit outstanding capabilities in terms of balance, and highly concentrated flavor and aroma, les Criots consistently offers the best value.

The commune also contains fourteen red and white wine-producing Premier Cru climats, of which Morgeot, Cailleret, and Grandes Ruchottes are particularly good in the production of quality white wine. Clos St.-Jean, Morgeot, la Boudriotte, and les Vergers are considered above average in the production of red wine. The reputation of Chassagne-Montrachet not withstanding, it is important to note that because more than half the total hectarage lies on inferior soil, most of the wine is sold with the communal label and offers little value.

The main producers are *Albert Morey, Ch. de la Maltroie, Dne. Delagrange-Bachelet, Bernard Morey, Gagnard-Delagrange, Dne. de Duc de Magenta, Jean-Noël Gagnard, Dne. Ramonet-Prudhorn, Dne. Bachelet-Ramonet, Claude Ramonet, André Ramonet, Marquis de Laguiche, Dne. Alphonse Pillot, Dne. des Vieilles Vignes, Roger Belland, René Lamy,* and *Marc Colin.*

St.-Aubin and Gamay

Totally surrounded by south-facing vineyards, St.-Aubin and Gamay are located in a narrow valley due west of Puligny-Montrachet. It is a little-known region with a high percentage of hectarage composed of Premier Cru climats, of which la Chatenière, les Frionnes, and les Murgers-des-Dents-de-Chien are the most important. Historically it is an area of Aligoté, Gamay, and other lesser grapes known for good, sound, but unspectacular wines. Over the past thirty years, however, hectarage under Chardonnay and Pinot Noir has doubled, and production now stands at more than 4,000 hectoliters. The red wine is full-bodied, coarse, grapey in flavor, good for blending, and usually sold as Côte de Beaune or Côte de Beaune–Villages. The white, particularly from Chardonnay, is acidic, well flavored, and considered by many superior to the red. The principal producers are *Hubert Lamy, Roux Père, Raoul Clerget, Gérard Thomas, Henri Prudhorn, Jean-Claude Bachelet, Marc Colin,* and *Dne. Aimé Langoureau.*

Santenay

The 13,000-hectoliter vineyard of Santenay lies at the southern end of the Côte de Beaune and formally terminates the famous Côte d'Or viticultural region. The wines are overwhelmingly red, robust, tannin-rich, dark, and excellent in giving backbone to the weaker sisters farther north. Because Santenay is not widely known, the wines are honest and occasionally offer good value. The commune also produces small quantities of coarse white wine. The commune has 400 hectares of vineland and seven Premier Cru climats: le Clos-de-Tavannes, Beaurepaire, le Passe-Temps, Beauregard, la Comme, la Maladière, and les Gravières, the last three being considered the finest. Near Santenay are the three minor wine communes of Dezize-les-Maranges, Cheilly-les-Maranges, and Sampigny-les-Maranges. Their combined AOC hectarage of less than 50 produces about 1,500 hectoliters. The wine is dark, acidic, coarse and used to strengthen weaker wines. *Dne. Mestre, Jessiaume Père, Prosper Maufoux, René* and *Paul Fleurot, Roger Belland, Dne. Lequin-Roussot, Michel Clair, Dne. Jean Girardin, Dne. des Hautes Cornières, Lucien Muzard,* and *Herve Olivier* are the principal producers.

THE WINES OF THE SAÔNE-ET-LOIRE

South of the Côte d'Or in the department of Saône-et-Loire are the two viticultural districts of Chalonnais and Mâconnais. Their 1984 combined hectarage of less than 9,000 produced but 13 percent of total Burgundian output. One hundred years ago, the viticultural hectarage was more than six times the present size, but after the *phylloxera* epidemic, hectarage and production steadily declined to only a handful of successful viticultural pockets. The department contains few large cities and little industry and continues to be the source of chronic outmigration, a condition not too dissimilar from other rural areas in central France. Of the 600 settlements in the department, nearly 500 contain varying portions of commercial vineyards.

The acceleration of economic depression since the middle of the 19th century is clearly reflected in the land-use patterns, particularly viticulture. Approximately 6 percent of all arable land was planted in vines in 1850, 4 percent in 1920, 3 percent in 1950, and only 1 percent in 1985. Simultaneously, land devoted to grazing increased from 130,000 hectares in 1850 to more than 475,000 in 1985, while arable land for the same period declined by 300 percent. Approximately one-third of the total land area in the department is officially classified as forest or scrubland, all of which reflects the serious decline in wine production. Eighty-five years ago, the department produced twelve times its present output and served as the principal area for the production of Burgundian *vin ordinaire*. In 1945, less than 30 percent of total vineland was officially classified as AOC, a figure that has since risen to 50 percent in 1957 and to 78 percent

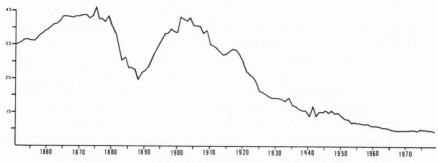

Figure 5.9   Saône-et-Loire: Vine Hectarage, 1850–1985
(in thousands of hectares)

in 1984. Quality appreciation not withstanding, the department is still responsible for one-third of all Bourgogne Rouge, two-thirds of all Crémant, and half of all Bourgogne Blanc and Aligoté.

The Saône-et-Loire is also an area of small, inefficient holdings and part-time farmers. In 1950, 78 percent of all growers owned less than 1 hectare, and only eight owned more than 20. This picture has improved in the past 35 years, but only marginally. The department is also the site of more unauthorized vines than any other in Burgundy. As recently as the 1950s, more than 6,000 hectares were planted in inferior Gamay Teinturières and hybrids, along with an additional 2,000 planted in Melon, Aligoté, and others. Over the past sixty years, the department has shifted from red to white wine production, particularly in the Mâconnais.

The Chalonnais begins 5 kilometers south of Chagny at Bouzeron and continues in an irregular fashion southward for 25 additional kilometers to Montagny. The small viticultural area takes its name from the old Roman colony at Chalon-sur-Saône, and the region has a rather favorable reputation. The Côte Chalonnais encompasses one regional AOC and four communal appellations: Bourgogne Aligoté Bouzeron, Rully, Givry, Mercurey, and Montagny. Rully produces near equal amounts of red and white, Montagny only white, while Givry and Mercurey are widely recognized as the most celebrated red wine regions south of Beaune. Representing only 2 percent of total Burgundian output, wine production is approximately 40,000 hectoliters. About one-quarter of regional output is white, equally divided between Rully and Montagny; the area's largest appellation, Mercurey, produces more than 50 percent of all red wine. Because of recent price increases in Côte d'Or, Beaujolais, and

Table 5.11 Major Grape Varieties Planted in the Department of Saône-et-Loire, 1968 and 1979

Grape varieties	1968		1979		As percent of national total
	Hectares	Percent[a]	Hectares	Percent[a]	
Gamay Noir	4,000	29.2	3,500	35.8	9.2
Chardonnay	3,100	22.6	3,100	31.7	23.7
Pinot Noir	1,500	10.9	2,500	25.6	14.5
Aligoté	600	4.4	300	3.1	25.2
Oberlin	600	4.4	100	1.0	
Gamays teinturiers	1,300	9.5	95	.9	
Plantet	400	2.9	50	.5	
Baco Noir	200	1.5	10	.1	
Melon	200	1.5	—		
Others	1,800	13.1	125	1.3	
Total	13,700	100.0	9,780	100.0	

[a]Percent of departmental total.

Source: French Ministry of Agriculture.

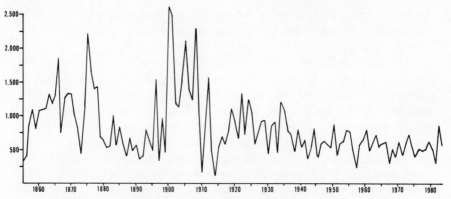

Figure 5.10   Saône-et-Loire: Wine Production, 1859–1985
(in thousands of hectoliters)

Chablis wines, the Chalonnais is an area of renewed interest providing a good, sound alternative to higher-priced Burgundy. As a result, hectarage and production have increased significantly within the past fifteen years, and large negociant firms such as Antonin Rodet, Chandesais, and Thénard have expanded operations.

Only Chardonnay and Pinot Noir are authorized for AOC wine production under the Rully, Givry, Mercurey, and Montagny appellation names. Aligoté is sold as Bourgogne Aligoté de Bouzeron. Gamay, used for Passetoutsgrains, accounts for about 20 percent of total regional output and is known for its harsh, acidic taste and early maturing character. While "Côte Chalonnais" is not a classified appellation, "Côte Chalonnais–Villages" is semi-official, and it encompasses at least five settlements, of which Bouzeron, Chassey, and Le Comp are the most important. In general, however, if the wine does not carry the Mercurey, Rully, Montagny, or Givry name, it must be sold as Bourgogne. Wines range from below average to above average in quality, are light to medium in body, and relatively early maturing. The reds are superior to the white,

Table 5.12   AOC Wine Production in the Côte Chalonnais, 1980

Appellation	Hectoliters	Percent of total	Appellation	Hectoliters	Percent of total
Mercurey Rouge	23,097	60.0	Rully Rouge	3,225	8.4
Mercurey Blanc	1,061	2.8	Rully Blanc	2,981	7.7
Givry Rouge	4,631	12.0	Montagny Blanc	3,002	7.8
Givry Blanc	516	1.3	Total	38,513	100.0

Source: French Ministry of Agriculture.

particularly those from Mercurey. White wines are dry, crisp, acidic, refreshing, and firm. Two wines—Crémant and Aligoté—are becoming increasingly important, and both carry the Bourgogne appellation. The former is a first-class underrated mousseux, and hence offers excellent value within the region. *Delormé-Meulien* is the largest producer, followed by *R. Chevillard* and *Parigot-Richard*. The second wine is a plain Aligoté from the small hamlet of Bouzeron. Although it lacks familiarity and glamor, Bouzeron is the home of *A. de Villaine,* a grower with an international reputation, a principal of Dne. de la Romanée-Conti, and maker of one of the finest Aligoté-based wines in the region. Other regional producers include *Chanzey Frères, Michel Derain, Michel Goubard,* and *Cave des Vignerons de Buxy.*

Rully

Rully, a good-sized village, lies at the foot of Montagne de la Folie, south of Bouzeron. It is a 200-hectare AOC district and the oldest vinegrowing settlement in the Chalonnais. The vineyard is composed of three physical sections; flat land of mixed agriculture in which long fields dominate east of the town; an intermediate zone of gentle foothills north of the town; and hilly portions in which vineyards stretch in a narrow belt along the steep portions of the Folie. The latter section, lying to the west of the city, is considered the finest of the three. Historically Rully was a red wine region, its reputation based on the cultivation of Pinot Noir, particularly in Marisson, Raboursey, Ptet, and Montpatais. After the *phylloxera* epidemic, production gradually shifted from Pinot Noir to Chardonnay, with white wine production now constituting half the total output. Since its name is unfamiliar to the average consumer, the vineyard lost a good deal of its reputation after 1923 when it lost its right to sell wine under the Mercurey banner. Between 1880 and 1950, hectarage declined from more than 1,100 hectares to less than 50 (AOC). Since then, the vineyard has grown to nearly 200 hectares, and the resurgence is expected to continue in the near future. Production has increased from fewer than 600 hectoliters in 1953 to more than 4,000 in 1982 (see Fig. 5.11).

Three types of wine are made in Rully: dry white, Crémant, and red, the latter considered the least distinguished. The white, made entirely from Chardonnay, is known for its distinctive dry, fruity, earthy, full and tart flavor and excellent golden-yellow color. Although not as distinguished as Côte de Beaune libations, it is good and almost always sound. The wine differs significantly from the Aligoté-ridden Mâconnais by being more elegant and fruity. Its more spirited, intense flavor and lingering bouquet are features that make Rully one of the best values in southern Burgundy. It is rarely flat, always clean, and offers considerable value. From lesser vineyards, a good deal of Crémant is made from

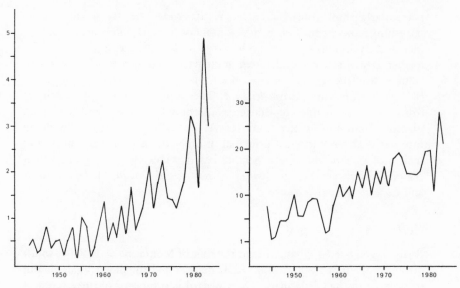

Wine Production in Rully (Fig. 5.11, *left*) and Mercurey
(Fig. 5.12, *right*), 1944–1982 (in thousands of hectoliters)

varying combinations of Gamay, Chardonnay, Aligoté, and Pinot Noir. The white Crémant (superior to the rosé) is brisk, well structured, underrated, and offers outstanding value in the producing region. Red Rully, similar to Mercurey, lacks refinement, and its flavor is marred by acidity and coarseness.

The principal climats are Grésigny, les Pierres, la Bressande, Mont Palais, Margotey, Raclot, Bas de Vauvry, Cloux, Pillot, Maix, Meix Caillet, Champ Clou, la Renarde, Raboursay, Ecloseaux, Chapitre, Marrissou, la Fosse, Préau, and Moulesne. The first four are widely recognized as the finest for white wine, and the last four are the most important for the production of red wine. Among the two dozen major growers and negociants, the most important are *Comte J. d'Aviau de Ternay, René Brelière, René Ninot Rigaud, Emile Chandesais, Jean-François Delorme, Henri Jacqueson, Armand Monassier, Noël-Bouton, Faiveley,* and *Leroy*.

Mercurey

Responsible for more than the combined output of Rully, Givry, and Montagny, Mercurey is the largest appellation in the Côte Chalonnais. Its 700 hectares produce more than 25,000 hectoliters (see Fig. 5.12), of which more than 90 percent is red wine. The vineyard begins half a kilometer north of the small town of Mercurey and stretches in an irregular fashion south to St.-Denis. The entire region is drained by two tributaries of the Saône and includes the settlements of Bourg, Bassot, Etroyes, Chamirey, St.-Martin, Mellecey, St.-Mard-de-Vaux, and St.-Jean-de-Vaux.

The somewhat compact, rugged area has a variety of aspect and soil. The best sites, located on soil geologically similar to that found in the Côte de Beaune, lie along protected slopes at altitudes between 220 and 230 meters that face south and southeast. The fragmented south-facing slopes of Mont Morin (called the "Chalon slope"), located south and east of Mercurey, along with the two sister parishes of Bourgneuf-Val-d'Or and St.-Martin-sous-Montaigu, produce the finest red wines south of Beaune. The major Premier Cru climats are Clos du Roi, Clos des Montaigus, Clos Marcilly, Clos des Fourneaux, and Clos Voyens. Considered slightly less fine are Clos de l'Evèque, Clos de Petit Clou, Byots, Champ Martins, les Crets, Nuagues, Tonnerre, and Vignes Blanches. In addition, the following monopole vineyards enjoy an above-average reputation: Clos de Myglands, Clos Rond, les Mauvarennes, Clos Rochette, la Mission, Clos du Château de Montaigu, Ch. Chamirey, Clos la Marche, and Clos Barrault.

Mercurey is distinguished by its sweet aroma, exquisite robe, strength, and pleasant flavor. It is generally darker in color than most red Beaune, more full-bodied, keeps well beyond eight years, but lacks the finesse and elegance of superior climats. Historically the wine was so good that it was sold as Côte de Beaune until the mid-1920s. Among the many growers and negociants, *François Protheau, Yves de Launay, Paul Bull, Louis Descombins, Louis Michel, Michel Juillot, Dne. Saier, Dne. du Château de Chamilly, Emile Voarick, Paul Granger, Hugues de Suremain, Dne. de Chamerose, Dne. Brintet,* and *Dne. Jeannin-Naltet* are all above average in quality. Wines evaluated by the Chante-Flute, the fraternal order of Mercurey, are usually of a high standard and reliable. Among the few but increasingly important negociants, *Antonin Rodet, Emile Chandesais, Faiveley, Bouchard Aîné,* and *Louis Latour* are the most prominent.

Givry

Givry, with approximately 14 percent of total production, is the second-largest AOC vineyard in the Chalonnais. It is located on a series of hills due south of Mercurey, separated only by the 450-meter-high Chatelet mountain. Composed of the villages of Russilly, Jambles, Poncey, Mont Borge, Cercot, St.-Désert, and Rosey, this south-southeast-facing vineyard is well protected from cold north winds. The producing sites are less compact than those in Mercurey and have to compete with other crops.

Givry, an old Roman garrison, is a picturesque town located between wooded uplands on the west and the Saône floodplain on the east. Vineyards, which were developed on a large scale by religious orders in the 13th century, soon became Burgundian favorites during the 14th and

15th centuries. The Cellier aux Moines and les Bois-Chevaux climats were first planted in the latter part of the 13th century, and Clos Salomon in the 16th. Between the 15th and the latter part of the 18th centuries it was an area of many large aristocratic holdings, whose production on the eve of the French Revolution is estimated to have exceeded 20,000 hectoliters, or four times the present output. After the *phylloxera* epidemic, wine production and vine hectarage steadily declined, until the post–1960 resurgence in white wine drove shippers and growers to take advantage of the area's underdeveloped potential. Until 1923 the wine was sold as Mercurey. Of the 6,000 hectoliters of wine made annually today, more than 5,000 are red and the remainder white. Both wines are alcoholic and often unbalanced, and the white is nearly always overrated. The red has excellent color, is well structured, assertive, often coarse, full-bodied on the palate and, when made by the *méthode ancienne,* contains plenty of extract and tannin. Although it can live longer than Mercurey, its intensity of flavor and bouquet are less fine and lack subtlety. Givry contains no Premier Cru climats, but the following are considered near equivalents by local aficionados: la Baraude, les Petits Pretans, les Bois-Chevaux, Clos Charlé, Cellier aux Moines, Clos Marolle, Clos Salomon, Servoisine, les Grands Pretans, Clos St.-Pierre, and Clos St.-Paul.

Despite its small size, Givry has a suprisingly large number of negociants, of which *Dne. Thénard, Antonin Rodet,* and *Louis Latour* are the most prominent. *Jean Maréchale, Du Gardin and Dumas, Dne. Joblot, Dne. Ragot, Jean Chofflet, Jean Morin,* and *Gérard Mouton* are widely considered the leading private producers.

Montagny

Of the four main appellations, Montagny, a white wine region, is the smallest and the southernmost of all Chalonnais vineyards. It consists of approximately 300 hectares, of which fewer than 100 are AOC. The producing sites lie at altitudes between 280 and 380 meters, with the best sites facing east-southeast and enjoying a superb view of the alpine Savoie peaks to the east across the Saône. The vineyard is widely scattered among the communes of Buxy, Montagny, St.-Vallerin, and Jully-les-Buxy. Although there are no officially classified Premier Cru sites, Vieux Château, les Roches, les St.-Ytages, les Bouchots, les Combes, and les Carlines are considered above average in the production of quality wine. Historically it was a red wine region, and although the reds still dominate, all AOC wine is white and made entirely from Chardonnay. The supple, gold-green wine has a fine bouquet, and characterized by the taste of hazelnuts. It is less elegant than Rully, yet substantial, fresh, appealing, much cheaper, and more reliable than Pouilly-Fuissé and Mâcon-Villages. Little known in export markets, it offers good value within the region. *Jean Vachet, Dne. M. de Laboulaye, Louis Latour,* and the

Coopérative des Vignerons de Buxy all enjoy a good reputation for crisp, fruity wines.

The Côte Mâconnais begins at Tournus, an ancient Roman outpost, and extends southward to Beaujolais. It is a prolific region with 11 percent of total Burgundian AOC wine production, and is the department's largest producer of white wine. Three-quarters of all the wine is white, and with but one exception (Pouilly-Fuissé) nearly all is quite ordinary. Red wine is not the equal of Beaujolais, Givry, or Mercurey, and as a consequence a lot of it is used in the making of plain Bourgogne, Crémant, or made into rosé. For the district as a whole, more than 40 percent is either plain Mâcon or Mâcon Supérieur, the two most basic appellations. At least 20 percent of all white wine is made from Aligoté and used to "stretch" Chardonnay production.

While Beaujolais, immediately to the south, is an "old" geologic region of rounded granite hills and gentle slopes, the Mâconnais is a limestone eruption of higher elevations exhibiting significant local relief, abrupt ravines, and jagged upland heights. Rarely are the vines grouped in vast homogeneous stands as in the Côte d'Or and Beaujolais; rather, they are widely scattered—separated by abandoned fields, wooded areas, and grazing land. The largest concentration of vineyards is in the area south of Fuissé, which contains more than 45 percent of total hectarage.

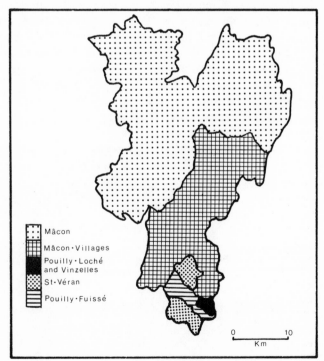

Figure 5.13　The Vineyards of the Mâconnais

Table 5.13   AOC Wine Production in the Mâconnais,
1980

Appellation	Hectoliters	Percent of total
Mâcon-Villages Blanc	87,869	44.0
Mâcon Supérieur Rouge	52,641	26.3
Mâcon Supérieur Blanc	6,757	3.4
Pouilly-Fuissé Blanc	32,748	16.4
St.-Véran Blanc	14,250	7.1
Mâcon Rouge	1,848	.9
Mâcon Blanc	707	.4
Pouilly-Vinzelles Blanc	1,790	.9
Pouilly-Loché Blanc	1,195	.6
Total Rouge	54,489	27.3
Total Blanc	145,316	72.7
Total	199,805	100.0

Source: French Ministry of Agriculture.

The entire producing district stretches north to south for 37 kilometers along the left bank of the Saône, with the best sites located on a limestone base.

The Mâconnais has produced wine ever since Roman legionnaires introduced the vine to the local population, a tradition that was continued and encouraged by the once large and highly influential ecclesiastical center of Cluny during the Dark Ages. Prior to *phylloxera,* more than 50,000 hectares were planted in vines, but only 5,000 remain today despite the energetic replanting efforts of the past thirty years. The poet-politician Lamartine remains Mâcon's most celebrated son and former grower at Château Monceau. Today most growers are too small to make and bottle wine, and instead sell grapes to negociants or belong to cooperatives. The twenty cooperatives are responsible for more than 80 percent of total production, and while they vary in emphasis, all but one produce AOC wine. The largest are located in Buxy, Viré, Verzé, Sologny, Igé, Lugny, Prissé, Chaintré, and Azé, with Lugny, Buxy, and Prissé the largest. Their output generally goes to major negociants like Louis Latour, Louis Jadot, Thorin, Georges Dubeouf, Piat, Joseph Drouhin, and other negociant firms that deal in large quantities of regional blended wine. Nicolas, the largest French wholesale/retail firm, buys substantial quantities and is a major factor in the domestic market. Blended Mâconnais wine has become a popular export wine, especially in Switzerland, West Germany, Holland, and the United States.

Mâcon-Villages Blanc

With nearly 50 percent of total output, the Mâcon-Village Blanc appellation is the single-most-important wine in the Mâconnais. The producing region encompasses 43 of what are considered the finest villages in the entire Mâconnais, aside from those producing Pouilly-Fuissé, Vinzelles, and Loché. The largest concentration occurs along the eastern portion of the region; Prissé, Clessé, Lugny, Viré, and Chardonnay are considered the finest, with the first three having the right to append their name to the appellation on the label. The wine, nearly all of it blended, is the product of Chardonnay and must have at least 11 percent alcohol. As the volume of production and overall quality are highly inconsistent, when the alcohol content proves insufficient it is sold as either Mâcon-Supérieur Blanc or plain Mâcon Blanc. At its best the wine is fresh, soft, appealing, and refreshing on the palate. At its worst it is dull, flat, tasteless, and lacking in character and fullness. Even when compared to Rully, it lacks harmony, roundness, and has become overpriced. Ninety percent or more is simple carafe wine, nothing more. Despite the above shortcomings, the soft, dry white wine is very popular in the United States, United Kingdom, and the Low Countries. Steady demand, improved vinification, and timeliness have encouraged significant replanting of abandoned vineland. It has become fashionable for French and continental restaurants to feature white Mâconnais, and the trend is expected to continue. In 1976, a group of growers from a limited 25-hectare region has produced a supposedly superior Mâcon-Villages wine called Mâcon-Fuissé. Thus far, the wine is below average and the nomenclature appears to have a limited future.

Among the major negociants, *Louis Latour, Mommessin,* and *Joseph Drouhin* produce a complete line, while the following are all considered the leading private producers: *Etablissement Chevalier, Pierre Santé, Dne. de Roally, Patrice de l'Epine, René Michel, Henri Lafarge, René Gaillard, Claude Mauciat-Poncet, Jean Signoret, Adrien Arcelin, André Bonhomme, Pierre Mahuet,* and *Dne. de la Condemine.* The cooperatives of Igé, Lugny, Prissé, Verzé, Chardonnay, and Charnay all make average to above-average-quality wine.

Mâcon Supérieur Rouge and Blanc

Both appellations account for nearly one-third of total regional output, of which the rouge represents one-quarter. While alcohol content is nearly always the same as that for Mâcon-Villages Blanc, the main quality difference between them lies in the location of the vineyards. Mâcon Rouge is also, because of a lack of delicacy, a lesser wine than AOC counterparts from the Chalonnais and Beaujolais, its main appeal being low price. Recently producers of Mâcon Supérieur Rouge and Mâcon Rouge have begun to ferment by the carbonic maceration process, with dramatic success; should the quality improve and prices hold steady, the wine will offer stiff competition to Beaujolais.

Mâcon Blanc and Rouge

Mâcon Blanc and Rouge account for 7 to 10 percent of total regional production, of which the rouge is nine times greater in volume than the white. Mâcon Blanc, with a minimum of 10 percent alcohol, constitutes about 1 percent of regional production. Theoretically coming only from limestone soils, it is occasionally marketed as Pinot Chardonnay de Mâcon. The wine is common, coarse, often unstable, and offers little value. Although Mâcon Rouge contains 9 percent minimum alcohol, the wine is nearly identical to Supérieur and offers little value no matter what the price.

Pouilly-Fuissé

The only area in the Mâconnais capable of producing above-average wine is Pouilly-Fuissé, an appellation whose vineyards are sited on limestone hills in the southcentral portion of the producing district. The area contains nearly 600 hectares of AOC vineyards, with an output of 40,000 hectoliters of Chardonnay-based wine. The soils are based on limestone, marl, and Kimmeridgian chalk whose incidence and depth vary significantly throughout the district. The best sites face east and southeast at altitudes between 250 and 400 meters. The production center is dominated by La Roche de Solutré, a huge, picturesque rock outcrop almost completely surrounded by vineyards. Only five communes, Fuissé, Pouilly, Solutré, Chaintré, and Vergisson, are allowed to produce grapes and wine under this appellation name. More than 50 percent of all exploitations are less than 3 hectares in size, yields are high, and more than 60 percent of total production is absorbed by major negociants like Louis Latour, Mommessin, and Louis Jadot (see Fig. 5.14).

The most important Premier Cru climats in the production of Pouilly-Fuissé by commune are Vergisson (les Crays, la Maréchaude, les Charmes, Carmentrat, les Croux); Solutré (la Frerie, les Crayes, les Quarts, Rousse-

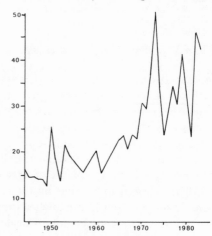

Figure 5.14   Pouilly-Fuissé:
Wine Production, 1944–1983
(in thousands of hectoliters)

lain, Vignerais, la Mure); Pouilly (les Bouthières, les Chailloux, Au Clos, Aux Morlays, Aux Peloux, Château Pouilly); Fuissé (les Clos, les Mene-trières, les Brules, les Champs, les Resses, les Perrières, en Chantenay, Château de Fuissé); and Chaintré (le Clos Ressier, les Chevrières, les Quarts, en Paradis).

At its best, Pouilly-Fuissé is a dry, clean, light, pale wine highlighted with green tones that has an expansive aroma and a very agreeable, refreshing taste. Its appeal is very obvious from its quaffable and satisfying character. At its worst the wine, thin and neutered of its individuality and character, can often be tasteless and disappointing. Despite a doubling of output since 1945, demand continues to outstrip supply, and prices have recently risen to outrageous levels, thus debasing its intrinsic value enormously. With overcropping and adulteration, the wine today is but a degraded fossil of its former *éclat* and, as a consequence, sales in the United States and Great Britain have fallen. Not only does Pouilly-Fuissé vary widely in quality, but the very best is no match for Chablis, Meursault, Montrachet, Sancerre, or Pouilly-Fumé.

The standard for all Pouilly-Fuissé is *Ch. de Fuissé,* a wine that is full, crisp, eminently refreshing, perfectly balanced, and substantial on the palate. Other above-average producers are *Ch. Pouilly, Guffens-Heynen, Clos de Bourg, Ch. de Beauregard, André Besson, Jean Goyon, Etablissement Loron, Roger Lassarat, Joseph Corsin, Ch. de France,* and *Dne. Bellenaud.* More than 55 percent of all Pouilly-Fuissé is produced by cooperatives, and more than three-quarters of total output is distributed by negociants.

St.-Véran

In the extreme southern portion of the Mâconnais, a group of villages have banded together to form a new appellation called St.-Véran. In existence since 1971, this geographically diffused but rapidly growing appellation makes 7 percent of all the wine in the Mâconnais region. Its producing areas lie along both banks of the small and shallow l'Arlois stream in the central Mâcon, where a confusing overlapping pattern of appellations is found. In general, however, the confines of the disjointed appellation roughly coincide with limestone outcrops not included within the Pouilly-Fuissé appellation.

The principal communes are Davaye (located north of Pouilly), Prissé (located in the extreme northeastern section of Mâcon), Chânes (in the extreme south), St.-Amour (in Beaujolais), St.-Vérand, Leynes, and Chasselas. It is probable that the confusion probably increases fraudulent practices, since a good portion of the wine can be sold legally as Beaujolais Blanc, Mâcon-Villages, or Bourgogne Blanc. If a village name is ap-pended, the alcohol content must be at least 12 percent. Due to the enormous variation in soil, aspect, and location, the character and quality of the wine vary significantly. When it is dry, crisp, and refreshing, it is softer and easier to drink than Rully and Pouilly-Fuissé, but scarcely better than simple Mâcon-Villages. Among the numerous negociants and growers, *Georges Chagny, Marcel Robert, André Chavet, R. Duperron, Georges Duboeuf,* and *Dne. Mondange* are all considered above average.

Pouilly-Vinzelles and Pouilly-Loché

The combined output of Pouilly-Vinzelles and Pouilly-Loché is less than 3 percent of total regional Mâconnais wine. The larger of the two, Vinzelles lies south of Loché and 3 kilometers southeast of Fuissé. Although its 60 hectares are admirably situated along east-facing slopes, the wine is weaker in flavor and body, more acidic, and less round than Pouilly-Fuissé. Outrageously overpriced, it offers no value whatever. Production hovers around 2,000 hectoliters, which is 50 percent more than the output of Loché. More than 90 percent of total production is made by one cooperative, and the leading grower is *Jean Mathias. Caves des Crus-Blancs* and *Charles Vienot* are two smaller properties with good reputations.

THE WINES OF BEAUJOLAIS AND COTEAUX DU LYONNAIS

The Beaujolais is not a department, river, major city, or industrial heartland, but an ill-defined viticultural region of rolling hills draped in vines that stretches for a distance of 50 kilometers from the southern portions of Mâcon to L'Arbresle, a large hamlet about 22 kilometers north of Lyon. Nearly the whole of the Beaujolais lies in the Rhône department and has a north-south orientation. The western foothills of the Massif Central being well rounded and forested, the hills of Beaujolais are more wide than high. Population is widely scattered and not clustered in large towns or next to medieval castles, as is the case along the Rhône. Viticultural land use, expressed as percent of total agricultural land, is more important in the Rhône than in the Yonne, Saône-et-Loire, or Côte d'Or departments. While vineyards covered nearly 14 percent of all agricultural land in 1870, its present 12 percent figure is hardly a significant decline when compared with other appellations to the north. Approximately one-tenth of the area is forested, one-third is arable, another one-third is pasture, and the remainder miscellaneous. About one-third of total arable land is planted in vines, which are responsible for more than one-half of the agricultural product of the department.

Viticulture in the Beaujolais, unlike the rest of Burgundy, developed significantly after the French Revolution, when many large grazing estates in the region were confiscated and parceled out to the citizenry. The subsequent improvement of transportation, and the elimination of toll stations along the tortuous route to Paris, rapidly transformed the land of Beaujeau into the largest Burgundian vineyard. Today the region has the highest population density of all Burgundian appellations and produces between 60 and 72 percent of all wine in Burgundy.

It is estimated that in the middle of the 18th century, there were fewer than 10,000 hectares of vineland, nearly all of which were subsistent in character. Hectarage increased steadily; on the eve of the French Revolution, about three-quarters of the approximately 38,000 hectares were located in the extreme southern portion. At that time, the Haut-Beaujolais region was underdeveloped and possessed no large-scale commercial hectarage. Figures 5.15 and 5.16 indicate the evolution of wine production and vine hectarage since 1850. The effects of *phylloxera* and the economic depressions of the first and third decades of the 20th century illustrate the "boom or bust" nature of the industry. For a brief period after World War I, total output peaked in 1922, whereas production between 1925 and 1970 remained relatively stable. Hectarage, however, continued to decline and reached a low of 16,000 hectares in 1964. While the percentage of total hectarage not classified as AOC has declined, AOC hectarage has grown from 12,500 hectares in 1949 to more than 21,000 in 1985. More than 70 percent of this increase occurred on flat, easily mechanized land in the Bas-Beaujolais. Given the current demand, the growers and negociants easily sell all the wine they make, no matter what the price.

Fifty years ago, nearly 80 percent of all growers were subject to a

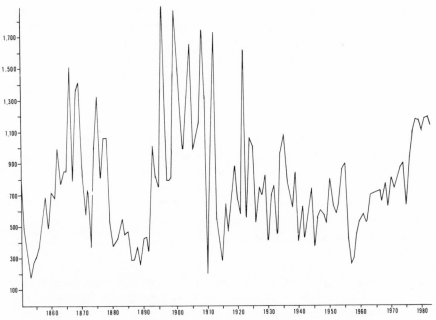

Figure 5.15   Beaujolais: Wine Production, 1850–1985
(in thousands of hectoliters)

Figure 5.16   Beaujolais: Vine Hectarage, 1850–1985
(in thousands of hectares)

variation of the *métayage* system locally called *vigneronnage,* a medieval form of sharecropping. The vigneron, who did not own land, attained the right to cultivate the land by sharing the proceeds with the landowner, who usually provided equipment and shared in the cost of harvesting the grapes. Historically more than three-quarters of the land was worked in this fashion, but after World War II land consolidation proceeded at a fairly rapid pace and reduced *vigneronnage* to 31 percent for the entire region. Today it is most prevalent in the Haut-Beaujolais and nearly extinct in the Bas-Beaujolais. In the entire region, about 50 percent of all holdings are smaller than 5 hectares, a figure that is below the economic solvency point, hence the high percentage of part-time farmers. One hundred years ago, 80 percent of all growers cultivated less than 1 hectare; today this figure has dropped to 16 percent. As of 1984, fifty growers owned more than 30 hectares, 40 of whom were found in the Bas-Beaujolais.

Soils and Climate

The Beaujolais is divided into two producing areas: the Haut-Beaujolais in the north, which includes all the Grand Cru communes, is the area recognized for the production of fine wines; the lower, or Bas-Beaujolais, region to the south is the larger-producing, although lower-quality, wine area. Two specific elements—relief and soil—separate the two districts in terms of wine quality, yield, and total production.

Villefranche (or the Nizerand valley, depending on the authority) separates the Haut from the Bas-Beaujolais. It is a rough dividing line between the dominance of granitic and limestone/clay soil, the latter a poor medium in which Gamay produces a much coarser, thinner, less fruity and flavorful wine than its more famous partner to the north. The Haut-Beaujolais contains soil of decomposed granite that is sandy, rocky, pinkish in color, and has excellent permeability. It dries out readily, warms up early in the season, is easily worked, and maintains heat during

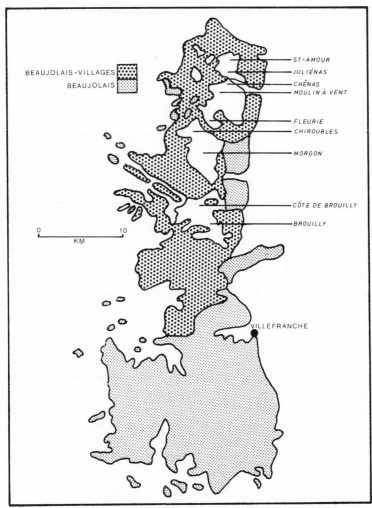

BEAUJOLAIS·VILLAGES
BEAUJOLAIS

ST·AMOUR
JULIÉNAS
CHÊNAS
MOULIN À VENT

FLEURIE
CHIROUBLES

MORGON

CÔTE DE BROUILLY

BROUILLY

0   10
KM

VILLEFRANCHE

Figure 5.17   The Beaujolais Vineyard

the evening better than the soils of the Bas-Beaujolais. The best sites contain sub and surface soils rich in iron, manganese, and potassium, as in Moulin-à-Vent and Morgon—two areas with the highest mineral concentrations. These soils are also more acidic and contain numerous outcrops of granite, schist, and sandstone, all of which are irregular in distribution throughout the region. The predominance of limestone and clay in the Bas-Beaujolais impairs drainage, inhibits root development, and results in wines that are less alcoholic, much coarser, and less supple on the palate than in the Haut-Beaujolais.

The climate is characterized by three seasonal air masses. The Mediterranean from the south brings hot, dry summer weather, and alternating continental and marine west coast air masses influence the late autumn, winter, and spring seasons. Continental air from the northeast is cold and dry, while the westerly oceanic winds are higher in temperature and more humid. June, July, and August are the hottest, driest months, while fall and spring are the most rainy with precipitation coming in downpours. Hail, the most notorious environmental problem, usually occurs when maritime humid air from the west meets drier, warmer air from the Mediterranean over central France. Winds are irregular in their occurrence and quite variable in their intensity. Northern winds called *la Bise,* characterized by low temperatures, predominate. A westerly wind called *la Traverse* crosses the Massif Central and is responsible for most of the precipitation, while winds from the Mediterranean are invariably higher in temperature but lower in humidity. Due to the persistency of winds in the Haut-Beaujolais, the hill summits are kept forested to protect the vineyards below, where the most favorable aspects face southeast to take advantages of the morning sun and lower the incidence of frost. Northern aspects are more humid, have a history of more disease, and are generally avoided, as are low-lying areas that are foggy and prone to frost. Because higher exposures get early sun, the soil warms up faster, and grape berries mature more evenly than those in valley locations.

The Wines of Beaujolais

Beaujolais exhibits a bewildering variation in flavor, color, ability to withstand bottle-aging, quality, and price. It ranges from the light-colored, watery, tasteless libations on the lower end of the quality spectrum to highly refined, even elegant wines (such as Moulin-à-Vent) that can rival a good number of Premier Cru from the more exalted slopes of Nuits and Beaune. At its best, Beaujolais is described as being similar to an envelope because it "surrounds and seals the pleasure." In addition to its fruitiness and mild grapey aroma, "being easy to drink" is its hallmark.

More than 96 percent of all Beaujolais is red with purple highlights of varying intensity. Although the wine appears to be light in body, it is high in alcohol and substantial on the palate. It usually has the pleasant sweet aroma and flavor of ripe fruit. When served cool, it can be refreshing, with the very best supple and eminently quaffable. While nearly all will not improve with age, the wines of the nine Grand Cru communes are distinguished by fullness, darker color, somewhat higher alcohol, and the potential to age. In addition to soil and climate, the character of the grape and the method of vinification play vital roles in determining the personality of Beaujolais. The wine is made by the carbonic maceration process, a method of vinifying grapes by placing uncrushed grapes in a closed container. Fermentation is rapid and usually without the aid of added yeast. The grapes are kept under anaerobic conditions for at least three days, during which time they undergo intercellular fermentation, a key element in the preservation of a good deal of fermentation bouquet. The resulting wine contains an intense fruity flavor, a low volatile acidity, and low levels of malic acid. Reducing production costs drastically, this process requires no barrel-aging and the wine matures rapidly. As it appeals to contemporary tastes, the carbonic maceration process is the "in" vinification method everywhere in the country for the production of early maturing, light, flavorful, fruity wines. Few bottles, except the very rare ones produced by the *méthode ancienne* and aged in wood, ever develop complexity with age.

Beaujolais is made only from clones of the Gamay Noir à Jus Blanc and not from the Gamay Noir à Jus Coloré, commonly referred to as Gamay Teinturier, a much inferior grape permitted in the Mâconnais that gives a bitter-tasting, coarse wine. The many clones of the Gamay Noir à Jus Blanc differ significantly in terms of growing features, size of berry and bunch, color, and texture of skin. Four principal types are Gamay de Gamays (a prolific clone grown for its yield, which appears to be inferior in the production of quality wine), Gamay Chatillon, Gamay Magnyx, and Gamay Goffray (current favorites due to their lower yields, fruitier taste, and resistance to disease and frost). Throughout the entire district, their proper selection contributes as much to the quality of the finished product as aspect, soil, and vinification techniques, hence the subtle differences between the wines of neighboring vineyards. Vialla, the most common rootstock, is popular because it has a special affinity for the lime-free granitic soil found throughout the central and northern portions of the appellation.

Minuscule amounts of rosé and a slightly larger amount of white are made, but the overwhelming sum—about 98 percent—is red, of which more than half is made in the nouveau style. In the final analysis, however, no matter what the color or nomenclature, Beaujolais can be divided into four specific types of wine: (a) "la réserve," the finest selections of the best cuvées made by traditional methods, which accounts for less than .2 percent of the total output: (b) domaine or estate production, less fine than "la réserve" wine, but superior to all others, which accounts for 5 percent of production; (c) Grand Cru, of average to above-average quality, which accounts for about 10 to 15 percent of total production; and (d) regional blended wine, of below-average to average quality, which represents 80 to 85 percent of total output. It is important to note that the wines of Beaujolais are classified under the Vin de Bourgogne appellation, therefore a varying portion may be sold as Bourgogne, depending on the vintage and the demands of the market.

Despite the seemingly unlimited demand for Beaujolais, the producing region is faced with a number of formidable problems. Excessive chaptalization produces off flavors and unbalanced wines: at least one-third of total output is considered unstable and barely palatable. A lot was and still is *Vin Bourru* ("stuffed wine"), Beaujolais blended with cheaper wine that originates outside the district. The issue of overproduction, ignored for years, is getting worse, and yields in the Bas-Beaujolais regularly exceed 100 hectoliters to the hectare, or twice the legal limit. Finally, unlike other fine wine-producing regions, Beaujolais completely disregards bottle- and wood-aging in favor of the quick turnover, cash-producing, nouveau style of wine. Producers will have a difficult time adjusting to the realities of the fickle marketplace once the craze for this type of wine subsides.

The Beaujolais Wine Trade

The Beaujolais wine market is a big business and getting bigger. Beaujolais produces approximately 1.5 percent of all wine in France, and if one judges by its availability and degree of advertising, as much as 4 percent of total French wine production may ultimately be sold as Beaujolais. The region produces roughly 8.5 percent of all AOC and 13.5 percent of all AOC red wine. In addition, as the third-largest wine-exporting region in the country, it accounts, in terms of volume, for 14 percent of all AOC wine exports and earns 8 percent of the total exportable value. Beaujolais is now called the "little wine that grew up," referring to the fact that the wine is no longer inexpensive and widely accepted as something more than *vin ordinaire*. The business is complicated and, in fact, very convoluted, with a large number of holding companies and numerous *sous marques*. There is a lot of speculation, since price and quality vary enormously and the authenticity of a good portion must be questioned. No other wine receives as much national and international attention; the name is universally recognized, and the wine is widely imitated.

The wine trade is centered in six principal towns, the largest and most important of which is Villefranche-sur-Saône. It is the largest city, a rapidly growing industrial area, a university town, the principal wholesaling hub, the locus for the principal wine agencies, and the home of at least three dozen negociants. The second largest is Bellevue, a small town with more than thirty negociants and the site of a rapidly growing industrial base. The third area for negociant activity is Beaujeau, the historical and geographical capital of the appellation. In a triangular area west, southwest, and south of Villefranche are the three small negociant towns of Denicé, Anse, and Le Bois d'Oingt, which collectively contain approximately 50 percent of all negociants, most of whom deal in the product of the Bas-Beaujolais.

Forty to 45 percent of all Baujolais is exported, one of the highest such export figures of any French appellation. It accounts for 57 percent of all Burgundian exports in volume and 35 percent of total value. The main importing countries are Switzerland, United States, West Germany, Belgium, Luxembourg, United Kingdom, Holland, and those of Scandinavia.

Beaujolais is a well-advertised and -promoted wine. Few wines enjoy the *sans souci* image of Beaujolais, and this image is no casual event. A number of regional organizations have one basic goal in mind: to propagandize the virtues of Beaujolais. According to the Union Interprofessionnelle des Vins du Beaujolais, there were twenty-three official tasting centers in 1985, all catering to tourists for the express purpose of increasing direct sales. More than 300,000 tourists annually get off the major north-south expressway to and from the French Riviera to sample, consume, and cart away as many as 200,000 hectoliters of Beaujolais. A common estimate is that between 15 and 20 percent of all Beaujolais is sold directly *(vente directe)*—a rapid rise from less than 5 percent in 1950.

The eighteen cooperatives in the region maintain a skilled public relations staff that works closely with the Credit Agricole Bank. These cooperatives, linked in an association known as the Federation des Caves Coopératives du Beaujolais, maintain thirteen tasting centers; their collective output is estimated to amount to more than 55 percent of all Beaujolais produced annually. The most successful of all organizations is the Union Interprofessionnelle des Vins du Beaujolais, a publicity organization working on behalf of the growers and the trade, whose sole purpose is to make the wine better known both within France and abroad. A smaller but no less influential organization is the Union Viticole du Beaujolais, an umbrella of all Beaujolais wine trade associations, for which there is at least one member in each major village. In addition, the Federation Regionale des Grands Cru de Bourgogne is an organization linking all the Cru producers of the Beaujolais, Chalonnais, and Mâconnais. Two smaller and less influential organizations are Amicale des Beaujolais-Villages and Groupement des Beaujolais. According to the Union Interprofessionnelle des Vins du Beaujolais, there are more than 866 négociants, cooperatives, viticulteurs, and manipulants, each of whom produces more than 500 cases of wine. The Confrérie de Beaujolais was founded in 1947 and does much to publicize the activities of wine chapters in many countries. The executive committee is widely traveled and quite sophisticated in its approach to marketing and spotting consumer trends.

Historically the distribution of Beaujolais occurred through Burgundian shippers, nearly all of whom blended wine and offered few estate wines. During the past thirty years, however, the business of Beaujolais has changed dramatically. Not only is there a noticeable rise of estate or domaine wines, but a small, energetic numbers of "specialists" have emerged who distribute these individual and more distinctive libations. Among the most prominent of the "new" style of negociants are Paul Beaudet, Georges Duboeuf, Sylvan Fessy, Louis Tête, Pasquier-Desvignes, Jean Bedin, and Trenel. The Eventail de Vignerons Producteurs, a syndicate of conscientious growers dedicated to quality Beaujolais production, make their own wine, but store, market, and distribute under a common central unit. Their wines vary in quality and price, but in general are above average and offer varying degrees of value for dollar.

One of the largest of all Beaujolais negociants specializing in average to above-average wine is *Mommessin,* the large Burgundian house that does about 50 percent of its business in Beaujolais and exports 60 percent of its turnover. The firm's reputation rests in the distribution of estate wines, of which the following are all above average in quality: Dne. de Lathevalle and des Charmes (Morgon); Castel du Cotoyant and Dne. de la Conseillere (Juliena); Clos de la Roilette and Dne. de la Presle (Fleurie); la Rochelle and Dne. de Champ-de-Cour (Moulin-a-Vent); and Ch. de Briante (Brouilly). The largest negociant, Georges Duboeuf, often known as "Mr. Beaujolais," buys wine from more than 100 growers. A major driving force in Beaujolais, he distributes more than 500,000 cases of wine annually, or about 4 percent of all Beaujolais made. He does not make wine, but buys, blends, and is the exclusive distributor for at least fourteen viticulteurs/manipulants with average to excellent reputations. The wines range from the most basic Beaujolais through nouveau, Villages, commune, single vineyard, to "special" bottlings. He has acquired an international reputation for fine Beaujolais, beautiful bottles, and exotic names—wines that are carried by fine restaurants and exclusive retail establishments. The following are all above average in quality: Ch. de Nevers (Brouilly); Dne. de Héritiers Tagent (Moulin-à-Vent); Ch. de Deduits (Fleurie); Dne. des Versauds (Morgon); Ch. de Javernand (Chiroubles); and Dne. Desmures and Dne. des Vignes (Juliénas). Among smaller but no less influential negociants are *Paul Sapin, Wildman, Valette, Robert Sarrau, Pellerin, Héritiers A. Quinson, Sylvain Fessy, Piat, Thorin, Henri de Villamont, Chevalier, Bouchacourt, Paul Beaudet, Loron, David & Foillard, Aujoux, Pierre Ferraud, Caves de Champelos,* and *Chanut Frères.*

THE BEAUJOLAIS APPELLATIONS

Beaujolais Rouge and Blanc

The most basic appellation, Beaujolais, is characterized by a minimum of 9 percent alcohol and a yield of 50 hectoliters to the hectare. More than 95 percent of it is red, minute quantities are rosé, and the remainder is white. Nearly all is blended wine, with few single-vineyard wines appearing under the simple designation of Beaujolais. Production, fluctuating between 400,000 and 550,000 hectoliters annually, represents about 45 to 60 percent of the total regional output. More than 80 percent of it originates from the rich flatlands of the Bas-Beaujolais. About

10,000 hectares are classified under this appellation, one-third on land newly expanded during the past twenty years. Its quality is low due to excessive chaptalization and overcropping. The chaptalization issue, however, is most critical, not because it is widespread but, as it is necessary to raise alcohol levels more than one degree, because it affects the wine's balance, flavor, and aroma adversely. Wine under this appellation rarely offers value.

With less than 1 percent of regional production, Beaujolais Blanc is the smallest Beaujolais appellation. Minuscule amounts are also produced under the Village and Supérieur designations, the only difference between the three being 1 percent alcohol. Beaujolais Blanc is produced only in the northern portion of the Haut-Beaujolais close to the Mâcon border where there is limestone in the soil. The wine is ideally made only from Chardonnay, but its recent popularity has prompted a number of producers to "stretch" the vintage with inferior Aligoté. A peculiar legal restriction dictates that its production may not exceed 10 percent of any vineyard. It is curious that the wine also has the right to be sold as St.-Véran. Another odd characteristic is that Beaujolais Blanc is not Beaujolais at all, since all authentic Beaujolais must be made from the Gamay grape. Despite its current popularity, production over the past ten years has fluctuated between 3,000 and 6,000 hectoliters. It is very rare and seldom encountered in export markets. The character of Beaujolais Blanc ranges from soft to hard, and from a light to medium-bodied wine. It is refreshing, often well balanced, mildly scented, and can, on occasion, offer better value than overpriced Mâcon Blanc. Some of the better producers and negociants with established reputations are *Louis Jadot, Prosper Maufoux, Bernard Ialicieux, Pierre & Paul Durdilly, Ch. de Loyse, Ch. de Chatelad,* and *Dne. de Sandar.* Although less Beaujolais Blanc is

Table 5.14   AOC Beaujolais Wine Production, 1980

Appellation	Hectoliters	Percent of total	Appellation	Hectoliters	Percent of total
Beaujolais Rouge	470,225	42.4	Juliénas Rouge	30,252	2.7
Beaujolais Blanc	4,246	.4	Moulin à Vent Rouge	34,083	3.1
Beaujolais Supérieur			Chiroubles Rouge	16,385	1.5
Rouge	13,453	1.2	Côte de Brouilly		
Beaujolais Supérieur Blanc	622		Rouge	15,363	1.4
Beaujolais-Villages			St.-Amour Rouge	14,057	1.3
Rouge	334,966	30.2	Chénas Rouge	12,630	1.1
Beaujolais-Villages Blanc	492		Total Rouge	1,103,381	99.5
Brouilly Rouge	66,729	6.0	Total Blanc	5,360	.5
Morgon Rouge	54,953	5.0			
Fleurie Rouge	40,285	3.6	Grand total	1,108,741	100.0

Source: French Ministry of Agriculture.

made than Rosé, the latter is not considered a serious wine, and its consumption is confined to the producing region only.

Beaujolais nouveau is the current rage in the turbulent history of Beaujolais. Made quickly by the carbonic maceration process, the wine is available for sale by December and quickly consumed within the next nine months. It differs from conventional Beaujolais only by having its fermentation accelerated to half the normal period; all the other necessary steps are the same. The wine is light in color, fresh, fruity in flavor, with no tannin and little extract. Often petillant and almost always unstable (although nearly all of it is pasteurized), it is not very consistent and deteriorates very rapidly.

Now officially an "in" wine, Beaujolais nouveau remains highly controversial and has taken on the ambiance of a cult; the United Kingdom alone consumed more than 244,000 cases in 1983. Beaujolais nouveau is also big business. In 1960 nouveau production accounted for less than 5 percent of total output, but had increased to 11 percent by 1965, to 17 percent in 1970, to 45 percent in 1980, and to 52 percent in 1984. About two-thirds is made by cooperatives. Eighty-two percent originates from the Beaujolais appellation and the remainder from Villages and Supérieur hectarage, with (theoretically) none from Grand Cru sites. Nouveau is popular with growers, shippers, and bankers because its easy to "move" and, since it is sold within three months of the vintage, represents the fastest return on money invested in the wine business. This is in sharp contrast to Bordeaux, where yields are lower and handling expenses high for two years while the wine matures in wood prior to shipment. Despite the rapid increase in the production of nouveau, a number of significant problems remain. In the rush to speed consumption and accelerate cash-flow, overall quality has declined. The wine at its best is thin, astringent, bitter, and unbalanced—some call it "pseudowine." Although good nouveau can be found, the overwhelming majority is poor, overpriced, and offers little value. The wine has, in many instances, approached the quality levels of American "pop" wine, and it is feared that once consumption peaks the market for traditional Beaujolais will suffer.

Beaujolais Supérieur

The only difference between this seemingly better (regional) appellation and plain Beaujolais is 1 percent more alcohol. But since the wine is the product of severe chaptalization and overcropping, the theoretical differences between the two are not reflected in the bottle and, hence, quality really varies with the producer. Beaujolais and Beaujolais Supérieur are, in effect, one and the same wine, despite the fact that the Supérieur designation commands a higher appellation and price. Production, varying between 2 and 5 percent of the regional total, is nearly all red with only tiny amounts of white and rosé.

Beaujolais-Villages

More than 300,000 hectoliters, or 30 to 35 percent of all Beaujolais, is classified as Beaujolais-Villages, nearly all of it red. While the alcohol content and yield are the same as Supérieur, its higher rank on the quality ladder is said to be caused by superior soil and microclimate. The irregular delimited area surrounding the nine Grand Cru communes covers approximately forty villages in the region between Beaujeau and Villefranche-sur-Saône. The most important are Beaujeau, Cercié, Charentay, Emeringes, Lancié, Lantigné, Leynes, Odenas, Le Perréon, Villié Morgon, Salles, St.-Lager, St.-Etienne-la-Varenne, St.-Etienne des Oullières, Romanèche Thorins, Rivolet, Pruzilly, and Montmélas.

While the wine at times is more concentrated, fuller on the palate, and a shade darker than plain Beaujolais and Supérieur, careful selection is necessary because up to 25 percent (and sometimes more) of all Beaujolais can be sold as Beaujolais-Villages. Under certain circumstances, the name of the village may be appended to the appellation name. Some of the better growers of Beaujolais-Villages include *André Vernus, René Miolane, Etienne Jambon, Claude* and *Michelle Joubert, Gilles Perroud, Jean Benon, René Berrod, Paul Cinquin, Joel Rochette, Paul Gauthier,* and *Vins Dessalle.* The following estate wines are also above average and offer good value: *Dne. de Niveaudières, Ch. Lacarelle, Ch. de Corcelles, Ch. du Thyl,* and *Dne. du Chapitre.*

Beaujolais Grand Cru

Beaujolais Grand Cru refers to wine originating from nine communes in the Haut-Beaujolais: St.-Amour, Brouilly, Côte de Brouilly, Chénas, Chiroubles, Fleurie, Juliénas, Morgon, and Moulin-à-Vent. All the communes lie on hilly terrain containing granitic and well-drained soils, and collectively they contain nearly all the most celebrated domaines. Located just north of Brouilly, Regnié-Durette, a commune known for strong, seasoned, and assertive wines, is slated to be officially designated the tenth Cru. Being higher in elevation, the Haut-Beaujolais avoids disastrous and deadly spring frosts because the vines delay their bud break until the danger of frost has passed. Here, a good deal of the vines are trained gobelet-style, and the yield is limited to 40 hectoliters per hectare. In the Bas-Beaujolais vines can be trained high on wires, and the yield is increased to 50 hectoliters per hectare.

The northernmost appellation in the Haut-Beaujolais, with a small portion lying within the Saône-et-Loire, is *St.-Amour,* which is a collection of four small hamlets. An AOC appellation since 1946, it is a small vineyard of 260 hectares that has doubled in size during the past twenty-five years. Production, which had varied between 4,000 and 6,000 hectoliters during the 1950s, now exceeds 15,000 hectoliters and is expected to increase soon to 20,000. (Total Cru Beaujolais production is shown in Figure 5.18.) The producing region, which dates back to the 10th century, is considered the "oldest" of the nine growths. A significant portion of the vineyard was owned by the Chapter of Saint Vincent of Mâcon in the 18th century, and historical accounts also verify that it was a staple wine for the Abbey of Cluny as early as the 14th century.

Because the producing region lies close to the southern margins of the Mâconnais, the soil contains some limestone; as a result the appellation is the largest single producer of white Beaujolais. Containing schist and sandstone as well as granite, the southern and eastern portions of the appellation are mainly planted in Gamay. The wines of St.-Amour, due to the variations in soil, are different from the other eight Grand Cru communes in that they are coarser, more variable, "hard" on the palate, and lack the softness, fragrance, and suppleness that is the hallmark of fine Beaujolais. The finest wine, containing 1 percent more alcohol than the rest, is said to originate from the hamlet of Bellevue. While the eastern portion of the appellation contains large vineyards on flatter, richer soil, the north section is hillier, and its vineyards are very fragmented. The vineyards with a considerable following are les Billards, le Clos, les Belouses, la Poulette, les Thevenins, les Breteaux, le Clos de Brosse, la Pirolette, and Champs Grilles. Some of the more important producers are *Dne. des Billards, Ch. St.-Amour* (by Piat), *Dne. du Paradis, Francis Saillant, M. Janin, Vins Mathelin, Paul Spay,* and *Finax Dervillaine.*

Juliénas, located to the south of St.-Amour on a series of fertile hills, is

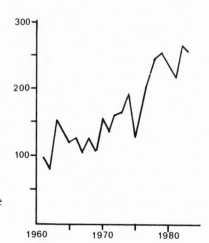

Figure 5.18   Cru Beaujolais: Wine Production, 1961–1983 (in thousands of hectoliters)

known for fatter, softer, spicier, sturdier, and darker-colored wines than its sister growth to the north. With 520 hectares and an output of 33,000 hectoliters, Juliénas is also a much larger vineyard than St.-Amour. Very old and very traditional, it is one of the more prosperous communes. It contains more than ten estates with 15 or more hectares of planted vines—a very unusual phenomenon in an area known for small, fragmented holdings. As vineyards straddle both sides of the narrow Mauvaise valley, the best of the individual sites, located on high ground facing south and southeast, are les Capitans, les Mouilles, la Bottière, les Chers, and Bucherots. Of the many producers, the following are all first class: *Dne. de Mouilles, Dne. de la Conseillere, Dne. de Beauvernay, Dne. de la Vieille Eglise, Ch. de Juliénas, Ch. de Capitans, André Pelleier, M.P. Poulachion, M.J. Perrachon, M. Foillard, Ernest Aujas, Louis Tête, Dne. des Poupets,* and *Vins Mathelin.* The *Cave Coopérative des Grands Vins de Juliénas,* an aggressive firm enjoying an above-average reputation, markets an agreeable wine under the label of Ch. du Bois de la Salle.

The town of *Chénas,* a 200-hectare vineyard producing 12,000 hectoliters, lies at the foot of a high, bow-shaped wooded hill sandwiched between Juliénas and Moulin-à-Vent. It is the smallest of the Grand Cru, in part because a good deal of the vineyard sites have the right to sell under the more prestigious Moulin-à-Vent appellation. Therefore, the best sites and the most intensely cultivated portions of the Chénas vineyard lie close to Moulin-à-Vent. Only the northeastern and western sections produce grapes that can be legally sold under the Chénas banner. All of the foregoing is of little consequence, however, as Chénas is a good wine. At its best, the wine is full, satisfying, of medium body, and capable of aging for four years, although wood-aged and estate bottlings have been known to last for as long as eight years. At its worst, it seems to lack the fruitiness and delicacy of Fleurie, and can, on occasion, be dull. *Dne. Champagnon, Ch. Bonnet, Dne. Chassignol. Ch. de Chénas, Pierre Perrachon, Emile Robin, Fernand Charvet, Ch. de Jean Loron, Cave du Château de Chênas, Charles Vienot, Dne. des Pins,* and *Paul Beaudet* all enjoy good reputations.

The indisputable king of the nine Grand Cru communes of Beaujolais is *Moulin-à-Vent.* It is the longest lived, most full-bodied, Burgundy-type wine of all—always rich and harmonious, with a depth of flavor and an explosive bouquet. It commands, and easily gets, higher prices than the other eight growths. Careful selection is necessary, however, since excessive demand and high prices have helped expand hectarage to less desirable vineland. With 700 hectares and more than 200 growers producing 35,000 hectoliters, Moulin-à-Vent is the fourth-largest appellation in Beaujolais. The staying power, dark color, concentrated flavor, and fragrance are all attributed to the peculiar nature of the soil in isolated areas within the producing region. In addition to granite rock, there are pockets of pink sandstone called "gres" that contain heavy accumulations of iron and manganese oxides. All the best sites lie on east-facing slopes and include les Thorins, le Moulin-à-Vent, la Roche, les Gros Vosges, les Carquelins, les Champs de Cour, la Tour du Bief, les Gimarets, la Rochelle and les Burdelines.

Among the many small estates and small growers, the following are considered above average: *Ch. du Moulin-à-Vent* (considered the standard for all Beaujolais), *Ch. des Jacques, Ch. Portier, Dne. de Champ de Cour, Dne. Sambin, Dne. de la Tour du Bief, Dne. Monrozier, Ch. des Gimarets, Jacques Depagneux, Dne. Jean-Marie Meziat, Raymond Siffert, Jean Brugne, Raymond Degrange, Dne. Desvignes, Marius Laforêt, Vigneronnage Picolet, Clos du Tremblay,* and *Dne. de la Rochelle.*

South of Chénas and Moulin-à-Vent lies *Fleurie,* the "land of flowers," the commune with the reputation for being the most perfumed and flowery of all Beaujolais—a wine locally described as "soft fruit." Of all the nine growths, this appellation is the most popular and probably the best known. Lighter in color and body than Moulin-à-Vent, the wine is characterized as supple, fruity, and very agreeable on the palate. Drained by two small streams, the producing area is quite hilly and in places very steep. With 770 hectares and an output of 40,000 hectoliters, Fleurie is the third-largest vineyard in the Beaujolais after Brouilly and Morgon. The best sites are located east, south, and west of the town and include les Moriers, Aux Quatre Vents, la Roilette, Au Rolet, la Biaune, le Vivier, le Garant, le Point-du-Jour, la Chapelle de Bois, and la Madonne. Fleurie is the first major casualty in an attempt to capitalize on the name of its famous appellation. The wine, historically light in color and body, supple, fruity, and very agreeable on the palate, has recently been debased by overcropping and the extention of the production area to undesirable land. *Cave Coopérative des Grands Vins de Fleurie, Dne. de la Grand Cour, Ch. de Fleurie, Dne. le Point du Jour, Bernard Paul, Chauvet Frères, Dne. de la Presle, Ch. des Bachelrads, Ch. des Deduits, M. Darroze, Logis du Vivier, Marcel Rollet,* and *Maurice Bruone* are among the better producers.

Southwest of Fleurie in the center of the Haut-Beaujolais, the exquisitely situated vineyard of *Chiroubles* lies on the side of a hill whose vineyards all face southeast. The highest of all the Grand Cru sites, its slopes are steep, and the soil is coarse and rocky. With 329 hectares and an output of 16,000 hectoliters, Chiroubles is the third-smallest in the region. The wine has excellent color but has maintained a reputation for being the lightest in body among the "big nine." Fruity, eminently drinkable, smooth, satisfying, with a faint taste of "terroir," it seldom lasts for more than three years. Bel-Air, Côte Rotie, les Côtes, le Bois, Bois de Chatenay, Grille-Midi, Temere, les Pres, Poulet, le Moulin, and les Rontets are considered first-rate vineyards. *Georges Passot, Dne. de Rausset, Dne. Cheysson-les-Farges, Ch. les Pres, Dne. du Moulin, Collin & Bourisset, Vins Mathelin, Vigneronage Durand, Ch. Javernand, René Bouil-*

lard, Jean-Pierre Desvignes, Jean Bedin, Philippe Govet, Jacques Depagneux, René Savoye, and *Christian Lafay* all enjoy above-average reputations.

With 983 hectares and an output of 60,000 hectoliters, *Morgon* is second to Brouilly in the production of Grand Cru Beaujolais. Although the appellation is dominated by the principal town of Villié-Morgon, there are three hamlets and a rather dense, widely scattered rural population along the hillsides of two small valleys. Unlike other Beaujolais villages, Morgon contains a schistous soil that is locally called *terre pourrie* ("rotten soil"). Well-drained with considerable gravel and sand, it produces wines that are described as "morgonne"-dark in color, full-bodied, tannin-rich, and capable of extended cellaring. While they are not as fruity as those of Fleurie and Chiroubles, they are highlighted by a distinct "cherry" and "terroir" flavor. Of all the Grand Cru sites, Morgon has shown the most consistent and rapid rate of growth within the past thirty years and, along with the wines of Moulin-à-Vent, enjoys an international clientele. South of Villié-Morgon lies the famous vineyard site of Mont du Py, of which les Gaudets, la Dependable, le Py, les Chintres, Aux Perrets, la Beche, and les Charmes are the most renowned. Of the many producers, the following have above-average reputations; *Ch. Gaillard, Jean Descombes, Ch. de Bellevue, Dne. du Py, Pasquier-Desvignes, Vigneronnage Jambon, Paul Collonge, Jean Ernest Demont, Louis Desvignes,* and *Louis Genillon.*

Separated by the small, meandering Ardière valley, the two southern-most Grand Cru communes of *Brouilly* and *Côtes de Brouilly* are not contiguous with the other seven. With more than 1,100 hectares, 460 growers, and an output of more than 70,000 hectoliters of wine, Brouilly is the largest of the nine growths. The extensive vineyard spreads over six different communes and covers nearly every square meter of Mount Brouilly, particularly the settlements of Odenas, St.-Lager, Cercié, Quincié, Charentay, and St.-Etienne-la-Varenne. Because of the large size of the producing unit and the prevalence of the *métayage* system, wine quality varies enormously and careful selection is absolutely essential. The wines of Cercié, for example, are the first to develop and lose their fruit; the wines of Odenas are richer, darker, and capable of aging; the wines of Quincié tend to be fruitier and more acidic than those of St.-Lager and Chartenay; and the wines of St.-Etienne-la-Varenne are coarse and not supple. The principal producers include *Cave Coopérative de Bel-Air, Ch. de la Chaize, Ch. de Pierreux, Ch. le Fouilloux, Dne. Cret des Garanches, J.-P. Ruet, Ch. des Tours, Ch. de Briante, Ch. de Ververs, André Large, Dne. de la Folie, Ch. St.-Lager, Claude Goeffray, Philippe Dutraive, André Ronzière,* and *Roger Verger.*

Côtes de Brouilly represents the weathered remains of an old volcanic porphyry plug. Nearly circular and forested at the summit, the middle and lower slopes are completely enveloped by vines. Despite the fact that it is not the highest elevation in the Haut-Beaujolais, its cone-shaped appearance represents the most spectacular physical aspect of all the Grand Cru vineyards. The best sites are located along the gentle slopes of the eastern boundary with Brouilly and include the vineyards of Bussières, Ecluse, le Pave, and les Ravatys. When compared with Brouilly, the Côtes de Brouilly wines have a deeper color, more body, more tannin, and higher alcohol. Its most distinctive characteristics are a rich, powerful bouquet and lingering flavor. Among the handful of above-average producers are *Lucien Verger, Jacques Depagneux, Dne. du Château Thivin, Ch. Delachanal, Mme. Veuve Joubert,* and *Alain Bernillon.*

The Wines of Coteaux du Lyonnais

As of 1984 the small, 9,000 hectoliter VDQS Coteaux du Lyonnais appellation has been upgraded to AOC status. While the appellation is known for red, rosé, and white wine, more than 95 percent of total output is red wine, not too dissimilar from Beaujolais, which it adjoins to the north. The principal grape varieties are Gamay à Jus Blanc and Chardonnay, but a good deal of non-AOC white wine is made from Aligoté. Nearly the whole of production emanates from vineyards in the southern portion of the Rhône department, north, south and west of the city of Lyon. Although most of the wine is made by the *Cave Coopérative Coteaux-du-Lyonnais, Robert Thollet* is considered by many as the standard for the production of young, fresh, early maturing wine, followed by *François Descotes, Pierre Jomard,* and *Lucien Boulieu.*

THE WINES OF THE RHÔNE

A LTHOUGH not well defined, the Rhône vineyard, stretching for
200 kilometers south from Vienne to the lower margins of the
Rhône, encompasses seven departments: Loire, Isère, Rhône,
Ardèche, Drôme, Gard, and Vaucluse. The first three are located in the
northern portion, but the last four, all in the south, are the most
important. The area includes more than 165 settlements with 12,000
growers. The 40,000 hectares of vineland produce between 2 and 3
million hectoliters of wine annually, or approximately 5 percent of the
national total. The region's eighteen AOC appellations contribute between 15 and 20 percent of all national AOC wine production and
represent, after the Gironde, the second-largest AOC area in the country.

For 200 kilometers between Lyon and Avignon, the vine is cultivated
on both banks of the Rhône River. Specific viticultural sites are influenced
by the element of shelter from the *Mistral* and other winds, exposure, and
type of soil. As a result, the wines of the Rhône vary from appellation to
appellation, vineyard to vineyard, even hillside to hillside. Because of its
geography, climate, and soils, the entire vineyard is divided into two
major zones. The northern Rhône, beginning just south of Vienne,
consists of tiny islands of greenery arranged in narrow ribbons on both
sides of the river (but primarily on the left bank), which continue at
irregular intervals as far south as Valence. These terraced vineyards, on
rocky soil derived from granite and limestone, are planted mainly in
Syrah, Roussanne, Marsanne, and Viognier vines. The finest red and
white wines are full-bodied, fragrant, flavorful, long-lived, and equal to
the best from other AOC appellations. Unfortunately they are little
known, underrated, undervalued, and overshadowed by Burgundy to the
north and Bordeaux to the west. The entire northern section produces

only 110,000 hectoliters, or about 4 percent of the Rhône valley's total wine output. Because the climate is more humid, the sun less intense, the average temperatures lower, the grape vines late-ripening, and the growing season more precarious, the wines contain less alcohol but are more complex and fragrant than those from the southern section of the producing valley.

Between Valence and Orange is a gap of 40 kilometers where no

Table 6.1   AOC Wine Production in the Rhône Valley, 1980

Appellation	Hectoliters	Percent of total
Northern Rhône		
Clairette de Die Blanc	46,489	2.0
Châtillon-en-Diois Rouge	1,330	
Châtillon-en-Diois Blanc	182	
Crozes-Hermitage Rouge	36,400	1.5
Crozes-Hermitage Blanc	4,383	.1
St.-Joseph Rouge	8,886	.4
St.-Joseph Blanc	683	
Hermitage Rouge	2,412	
Hermitage Blanc	2,170	
Côte-Rôtie Rouge	3,378	
St.-Péray Blanc	1,981	
Cornas Rouge	1,894	
Condrieu Blanc	367	
Château Grillet Blanc	116	
Total	110,671	4.7
Southern Rhône		
Côtes du Rhône Rouge	1,672,664	71.1
Côtes du Rhône Blanc	25,299	1.1
Côtes du Ventoux Rouge	169,044	7.2
Côtes du Ventoux Blanc	1,434	
Côtes du Rhône–Villages Rouge	99,505	4.3
Côtes du Rhône–Villages Blanc	1,915	
Châteauneuf-du-Pape Rouge	98,450	4.2
Châteauneuf-du-Pape Blanc	2,683	
Coteaux du Tricastin Rouge	66,700	2.8
Coteaux du Tricastin Blanc	420	
Gigondas Rouge	37,116	1.6
Tavel Rouge	35,411	1.5
Lirac Rouge	19,785	.8
Lirac Blanc	303	
Rasteau Rouge	156	
Rasteau Blanc	3,964	
Muscat de Beaumes-de-Venise Blanc	7,562	.3
Total	2,242,411	95.3
Grand total	2,353,082	100.0
Total Rouge	2,252,915	96.3

Source: French Ministry of Agriculture.

vineyards of significance are found. The southern Rhône vineyard, producing 95 percent of all Rhône wine, is found south of Orange where, due to the more variable microclimates, soil, and topography, the area makes a large number of wines from a much longer list of grape varieties than the northern producing district. The soils, mainly of glacial and fluvial origin, rest on former river and glacial terraces. Here the vines, "méridional" in character (early maturing, higher in sugar, and essentially non-aromatic), consistently produce wines with a higher alcohol content than the northern portion of the producing valley. Instead of Syrah dominating red wine production, Grenache Noir is the *cépage de base,* followed by a dozen others. Approximately 85 percent of the wine is red, 13 percent rosé, and less than 2 percent white.

The entire valley is drained by the Rhône, the only major river with a north-south axis. Originating in southwestern Switzerland, it flows through the Valais, enters France from Lake Léman, and then proceeds in a southwesterly course through a series of narrow gorges to join the Saône at Lyon. Between Vienne and Valence, six tributaries converge—Varèze, Dolon, Galaure, Herbasse, Isère, and Doux; and between Valence and Avignon the Lèz, Gard, Cèze, Bèrre, Ardèche, Drôme, Augues, Ouvèze, and Durance are found. To the east lie the Rhône-Alps, a region for freshwater sports, eighteen thermal water resorts, innumerable hydroelectric stations, and the largest concentration of public parks in the entire nation. To the west is the Massif Central, a large plateau covering one-seventh of the country's land area. With an average height of 1,000 meters, it is highest along the eastern margins where it is characterized by exposed limestone, scattered brush, and quick-flowing streams before it ends abruptly in the Rhône basin. Between these two formidable mountainous regions is the thin silver of the Rhône and its fifteen major tributaries. Throughout, vineyards are never located on moist, rich, floodplain soils, but on terraces and hillsides containing rocky, colluvial material, or areas of fluvial and glacial deposition. The extreme southern portions of the Gard and Vaucluse departments contain very fertile alluvial soil that produces all manner of fruit and vegetables on an extensive scale, but is marginal in the production of quality wine.

Despite the fact that the Rhône, dotted with Roman and medieval artifacts, has long been a major corridor for the north-south flow of ideas and people, the viticultural portion of the valley is generally an area of declining population, small, poor villages, and backwater pockets of isolated existence. Along the entire course, it has but four cities, of which Avignon is the largest in population, followed by Valence, Vienne, and Orange. Like a good portion of the Midi, the Rhône lacks energy resources, mineral wealth, and a solid industrial base. Its agricultural history has been one of vine, olive, fruit, and garden vegetable production of small dimensions, due to the lack of significant arable land, the availability of irrigated water, and the lack of proximity to large urban markets.

History

Because the Rhône is the only north-south valley in the country linking the Mediterranean Sea with northern France, it has served, throughout history, as the most important avenue for invasion. As a result, it breathes a continuous history of former civilizations. The Rhône, after the Midi and Provence, is widely considered to be the third-oldest vineyard in France. In the 6th century B.C., the Phocaean Greeks brought the vine and olive to the Rhône, and the Romans, who arrived in the 2nd century, quickly extended viticulture and founded all the largest settlements, including Orange, Vienne, Valence, Arles, Aix, and Nîmes. Under Roman domination, viticulture became so widespread that in the 1st century A.D. Emperor Diocletian ordered that vines be uprooted because wheat was more important. Roman artifacts, including countless outdoor theaters, aqueducts, arenas, and public monuments, are ubiquitous throughout the region. In the 5th century the Franks, a Germanic tribe who were to give France its name, overran large portions of eastern and southern France. Soon after, during the "monastic period" of French history, religious orders revived and maintained viticultural traditions, particularly during the reign of Clovis. The Benedictines established vineyards in Chusclan, St.-Péray, Gigondas, and Cornas; and the Cistercians in Gigondas and Vacqueyras. The isolated and religious orientation of the industry lasted through the crusading period, when the Knights Templars and other religious orders increased holdings throughout the region, especially in Châteauneuf-du-Pape and Cairanne.

The most eventful viticultural development occurred in the 14th century, when Pope Clement V moved the Papacy to Avignon. His successors furthered the cause of viticulture and raised, over the next three centuries, the name of Châteauneuf-du-Pape to the rank of a top French red wine-producing region. During the Wars of Religion in the 15th and 16th centuries, the region suffered from large-scale depopulation, the vineyards were destroyed, and those that survived were quickly abandoned. The industry recovered in the middle of the 19th century, only to be decimated by the *phylloxera* aphid in the 1870s. As vineyard rehabilitation after *phylloxera* was slow, the wines remained obscure and underpriced, the very best being used as *vin de medicin* to improve weak Burgundian libations. The devastating world depression of the 1930s was followed by a particularly bizarre governmental action during the Vichy administration of World War II when, in an effort to make the region more self-sufficient, close to 16,000 hectares of vineland were plowed under and planted in wheat and other crops. Since 1950 the wines of the

Rhône and, in particular, the Côtes du Rhône and Côtes du Rhône–
Villages appellations have experienced unparalleled growth.

Climate and Soils

The variable climate of the Rhône is a combination of continental and
Mediterranean influences and, since it is sheltered by the Massif Central,
it experiences minimal maritime weather activity. While the entire region
is characterized by significant annual and diurnal temperature extremes,
erratic and torrential rainfall, brilliant sunshine, summer drought, and
violent winds, the northern and southern vineyards experience subtle but
distinct differences. In general, the area north of Valence is dominated by
continental air masses, which produce a climate similar to that of
Burgundy with a natural vegetation pattern of broadleaf deciduous forest.
Here winters are longer, colder, and drier, and the lifecycle of the vine is
more precarious than areas south of Valence where the full impact of
Mediterranean weather emerges: walled towns located on hilltops, tiled
roofs, xerophytic and less dense vegetation, a longer, drier summer, and
shorter, milder winters. The north is more foggy and colder, with wider
annual fluctuations in temperature and a more even distribution of
precipitation during the year. The fewer than 200 sunny, dry days in the
Côte-Rôtie are replaced in the south by a Mediterranean climatic pattern
of sunny skies and reduced humidity that dominates the weather patterns
for more than 260 days.

The principal wind in the Rhône valley is the *Mistral,* which is bitterly
cold in winter and warm and arid in summer. A dense, katabatic wind
that forms in the upper, exposed elevations of the French Alps and the
Massif Central, it flows toward the Mediterranean Sea. To combat its
lower temperatures in winter and increased evaporation rate in summer,
house entrances face south rather than north, the animal population is
reduced, and commercial agriculture is sheltered by windbreaks. The
Mistral blows annually for about 80 days in the northern section and
between 100 and 125 days in the southern portion of the valley,
sometimes for days at a time. Because it is a dry, dense, air mass, it hugs
the river bottom as it flows southward and rarely rises more than 100
meters from the level of the Rhône. Therefore, a large number of
vineyards remain unaffected by the *Mistral* because, although unpro-
tected, they are situated above the flow of the coldest and densest portion
of the moving air mass.

The Rhône vineyard soils vary from colluvial debris in hilly regions, to
fluvial and glacially deposited stone on former river terraces, to clay
deposits in low-lying areas. A good portion of the northern vineyards lie
on hilly terrain with granite- and limestone-derived soils; few, if any, are
situated on alluvial material. In the southern portion of the producing

valley the soils are more complex than along the narrower northern section. There the Rhône and its tributaries have eroded surface stone into terraces. In places, local relief is sharp and the loose, unconsolidated material clinging to hillsides is well drained. Soils in general are stony, sandy and, because of a complicated geologic history, multivarigated without uniform patterns, which explains the large number of appellations and the diversity of wines made in this area.

THE NORTHERN RHÔNE APPELLATIONS

The northern Rhône vineyard includes the appellations of Côte-Rôtie, Château Grillet, Condrieu, St.-Joseph, Hermitage, Crozes-Hermitage, Cornas, St.-Péray, Clairette de Die, and Châtillon-en-Diois, the last two located in the Drôme valley southeast of Valence on the lower margins of the French Alps. In addition, minor hectarage devoted to the production of Côtes du Rhône and Côtes du Rhône–Villages lies mostly to the east of Cornas, St.-Péray, and the hilly locations of St.-Joseph. Collectively, this northern vineyard is little known because its limited production and hectarage represent only 4 percent and 5 percent, respectively, of the entire Rhône valley. Its annual production, between 100,000 and 125,000 hectoliters, approximates that of Châteauneuf-du-Pape or the Haut-Médoc. What it lacks in size, however, it more than makes up in quality; the northern Rhône consistently produces the Rhône valley's finest red and white table wines. Therefore, the wines are extremely scarce and very expensive in foreign markets, but are worth seeking out. While Condrieu and Château Grillet are outrageously priced and offer little value, white Hermitage, still reasonably priced and extremely durable, offers outstanding value among dry, white table wines. Côte-Rôtie, of which only 40,000 cases are produced in an average year, is not only the finest red wine in the Rhône but rivals the finest Bordeaux and Burgundian growths.*

Grapes and Wines

Red AOC wine production in the northern Rhône is totally dominated by the Syrah vine. It is overwhelmingly concentrated in Côte-Rôtie, St.-Joseph, Hermitage, Crozes-Hermitage, and Cornas, where it constitutes more than three-quarters of the total planted area. The element of concentration is directly associated with the Syrah's affinity to granitic and limestone soils; hence, its principal area of localization is Côte-Rôtie and Hermitage where it has adapted well to the rocky, well-drained soils of both appellations. The small, thick-skinned berry, full of tannin, pig-

* For comparison, 1 hectoliter = 100 liters = 26.4 U.S. gallons = 11 cases (or 9 liters per case).

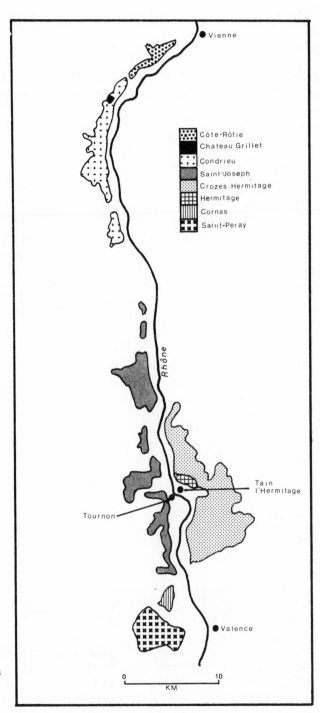

Figure 6.1
The Northern
Rhône AOC
Appellations

mentation, essence, and flavor, produces wines that are known for their dark color, pronounced aroma, bouquet, and assertive flavor of cherry, raspberry, and violet. The wine in its youth is hard, chewy, unyielding, austere, and astringent, but after ten to fifteen years of bottle-aging it becomes a sublime libation rivaling any in France. Unlike other Rhône grapes, the Syrah is very consistent in its ability to produce excellent wine.

Although not extensive in hectarage, the two principal quality white grapes of the northern Rhône are the Marsanne and Roussanne. The former, much the better vine and widely planted because it is more resistant to disease, is hardy, vigorous, and a high yielder—features that make this grape far more attractive than the Viognier and Roussanne. The Marsanne, the essential ingredient in the production of the best Hermitage and Crozes-Hermitage, is also the base for St.-Péray and St.-Joseph. When well made, the wine is big, powerful, full of flavor and scent, and is one of the longest-lived white wines of France. The Roussanne, like the Viognier, is a fragile grape, prone to disease and, because it does not age as well as the Marsanne, used as a blending wine.

The third-most-important white grape is the Viognier. A very difficult vine to grow, it has the capacity to give low yields of intensely flavored and scented wine. One of the better "fossil" grapes, it has adapted well to one small corner of the northern Rhône, where its cultivation is almost exclusively confined to Condrieu and Château-Grillet. Although now subjected to overcropping and not as concentrated and flavorful as it once was, it remains one of the most unusual and expensive of all French white wines. Another white vine is the Rousette, a minor but growing element in the production of still and sparkling white wine in St.-Péray and St.-Joseph. It is much more prevalent than people realize or growers are willing to admit. Other white grapes include Clairette, Villard Blanc, Aligoté, and Chardonnay.

Côte-Rôtie

The importance of Côte-Rôtie as a quality viticultural region has been known ever since the Phocaean Greeks established a colony on what is the small village of Ampuis. This appellation, located south of Vienne on the left bank of the Rhône, is centered on the small village of Ampuis and two additional hamlets: Tupin-Semons and St.-Cyr-sur-Rhône. The vineyards lie on two hills to the west and north of Ampuis whose combined hectarage is but 100. Their total production varies between 2,500 and 4,500 hectoliters, or the same as a large Bordeaux property (see Fig. 6.2).

Only two grapes are grown, the Syrah and Viognier, both of which were introduced in the region, it is said, by the Phocaean Greeks. The Syrah, staked on four posts to increase exposure, prevent rot, and shade the grapes, is a low-yielding, fragile, tender vine that is very sensitive to

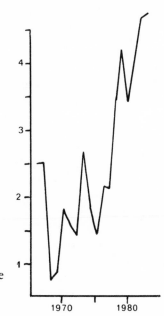

Figure 6.2   Côte-Rotie: Wine
Production, 1966–1984
(in thousands of hectoliters)

the ferocity of the *Mistral*. Two different vines are recognized—the Petite Syrah and the Grosse Syrah. Although the latter has a heavier yield, the Petite Syrah, as the name suggests, has a smaller berry which makes the higher quality wine. Although up to 15 percent of Viognier grapes may be added for finesse, the actual percentage varies according to the vintage, with most quality-oriented producers adding no more than 10 percent or even none at all. The Viognier, an uncertain producer, dislikes clay soils and hence prefers the lighter Côte Blonde rather than the Côte Brune that supports the Syrah. It produces a comparatively long-lived wine and, when added in small quantities to Syrah, it adds considerable complexity to the final blend. Because it produces a wine with a hint of pine in it, its use is a matter of contemporary debate, the actual amount used being a function of vigneron preference and the character of the vintage.

The Syrah produces full-bodied, elegant wine, highly concentrated in extract, perfectly balanced, and with an uncanny ability to age magnificently. It has a deep ruby color, a strong penetrating scent of violet, and a savory flavor of spice and blackcurrant that makes it an ideal accompaniment to game and tangy cheese. Côte-Rôtie when young is austere and forbidding, but after ten to fifteen years of bottle-aging it loses its harshness and develops into an assertive, generous wine filled with blackcurrant flavor. Improving with age as no other Rhône, it is one of the most durable wines in the entire country. Certainly the biggest of all Rhône red wines, it rivals, and usually offers better value than, Grand Cru Burgundies. For the ideal, comprehensive cellar, a case or two of good

Côte-Rôtie is imperative. Since the steep slopes, not suitable for mechanization, are costly to maintain, the wine is scarce and always expensive.

Three specific geographic elements make Côte-Rôtie an unusual wine-producing region. The first is the nature of the granitic soil, which has small infusions of *limon,* micaschist, limestone, slate, and gneiss. Second, the vineyards are located on south-facing terraces, with the best sites located on high, ventilated exposures that create an effective suntrap; because of the elevation, gentle breezes mitigate the negative effects of frequent fog and mist. These conditions are maximized on two hills appropriately called, from the color of their soil, "Côte Brune" and "Côte Blonde." The former, containing clay rich in iron oxide, produces tannin-rich, long-lived wines, while the latter, because of limestone accumulations, makes lighter, faster-maturing wine. Third, Côte-Rôtie cultivates the original Syrah vine and not the more productive clones widely planted in other areas. The original produces, besides lower yields, a superior, more consistent fragrance, softer tannins, higher extract due to a smaller grape berry, and more concentrated flavors.

All the foregoing refers to the original 48-hectare vineyard where individual plots were fragmented into small, narrow, discontinuous terraces whose rocky soil was held in check by walls locally called *murgets.* Over the past fifteen years, however, thanks to ever-rising prices and an insatiable demand, the original boundaries have been expanded to include an additional 52 hectares, thus doubling the planted area and nearly tripling total output. Because the expanded area lies on a plateau to the west of Ampuis, it is widely considered to be a less desirable area due to richer, more productive soils with poor exposure. The "old guard" maintain that sugar levels from those grapes are lower and the resulting wines less concentrated and incapable of extended cellaring. Although vineyard names are rarely displayed on labels, the following are considered above average in the production of quality wine: in the Côte Blonde, la Mouline, les Clos, and la Châtillone; in the Côte Brune, la Chevalière, la Côte Boudin, la Châtillonne, la Viria, la Turque, la Pommière, and la Landonne.

A true democracy, Côte-Rôtie lacks the pretense of elaborate château or majestic domaines and contains fewer than twenty-six small growers, none of whom cultivates more than 8 hectares, and the majority cultivating smaller than a 1-hectare plot. The wines, which vary in quality and style, are extremely hard to find because an overwhelming number are sold to smart restaurants and private clients. The following dominate production and are most often encountered in foreign markets. *E. Guigal,* property owner and negociant, is widely considered the leader in the production of Côte-Rôtie and fine Rhône wines. The house make Côte-Rôtie Blonde and Brune, la Mouline, and la Landonne, all of which are consistently well made and absolutely marvelous. La Mouline, in particular, because of its dark color, tannin, impressive, overpowering flavor and bouquet, should rank among the finest wines of France. *Pierre Barge* is a small producer making average to above-average wines portrayed by a full, spicy, tannin-rich, robust character. *Robert Jasmin,* a well-known and respected vigneron, makes fewer than 2,000 cases of wine from less than 4 hectares. Above average in quality, the wines are supple, well flavored, often sublime, early maturing, and expensive. *Vidal-Fleury* (now part of Guigal), the oldest and largest property holder in the Côte-Rôtie, makes 3,000 cases from 8 hectares in the Côte Blonde and Brune, all of which are much lighter in body than formerly and very expensive. *A. and L. Drevon* own less than 3 hectares and make 1,200 cases of excellent, wood-aged, alcoholic, spicy, complex wines. *Dne. Marius Gentraz-Dervieux* is a small house that owns less than 1 hectare and produces outstanding *vin de garde* wine.

Dne. A. Dervieux is a 3-hectare property that makes exceptional wine from 100 percent Syrah. Mainly found in stylish restaurants, these excellent *vin de garde* wines should not be missed. *Paul Jaboulet,* the largest negociant firm, makes one of the finest wines in the appellation: les Jumelles, a wine known for its longevity, rich taste, and long, lingering finish. *R. Rostaing,* a small house known for distinctive Côte Brune, makes very spicy, tannin-rich wines. *Emile Champet* is a small house that makes soft, forward, appealing wine that lacks the consistency of Guigal. *Dne. Gerin,* located in a small hamlet near Ampuis, makes 3,000 cases of below-average to average wine. Other growers include *George Vernay, Edmond Duclaux, Chol, Joseph Jamet, L. de Vallouit, Bernard Burgaud, A. Gerin,* and *Jean Clusel. Max Chapoutier* and *Delas Frères,* two large negociant houses, distribute average-quality wines offering good value.

Condrieu and Château Grillet

Just south of the Côte-Rôtie appellation are Condrieu and Château Grillet, two tiny vineyards whose combined hectarage is a miserly 17 hectares. Condrieu, with 14 hectares, takes its name from a small, unpretentious village founded by a migrating Swiss tribe during the early Middle Ages. Château Grillet is an enclave within Condrieu, but maintains a more celebrated history. Only the Viognier grape is allowed for both. With yields restricted to 30 hectoliters (32 for Château Grillet), the vines are confined to the granite, gneiss, and micaschist soils that weather into a powder locally called *arzelle.* Due to topographic irregularity, the entire producing district is scattered in four small settlements: Condrieu, Verin, St.-Michel-sur-Rhône, and Limony. The two appellations produce white wine that is intensely flavored and scented, highly concentrated, rich, and very distinctive.

Château Grillet, a 3-hectare vineyard that attained AOC status in 1936, has the distinction of being the smallest AOC appellation in the Rhône valley. The wine is made solely from the Viognier Doré, considered to be a superior clone. The vineyard, between 170 and 250 meters in elevation, overlaps the parishes of Vérin and St.-Michel. The *Neyret-Gachet* family, the sole owner of Château Grillet since 1825, has enlarged its dimensions from 1.7 hectares in 1971 to 2.3 hectares in 1977, and to 3 hectares in 1982. Production is about 10,000 bottles annually. Sold in a distinctive brown bottle, the wine has a marvelous flavor and an outstanding finish. Very alcoholic in great years, it is ideal at four to six years but begins to deteriorate after its eighth birthday. It is said to be marginally better than Condrieu, but it takes a great nose and a highly sophisticated palate to distinguish between the two. Aged in wood for as long as 18 months, the wine, very light in color, turns dark gold and amber with time. The bouquet varies, with faint nuances of nut, honey, honeysuckle, and apricots. Château Grillet is equated with high prices and the finest Montrachet and Sauternes.

The Condrieu vineyard is widely scattered and divided among two dozen growers, all of whom are part-time farmers. Condrieu is made in two styles, dry and half-dry, but the former dominates production and is by far the better. A remarkable wine, full-bodied yet supple, with a strong scent of violets, fruit, and nuts, it is absolutely magnificent with rich paté, fowl or strong cheese. While Château Grillet is the more expensive wine, both sell for two to three times the price of a white Hermitage, and it is debatable whether either offers better value. *Georges Vernay,* the largest grower in Condrieu with nearly 8 hectares, makes fresh, well-balanced, crisp, but expensive wine. The Coteaux de Vernon Condrieu, made from a small plot of old vines, is a premium, complex cuvée of consequence. *E. Guigal* makes an outstanding Condrieu—full-bodied, highly scented, well flavored, and drinkable almost immediately. *Pierre Dumazet* makes a rich, highly complex wine that offers outstanding value. *André Dézormeaux* and *Ch.-du-Rozay* both make luscious, barrel-fermented, fat, complex wines. Slightly less fine, but well above average in quality, are the wines of *Jean Pinchon, Pierre Perret, Robert Jurie-des-Camiers,* and *Delas Frères.*

St.-Joseph

A 610-hectare appellation, St.-Joseph makes more than 15,000 hectoliters of wine, 90 percent of which is red. The producing region, stretching over 50 kilometers along the western bank of the Rhône, encompasses more than twenty villages, of which St.-Désirat, Chavanay, Châteaubourg, Mauves, Tournon, and St.-Jean-de-Muzols are the most important, particularly the last three. The appellation has grown rapidly over the past thirty years from fewer than 200 hectares in 1965 to more than 610 in 1985. Historically, fruit trees, particularly cherry and apricot, provided employment, and until recently vines were considered a secondary cash crop.

Soils are a mixture of granite, sand, and clay. The latter is found mainly in the less desirable, low-lying areas, and the best sites are located in more hilly locations. As the principal sites do not enjoy the superior aspect of Hermitage, the wines, although less aromatic, refined, and elegant, tend to be fruitier and early maturing. Red wines are made from Syrah, with an added 10 percent maximum of Marsanne and Roussanne to lighten and "freshen" the otherwise *vin de mauve* wine, as good St.-Joseph is called. It is an easy, uncomplicated wine, excellent for light stews and grilled meat, particularly chicken. In most instances, it is ready to drink by its fourth year, although excellent vintages can last for as long as ten years. White wine, made principally from Marsanne with small additions of Roussanne, is light and refreshing, but can often be flat, heavy on the palate, oxidized, and not the equal of white Hermitage or even St.-Péray, although there are exceptions. Recently, a number of growers and the main cooperatives have increased production of sparkling wine.

The largest producers in the appellation are the cooperatives of St.-Désirat and Ruoms, both of which make at least 60 percent of the appellation's total output and have experimented with carbonic maceration techniques in an effort to produce light, supple, fruity wines. The largest private producer, *Bernard Gripa,* owns a domaine of nearly 14 hectares in St.-Joseph and St.-Péray. The highly fragrant, fruity and flavorful wine is aged for one year in wood and exhibits *vin de garde* features. White wine made from Marsanne is less good. *Pierre Coursodon,* with 7 fragmented hectares, is known for robust, full-bodied, strapping red wine capable of extended bottle-aging; the white, given some barrel-aging, is considered one of the best in the appellation. The red and white wines of *Jean-Louis Grippat* are well made, soft, and supple, and offer excellent value. *Raymond Trollot,* considered a standard in the appellation, makes superlative fruity, well-flavored red wine. Other producers include *Jean-Louis Chave, Maurice Courbis, Delas Frères, M. Chapoutier,* and *Paul Jaboulet,* the latter known for the superb Le Grand Pompée.

Crozes-Hermitage

Surrounding Hermitage is the 850-hectare Crozes-Hermitage appellation. Widely dispersed north, south, and east of Hermitage, it encompasses the communes of Crozes, Tain, Chanon-Curson, Beaumont-Monteux, Larnage, Erôme, Mercurol, Gervans, Roche-de-Gum, Serves, and Pont-de-l'Isère. Gervans (located on steep, well-exposed slopes), and Mercurol enjoy the best reputations for quality wine production. Although Crozes-Hermitage is not as illustrious as its more famous neighbors, vine hectarage has nearly doubled over the past thirty years and will probably increase to 1,000 hectares by the end of this century. The principal focal point for the wine trade in the northern Rhône is Tain, a town known in the engineering world for the first suspension bridge, originally constructed in 1824, joining it with Tournon across the river.

Soils in Crozes-Hermitage are variable, with chalk and clay being more prevalent in the north, and sand and clay dominating in the southern portions of the producing region. The vineyards occupy less favorable exposures than Hermitage and are located on flatter land that is poorly drained. This explains why the wines, although made from the same grapes, are not as concentrated or flavorful as those of Hermitage and Côte-Rôtie.

Syrah (with small additions of Marsanne) is the dominant grape for the production of red wines that are similar in character to other northern Rhône wines. But the tendency today is to vinify more and more by carbonic maceration and to produce fruitier, lighter-colored, and shorter-lived wines than formerly. Although similar to Hermitage, the wine lacks complexity and depth and, on the whole, is rather dull. It varies enormously in quality because there is no consensus on what good Crozes-Hermitage is supposed to taste like. Therefore, fermentation techniques, aging, and handling practices vary significantly by producer and negociant. The final product can either be supple and fruity in style, or similar to classic Hermitage. In the former category are *Dne. de Thalabert, Dne. des Ramizières,* and *Dne. St.-Jemms,* all of which like to limit their barrel-aging to six months or less. In sharp contrast, *Albert Bégot* and *Raymond Roure* age their wines in wood for up to three years, which reduces the fruit content of the finished product significantly. Although not common knowledge, those wines that are traditionally made are just as age-worthy as Hermitage, especially those that are unfiltered and not heavily fined. It is unfortunate that instability, a common problem, makes a good percentage of total output murky and cloudy. Lacking the history, romance, and propaganda of other more famous names, the wines remain obscure in the United States, but they often offer good value because they are reasonably priced. Approximately 3,500 hectoliters (or 10 percent of total output) is white wine produced mainly from the Marsanne vine. Light yellow in color, fresh, dry, and nutty in flavor, it is modestly priced, but does not compare with the finest white wines of Hermitage in terms of flavor, scent, or balance.

Most of the wine is made by four negociant firms (*Paul Jaboulet, Max Chapoutier, Delas Frères,* and *Léon Revol*), and *Cave Coopérative de Vins Fins,* the largest producer. Important private producers include *Dne. Pradelle, Dne. St.-Jemms, Albert Bégot, Raymond Roure, Tardy and Ange, Jules Fayolle, Robert Rousset, Bernard Bied,* and *L. de Vallouit.*

Hermitage

Hermitage, the only quality appellation lying along the right bank of the Rhône, is a 150-hectare vineyard producing between 4,000 and 5,000 hectoliters of wine, of which one-quarter is white. Although wine was made here since the Roman occupation, serious commercial production did not take place until 1224 (so the locals say), when the legendary knight Gespard de Sterimberg established vineyards. Local folklore notwithstanding, the wine of Hermitage was little known until Louis XII served it at Versailles in 1642. Demand and fame soon soared; Hermitage, sold to many royal courts throughout Europe, became the favorite of Alexandre Dumas, many Czars, and English kings. It was widely used to fortify Burgundy, and by 1860 more than half of all Hermitage was sold in Bordeaux for the same purpose. Its demand on the eve of the *phylloxera* epidemic was so high that it was one of the most expensive wines of France. Of the 150 hectares, the negociant houses of Paul Jaboulet, Max Chapoutier, and Delas Frères own or control 80, Jean-Louis Chave 10, and Henri Sorrel 4; the remaining 56 hectares are fragmented among 82 other growers. Thus it is interesting to note that with half of the entire vineyard owned by three large negociant firms, prime vineland in Hermitage is very scarce. Moreover, the entire planted area, within reasonable limits, cannot be extended by more than 5 percent from present levels, although there have been repeated attempts to do just that in recent years.

Hermitage, named after a crusading knight who retired as a hermit, is a 300-meter block of granite that is geologically the eastern extension of the Massif Central. The quite small producing vineyard, barely measuring one-half by one kilometer, begins on the northern edge of Tain and spreads over the entire south-facing portion of the "Hermitage" hill. The entire stone monolith, devoid of any tree vegetation, stands totally naked except for grape vines and stone walls. The soil is granite with a thin mantle of sand, with only the eastern portion containing limestone suitable for white wine production. The entire vineyard is superbly positioned to the south and is completely sheltered from cold northerly winds. Although rarely used on labels, the most prominent vineyard sites (called *mas*) are les Bessards, le Méal, les Greffieux, la Chapelle, les Murets, la Croix, l'Homme, la Pierrelle, le Gros de Vignes, l'Ermite, and la Varogne. Les Bessards, located in the extreme western section, produces dark, tannin-rich wine; le Méal, its immediate neighbor, contains more chalk and makes decidedly lighter, raspberry-scented wine. Les Greffieux, near the bottom of the slope, and la Chapelle, near the top, both maintain above-average reputations. For white wine, the best sites are les Murets (known for fine, elegant wine), les Rocoules (for fruity and nutty-flavored wine), and Chante Alouette (for robust, nervous, zesty wine); the latter is not an individual site but is part of le Méal.

Red Hermitage is made from Syrah, a maximum of 15 percent Marsanne, and minute quantities of Roussanne. The best wines, certainly those that are *vin de garde* libations, are usually made from 100 percent Syrah, with perhaps traces only of the glycerine-rich Marsanne. Unlike Côte-Rôtie, Hermitage does not permit the white Viognier, a curious departure since the microclimate and soils are similar. Minimum alcohol strength is 10 percent, and the yield is limited to 40 hectoliters to the hectare. Usually the wine is alcoholic (13%), rich, mouth-filling, and well-scented with a noticeable touch of wood, complex, and full-bodied. This makes it one of the longest-lived wines of the Rhône and just a shade less elegant than Côte-Rôtie. Quality is consistently high, and the wine regularly offers excellent value in foreign markets.

White Hermitage is made from Marsanne with small infusions of Rousanne, usually from areas that have heavier accumulations of clay derived from limestone, chalk, and flint. It is golden in color, full-bodied, dry, and often hard, but the best bottles are well balanced and very impressive in the magnitude of their bouquet and multilayered flavors on the palate. Because of its comparatively high alcohol and glycerine content, white Hermitage is one of the longest-lived white wines of France. It is a perfect accompaniment for grilled meat such as chicken, pork, or fish. Never a "summer wine" nor one for casual sipping, white Hermitage, because of its full and powerful character, is the classic "winter" white—perhaps like no other. Over the past ten years, all premium white Hermitage has been moderately priced and, as such, offers better value than weak, watery, low-acid white Burgundy at three times the price. Among the top producers, Paul Jaboulet, Jean-Louis Chave, Jean-Louis Grippat, and Max Chapoutier are very reliable.

Max Chapoutier is the largest owner of Hermitage, the second biggest in the Côte-Rôtie, and among the largest in Crozes-Hermitage. Founded in 1808, the firm owns more than 71 hectares and is one of the largest negociant houses in the Rhône, known for big, powerful, traditionally made wines. La Sizeranne is the principal quality red wine and Chante Alouette the white, both of which are outstanding. The house of *Paul Jaboulet,* founded in 1834, has established a good reputation over the years for quality wine production, particularly for Hermitage. Two outstanding wines are Chevalier de Sterimberg (a white wine) and la Chapelle, one of the finest red wines of the Rhône that can be described only in superlatives. *Delas Frères,* one of the three largest northern Rhône negociants, is a major vineland owner in several appellations and part of the Champagne Deutz group. Most of the wines are good, sound, average to above-average in quality, and underrated. The small but good negociant firm of *Léon Revol* also offers an excellent line of red and white Hermitage.

The following are among the most important of the small private producers. *Dne. Jean-Louis Chave,* a winemaking family through five generations, is considered the standard in the appellation. From 7 hectares the house makes a superb *vin de garde* wine that is worth the asking price and should be part of any serious cellar. *Bernard Faurie* is a small quality-minded house known for full-bodied, traditionally made red, and fresh, crisp, well-flavored white wines that offer good value. *Jules Fayolle* is a little-known small grower who produces first-class wine that is big, powerful, and some of the finest in the appellation. Equally good and reliable is *E. Guigal,* known for rich, flavorful wines. *Henri Sorrel* is a small grower who makes above-average red and white wines from 4 hectares. *Jean-Louis Grippat,* a good-sized grower with interests in several neighboring appellations, makes outstanding white and spicy, flavorful red wines. *Dne. des Remizières, Jean and Michel Ferraton,* and *Terrance Gray* are three additional growers with good reputations.

Cornas

A small village with a viticultural history that goes back to the 9th century, Cornas lies across the Rhône River from Valence and adjoins the St.-Péray appellation to the south. With 81 hectares and an annual output of 2,500 hectoliters, Cornas is the third-smallest appellation in the northern Rhône. Present hectarage, more than double the 1938 planted area, is still significantly less than the 350 hectares it occupied on the eve of the *phylloxera* epidemic. The wines of Cornas are all red and made entirely from the Syrah. The minimum alcohol content is 10.5 percent, and the yield is restricted to 35 hectoliters to the hectare. What makes Cornas a unique vineyard is the fact that the area is well sheltered from the Mistral, which produces a microclimate that is a tiny air pocket of above-average temperature. This condition enhances grape berry maturation in a consistent and predictable manner, yielding wine that is full-bodied, concentrated, and high in alcohol. Second, the soils are not homogeneous but a combination of granitic stone, scattered limestone, chalk, sand, and clay, all of which are very dry and pale in color, providing the origin of the name from the ancient Celtic word for "burnt earth."

The combination of higher than normal temperatures, excellent exposure, and variable soils produces a highly alcoholic wine capable of extended aging. It is also dark in color, well structured, fruity, flavorful, and concentrated in extract. The very best *vin de garde*-type wines, from areas where granite dominates, are characterized by a pleasant raspberry flavor and aroma. Because the wines are underrated and so little known, they offer excellent value. Eight growers—*Delas Frères, Auguste Clape, Robert Michel, Alain Voge, Marcel Juge, Jean Lionnet, Noël Verset,* and *Guy de Barjac*—all above-average quality producers, own close to 50 percent of the planted area and produce most of the wine.

St.-Péray

St.-Péray, the most southerly of the "River appellations," is situated west of Valence and below Cornas on the left bank of the Rhône. It takes its name from the principal village of the region, St.-Péray, located at the foot of the medieval castle of Crussol. Unlike its neighbors to the north, St.-Péray produces only white wine, 75 percent of which is mousseux made by the *méthode champenoise.* It is made from 90 percent Marsanne, 10 percent Roussanne, and minute amounts of the controversial Roussette. The yield is limited to 40 hectoliters to the hectare, and the minimum alcohol content is 10 percent. The soil, unlike most other sparkling and white wine regions, contains granite, clay, and sand, with only small amounts of limestone, a significant factor in the distinctive flavor and aroma of the wine.

The mousseux is light, fruity, crisp, and refreshing, but not above average quality. Its reputation is much larger than it warrants because it is the only one made along the Rhône. Golden-yellow in color, it has a pronounced *goût de terroir,* with a long, respectable finish. The tart and unreliable still wine is not the equal of Hermitage or even Châteauneuf-du-Pape. Of the more than twenty growers, four control more than 50 percent of the hectarage. The most important, *Jean-François Chaboud,* is widely recognized as the leader in quality production. Additional names include *Darona Père, Auguste Clape, Alain Voge, René Milliand, Jean Teysseire,* and *Paul Etienne Père.*

Clairette de Die

A 1,200-hectare vineyard, Clairette de Die is almost unknown in France and unheard of in traditional export markets despite the fact that it is the third-largest AOC appellation in the Rhône and the fourth-largest producer of AOC sparkling wine made by the *méthode champenoise.* The 2,000-year-old town of Die, 60 kilometers southeast of Valence along the foothills of the French Alps, is an obscure white wine region making more than 50,000 hectoliters of respectable mousseux.

Die is a small, medieval, stone and ceramic-tiled village, whose only claim to fame is Hannibal's sojourn across the Alps. The producing region lies in the middle valley of the Drôme, an alpine tributary of the Rhône, where most vineyards are situated near the valley floor, framed by bare mountains and lavender-clad foothills. The dominant soil is derived from limestone, chalk, and clay. Upstream from Die are four important vinegrowing communes: Barnave, Châtillon, St.-Romain, and Menglon; downstream are the communes of Aurel, Barsac, Espenel, Saillans, and Vercheny. The most important economic activity is vinegrowing, and the local cooperative is the principal employer of the region. Of the 500 growers widely distributed in thirty-two villages and hamlets, 350 sell their grapes to the cooperative.

While the Clairette de Die vineyard has been making wine since Ror. .n times, sparkling wine was not made in large commercial quantities until the second half of this century. Clairette de Die, despite its inference to the Clairette grape, is made primarily from Muscat Blanc à Petits Grains when Demi-Sec, and from Clairette grape for Brut. More than 50 percent of total output is made in a Demi-Sec style, heavily scented with Muscat and not altogether trivial. The Brut style, made lighter in color with a more subdued Muscat flavor and aroma, is surprisingly refreshing and characterized with excellent carbonation. More than 80 percent of total production is made by *Cave Coopérative de Die,* a highly energetic firm that has done much to revitalize the regional economy. *Buffardel Frères,* a small producer, is known for meticulous, well-crafted wines that deserve to be better known.

Châtillon-en-Diois

The 65-hectare Châtillon-en-Diois appellation centered around a small number of villages southeast of Die is totally surrounded by the Clairette de Die–producing region. The appellation produces red, rosé, and white wines, almost all made by the Die cooperative. Although closer to Hermitage and other northern Rhône vineyards, the wines of Châtillon-en-Diois have a decided Burgundian orientation, since the red and rosé are made from Gamay and the white from Aligoté and Chardonnay. Because it is fuller and the more flavorful of the three, red wine appears to generate the most interest. Until the producing area became an AOC appellation in 1974, the red wines were called "Côtes du Bez" after a small local stream.

THE SOUTHERN RHÔNE APPELLATIONS

The southern Rhône vineyard of thirteen appellations produces approximately 96 percent of all wine in the Rhône valley, three-quarters of which is Côtes du Rhône and Côtes du Rhône–Villages, followed by Côtes du Ventoux, Châteauneuf-du-Pape, and Coteaux du Tricastin.

While grape varieties are more varied in the southern Rhône than in the northern portion of the producing region, AOC hectarage in the south is dominated by Grenache Noir for the production of both red and rosé wines. In its northernmost area of penetration in France, Grenache Noir is limited to those areas that exhibit hot, dry, and windy microclimates. Grenache Noir, plus minor plantings of Grenache Gris and Blanc, is the base for all southern quality red and rosé, including the famed Châteauneuf-du-Pape. Its main attributes are its ability to adapt to the Mediterranean climate and to produce high yields, its uncanny propensity to blend well with other grapes, and its high alcohol levels. Furthermore, because of its low color intensity, it is ideal for the production of rosé wine. Its main disadvantages are low acid levels, a disposition to oxidize, and a lack of assertive flavor and bouquet, which are balanced by the addition of Bourboulenc for freshness, Clairette for a touch of elegance, Mourvèdre for structure, and Syrah for color and flavor. To make rosé wine, Grenache Noir is usually mixed with Cinsault, Carignan Noir, and small quantities of Bourboulenc and Clairette.

The second-most-important "meridional" vine, the Cinsault, is rapidly

Table 6.2   Major Grape Varieties in the Ardèche Department, 1968 and 1979

Grape variety	1968		1979		As percent of national total
	Hectares	Percent[a]	Hectares	Percent[a]	
Couderc Noir	3,300	14.0	1,500	11.5	19.5
Carignan Noir	1,900	8.1	1,400	10.8	
Aramon	2,900	12.3	1,300	10.0	
Villard Noir	1,600	6.8	1,300	10.0	16.5
Grenache Noir	800	3.4	1,200	9.2	
Cinsault	700	3.0	1,200	9.2	
Syrah	1,300	5.5	1,200	9.2	9.8
Villard Blanc	500	2.1	300	2.3	
Alicante Bouschet	500	2.0	100	.8	
Others	10,100	42.8	3,500	27.0	
Total	23,600	100.0	13,000	100.0	

[a]Percent of departmental total.

Source: French Ministry of Agriculture.

Table 6.3   Major Grape Varieties in the Drôme Department, 1968 and 1979

Grape variety	1968		1979		As percent of national total
	Hectares	Percent[a]	Hectares	Percent[a]	
Grenache Noir	4,200	23.3	7,800	50.3	10.1
Syrah	500	2.8	2,100	13.5	17.0
Carignan Noir	1,600	8.9	1,600	10.3	.8
Cinsault	300	1.6	700	4.5	
Clairette	500	2.8	600	3.9	
Muscat Blanc à Petis Grains	400	2.2	400	2.6	
Couderc Noir	2,100	11.7	300	1.9	
Mourvèdre	300	1.7	200	1.3	
Gamay Noir	100	.5	200	1.3	
Marsanne	100	.5	100	.7	
Alicante Bouschet	300	1.7	100	.7	
Villard Noir	1,200	6.7	100	.7	
Villard Blanc	300	1.7	100	.6	
Aramon	400	2.2	100	.6	
Other	5,700	31.7	1,100	7.1	
Total	18,000	100.0	15,500	100.0	

[a]Percent of departmental total.

Source: French Ministry of Agriculture.

Table 6.4 Major Grape Varieties in the Vaucluse Department, 1968 and 1979

Grape variety	1968		1979		As percent of national total
	Hectares	Percent[a]	Hectares	Percent[a]	
Grenache Noir	17,700	43.9	24,700	56.3	31.8
Carignan Noir	7,400	18.3	6,700	15.4	
Cinsault	1,800	4.6	3,000	6.9	
Syrah	300	.8	2,100	4.8	17.2
Ugni Blanc	1,700	4.2	1,700	3.9	
Aubun	1,200	3.0	1,100	2.4	19.0
Mourvèdre	300	.8	900	2.1	28.6
Clairette	1,400	3.4	700	1.7	
Aramon	1,700	4.2	600	1.3	
Alicante Bouschet	400	.9	400	1.0	
Courderc Noir	2,500	6.0	400	1.0	
Muscat Blanc	100	.2	200	.5	
Villard Blanc	700	1.7	200	.4	
Villard Noir	700	1.7	100	.2	
Grand Noir	400	1.1	100	.2	
Other	2,100	5.2	900	2.0	
Total	40,400	100.0	43,800	100.0	

[a] Percent of departmental total.

Source: French Ministry of Agriculture.

Table 6.5 Major Grape Varieties in the Gard Department, 1968 and 1979

Grape variety	1968		1979		As percent of national total
	Hectares	Percent[a]	Hectares	Percent[a]	
Carignan Noir	16,700	19.6	22,400	27.2	11
Aramon	31,500	37.2	18,200	22.1	29
Grenache Noir	4,000	4.7	11,700	14.2	15
Cinsaut	1,900	2.3	9,000	10.9	17
Alicante Bouschet	2,900	3.4	3,000	3.7	14
Couderc Noir	6,500	7.7	2,800	3.5	36
Syrah	100	.1	2,600	3.1	21
Villard Blanc	3,700	4.5	2,300	2.8	39
Ugni Blanc	500	.6	1,600	2.0	
Clairette Blanc	2,200	2.6	1,300	1.6	24
Auburn	400	.4	1,200	1.4	24
Villard Noir	2,300	2.7	1,000	1.2	13
Cabernet Sauvignon			600	.7	
Grand Noir	3,300	3.9	400	.4	
Mourvèdre	300	.3	400	.5	
Others	8,500	10.0	3,849	4.7	
Total	84,800	100.0	82,349	100.0	

[a] Percent of departmental total.

Source: French Ministry of Agriculture.

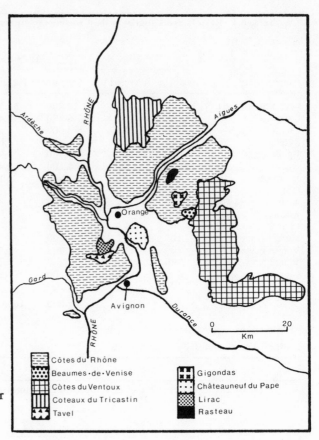

Figure 6.3 Major Southern Rhône Appellations

Côtes du Rhône
Beaumes·de·Venise
Côtes du Ventoux
Coteaux du Tricastin
Tavel
Gigondas
Châteauneuf du Pape
Lirac
Rasteau

being recognized as a quality variety and is fast replacing Carignan Noir for the production of both red and rosé wine. Vinified by carbonic maceration, Cinsault yields fresh-tasting wine with excellent quaffing characteristics and a mild, pleasing fragrance. Although it fades quickly and is meant to be consumed young, it is nevertheless soft and supple and exhibits no hard, tannin-rich features of a Mourvèdre or Syrah. It adapts well to the dry, stony, hot regions of the southern Rhône and is a good table grape. Along with Ugni Blanc, it is the only quality, or at least acceptable, "two-way" grape in the region. As Cinsault produces supple, well-scented wines with some measure of finesse and blends well with tannin-rich grapes, its hectarage will probably continue to increase.

The Mourvèdre has properties that are similar to Syrah but demands higher temperatures, plenty of underground water, brilliant sunshine, and a hot, deep, friable soil; it is essentially confined to Provence and the Midi. This late-ripening vine, by its ability to impart firmness, color, flavor, and aroma (features lacking in Grenache Noir and Carignan Noir), is an excellent blending grape in limited amounts for weak, unstructured southern wines. Historically it was highly localized in the Bandol region, but over the past twenty years it has spread throughout southern France. Considered a quality grape comparable to the Syrah, its wine, always tannin-rich, dark, fragrant, and high in alcohol, requires time to reach its full potential.

Because the Syrah is less demanding than the Mourvèdre, its hectarage has increased in the southern Rhône from fewer than 1,000 hectares in 1965 to more than 8,500 in 1985. Quality producers, especially those making Côtes du Rhône–Villages wines, have increased their Syrah plantings more than 15 percent, expecting that as much as one-third of total hectarage will be composed of this variety in the near future. The other major red grape, the Carignan Noir, is increasing hectarage in the department of Gard, holding steady in the Drôme, but showing slight reductions in the Ardèche and Vaucluse. Although ubiquitous everywhere in the south of France and known for bland, often dull wine, Carignan Noir manages to produce above-average wine in areas that are well suited to its growing habits, particularly from vines that are more than 50 years old.

The dominant white grape varieties for the production of AOC wine are Clairette, Grenache Blanc, Grenache Gris, Bourboulenc, Marsanne, Roussanne, and Ugni Blanc. The Bourboulenc, which has responded well to new vinification methods that produce fresh and light wines, is currently considered a vine with a bright future; as a result, hectarage is expected to increase in the coming decades. The Clairette, found throughout the southern vineyard, grows particularly well along the northern fringes of the producing district and is considered an elegant grape, compared to the ubiquitous but common Ugni Blanc. The Clairette is an old Mediterranean variety that has adapted well to dry limestone and stony soils. While it is moderately vigorous and produces alcoholic wines often with a pronounced bouquet, it ages rapidly and turns dark, bitter, and flat-tasting within two years. Even though it does best in higher elevations that are protected from dessicating winds, about one-quarter of the national hectarage is planted in the flat portions of the Gard department and represents the single largest area of concentration in the nation. Ugni Blanc is also successful in the hot, dry climates of southern France. Because it adds strength and firmness to blends, it forms the base for most white wine production.

The southern Rhône vineyard produces red, rosé, white, sparkling, and VDN wines with considerable variation in quality, style, and price. In general, however, the northern portion makes the finest red and white wines from "varietal" grapes, while the southern portion makes a wider range of wines from *cépages d'assemblage,* or "blending" vines. As a result, wine quality in the southern portion varies more than in the northern district not only because more grape varieties are grown, but because there exist more microclimates, a greater diversity of soil, and a lack of standardized vinification and aging procedures.

Approximately 88 percent of all wine is red, 7 percent is rosé, and 5 percent is white, of which the red, without question, is the best. It is divided into three types: old-fashioned *vin de garde* wines that are wood-aged and characterized by a dark color, fullness, and concentrated flavor and bouquet; young "nouveau-type" wines that are the product of carbonic maceration techniques very much in the manner of Beaujolais; and an in-between version of limited or no-wood aging made for consumption within three years. The tendency over the past twenty years has been to concentrate on the last type, which is made by complete destemming and by total or partial fermenting by carbonic maceration to emphasize freshness and fruit. It is unfortunate that more than three-quarters of total output lacks character and individuality and offers little value. When the process of carbonic maceration is abbreviated, "nouveau" wines are produced, which are currently the rage. Whether the trend will persist is problematic, because the wines lack the individuality, flavor, and subtle sweet scent of authentic Beaujolais.

Rosé production has benefited greatly from improved vinification methods in recent years. Made from Grenache Noir, Cinsault, Carignan Noir, Clairette, Vaccarèse, Couderc Noir, and Mourvèdre, usually in that order, the wine tends to be light, fresh, fruity, and flavorful. The finest producing districts, of which Tavel and Lirac have established reputations, are all located on skeletal soils, alluvial rock, and sand. In general more successful than white, rosé production is increasing. White production, constituting less than 5 percent of total output, is restricted to those areas with a unique microclimate, peculiar soil, and a dedicated winemaker, who is extremely important due to the difficulty in making good to above-average white wine in a hot climate. Except for Châteauneuf-du-Pape, few can be referred to even as average in quality, since the wines suffer from reduced acid levels, high sulfur additions, oxidation problems, high alcohol levels, and the perennial presence of "oiliness." Although there are occasional surprises, nearly all offer poor value.

Historically, southern Rhône wines had a poor reputation and suffered from all the above drawbacks, plus unreliability, heavy filtration and sulfur, coarseness, and lack of substantial fruit and flavor. They were the product of overcropping and chaptalization, which is a particularly nasty practice in hot climates. Under appellation laws the *dérogation,* or the right to sell "excess production" under the appellation label, is rather liberal. Although it varies with the vintage, it is usually twice as high for southern Rhône appellations as for those in the northern portion of the valley. Because there is a vast sea of Côtes du Rhône "générique," nearly all of it palatable but undistinguished, the reputation of the entire southern producing district has suffered. But grape variety changes, recent improvements in viticultural and vinification practices, and the rise of domaine bottling have elevated wine quality levels in most districts. During the intercensal period (1968–79), in a major attempt to upgrade the quality of vine cultivation, Grenache Noir nearly doubled its hectarage in the four southern departments at the expense of such inferior grapes as Couderc Noir, Aramon, Alicante Bouschet, Grand Noir, and Villard Noir and Blanc (as well as other hybrids). While all the aforementioned have declined by more than 31,000 hectares, superior grapes, such as Syrah, Cinsault, and Mourvèdre, have increased in hectarage by more than 17,000 hectares.

Of the 257 cooperatives in the four principal departments, nearly 100 are in the business of making some percentage of Rhône wine, collectively perhaps by as much as 80 percent of total output. Given the large number of individual styles and quality standards of cooperative wine, the contemporary reputation of quality wine production rests entirely with private vignerons. The largest concentration of estate-bottled and privately produced communal wine is mainly confined to the northern portion of the Rhône, with only a few additional, select locations in the southern portion. In this respect, grower-produced wine dominates in the Côte-Rôtie, Condrieu, and Hermitage appellations in the north, and Châteauneuf-du-Pape, Tavel, Lirac, Gigondas, and Rasteau in the south.

Coteaux du Tricastin

Located just north of the main Côtes du Rhône producing region, Coteaux du Tricastin is a rapidly growing appellation of nearly 2,000 hectares. This predominantly red wine vineyard of 75,000 hectoliters is centered around the villages of Donzère, Les Granges-Gontardes, Grignan, and La Baume-de-Transit. The topography is hilly, the soils are stony, and the entire producing region is severely buffeted by the *Mistral*. Prior to the arrival of *pied noirs* in the early 1960s, the area was known for nothing better than *vin de pays,* but since then wine quality has improved rapidly, and AOC status was attained in 1973. The most prominent vine is the Grenache, followed by Syrah, Cinsault, and Mourvèdre. Although the finest wines can be soft and supple, the majority tend to be more robust, darker in color, and more full-bodied than those from the Côtes du Rhône appellation. Despite the fact that nearly all wine is made by cooperatives, *Dne. de Grangeneuve, Dne. la Curate,* and *Dne. de Raspail* have generated above-average reputations.

Muscat de Beaumes-de-Venise and Rasteau

Muscat de Beaumes-de-Venise and Rasteau are two VDN wine-producing appellations that collectively make 2 percent of all VDN wine. Some experts maintain that Muscat de Beaumes-de-Venise is the finest VDN wine in France. Surrounded by olive groves, it is produced in the sleepy town of the same name and is situated along the foothills of the Dentelles de Montmirail. While Banyuls and Muscat de Frontignan (other VDN wines) enjoy something more than a regional reputation, Beaumes-de-Venise is generally found in foreign markets and smart restaurants.

The cultivation of the Muscat grape has long been indigenous in this area. Pliny mentioned it nearly 2,000 years ago, and the popes of Avignon, in particular, appreciated its quality, which gave rise to the medieval name "Muscat des Papes." It has a beautiful orange-amber color, a pronounced bouquet, and a fruity, apricot-almond flavor. At its best, it has a marvelous aroma, multiple layers of fruit on the palate, and is rich and sweet. At its worst, it is flat, unbalanced, and oxidized. It is generally consumed slightly chilled as an aperitif with ripe figs or melon.

The popularity of Muscat de Beaumes-de-Venise and of other VDN wines has recently soared to record levels. Land area has increased from fewer than 85 hectares in 1945 to more than 235 today, with every indication that the planted area will continue to grow in the future. Made solely from the Muscat Blanc à Petits Grains, with a restricted yield of 30 hectoliters to the hectare, the wine contains a minimum alcohol content of 15 percent. The grapes growing in sandy, limestone, and red marl soils are picked as late in the season as possible and are usually cultivated as a sideline by about three dozen growers.

With about 95 percent of total production, the largest producer of Muscat Beaumes-de-Venise is the local cooperative,* a firm that maintains high standards and usually makes above-average-quality wine. Among private producers, *Dne. Durban,* the unquestioned leader in the production of quality wine, is a comparatively small property located in an isolated and hilly area with a unique microclimate. Nearly as good are *Dne. des Bernardins* and *Dne. St.-Sauveur.*

The second southern Rhône VDN wine-producing region is Rasteau, a small, picturesque village of 650 inhabitants, which dates back to the Romans. It contains 750 hectares of vineland (increased from 190 in 1960), approximately half of which is officially delimited for the production of VDN wine. It is one of the seventeen Côtes du Rhône–Villages communes, hence approximately 90 percent of total wine production is officially classified as Côtes du Rhône. The entire appellation consists of fewer than 120 hectares producing 4,000 hectoliters of red and white VDN, the latter the most important in terms of quantity of output. The best portion of the appellation contains fluvial debris very similar to that found in Châteauneuf-du-Pape.

Both white and red Rasteau VDN are made from all three Grenache grapes (with the red dominating). Alcohol content usually varies between 20 percent and 21.5 percent, while the yield is limited to 35 hectoliters

---

* It is important to note that most southern Rhône producers, no matter what their location, make wine from more than one appellation.

to the hectare. According to the original delineation of the AOC producing region in 1944, portions of the neighboring communes of Cairanne and Sablet may also market their wine as Rasteau VDN. Although good and reliable, the red is never the equal of Banyuls, and the white does not approach the richness of Beaumes-de-Venise. The white is made for early consumption; the more complex red is made in two styles: with or without wood-aging, the former developing a strong *rancio* (oxidized) bouquet and flavor after spending as many as seven years in wood.

Although more than three dozen vignerons grow grapes for the production of VDN wine, the cultivation of grapes (including the extra work involved in picking late-harvested grapes) is considered a part-time activity for most of them. The Rasteau cooperative, the largest producer in the village, makes more than 90 percent of the total, nearly all of it sound, well made and, because it is so little known, offering excellent value. Among private producers, *Dne. de la Grangeneuve*, a 16-hectare property considered the standard in the appellation, is the only estate making *rancio* wine. All of the following properties are in the business of making Côtes du Rhône wine, with only small amounts of VDN: *Dne. de Char-à-Vin, Dne. la Soumade, Dne. de Trapadis, Dne. de la Girardière, Dne. Wilfred, Dne. des Coteaux des Travers, Dne. Girasols, Dne. des Escaravailles, Dne. de la Garriquette, Dne. de Verquière, Dne. du Sommier,* and *Dne. des Nymphes.*

Gigondas

Gigondas is an obscure, little-known, 1,600-hectare vineyard located 16 kilometers northwest of Châteauneuf-du-Pape. Sandwiched between Rasteau and Vacqueyras, its vines are perfectly situated and sheltered by the "Dentelles de Montmirail." The appellation, which takes its name from the village of Gigondas, is nearly surrounded by vines, of which at least one-fourth are situated between 300 and 400 meters above sealevel, a comparatively high elevation for a southern Rhône vineyard. It is a red and rosé region whose quality and standards are above average in the production of full-bodied, robust wines whose minimum alcohol content is 12.5 percent. From a yield of 35 hectoliters to the hectare, average production is approximately 30,000 hectoliters and rising.

The vineyard was developed by Romans in the first century A.D., but until recently the vine did not compete effectively with the olive, especially after the *phylloxera* epidemic. Every time local vignerons began replanting efforts, a major domestic or international crisis negated replanting efforts. As recently as 1929, a major frost destroyed the entire vineyard. Ever since appellation status was awarded in 1971, hectarage has expanded rapidly, with expectations that by 1995, more than half of the available 4,500 hectares within the officially delimited area will be planted. The present hectarage represents a fourfold increase since the early 1960s and an eightfold rise in the planted area since 1919. Its recent popularity is partly related to tourism and partly to the quality of wine made under its own appellation name. As a result, Gigondas has become one of the better southern Rhône appellations and perhaps ranks third to Côte-Rôtie and Hermitage for consistency and value.

The appellation has excellent, well-drained soil that is highly diverse, but in some instances nearly identical to the quality of the surface and subsurface soils of Châteauneuf-du-Pape. Large stretches of viticultural land occur that are calcareous, with significant accumulations of yellowish clay, sand, gravel, and pebble. All the best sites enjoy excellent aspect and are completely protected from the full force of the Mistral and other local winds.

For a wine to carry the Gigondas name on the label, the Grenache Noir must dominate but not exceed 65 percent of the total blend. The Syrah, Mourvèdre, and Cinsault are collectively restricted to 25 percent, while the remainder may include any other AOC–approved vine except Carignan. More than 95 percent of all wine is red, the very best having a pronounced cherry-raspberry-cinnamon flavor and aroma. The wine spends between 8 and 32 months in wood, depending on the vintage, and requires another three years to round out, with good to excellent bottles demanding an additional five years. At its best, the wine is big, chewy, spicy, and concentrated in extract and flavor. With a distinct touch of *goût de terroir,* it is assertive and alcoholic on the palate, and although rustic, robust and brawny in youth, has the capacity to age magnificently. Highly underrated, good Gigondas nearly always provides superior value to the more sophisticated but overpriced Châteauneuf-du-Pape. The rosé, less fine than the red, is consumed locally or blended with Côtes du Rhône rosé. Minute amounts of white are also made, most of it undistinguished and consumed within two years of the vintage. A massive, heady, coarse wine, it is made primarily from Clairette, Bourboulenc, Ugni Blanc, and Picpoul.

There are 220 vignerons, more than three-quarters of whom are part-time farmers, three good cooperatives, and several large negociants. Of these, the largest is *Etablissement Gabriel Meffre,* the nation's largest single owner of AOC vineland, and several prestigious properties in four southern Rhône appellations. In Gigondas, it owns *Dne. des Bosquets,* an 18-hectare estate known for consistency. Two other large negociant houses are *Pierre Amadieu* and *Pascal,* the latter the owner of *Dne. de Grand Montmirail* and the exclusive agent for three adjoining properties—*Dne. St.-Gens, Dne. du Pradas,* and *Dne. Roucas St.-Pierre.* Among the many individual producers, the following enjoy good reputations and are widely exported: *Dne. St.-Gayan* (a 15-hectare property owned by a member of the Meffre family, which can only be described in superlatives); *Dne. les Goubert* (a 6-hectare property making excellent *vin de garde,* spicy wine); *Dne. de Longue-Toque* (a 23-hectare property known for big, well-flavored wine); *Dne. les Pallières* (a little-known 26-hectare property making outstanding *vin de garde* wine); *Dne. de St.-François-Xavier* (once part of the domaines of the Prince of Orange, a 20-hectare property making exceptional, well-flavored wine); *Ch. de Montmirail* (a 35-hectare estate dating back to the 10th century and making robust, full-bodied wine); *Roger Combe; Dne. Raspail-Ay; Dne. du Pesquier; G. Faraud; Ch. St.-André; Dne. du Pourras; Ch. du Trignon; Dne. de St.-Cosme; Dne. de la Tuilière; Clos du Joncuas;* and *Dne. les Chênes Blancs.*

Châteauneuf-du-Pape

Châteauneuf-du-Pape is a vineyard of 3,000 hectares that makes 100,000 hectoliters of wine annually, 98 percent of which is red and the remainder white. The producing region, located 16 kilometers north of the papal city of Avignon (known as *Avenio* in Roman days, or the "city of strong winds"), is the most celebrated, important, and widely recognized of all Rhône vineyards. Although viticulture was not new to the area, it was the Knights Templars and other religious orders who began vinegrowing and winemaking on a large scale in the 12th century. The reputation of the wine grew when Pope Clement V started to spend summers on one of the highest hills in the region and expanded the papal vineyards. Before the 14th century, Avignon was successively a small Roman settlement, a fortified feudal town, a republic, and finally the seat of the "new popes." The red wines of Châteauneuf-du-Pape became an instant success in the second half of the 14th century and were widely distributed throughout France. Avignon was home base for a succession of seven popes, but after the papacy returned to Rome in 1378, four centuries of civil and religious turbulence reduced the once-important vineyard to insignificance, until the vineyards were reconstructed in the 19th century. Hectarage increased from fewer than 500 in 1800 to 1,000 on the eve of the *phylloxera* epidemic. Afterwards growers shifted to tree crops, such as olives, apricots, almonds, and cherries, all of which were short-lived enterprises. After 1890 vine hectarage began to expand and now stands at its alltime peak of 3,000. The total planted area is approximately double that of the quality regions of the northern Rhône, and its annual production is about four times what it was in 1950. Nearly the whole of the delimited region is currently in production.

The Châteauneuf-du-Pape vinegrowing region is delimited by the limits of a small plateau surface covered by fluvial and glacial debris. In the heart of the producing district, in an area that measures barely 6 by 8 kilometers, the soils are composed of "cailloux roules" (or "galets")—rounded pebbles and stones laid down by alpine glaciers and rivers. They attract solar radiation during the day and radiate it back to the atmosphere at night, thus intensifying diurnal temperatures, raising sugar, and lowering grape acid levels. Soil, in the conventional sense of the word, is absent, the ground surface being composed of stones the size of oranges and grapefruit. The reddish subsoils, which indicate the presence of iron, are rich in silica and, in places, contain appreciable amounts of calcareous material. Conditions change radically north, east, and south of the center of the district. Gravel dominates near Sorgues, toward the east sand is prevalent, and toward the north calcareous clay is the dominant soil constituent. The subsoil throughout the plateau consists of varying amounts of gravel, clay, and sand. Climate is characterized by chilly, damp, cloudy winters; Mediterranean features in summer; usually pleasant and sunny falls; and unpredictable springs often marred by frost and torrential downpours.

The production zone spreads outward from Châteauneuf-du-Pape proper to portions of the four adjacent communes and towns of Orange, Sorgues, Bédarrides, and Courthézon, the latter being widely considered, along with Châteauneuf-du-Pape, better than the rest. By Rhône standards, land holdings are quite large: three-quarters of the properties in the vineyard are larger than 15 hectares, one of the highest figures in France.

Appellation laws permit thirteen different varieties to be blended in the production of red and five to make white wine. In the extensive list, Grenache Noir dominates hectarage, followed by Cinsault, Syrah, and Mourvèdre. Locally it is said that Grenache Noir and Cinsault provide flavor and alcohol; Mourvèdre, Syrah, Muscardin, and Vaccarèse lend firmness, aging potential, color, and flavor; and Counoise and Picpoul impart vinosity, freshness, and bouquet. It is interesting to note that only a handful of growers cultivate and make wine from all thirteen grape varieties (most make wine from at least 85 percent Grenache Noir). The grapes, in terms of importance, are officially ranked as follows: Grenache Noir and Cinsault are considered primary; Mourvèdre, Syrah, Muscardin, and Vaccarèse are secondary; Counoise and Picpoul fall into the third category; the fourth group includes Clairette and Bourboulenc; and the remainder (Terret Noir, Roussanne, and Picardin) are limited to 10 percent of the total blend.

All varieties except Syrah are trained gobelet-style and pruned in such a way that grape bunches grow close to the ground and are well sheltered by dense, leafy growth. Production is limited to 35 hectoliters to the hectare, with the legal stipulation that each grower can produce a supplementary quantity from 5 percent to 20 percent above the appellation minimum. This proportion of wine, routinely exceeded, is not entitled to appellation status, although a good deal of it sold as such.

The wide choice of grape varieties and the absence of precise percentage limits for each leads to wide fluctuations in the wine's physical character in terms of color, extract, alcohol, and other essential constituents. Just how Châteauneuf-du-Pape is supposed to look, taste, and smell varies widely within the appellation. Furthermore, vinification techniques do not conform to a standard but vary from "nouveau" to traditional—from quick carbonic maceration to "la méthode ancienne." Post-fermentation aging techniques also vary: the "old school" maintains that two years of wood-aging is mandatory, while the "new" advocates either none or limited wood contact prior to bottling. But the wines do fall into three broad style categories. The first is a light, fruity, and early maturing wine made by carbonic maceration primarily from Grenache Noir and Cinsault. It lacks the complexity, color, tannin, and extract of old-fashioned wines and is ready to drink almost immediately. Perhaps as much as 60 percent of all wine is now made in this style, and nearly all of it is not much better than Côtes du Rhône–Villages.

The second style is a wine made by a slow three-week fermentation, then aged in wood for two to three years. It is made from a smaller percentage of Grenache Noir and Cinsault and includes not only Syrah and Mourvèdre, but Counoise, Vaccarèse, and Muscardin—three unheralded but essential grape varieties in the production of first-class wine. The Counoise, a very rare grape of Spanish origin, has a spicy flavor and aroma that, in small quantities, adds considerable complexity to the final blend. Vaccarèse and Muscardin, obscure grape varieties difficult to grow in the producing region, are above average in quality and impart firmness, color, and flavor. This traditional style of wine is characterized by a dark color, tannin, and extract, and requires more than ten years to mature fully into a luscious libation known for a unique combination of penetrating fragrance, multiple flavors, and long, lingering finish. At its best, the wine has a beautiful ruby color and satisfying rich taste, and is always better older than younger. Probably less than 5 percent of total production is currently made in this fashion.

The third type is an in-between version of moderate astringency, body, and staying power. It is a popular style for those growers who wish to bridge the gap between the diversity of the first two. It is usually ready to drink after the second year and will last for an additional five. For all three styles, the minimum alcohol content is 12.5 percent (one of the highest in France), a figure that must be achieved naturally since chaptalization is officially forbidden.

A good deal of Châteauneuf-du-Pape currently available in export markets is below the standards of average AOC wine from Burgundy and Bordeaux. At least half of production of any vintage is alcoholic, unbalanced, oxidized, or otherwise unpalatable, and nearly all is overpriced. The reasons for this sad state of affairs are sloppy vinification and careless handling, overcropping, chronic adulteration, and inconsistency. Yet, despite its obvious faults, the wine continues to sell well primarily because the 500,000 tourists in the greater Avignon region each year find the "new," fresh, light-bodied wines very appealing. Over the past twenty-five years, 1963, 1965, 1968, 1969, 1975, and 1977 are considered average vintage years. Above-average to excellent are 1976, 1978, 1979, 1980, 1982, 1983, and 1985.

White wine, accounting for less than 3 percent of total production, is made primarily from Clairette and Bourboulenc, with Grenache Blanc, Picpoul, and Roussanne considered secondary varieties. Golden-yellow in color, it must be consumed young to take full advantage of its freshness and fruit. With extended bottle-aging it quickly darkens, turns bitter, and declines rapidly after its third birthday. At its best it is the equal of other southern Rhône white wines, but not superior to Hermitage, Château Grillet, or Condrieu. It is usually expensive and offers little value. Under appellation laws, rosé wine cannot be made under the Châteauneuf-du-Pape name.

The producing properties are large, contiguous vineyards and include the following: *Dne. de Beaucastel,* located in the extreme northern portion of the district, is a 130-hectare property considered by many to be the finest in the appellation. With a reputation for powerful, often extraordinary wine, it attracts attention because of high standards, consistency, and outstanding value. In above-average vintages, the domaine manages to produce superb, classic, long-lived wines with great depth of flavor and a complex bouquet that should not be missed. The white, consistently above average in quality, is one of the finest in the appellation. The domaine makes more than 60,000 cases, including Côtes du Rhône. *Dne. du Vieux Telegraphe,* a 40-hectare property that historically produced dark, tannin-rich, long-lived wines, has recently changed to a lighter, fruitier, smoother, early maturing style that is very appealing. *Ch. de la Nerthe,* situated on a wooded knoll, is a well-regarded 65-hectare domaine that dates back to the 16th century and produces one of the most durable of all wines. In outstanding years a special cuvée, called "des Cadettes," is extraordinary in terms of body, color, and fragrance. *Clos du Mont-Olivet* is an 18-hectare property with an excellent reputation for dark, full-bodied, spicy and highly satisfying *vin de garde* wines. *Clos du Papes* is a 30-hectare property that makes big, rich, well-structured, meaty wines. *Les Clefs d'Or,* a 24-hectare property, makes concentrated wines with considerable depth of flavor.

Slightly less fine but still above average in quality are the wines of the following: *Ch. Fortia,* a 30-hectare estate, makes well-scented, elegant, expensive wines. *Ch. Rayas,* a 16-hectare historic property that once made wine from 100 percent Grenache Noir, has had a checkered history over the past twenty years. At its best, the wine, with a distinctive bouquet and rich, expansive, array of of flavors, has the potential to rank among the top ten in the appellation. *L. Barrot,* a small grower, makes big, powerful, tannin-rich wines with considerable depth of flavor. *Dne. de Cabrières,* a 60-hectare property, makes big, expansive wine from very old vines. *Clos de l'Oratoire des Papes,* a 40-hectare property, makes fragrant, complex *vin de garde* wine that is often marred by inconsistency. Also known are *Dne. Chante-Cigale; Dne. Chante-Perdrix* (well-aged, powerful, but inconsistent wines); *Felicien Diffonty* (a 17-hectare property making powerful wines that are often ranked among the top ten in the appellation); *Dne. du Haut des Terres Blanche* (classic, round, warm, highly concentrated wine with strong assertive flavors); *Dne. Roger Sabon* (complex wines that offer excellent value); *Dne. de Nalys* (in good vintages, complex and well-scented wine); *Ch. de la Gardine* (a large 72-hectare property making early maturing wine); *Dne. du Grand Tinel* (soft, supple, well-scented wine); *Dne. de la Roquette* (full-bodied, complex wine); *Ch. de Vaudieu* (light, early maturing wine); *Dne. de Beaurenard* (fruity, supple, early maturing wine that is often dull); *Dne. Font-de-Michelle; Dne. de la Serrière; Berard Père; Dne. du Vieux Lazaret; Dne. Trintignant,* and *Dne. de Mont-Redon.*

Less consistent but occasionally above-average in quality are the wines of *Dne. Durieu, Ch. des Fines Roches, Dne. de la Solitude, Dne. du Père Caboche, J.-P.Brotte, Dne. de Palestor, Dne. de Montpertuis, Pierre Jacumin, Dne. Mathieu,* and *Dne. de la Vielle-Julienne. Le Cellier des Princes,* founded in 1924, the only cooperative in the appellation, makes average-quality, uninspired wine. Among the many negociants, *Père Anselme* makes and distributes a complete line of southern Rhône wines; *Paul Jaboulet* distributes Les Cedres, a popular label; *E. Guigal,* always consistent, offers good value; *Caves Bessac,* a large firm, handles solid, firm, well-matured wines; *Caves St.-Pierre-Sefivin,* one of the largest negociants in the southern Rhône, in known for reliability; and *Max Chapoutier* is best known for La Bernardine, an early maturing, spicy wine that offers good value.

Lirac

Lirac, a 25,000-hectoliter red, rosé, and white wine region, adjoins Tavel along its southern border on the left bank of the Rhône. Included within the irregular appellation boundaries are the communes of Lirac, St.-Laurent-des-Arbes, St.-Geniès-de-Comolas, and Roquemaure. The latter, the most important, produces more than one-third of total appellation output. The soils, not too dissimilar to portions of the Vaucluse department across the Rhône, are largely derived from limestone and contain clay with considerable fluvial gravel and sand. The best sites lie on a ridge approximately 100 meters above the level of the Rhône. It is an area of fresh, modestly priced, unpretentious wines that are easily quaffed and most often quite enjoyable. After AOC status was awarded in 1947, the planted area steadily increased from 280 to 760 hectares in 1983. Spectacular quality improvements in the wines and the significant progress in the enlargement of the planted area are directly related to the arrival of *pied noirs* in the early 1960s. As a result, wine prices have increased, more than half of production is sold in bottles, and the wines are selling well.

Lirac produces equal amounts of red and rosé, and only minute quantities of white wine. For all three colors, the minimum alcohol content is 11.5 percent, and the yield limited to 35 hectoliters to the hectare. Of the three wines, the finest is the red, made primarily from Cinsault, Mourvèdre, and Grenache, the latter representing a minimum of 40 percent of the blend. Secondary varieties include Syrah, Clairette, Bourboulenc, and Ugni Blanc. Macabeo, Picpoul, Calitor, and Carignan, the latter limited to less than 10 percent of the total blend, are slowly disappearing. The wine is consistently soft, fruity, devoid of any rough edges, and ready to drink after its second birthday. Almost a quaffing wine, it is very satisfying and offers excellent value. Lirac Rosé, little known and scorned by many, is the only true rival to Tavel in the southern Rhône vineyard. In contrast to Tavel, Lirac Rosé is more flowery, perhaps a bit coarser, and lacks the "tang" of a superior Tavel, but its color, aroma, and flavor are very appealing. It is made with the same grape varieties as the red, only with greater infusions of Cinsault. White Lirac is made from at least one-third Clairette, followed by varying percentages of Bourboulenc, Picpoul, Ugni Blanc, Calitor, Grenache Blanc, and Macabeo. The wine, light in color, is alcoholic, fresh, tart, fruity, and surprisingly good. According to appellation regulations, white wine is aged for six months, rosé for ten or eleven months, and the red between twelve and twenty-four months, depending on the vintage.

Of the two dozen primary producers, the following have established reputations: *Dne. de Castel-Oualou* (a 52-hectare estate, makes excellent red, rosé, and white wine), *Ch. de Ségriès* (a 17th-century property, makes above-average red, rosé, and white wines), *Dne. du St.-Roch* (a 25-hectare property, has an excellent reputation for *vin de garde* red and lighter rosé wines), *Ch. de Clary* (well regarded but does not bottle its own wines), *Dne. de la Tour de Lirac, Les Garrigues, Dne. du Devoy, Dne. de la Clairetière, Dne. Sabon,* and *Les Carabiniers.*

Tavel

The most southerly of the Rhône commune appellations, and long considered the source of the finest rosé in France, Tavel sits on the west bank of the Rhône 15 kilometers southwest of Avignon. The appellation takes its name from the principal town, an unpretentious, one-street affair surrounded by denuded hills with scattered olive and apricot trees. Although in existence as a viticultural region since the 1st century and recognized as an above-average-quality wine region since the 13th century, it has long been overshadowed by Châteauneuf-du-Pape. Geographically quite extensive, the Tavel vineyard has shown a proclivity for instability: the area had 720 hectares under vine in 1825, 846 in 1870, 50 in 1880, 196 in 1955, 692 in 1975, and 765 in 1985. Its recent resurgence is a manifestation of modern vinification practices, the arrival of *pied noirs,* and a local effort to improve overall quality. Annual production regularly exceeds 25,000 hectoliters, all of it rosé.

The producing region is a mixture of alluvial material composed of gravel, sand, and clay, a good portion of which rests on a limestone base. To the west the area is flat with highly absorbent limestone and clay soil. To the east sand prevails, and to the north and northwest, gravel of alluvial origin. As a general rule, grapes growing on limestone produce wines that are fresher, lighter in alcohol, and better balanced, while those growing in clay soil mixed with gravel produce wines of higher alcohol content. While the better growths are located to the north and northeast of the town of Tavel, with few exceptions the growers blend grapes from all three areas. It is also important to note that about one-third of all vignerons also own vineland in neighboring Lirac.

The wine is made from a combination of Grenache Noir, Cinsault, Clairette Blanc, Clairette Rosé, Picpoul, Calitor, Bourboulenc, Mourvèdre, Syrah, and Carignan, of which the first two are the most important. Grenache Noir is restricted to 60 percent of the blend, Cinsault to 15 percent, Carignan to 10 percent (but most of the top growths have eliminated it entirely), and the remainder varies widely by grower. The minimum alcohol content is 11 percent (most Tavel varies between 12 percent and 13.5 percent), and the yield is limited to 42 hectoliters to the hectare. Historically Tavel produced austere, dry, often dull, full-bodied, alcoholic wine from Grenache Noir, Carignan, and Cinsault. The tendency over the years has been to reduce (and eventually eliminate) Carignan, to increase the percentage of Cinsault and other more "aromatic" varieties like Syrah and Mourvèdre, to reduce the alcohol content, and to make the wine fruitier. The more traditional vignerons also attempt to maintain depth of flavor by wood-aging from six to twelve months before bottling. With its very pleasing color and fine, subtle bouquet with floral highlights, Tavel at its best should be consumed within three years. It differs from other southern rosés by its refinement, depth of flavor, bouquet, and lingering finish. It is always vinified bone dry, but because of the diversity of vinification methods, the large number of grape varieties, and soil differences, the wines differ widely in color, alcoholic strength, and ability to improve in bottle.

The principal producers are *Les Vignerons de Tavel* (with 140 members, it controls 400 hectares and makes nearly two-thirds of all appellation wine, most of which is sold to negociants), *Ch. d'Aquéria* (a 50-hectare property capable of producing full, well-flavored, and scented wine), *Dne. de la Genestière* (a 30-hectare property making supple, refined, reliable wine with a delicate aroma), *Dne. le Vieux Moulin* (above-average light to medium-bodied yet firm, fruity wines), *Dne. de la Forcardière, Ch. de Trinquevedel* (impeccably made, well-flavored, and delicate wine), *Dne. du Vieux Relais* (smooth, early maturing wine), *Dne. de Tourtouil* (concen-

trated, flavorful wine from old vines), *Adolphe Roudil* (excellent wine from
6 hectares), *Dne. des Lauzes* (delicate wine with a distinct *goût deterroir*),
Dne. de Lanzac (fruity, early maturing, supple wine), *Dne. de Corne-Loup*
(robust, full-bodied, well-structured wine), *Clos Canto-Perdrix* (full-flavored Tavel, above-average red Lirac, and assorted *vin de table*), *Dne. les
Trois Logis* (average but often dull wine, despite its excellent location), *Ch.
de Manissy* (above-average wood-aged but fresh, fruity wine), *Prieuré de
Montézargues* (distinctive, well-flavored wine), *Dne. de Roc-Epine* (full-
bodied and often complex wine), and *Seigneur de Vaucrose* (full-bodied,
robust, "woody" wine that is often unbalanced).

Côtes du Rhône

The Côtes du Rhône appellation, located on both banks of the Rhône,
stretches south from Vienne, in the extreme northern portion of the
producing district, to Beaucaire in the department of Gard. It produces
approximately three-quarters of all the wine in the Rhône valley, encompasses 150 settlements, nearly 10,000 vignerons, and sixty-six cooperatives. The area south of Montelimar, with nearly 98 percent of the total
hectarage, is the primary area of production, particularly the river valleys
of the Aigues, Ouvèze, Ardèche, and Cèze.

With Châteauneuf-du-Pape and Tavel the two notable exceptions,
southern Rhône wines were ignored until the formation of the Interprofessional Wine Committee of the Côtes du Rhône in 1955. This large
organization has broad powers to assist growers and winemakers in
technical matters and public affairs. The committee is largely responsible
for popularizing the appellation in Switzerland, West Germany, and
Belgium, and it is expected to help triple exports over the next fifteen
years. It is very active in promoting the wine to tourists, and has
introduced a new and distinctive bottle called "La Rhodanienne." Figures
6.5 and 6.6 show the growth in production and exports between 1950
and the present decade.

The appellation has grown rapidly during the past thirty years and
ideally fills the void for average-quality, inexpensive, everyday table wine.
When carefully selected, it is generally a good value; but more often than
not the wine is just barely palatable, dull, unbalanced, overly filtered and
fined. Ninety-five percent of the wines, which originate in diverse soil and
microclimates, are red in color. Minimum alcohol content is 11 percent,
and the yield, the highest in the Rhône valley, is 50 hectoliters to the
hectare. Because the latter is chronically exceeded, nearly all appellation
wine is called *générique,* which refers to wine that is the product of
overcropping and is characterized by low intensity of flavor, scent, and
extract. Less than 5 percent of all wine is estate-bottled.

Grape varieties vary by department and include Cinsault, Gamay Noir
à Jus Blanc, Marsanne, Pinot Noir, Roussanne du Var, Syrah, Grenache

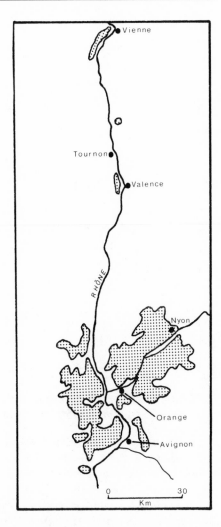

Figure 6.4
The Côtes du Rhône Appellation

Noir, Grenache Blanc, Grenache Gris, Clairette, Mourvèdre, Picpoul, Picpoul Noir, Terret Noir, Terret Blanc, Terret Gris, Oeillade, Bourboulenc, Carignan Noir, Carignan Blanc, Counoise, Muscardin, Vaccarèse, Mauzac Blanc, Mauzac Rosé, Ugni Blanc, Calitor, Marsanne, and Viognier, and others. The only major restrictions limit Carignan Noir and Blanc to 30 percent of the blend and forbid the inclusion of any hybrids. The tendency among the better growers is to reduce the proportion of Grenache and Cinsault while increasing Syrah and Mourvèdre.

Côtes du Rhône Rouge is by far the better wine made, but its quality varies enormously. Made by carbonic maceration, the wine is light in color and body and practically devoid of flavor and scent. The rosé constitutes about 4 percent of total production, and although pretty in color, does not compete well with equivalents from Tavel and Lirac, either

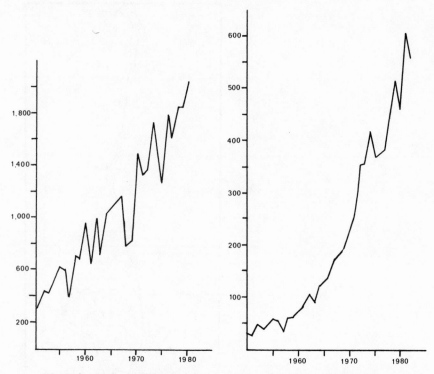

Côtes du Rhône: Wine Production (Fig. 6.5, *left*) and Exports
(Fig. 6.6, *right*), 1950–1983 (in thousands of hectoliters)

in quality or price. Constituting only 1 percent of total output, Côtes du
Rhône Blanc is characterized by a tendency to oxidize and turn bitter
within a year. The finest wine (not entirely made by carbonic maceration)
is from grapes grown only in gravelly soils. Light, flavorless wines are
always made by carbonic maceration and are made from grapes grown in
clay-dominated flatland. More than 90 percent of all Côtes du Rhône wine
is made by the 66 cooperatives in the region. By department, their
distribution is Gard 30, Vaucluse 22, Drôme 11, and Ardèche 3. The
principal negociants distributing more than three-quarters of all Côtes du
Rhône wine are *Le Cellier des Daupins, La Vieille Ferme, Bellicard, A. Ogier,
Société Nouvelle des Vins Fins Salavert, David & Foillard, Pascal, Etablissement
Meffre, Léon Revol, Paul-Etienne Père,* and *Abbaye de Bouchet.*

In the of Gard department the following properties have generated
considerable interest: *Ch. de Domazan, Dne. le Haut Castel, Dne. de Cocol,
Dne. de l'Amandier, Ch. de Boussargues, Dne. des Moulins, Dne. de la
Réméjeanne, Dne. Comte de Pontmartin, Dne. de la Charite, Dne. de la Rouette,
Dne. de St.-Libel, Ch. de Bosc, Ch. de Farel,* and *Dne. de Lascamp.*

The principal properties in the department of Vaucluse are *Ch. de
Fonsalette, Ch. Rayas, Ch. de St.-Estève, Dne. de la Guicharde, Dne. de la*

Grand Ribe, Dne. de la Chapelle, Dne. de la Girardière, Dne. Martin, Dne. de l'Espigouette, Ch. de Ruth, Dne. Ste.-Apollinaire, Ch. Malijay, Dne. des Richards, Dne. St.-Michel, Dne. Mitan, Ch. de Gourdon, Ch. du Grand Moulas, Dne. du Grand Prébois, Dne. du Vieux Chêne, and *Dne. de la Renjarde.*

In the department of Drôme the principal properties are *Ch. de L'Estagnol, Ch. la Borie, Cave Jaume, Dne. A. Mazud, Dne. du Petit Barbaras, Dnr. des Treilles, Dne. du Gourget, Dne. de la Taurelle, Dne. de St.-Luc,* and *Dne. du Bois de la Tour Couverte.* In the department of Ardèche, the principal properties are *Ch. Rochescolombe, Dne. de l'Olivet,* and *Dne. des Amoureuses.*

Côtes du Rhône–Villages

While the Côte du Rhône appellation has been in existence since 1937, the Côtes du Rhône–Villages designation dates to 1953, when four villages—Cairanne, Laudun, Chusclan, and Gigondas—were given the right to append their village name to the Côtes du Rhône designation. Over the next fourteen years, thirteen additional villages were added, and in 1967, all of them were given the separate appellation name of Côtes du Rhône–Villages. These seventeen villages are distributed in three departments as follows: in Vaucluse—Valréas, Visan, Cairanne, Roiax, Rasteau,

Plate 6.1   The cellars of Ch. St.-Estève

Séguret, Vacqueyras, Sablet, and Beaumes-de-Venise; in the Drôme—St.-Maurice-sur-Aygues, Rousset, Rochegude, St.-Pantaléon-les-Vignes, and Vinsobres; and in the Gard—Laudun, Chusclan, and St.-Gervais. Vignerons in all of the above-mentioned villages have the right to sell their wines as Côtes du Rhône, under the village name, or as Côtes du Rhône–Villages. If the vigneron chooses to market the wine under the last two designations it must contain a minimum of 12.5 percent alcohol, the yield must be limited to 35 hectoliters to the hectare, and the wine is subjected to a compulsory tasting. For the production of red wine, the Grenache is limited to 65 percent, followed by Syrah, Mourvèdre, and Cinsault, and all other varieties are restricted to 10 percent of the final blend. For rosé production, Grenache is limited to 60 percent of the final blend, Vaccarèse and Cinsault to 15 percent, and all others to 10 percent. For white wine production, Clairette, Roussanne, and Bourboulenc collectively account for 80 percent, Grenache Blanc for 10 percent, and other varieties for 10 percent. The "Villages" designation, in an attempt to upgrade the quality of Côtes du Rhône wine, has introduced more limiting requirements, which presumably results in a better wine, although comparative tastings do not always substantiate quality on a regular basis. While quality for the "Villages" appellation is highly variable, the very best wines are full-bodied, well flavored, and well scented. Total production from 1965 to 1984 is shown in Figure 6.7.

The following listing of principal villages and their growths starts along the right bank of the Rhône and proceeds southward. *Rousset-les-Vignes* and *St.-Pantaléon,* the most northerly of the seventeen villages, are located in hilly and mountainous terrain. Nearly all the wine is produced by the cooperative of St.-Pantaléon, and most of it is sold in bulk to negociants. The wines are full, firm, dark, and above average in quality. With approximately 1,400 hectares, *Valréas* is one of the most important communes in the "Villages" appellation. The wines have a reputation for being soft, supple, warm, and well-flavored. In addition to one large cooperative with a good reputation, there are a small number of private growers. Dating back to 1317, *Dne. du Val-des-Rois* is a 15-hectare property that was once owned by the Avignon popes. The vineyard is located 350 to 400 meters above sealevel on sloping and windy slopes whose soils are a varying mixture of limestone, clay, and sand. This conscientious property produces 5,500 cases of excellent red and rosé wines offering good value. Four other small, but above-average growths are *Dne. de la Prévosse, Dne. de St.-Chetin, Dne. de la Fuzière, Dne. des Grands Devers,* and *Notre Dame de Vieille.*

Vinsobres is a small medieval village of 1,240 hectares that overlooks the Aigues River. It has two cooperatives and a handful of private growers who produce full-bodied, alcoholic wines: *Dne. de la Bicarelle, Dne. du Coriançon, Dne. du Moulin, Dne. des Escoulaires,* and *Dne. les Aussellons.* The medieval town of *Visan,* with more than 2,000 hectares, is one of the

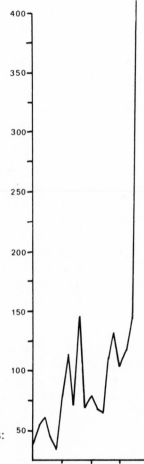

Figure 6.7   Côtes du Rhône–Villages:
Wine Production, 1965–1984
(in thousands of hectoliters)

biggest producers of red wine in the entire Rhône. In addition to the large cooperative that makes nearly all the wine, there are two small growths with a good reputation, *Dne. de la Cantharide* and *Clos du Père Clément. St.- Maurice-sur-Aygues,* located along the Aigues River, produces wine that has a reputation for being alcoholic, full-bodied, and good for blending. All the wine is made by the local cooperative. The village of *Rochegude,* one of the better communes in the appellation, makes only red wine, all of which is produced by the local cooperative. The medieval village of *Roaix* lying along the Ouvèze River is known for the production of undistinguished red and small quantities of white wine. In addition to the local cooperative, the only other property of importance is *La Fiole du Chevalier d'Elbène.*

With 900 residents, the village of *Cairanne* is located in the high Vaucluse, 16 kilometers from Orange. Historically it was the site of an important Knights Templars commandery. One of the most important, quality producing villages of the appellation, it is located in the center of the Villages appellation and contains more private Côtes du Rhône–Villages producers than any other commune. Maintaining an excellent reputation for quality and value, the local cooperative makes more than 650,000 cases. The red wine is firm and keeps well for four years. Among the many private producers are *Dne. des Travers, L'Oratoire de St.-Martin, Dne. du Grand Chêne, Dne. de Banvin, Dne, de la Fauconnière, Dne. Rabasse-Charavin, Ch. de Cairanne, Dne, de la Gayère, Dne. Richaud, Dne. de la Présidente,* and *Dne. d'Aeria.*

Rasteau, Séguret, and *Sablet* are three small medieval towns located in the fertile Ouvèze valley. Because vineyards suffer from truck garden and fruit tree competition, vignerons cultivate small vineyard plots and are mainly members of the local cooperatives. Of the four villages, Rasteau has as many private producers with a quality reputation as the other three combined. One of the principal properties in Rasteau is *Dne. des Girasols,* a recently developed property of 15 hectares that makes 7,000 cases of *vin de garde* wine. The principal growth in Sablet is the 60-hectare, 16th-century *Dne. de Verquière.* Other popular properties include *Ch. du Trignon, Dne. de la Soumade, Dne. de Cabasse, Dne. le Souverain, Dne. des Couteaux les Travers, Dne. de Wilfried, Dne. Roumanille,* and *Dne. du Sommier.*

Vacqueyras, one of the finest communes in the producing area, is expected to be elevated, like its neighbor Gigondas, to a separate village appellation in the near future. While there are more than fifteen outstanding growths, the standards of all producers in the commune are high, particularly for wine made by the *méthode ancienne.* The principal properties are *Dne. de la Fourmone, Vieux Clocher, Dne. du Clos des Cajaux, Ch. des Roques, Dne. de Montvac, Dne. du Pont du Rieu, Dne. de la Garrigue, Le Mousquetaire, Dne. le Colombier,* and *Dne. du Couroulou.* Adjacent to Vacqueyras is *Beaumes-de-Venise,* the most important properties of which were discussed previously.

Of the seventeen Côtes du Rhône–Villages appellation communes, only three are located along the left bank of the Rhône—*St.-Gervais, Chusclan,* and *Laudun.* The northernmost in the Cèze valley, St.-Gervais is a 200-hectare vineyard of small growers, nearly all of whom belong to the local cooperative. The only significant private property is *Dne. Ste.-Anne.* Chusclan contains 560 hectares of vineland, one major cooperative, and no important vignerons making or bottling wine. Laudun, one of the oldest of the Côtes du Rhône–Villages communes, is half the size of Chusclan and the site of one important property, *Dne. Rousseau.*

Côtes du Ventoux

With an annual output of 200,000 hectoliters from 3,500 hectares, Côtes du Ventoux is the second-largest appellation in the Rhône valley. The vineyards are located along the upper margins of the productive valley of the Coulon River and the western foothills of the 1,800-meter Mont Ventoux. Facing south, the region is a highly fertile, well-irrigated stretch of recently reclaimed land that is also the center of a large and growing table grape industry. The hilly portion, which is the most important area, trends in a north-south direction that begins in the Ouvèze valley and proceeds southward in an irregular manner to the town of Coustellet. The appellation embraces more than thirty villages, of which St.-Saturnin, Carpentras, Caromb, Flassan, Mazan, and Villes-St.-Auzon are considered the most important.

Unlike neighboring appellations, the wines (70 percent red, 25 percent rosé, and 5 percent white) are overwhelmingly of *vin ordinaire* quality: light in color, early maturing, and devoid of any distinctive character (the rosé, however, often can be fresh, fragrant and quaffable). Not only are the wines undistinguished, but the AOC status awarded in 1973 seriously undermines the integrity of other producing districts in the southern Rhône. This controversial appellation was faced with adverse publicity when prices rose by 30 percent the year the appellation status was awarded, only to fall and remain at present depressed levels. More than 95 percent of the wine is the product of cooperative efforts. The largest producer, *Dne. de Beaucastel,* bottles under the La Vieille Ferme label, which is a highly successful wine in overseas markets. *Pierre Amadieu* and *Pierre André* are two competent negociants, while *Dne. du Vieux Lazaret, Dne. de Tenon, Dne. Ste.-Croix, Dne. des Anges,* and *Dne. St.-Saveur* rank among the more prominent growers.

Other Producing Regions

In addition to the above AOC appellations, the southern Rhône contains two large and increasingly important VDQS appellations: Côtes du Luberon and Côtes du Vivarais. The first, a 3,000-hectare vineyard, makes more than 140,000 hectoliters of red, rosé, and white wine, of which the first two contribute more than 85 percent of total output. This hitherto unknown appellation is located north of Aix-en-Provence on cool, hilly, and mountainous terrain between the Coulon and Durance rivers. The best sites contain soils that are colluvial in origin, dry, and well drained. Properties are large and well mechanized.

Although "méridional" grapes dominate, the recent introduction of Syrah, Cabernet Sauvignon, and other Bordeaux and Burgundian varieties have improved overall quality tremendously. A good deal of the wine has considerable polish, is capable of aging, and is far better and more consistent than the wine of the overrated Côtes du Ventoux appellation immediately to the north. Of the three colors, the red is by far the finest, particularly if made with larger percentages of nontraditional grapes. The color ranges from very dark to medium ruby, the flavor is vinous, the aroma is pronounced, and it is surprisingly supple and well balanced. Cooperatives are responsible for more than 90 percent of total output, the largest being the *Union des Vignerons des Côtes du Luberon*. The showpiece in the region and one of the largest properties is the superbly run 1,000-hectare *Ch. Val-Joannis*, followed by *Ch. de l'Isolette, Ch. la Canorgue, Ch. Turcan*, and *Ch. de Mille*.

One-fifth the size of Côtes du Luberon and less good are the wines of the Côtes du Vivarais appellation. This little-known, predominantly red wine district consists of eight communes, all of which lie just north of the Côtes du Rhône appellation in the Ardèche department. Although the official status is VDQS, quality is hardly above *vin ordinaire* standards. The wine made primarily by the *Union des Producteurs Orgnac l'Aven,* is heavily filtered and fined, fruity, light-bodied, and made entirely by the carbonic maceration process. *Dne. Gallety,* a relatively large property, is the most prominent of several which bottle their output.

THE WINES OF PROVENCE

LOCATED in southeastern France, Provence is a somewhat ill-defined region bordered by Italy, the Mediterranean Sea, and the vineyards of southern Rhône. Along with Corsica, Languedoc, and Roussillon, it is part of the Mediterranean climatic region and one of the oldest viticultural regions of the nation. Its 45,000 hectares of vineland produce about 2.5 million hectoliters, about 4 percent, of the country's annual wine output. Its importance lies in the fact that it makes about 5 percent of all AOC wine and 65 percent of all AOC rosé wine in France. Historically Provence, poor in agricultural and mineral resources, was one of the most economically and culturally deprived areas of France. The population was low, the coastal areas were malarial, and agriculture was neither developed nor well mechanized. Until the middle of the 19th century, the dominant agricultural activity was sheep and goat herding, with scattered olive and wheat production. But with the advent of refrigerated ships, railroads, and efficient truck transportation, vegetables, citrus fruit, and a significant flower and perfume industry emerged. Today, slowly eclipsed only by vegetable production in newly irrigated areas, vinegrowing, winemaking, olives, and flower production are equally important.

The producing regions encompass all the departments of Var, the Alpes Maritimes, and portions of Bouches-du-Rhône. There are seven AOC appellations (Côtes du Provence, Bandol, Cassis, Ballet, Palette, Coteaux des Baux, and Coteaux d'Aix-en-Provence) (see Fig. 7.1), two VDQS (Coteaux Varois, and Coteaux de Pierrevert), and several *vin de pays*. For the region as a whole, approximately 60 percent of output is rosé (the highest percentage of any major producing region), 35 percent is red, and 5 percent is white. Although Provençal wines are rather uniform in style,

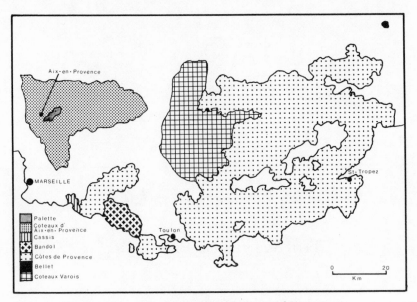

Figure 7.1   The Major Appellations of Provence
(Coteaux des Baux not shown)

quality and consistency vary widely. Approximately 10 percent of production is made by growers who, in general, make a superior product in
comparison to the many cooperatives. As of 1981, at least 144 cooperatives made highly variable *vin ordinaire* and AOC wine whose quality was
often not up to classified standards. Within the Var department alone, the
99 cooperatives control 34,000 hectares, have a storage capacity of 3.5
million hectoliters, and produce nearly all VDQS and *vin de pays* and more
than half of all AOC wine.

In Provence is one of the most geographically diverse vineyards in France;
it includes coastal lowlands, interior basins, high mountains, and totally
lacks physical unity, a common history, or a clear economic focus.
Marseilles, the nation's second-largest city and chief economic and urban
center in the south, lies on the western edge of the producing region, but
its main function is to serve as an entrepôt for the industrial areas of
central and northern France. The rest of Provence is a cluster of
fascinating resorts, mountain villages, and small interior cities, all of
which have curious and captivating histories.

In the extreme western portion lies the lower Rhône basin, and near the
Italian border are a series of diverse mountain ranges. Along the coast are
the mountain ranges of Estaque, Ste.-Baume, Maures, and Esterel, all of
which predate the central European Alps. The narrow and discontinuous
coastal region reflects the nonaligned character of the mountainous
interior. Between Marseilles and Toulon and near the Italian frontier are a
number of very picturesque fjord-like inlets called *calanques,* the focal
point of important tourist attractions. The entire region falls well within

Table 7.1 AOC Wine Production in Provence, 1980

Appellation	Hectoliters	Percent of total	Appellation	Hectoliters	Percent of total
Côtes de Provence Rouge	586,258	74.0	Coteaux d'Aix Route[a]	94,840	12.0
Côtes de Provence Blanc	58,762	7.4	Coteaux d'Aix Blanc	5,929	.7
Bandol Rouge	22,898	2.9	Coteaux des Baux Rouge[a]	15,516	2.0
Bandol Blanc	1,212	.2	Coteaux des Baux Blanc	90	
Cassis Rouge	1,763	.2			
Cassis Blanc	3,589	.4	Total Rouge	722,550	91.2
Bellet Rouge	782	.1	Total Blanc	70,057	8.3
Bellet Blanc	324				
Palette Rouge	493		General total	792,607	100.0
Palette Blanc	151				

[a] AOC status granted in 1985.

Source: French Ministry of Agriculture.

the Mediterranean climatic pattern of cool, humid winters and hot, dry summers. The only deviation from this paradigm are the interior basins and the mountainous uplands, the first receiving less precipitation and the latter more, along with lower annual and greater diurnal variations in temperature. Significant portions of the producing area, however, are buffeted by many local and regional winds: *Mistral, Gregal, Tramontane, Paunen, Lebech, Eisserog, Levant* and *Miegiou.*

Since the area is not homogeneous in terms of geology, topography, or climate, soils vary widely. When compared to the deeper and more uniform alluvial soils of the Languedoc, Roussillon, or southern Rhône, Provence offers a wide assortment of skeletal, colluvial, and alluvial soils that are highly mineralized, light in color, and rocky, with little sand or organic matter. In general, soils reflect the complex geology of granitic massifs with numerous granite, schist, and limestone outcroppings. In the final analysis, the soil is important only in conjunction with aspect, altitude, and microclimate. Throughout the Provençal region, wine quality is the direct result of the altitude at which it was produced: the higher altitudes produce better, crisper, more acidic, and fruitier wines. In sharp contrast, the low-lying, clay-filled interior basins produce coarser, flatter, more alcoholic *vin ordinaire* wines.

Despite the fact that wild vines were known to the indigenous Ligurians, it is widely believed that the ancient Phocaean Greeks, the founders of Marseilles, Nice, and other coastal settlements, taught the inhabitants of southern Gaul the art of pruning vines and making wine. In the 2nd century B.C. vinegrowing assumed considerable importance under Roman Imperial rule; but as Roman influence weakened, the region was invaded by several central and northern European barbarian tribes who did little to foster the continuity of viticulture. The entire coastline was ravaged by Moorish pirates (hence the ubiquitous name "Maures" throughout coastal Provence). This invasion, combined with a serious malaria epidemic, contributed to the depopulation of the coastal areas and forced the remaining population to establish new hilltop settlements in the interior.

The economic and political fortunes of Provence improved somewhat during the period of the Crusades in the 11th and 14th centuries, but only in a minor way and only in the western portion near Aix-en-Provence, a region lying along the north-south route between the Mediterranean and northern France. As the Crusaders bypassed a good portion of Provence, few vineyards were established by religious orders, in sharp contrast to the many founded in the lower Rhône and in western and northern France. The small scale and subsistent character of viticulture in Provence continued until the end of the 18th century, when portions of the Mediterranean coast were reclaimed. Long forgotten, the full-bodied, alcohol-rich rosés reemerged for a short time in the latter part of the 17th and 18th centuries in Paris. Real growth did not materialize until the middle of the 19th century, when a good portion of Provence was incorporated with France. As a consequence, vine hectarage had reached 65,000 hectares by the time *phylloxera* struck, only to fall steadily to the present level of 45,000 hectares. There are expectations that major intraregional shifting in the present distribution pattern will take place. For example, over the past 100 years, vine hectarage in the Alpes-Maritimes department has declined by more than 12,000 hectares, in the Bouches-du-Rhône by 3,000 hectares, and in the department of Var by 5,000 hectares. The latter is highly significant because it is a *net* figure and does not include the 14,000 hectares that have been abandoned in less productive areas. The process of abandonment and redistribution along the coastal margins is expected to continue because vines cannot compete with tourism and fresh flower production.

The ampelography of Provence is fascinating for both vigneron and historian as it is the site of perhaps more remnant grapevines than any other viticultural region of France. Major grape varieties for the department of Var for the years 1968, 1979, and as a percent of national total are given in Table 7.2. It is interesting to note that for 1979, three-quarters of total hectarage was composed of just four grape varieties and that about one-third of all plantings were white grapes. This is an unusual feature because less than 10 percent of total wine production is of that color. Two grape varieties, Mourvèdre and Roussanne, represent 92.2 and 86.9 percent of all national plantings. In an attempt to increase overall quality, Cinsault, Grenache Noir, Mourvèdre, Syrah, and a number of Gironde varieties, most notably Sauvignon Blanc, Cabernet Sauvignon, and Merlot, are expected to increase. While Carignan, Aramon, Alicante Bouschet, and Couderc Noir are expected to decline in the coming

Table 7.2 Major Grape Varieties in the Var Department, 1968 and 1979

Grape variety	1968		1979		As percent of national total
	Hectares	Percent[a]	Hectares	Percent[a]	
Carignan Noir	17,800	29.3	12,500	30.2	6.0
Ugni Blanc	10,100	16.6	6,600	15.9	5.2
Cinsault	4,600	7.6	6,000	14.6	11.6
Grenache Noir	3,200	5.3	5,000	11.9	6.4
Aramon	5,700	9.4	2,100	5.1	5.3
Mourvèdre	300	.5	1,200	2.9	92.2
Clairette	3,400	5.6	1,100	2.6	20.6
Roussane	1,600	2.6	1,000	2.5	86.3
Alicante Bouschet	1,500	2.5	800	1.9	3.7
Couderc Noir	3,000	4.9	700	1.8	9.0
Syrah	100	.2	700	1.6	6.0
Aubun	500	.8	500	1.0	8.6
Villard Blanc	1,400	2.3	200	.5	
Grand Noir	1,500	2.5	200	.5	
Villard Noir	900	1.5	100	.3	
Others	5,124	8.4	2,796	6.7	
Total	60,724	100.0	41,496	100.0	

[a]Percent of departmental total.

Source: French Ministry of Agriculture.

decades, the ancient Mourvaison, Brun-Fourca, Fuella, Mayorquin, Bouteillan, Teoulier, and Valentin are destined for extinction.

In general, the wines have good color but lack fruit, extract, and bouquet and are burdened by excess alcohol. They age quickly, are often "oily," bitter, and overly sulfured. They do, however, complement the grilled meat and spicy regional cuisine. Rosé wine, the life blood of the region, which is dry and occasionally fruity and citrus-flavored, dominates production throughout the entire area. Yet more than 50 percent is no better than *vin ordinaire,* with less than 10 percent considered worthy of AOC status. The main redeeming features are that it looks nice and can be attractively priced. The quality of red wine ranges from dull, lifeless, and tasteless, to full-bodied, highly flavorful potions, especially from Bandol and Aix-en-Provence. White wine suffers from a lack of freshness, balance, and aroma. The very best, which is only average, comes from Bellet, Aix-en-Provence, Bandol, and Cassis.

Côtes de Provence

The Côtes de Provence appellation, stretching over the departments of Bouches-du-Rhône, Var, and portions of Alpes-Maritimes, was historically the largest VDQS appellation in the nation, but since 1977 it has become the most important AOC vineyard in Mediterranean France.

More than 90 percent of total production occurs within the Var department, one of the largest in the country. The heart of the producing region
is uncommonly massive, measuring more than 200 kilometers along the
Mediterranean coast by 150 kilometers inland. Within this vast region are
several mountain ranges, numerous valleys, and soils that vary from low-
lying clay deposits derived from limestone, to granitic stone, schist,
sandstone, and wholesale quantities of colluvial material. Despite the
notoriety of the Côte d'Azur, more than 80 percent of total output occurs
in small interior valleys mentioned earlier and in the communes of Cuers,
Lorgues, Tradeau, Gonfaron, Pierrefeu-du-Var, Puget-Ville, Le Luc,
Vidauban, Les Arc, La Motte, Correns, Cotignan, and Cannet-des-
Maures.

Total hectarage for the production of red, rosé, and white Côtes de
Provence wine is estimated to be about 15,000 hectares, which produce
from 700,000 to 1 million hectoliters, up sharply from 300,000 hectoliters during the immediate post–World War II period. The wines,
commonly called "vacation wines," are served chilled and are readily
quaffed by more than 20 million foreign tourists who visit the area
annually. Approximately 65 percent of total output is rosé (declining), 28
percent red (increasing), and only 7 percent white (increasing)—all of
which are dry. While the appellation seems to make good to excellent red
and rosé, the overwhelming amount is plain *vin ordinaire,* the source of
much controversy over the AOC status awarded in 1977. Within the
department of Var are 99 cooperatives, most of which produce some AOC
Côtes de Provence, and at least 35 produce hugh quantities of *vin de pays.*
With only minor exceptions, cooperative wine is always strong in alcohol,
robust or flat on the palate, and totally devoid of delicacy, subtlety, and
consistency. Of the 100 major private growers, less than half enjoy a
regional and national reputation, and less than a dozen are known outside
France. An estimated 20 percent of all privately produced wine is sold
directly at the winery, a figure that increases beyond 50 percent for those
growers fortunate to be near prominent tourist attractions. As appellation
restrictions have tightened, a number of new, large, professionally
managed estates have been created throughout the region.

Provençal rosé lost its panache after the world depression of the 1930s,
when it became stale, flat, inconsistent, and outrageously expensive in
relation to other wines. Furthermore, because the number of large capital-
intensive properties were few, the wine was made primarily by cooperatives who did little to improve the product. To this day, the wine varies
from bland and dull to distinctive and individual, with the former
dominating production. It is usually consumed before its first birthday
and, with only a few minor exceptions, is never allowed to age. The very
best is fruity, bone dry, crisp, refreshing, and in some instances has a
pronounced bouquet; the overwhelming majority, however, is very unin-
teresting.

Rosé is made from a large number of grape varieties and a complicated two-tier system of vine allocation based on percentages. The first tier, called "principal varieties," accounts for 70 percent of the blend and includes the red varieties of Cinsault, Grenache Noir, Tibouren, Mourvèdre, Carignan, and three white grapes—Ugni Blanc, Clairette, and Rolle. The remaining 30 percent, or "complimentary varieties," include Barbaroux, Roussanne, Mourvaison, Cabernet Sauvignon, Syrah, Calitor, and two white grapes—Muscat and Sémillon. Within this second tier, Barbaroux must not exceed 10 percent of the blend, and as of 1986 Roussane was banned from the group of authorized grapes. As of 1984, at least 10 percent of the final blend must be Mourvèdre and Syrah. In an effort to improve wine quality, appellation restrictions have been tightened to ensure or at least to mitigate the possibility of abuse. Official permission is now required before vignerons may uproot and replant vines or expand their hectarage. Not only is overcropping frowned upon, but a strong effort is being made to punish offenders. More important, the area has been moderately successful in reducing hectarage devoted to undesirable vines such as Carignan (35 percent decrease in the past 15 years), Aramon (70 percent), Ugni Blanc (40 percent), Couderc Noir (90 percent), Alicante Bouschet (60 percent), and nearly all hybrids. In addition, a conscious effort has been made to match the grape variety with soil and microclimate. It was found, for example, that the Syrah vine does well in the clay soils of the Argens valley, that Cabernet Sauvignon adapts well to the cooler uplands, and that the Mourvèdre thrives in areas with deep soil and brilliant sunshine. Another important evolution in the improvement of Provençal wine is the use of carbonic maceration methods to produce fruitier and more stable wine.

Red wine is made primarily from Carignan, Cinsault, Grenache Noir, Tibouren, Mourvèdre, and Syrah. The percentages of Carignan and Tibouren have dropped sharply, while the remainder, particularly Grenache Noir and Cinsault, have risen. Historically Carignan accounted for nearly 70 percent of the final blend, but by 1995 it is expected to account for no more than 30 percent. Red wine amounts to nearly 30 percent of total output and, as it is so little known, it offers the best values in the producing region. While the wine is no match for Bandol and the better growths of Aix-en-Provence, it is well flavored and not coarse. White production since 1960 has doubled, and by 2000, it will probably account for 15 percent of regional output. The principal grape varieties are Ugni Blanc, Clairette, Sémillon, and Rolle. The better areas are the upper Argens valley and isolated hilly regions along the coast between Toulon and St.-Tropez. While quality is highly inconsistent, a small number of producers are now making fruitier, fresher, more acidic wine through better vinification methods.

The following are the main producers along the Mediterranean coast: *Dne. de la Tour,* a 13-hectare property, making firm, robust, flavorful red, rosé, and white wines; *Dne. du Peymain,* known for concentrated, light, more delicate wines; *Dne. des Mouliers; Dne. le Castel; Clos Cibonne; Dne. des Embiez; Dne. des Fouques; Dne. de Porquerolles,* located on a picturesque off-shore island; *Clos Mireille,* a 60-hectare property making 17,000 cases of expensive but outstanding white wine; *Dne. St.-André de Figuiere,* a 14-hectare, highly aggressive and quality-oriented property, making excel-lent red, rosé, and white wines; *Dne. de St.-Honoré; Dne. du Galoupet; Dne. des Campaux; Dne. de la Malherbe; Ch. de Leoubes; Dne. de la Croix,* a 200-hectare property making full-bodied, robust, brawny red wine from Cabernet Sauvignon and Mourvèdre; *Dne. des Garcinières; Dne. de St.-Maur; Les Maitres Vignerons de la Presque'ile de St.-Tropez,* a firm that bottles and distributes wines from nearly two dozen wineries; *Ch. Minuty; Dne. de St.-Antoine,* known for full-bodied, concentrated, and well-flavored wines; *Dne. du Bourrian; Ch. Barbeyrolles;* and *Dne. de Curebeasse.*

The principal properties along the southwestern portions of the Côtes de Provence appellation are *Ch. Montaud, Dne. de l'Aumerade, La Gor-donne, Ch. de Gairoird, St.-Pierre-des-Baux, Dne. de Rimauresq, Dne. de la Bernarde, Dne. de la Grande Lauzade,* and *Commanderie de Peyrassol.* In the extreme northern portion of the region, the principal properties are *Dne. de Nestuby, Ch. de Mentonne, Dne. de Feraud, Ch. de St.-Juline d'Aille, Ch. de Selle, Ch. St.-Martin, Ch. Clairettes, Dne. de la Bernarde, Dne. de St.-Baillon, Dne. St.-Romans-d'Esclans, Dne. Christiane Rabiega, Dne. du Dragon, Dne. des Grands Esclans, Dne. de Clastron, Ste.-Roseline, Dne. du Ch. du Rouet, Dne. des Planes,* and *Ch. St.-Pierre.*

Bandol

The Bandol vineyard, a 20-kilometer stretch of rugged coastline and interior hills located west of Toulon, contains 810 hectares of vineland, produces 30,000 hectoliters and, although the third-largest AOC appella-tion in Provence, makes only 4 percent of all AOC wine. Approximately 90 percent of production is red, 9 percent is rosé, and 1 percent is white. Historically Bandol produced the finest red wine of Provence, but now faces stiff competition from the "newer" red wine regions of Aix-en-Provence. The wines, consistently good, well flavored, dark in color, chunky in texture, and often blessed with a touch of elegance, are well above average for the south of France.

Although vines were cultivated as early as the 6th century B.C. under Greek auspices and were further encouraged by the Romans, the Bandol region proved too poor for effective, dense, human settlement. During the medieval period, barbaric invasions, Saracen occupation, pirate activity, and political and economic uncertainty kept extensive vine cultivation to a minimum. With the development of tourist activity along the Côte d'Azur in the 19th century, the industry was rejuvenated for a brief period before the *phylloxera* devastation in the 1870s. By 1920 there were fewer than 45 commercial hectares, but by 1945, four years after AOC status was attained, hectarage had increased to 100 and commercial production had risen to 2,400 hectoliters. Since then, production has increased elevenfold and hectarage eightfold, with output expected to approach 50,000 hectoliters by 1995.

The entire vineyard is an irregular amphitheater of basalt hills surrounded by modest "mountains," 450 meters above sealevel, that receive 3,050 hours of sunshine annually. Precipitation during late autumn and winter averages less than 650mm a year. During the long, dry summer season, mountain breezes moderate temperatures and help create a peculiar microclimate. Although the producing area is widely scattered and contains only 810 hectares of vineland, the finest sites are all located on south-facing slopes framed by a ring of rolling hills that are affected by the souwesterly *Lebech* wind. The vineyards start from the Gulf of Lexques, rise to the Plateau du Camp near St.-Cyr-sur-Mer and Le Castelet, curve toward Le Beausset south to Ollioles, then continue to Samary-sur-Mer overlooking the Mediterranean Sea. The entire region

Plate 7.1   Part of the Bandol vineyard (courtesy Moulin des Costes)

contains calcareous rock and is very stony, with only a thin mantle of reddish or dark-gray topsoil. The best sites, which contain high concentrations of calcium carbonate, are located on terraces called *restanques*. The dry summer climate, intense sunshine, and wind activity produce dry soils, which results in rather low yields—often as little as 15 hectoliters to the hectare. Despite the severe aridity, the Bandol region is a pleasant and picturesque area of pine, wild thyme, herbs, and scattered vineyards.

For red wine, three grape varieties, Mourvèdre, Cinsault and Grenache Noir, are cultivated for bouquet, body, and color. Of the three, the low-yielding Mourvèdre is the most important because its small berry produces a thick, dark, highly concentrated, well-flavored and scented wine that is both fresh and fruity on the palate. Brought from Spain in the 16th century, it has adapted extremely well to areas with high temperatures, brilliant sunshine, and mineralized, calcium-rich soil. Approximately 92 percent of national Mourvèdre plantings are located in the Var department, with the highest concentration in Bandol. The minimum allowable percentage of Mourvèdre in the production of Bandol is 50, but several houses increase the amount to 80 percent or more. Secondary varieties, in addition to Cinsault and Grenache Noir, include Carignan, Syrah, Pinot Noir, Tibouren, and others, all of which must amount to less than 40 percent of the total blend. Appellation laws also allow up to 20 percent of white wine to be blended, a practice not followed by better producers. The yield is limited to 40 hectoliters to the hectare, and the minimum alcoholic strength is 11 percent.

Red wine, made from a rather long vatting period, must be aged in oak barrels for a minimum of 18 months. The resulting wine is very dark in color, tannin-rich, well flavored, full on the palate, and surprisingly fragrant. The wine, known for its balance, complexity, elegance, and firmness, is capable of aging for as long as twenty years. Not only is the wine well flavored with spice and truffle, but its bouquet retains its flowery character even after ten years of bottle-aging. The rosé, one of the very best and most expensive in Provence, is made primarily from Grenache Noir, Cinsault, and Mourvèdre (60 percent combined), with the remainder coming from Carignan, Calitor, Pinot Noir, Tibouren, and others. The wine, though fresh and fruity, is better known for its "accessibility" and, although it is firm on the palate, it is much smoother and quaffable than most from southern France. White Bandol, the least popular of the three appellation wines, is made from a varying combination of Clairette and Ugni Blanc (locally referred to as "Blanc de Blanc"). Although the best bottles are absolutely dry, clean, round, and refreshing, they mature quickly and acquire a bitter aftertaste. Recently growers have begun planting small quantities of Sauvignon Blanc and Bourboulenc to heighten aroma and improve overall balance.

Of the two dozen major producers, five account for more than 60 percent of total production and nearly 95 percent of that which is exported. The largest and most important is the *Cave du Moulin de la Roque* cooperative founded in 1950. This quality-oriented firm affirms a progressive philosophical perspective on the future of Bandol and serves as an excellent model for all Provence. The wines are all expertly made and offer excellent value. *Dne. Tempier*, belonging to the Peyraud family since 1834, is located just north of the small port of Bandol in the rugged hills of Castellet. The 25-hectare estate, fragmented into three separate parcels sited on sloping land, is widely considered the premier quality property in the appellation. It produces about 8,000 cases of outstanding red wine that should not be missed. *Bunan Vignerons*, the largest of the private producers with headquarters in Moulin des Costes, makes more than 25,000 cases of red, rosé, and white under a number of distinctive labels. This very aggressive, reliable house currently revolutionizing the character of Bandol wines makes flavorful, well-balanced libations that offer excellent value. *Dne. du Val d'Arenc*, located in Beausset, is a 60-hectare property making more than 20,000 cases of well-made, consistently good, and moderately priced wines. *Ch. Pradeaux*, a large 120-hectare property, is part of a stable of properties that makes 20,000 cases of dark, heavy, tannin-rich, red Bandol. Much smaller but equally good is *Ch. des Vannières*, a 52-hectare property that makes 13,000 cases of Bandol plus other wines. *Ch. Romasson*, an old estate of 51 hectares, makes above-average red, rosé, and white wines. Other properties include *Dne. du Cagueloup, Ch. Milhière, Dne. de Fregate, Dne. le Galantin, Dne. de l'Hermitage, Dne. de la Noblesse, Dne. de la Laidière, Ch. de Pibarnon, Dne. Lafran-Veyrolles, Dne. de la Tour-du-Bon, Dne. la Borrasque, Dne. de l'Olivette*, and *Ch. Ste.-Anne*.

Cassis

Cassis, a small vineyard of 300 hectares, makes 6,000 hectoliters of red, rosé, and white wine, or about 1 percent of all AOC Provençal wine. The wine takes its name from a small, quaint, picturesque fishing village located 15 kilometers east of Marseilles along the Côte d'Azur. The widely scattered vineyards compete with sheep-grazing and summer home activities, and while the area enjoys considerable natural beauty, the port of Cassis lacks the panache of St.-Tropez or other coastal resorts farther to the east.

White wine is made from a varying mixture of Ugni Blanc, Sauvignon Blanc, Doucillon, Clairette, Marsanne, and Pascal Blanc, and although considerably better and more individual than red and rosé, it is, as the French say, very *corsé*, requiring several years of bottle-aging to round out fully. The most noticeable elements are its pronounced bouquet, dry taste, and firmness. Red and rosé wines are made from Carignan, Mourvèdre, Cinsault, and Barbaroux grapes with a maximum of 5 percent Terret Noir. Of the two, the rosé is marginally better, well scented, and an excellent accompaniment to grilled meat. The red, coarse but fragrant, is otherwise undistinguished and the lesser of the three wines. Six producers enjoy a local and regional reputation: *Dne. de la Ferme Blanche, Ch. de Fontblanche, Mas Calendal, Dne. du Paternel, Clos Ste.-Magdeleine,* and *Clos Boudard,* the last four widely known for above-average white wines with lofty prices.

Bellet

Bellet, an obscure and forgotten appellation of 125 hectares, makes less than 4,000 hectoliters of wine. The wines are produced by several villages located along the middle course of the Var River in the department of Alpes-Maritimes. The appellation makes red, rosé, and white wines, the latter considered the finest in Provence and perhaps in the entire Midi. The dominant grape for the production of white wine is Rolle, a rather obscure but highly fragrant grape that produces balmy and ambrosial wine. Other vines include Ugni Blanc, Listan, Clairette, and Chardonnay. The wine, which is highly variable, is nevertheless noted for its richness, delicate flavor, pronounced bouquet, and fresh, brisk character—rare features for a southern wine. The principal property in the appellation is *Ch. de Crémat,* known for pale yellow, dry, fragrant, well-balanced, highly satisfying wine that is very rare and expensive. The second, smaller but equally good property is *Ch. de Bellet,* known for well-structured, medium-bodied, and moderately priced wine.

With a beautiful color and a superb bouquet, red Bellet is made from the obscure Braquet and Fuella grapes, Cinsault, and a maximum of 40 percent Grenache Noir. Although above the level of average Provençal red wine, it fails to compete with Bandol. Quality has recently improved with the introduction of Cabernet Sauvignon, Syrah, and Mourvèdre in the final blend. The rosé, like the red, has excellent color and a host of pleasant assertive flavors. It is made from the same grape varieties plus Grenache Blanc, Ugni Blanc, Rolle, and others.

Palette

Palette, a postage-stamp appellation of less than 90 hectares, makes more than 4,000 hectoliters of red, rosé, and white wines. Small by any standard, the producing district is spread along the eastern margins of Aix-en-Provence, particularly in the communes of Palette, Meyreuil, and Tholonet. Of the three wines made, the white is considered the finest— full on the palate and with considerable staying power. The rosé, light and undistinguished, is the complete antithesis of the substantial yet supple red. The white is made from a minimum of 55 percent Clairette and a host of secondary vines, including Ugni Blanc and Grenache Blanc. The eastern outskirts of Aix-en-Provence are known for the one famous estate in the appellation: *Ch. Simone,* a modest property of 15 hectares with a long and well-established reputation for quality wine production. The vines, which grow on calcareous rocky soil, produce red, rosé, and white wines, all of which are complex and intense in flavor and aroma. The house makes two types of white wine. The finer and more delicate is a "Blanc de Blanc" made entirely from Clairette, and the other is a blend of several varieties and lesser cuvées. The red, primarily the product of Grenache and Cinsault, is a good, distinctive wine worth seeking out.

Coteaux d'Aix-en-Provence and Coteaux des Baux

Coteaux d'Aix-en-Provence is an irregular, widely diffused, and ill-defined appellation (mainly confined to limestone soils) of less than 2,000 hectares making above-average red and average rosé and white wines. First established as a VDQS appellation in 1972, the region has grown rapidly in hectarage as the quality of wines produced has established an excellent reputation for surprisingly soft, well-balanced, and superbly flavored wines. Appellation boundaries stretch northwest and north of Aix-en-Provence to the Durance River, east to St.-Maximim-la-Ste.-Baume, and south to Allauch. With the exception of two important communes, Rians and Artigues, both located in the department of Var, the rest of the appellation's hectarage is located entirely within the Bouches-du-Rhône department.

Unlike the Côtes de Provence appellation, red wine, with 85 percent of total output, is far more important than rosé and white wine production. In addition, more than three-quarters of production occurs in private cellars and not in cooperatives. The type of grape varieties used and the character of the wine are two other areas of departure from the usual Provençal enological picture. For red and rosé wines, the dominant grape varieties are Cabernet Sauvignon (limited to 60 percent), Grenache Noir, Syrah, Cinsault, Mourvèdre, and Counoise. Carignan, Tibouren, and other lesser vines are considered secondary and are slowly being phased out of production. Red wine, although varying dramatically by producer, is of high standards, is consistently well made, reliable, and often quite supple. The best properties emphasize a trilogy of superior grapes—Cabernet Sauvignon, Syrah, and Grenache Noir—and age the wine in wood for at least twelve months. The resulting libation is dark in color, fragrant, silky in texture, firm, and concentrated in flavor. It competes well in quality with any Provençal red, including Bandol, and all southern Rhône, including Châteauneuf-du-Pape. The main white vines include Clairette, Bourboulenc, Grenache Blanc, Ugni Blanc, Sémillon, and Sauvignon Blanc. Among the three dozen major properties, eighteen have established good reputations, of which *Ch. Vignelaure,* an 100-hectare property located at an altitude of 300 meters northeast of Aix-en-Provence, is the most important. Developed by the former owner of Ch.

La Lagune, this newly established, expertly managed vineyard contains a superb, modern, sophisticated winery that has generated an outstanding reputation for firm, multifaceted, *vin de garde* wines. Other properties include *Ch. de Beaulieu*, *Ch. la Coste*, *Dne. de la Grande Seouve*, *Dne. de Fonscolombe*, *Dne. de la Crémade*, *Dne. de la Tour Campanets*, *Ch. Picoudet*, *Dne. Richeaume*, *Charles-Marie Gruey*, *Mas de la Dame*, *Commanderie de la Bargemone*, *Dne. de la Lauzières*, *Dne. de la Semencière*, *Ch. du Seuil*, and *Ch. Mas de L'Hopital*. Coteaux des Baux, located east of Arles in the department of Bouches du Rhone, is known for red and rosé wines that are similar but of lesser quality than those of Coteaux d'Aix.

The largest of the two VDQS appellations, Coteaux Varois, a sizable 65,000-hectoliter vineyard, is a predominately red wine district that acquired its VDQS status in 1984. It stretches from the north and northwest of the Les Maures *vin de pays* area to the northwest portion of the Var department, and overlaps with a large section of the Côtes de Provence appellation. The producing region was formed with the specific purpose of upgrading the quality standards of red as opposed to Côtes de Provence rosé. Two large properties, both part of the vast holdings of Domaines Viticoles des Salins du Midi—*Dne. de l'Abbaye* and *Ch. la Gordonne*—dominate production from nearly 300 hectares. The wines (red, rosé, and white), all made from superior grape varieties, are expertly made and offer good value. Other properties include *Clos de la Truffière*, *Dne. de St.-Jean*, *Cave St.-André*, *Dne. du Loou*, and *Dne. de la Lieue*.

The remaining, small (10,000 hectoliter), little-known, and mainly red and rosé appellation of Coteaux de Pierrevert, located in mountainous terrain in the department of Alpes-Haute-Provence, enjoys the better reputation. Produced from traditional meridional grapes, the rosé wine is particularly fresh, fragrant, and above average in quality for the region.

THE WINES OF CORSICA

O NE of the more beautiful islands in the Mediterranean, Corsica
(Corse) is verdant, rural, picturesque, with no autostradas nor
other major manifestations of 20th-century urban-dominated
economics. With approximately 23,000 hectares of vines and an output of
2 million hectoliters of wine, Corsica produces from 4 percent to 5
percent of the nation's total wine output. The cultivation of grapes and
the production of wine represent 20 percent of the island's agricultural
product and employ more than 20,000 people.

Corsica measures 75 by 150 kilometers, and has an area of 8,700 sq.
kilometers and about 240,000 inhabitants. It is the third-largest island in
the Mediterranean and, with forty peaks above 2,150 meters, the most
mountainous. It is the sixth-largest French department in terms of size
and is composed of granite and schist rock similar to Provence 140
kilometers to the northwest.

The west-central portion of the island consists of a large, rugged,
granite massif whose coast is submerged, with deep rias and fragmented,
narrow slices of flatland. The eastern section, composed of schist rock, is
of lower elevation, contains the only large coastal plain, and is the main
food-producing area of the island. With nearly 80 percent of the entire
population living within 20 kilometers of the coast, the interior is less
developed and contains few settlements. The main agricultural areas other
than the eastern plain are Cap Corse, Balagne, the Ajaccio region, and the
immediate area surrounding Porto Vecchio.

Although the island has a typical Mediterranean climate, modification
by altitude is significant. The productive coastal region contains 19
percent of the island's total land area and 22 major communes. Historically heavily infested with malaria, it was reclaimed during the post—

World War II period and now accounts for the bulk of annual crops and nearly two-thirds of all vineyards, most of which are located along the east coast (see Fig. 8.1). The littoral also contains the island's two largest cities, Ajaccio, the capital, and Bastia, the principal port. Between 100 and 600 meters in elevation, the "Mediterranean region," with 42 percent of the total land area, is the most intensively used section and contains 238 communes. Originally it contained the wheat-producing areas (until 1965 the island's most important agricultural crop), nearly all the tree crops, and the principal vine cultivation area. But once the eastern littoral was developed in the early 1960s, its overall importance has declined drastically. The subalpine region, with 26 percent of the island's land area and 104 communes, is mainly devoted to pasture activities, contains few vines, and is the hub of a thriving tourist industry. Above 1,200 meters, the alpine region, with 11 percent of the total land area, is largely underdeveloped and contains only a handful of villages.

Figure 8.1
The Vineyards
of Corsica

Historically, Corsica was the least developed of all French departments as measured by per capita income, quality of transportation, education, and housing. The population was overwhelmingly agricultural, and settlement was isolated, fragmented, and located on malaria-free hill or mountain tops. The inefficient system of transhumance (the seasonal movement of man and animal between uplands and lowlands) was endemic over much of the island before it was eliminated in the middle of the 1960s. Finally, Corsica has, for the past 200 years, been an area of massive outmigration to mainland France.

The Grapes and Wines

The historic grape varieties of Corsica have Italian and Spanish ancestry. Among the "recommended" vines are Nielluccio, Sciacarello, Montanaccio, Caniaolo, Nero, Aleatico, Muscat Blanc à Petits Grains, Rossola Neras Riminese, Barbarossa, Vermentino, and Ugni Blanc. The newer varieties arriving with the *pied noirs* from Algeria in the early 1960s include Grenache Noir, Cinsault, Carignan Noir, and Alicante Bouschet. Within the last ten years, Mourvèdre, Syrah, Cabernet Sauvignon, Merlot, Pinot Noir, and Sauvignon Blanc have been introduced and are increasing their hectarage. Also grown is a bewildering list of additional, obscure, local and Italian varieties.

The most important "Corse" vines are the red Nielluccio and Sciarcarello and the white Vermentino. A variant of the famous Chianti Sangiovese, the Nielluccio, doing best in Bastia, is the historic workhorse of red and rosé wine production. It produces fragrant, full-bodied, and

Table 8.1   Major Grape Varieties Planted in Corsica, 1979

Grape variety	Hectares	Percent[a]	As percent of national total
Carignan Noir	5,400	23.1	2.6
Cinsault	5,200	22.3	10.1
Grenache Noir	3,600	15.4	4.6
Niellucio	2,500	10.7	100.0
Alicante Bouschet	2,500	10.7	11.4
Sciacarello	700	3.0	97.1
Malvoisie	700	3.0	85.2
Ugni Blanc	600	2.6	.4
Vermentino	300	1.3	96.0
Syrah	300	1.3	2.4
Others	1,531	6.6	
Totals	23,331	100.0	

[a]Percent of departmental total.

Source: French Ministry of Agriculture.

flavored wines but lacks subtlety, finesse, and harmony. As a result, it is rarely vinified alone but is blended with other "softer" varieties. The Sciacarello is not only good for wine, but is an admirable table grape as well. The wine is of medium color, has a marvelous fruity, spicy bouquet, and is able to age well, particularly when it comes from Tallano. The Vermentino acquires an exceptionally high sugar content but is subject to rapid oxidation. When vinified early in the season under ideal conditions and consumed early, the wine is fresh, zesty, and quite good as an aperitif or with seafood. If allowed to become overripe, it can be used only to make sweet wine. When mixed with Ugni Blanc, it is very successful, particularly in the limestone soils of Patrimonio.

Of the 2 million hectoliters of wine produced in Corsica, approximately 60 percent is red, 30 percent is rosé, and 10 percent is white. Of the total, only 90,000 hectoliters is AOC, with a similar color breakdown. An overwhelming percentage of wine produced is described as *vin de paysans*—the robust, full-flavored wine of small producers intended for local consumption. The better versions, *vins de chaudière,* are slightly higher in alcohol, deeply colored, and only marginally better. A good deal of red, rosé, and white exhibits the characteristics of old-fashioned Spanish and Italian "rancio" wines. A certain percentage is *pateux*—that is to say, thick and clammy, with a distinctive taste and aroma, and not at all "light" in the modern sense. Due to excessive chaptalization to boost alcohol levels, unwarranted use of sulfur, an overindulgence of grape concentrate, and the importation of Italian must of inferior quality, Corsica wines developed a bad reputation. On a slightly higher plane is an undetermined amount of wine currently being produced in the eastern section of the island that is officially called *vins du pays* and marketed under the name of "Ile-de-Beauté." Vinified in large cooperatives under modern technology, it is stored in stainless steel or glass containers and exhibits a taste that is nearly identical to all *vin du pays* libations—bland, with a muted bouquet, light color and alcohol, and easily drinkable.

Of the 90,000 hectoliters officially classified as AOC, most originate from the "old" areas of the island and are vinified mainly from "traditional" grape varieties. These wines are sold as "Vins de Corse" AOC by the following appellations: Coteaux-du-Cap-Corse, Patrimonio, Sartène, Figari, Porto Vecchio, Calvi, Ajaccio, or Coteaux d'Ajaccio. Of the 12,000 hectares of vineland in these regions, only 2,000 are officially classified as AOC, with the largest concentration in Sartène, followed by Calvi and Patrimonio. The finest AOC white wines, or those with more character and individuality, come from the limestone soils of Patrimonio. The rest are easily oxidized, flat, or worse. The rosé is spicy, fresh, full, and very popular. The red is big, full, alcoholic, and far superior to the rosé and the white. All owe a good measure of individuality to the flavor of the local grape varieties. The finest red wines come from selected areas in Sartène, Figari, and the southern tip of the island.

History of Wine Production

Wine has been made in Corsica since the Greeks introduced the vine in the 6th century B.C. Over the centuries it became, after the olive and wheat, the third most important commercial crop, followed only by chestnut, fig, and mulberry. The vine was widely distributed throughout the island except in the poorly drained, malarial coastal regions and the highest altitudes. Production under the Genoese and after 1768, when the island was sold to France, remained small and subsistence in character. Hectarage increased dramatically after the ascendency of Napoleon Bonaparte, who did much to encourage wine production. New vineyards were established in Balagne, Ajaccio, Patrimonio and Cap Corse, with surplus exported through the principal port of Bastia. In 1874, for example, on the eve of the *phylloxera* invasion, nearly one-third of the population was economically dependent on the production of grapes and wine. Since then, hectarage has varied enormously: in 1790 there were 9,050 hectares; in 1815, 11,920; in 1873, 16,900; and in 1890, 4,900. Production after *phylloxera* declined by three-quarters, forcing Corsica to become a net importer of wine for the first time in its history. Hectarage and production recovered somewhat during the 1890s, but during World War I Corsica was drained of manpower, and production once again declined. The 1919 to 1959 period was characterized by net outmigration and general economic stagnation. Only after malaria was eradicated and Corsica was targeted as a major development region did the general economic level of the island begin to improve.

Due to very favorable terms under de Gaulle, many *pied noirs* settled on the island, with an overwhelming number along the east coast. Between 1959 and 1969, the migrant flow accelerated and vine hectarage increased from 12,000 to 30,000. The influence of the *pied noirs* cannot be overstated: they brought capital, expertise, new varieties, and scientific vinification techniques and a dramatically improved wine quality. In a short time the geography of viticulture changed. At one time 80 percent of all wine was primarily made in the "old" producing regions. Now, the greatest concentration of large viticultural estates is along the east coast between Marana and Porto Vecchio. These are presently in a position to outperform the traditional areas and even put them out of business. This rapid growth was followed by a period of uncertainty and confusion in which governmental authorities tried to stabilize a situation that seemingly had few restraints to producing cheap, ordinary wine. Between 1974 and 1976, more than 8,000 hectares, located mostly in economically marginal areas, were uprooted in an attempt to stimulate the production of higher quality wine. In 1976, a compromise was struck between the "old" and *pied noir* producers in which the historic regions would lose their VDQS status, while a limited number of hectares would be labeled AOC and marketed under the "Vin de Corse" banner. The

newer regions of the east coast would be given the humble appellation of
vin du pays and would restrict their total hectarage for an unspecified
number of years. In the meantime, marginal producing regions in the
older areas would be slowly phased out of production, while obscure and
poor-quality-yielding varieties would be replaced by better varieties.

The east coast, with 63.3 percent of total hectarage and more than 70
percent of production, is the largest viticultural region in Corsica. It is
made up of five vineyards of which the Côte Orientale, located north,
south, and west of Aleria, is the largest single vineyard on the island,
with 9,000 hectares or 41 percent of the total. Although the entire region
is an area of bulk wine production with few redeeming attributes other
than low price, the valley of Tavignano is known for above-average red
wine made from the Nielluccio grape. A newly emerging quality region is
Porto Vecchio, located in the extreme south. The vineyards of Marana, La
Casinca, and Cervione are undistinguished and produce *vin ordinaire* and
vins de pays. The largest cooperative, and the single largest producer on
the island, is the *Coopérative d'Aleria,* founded in 1959. It makes more
than 90,000 hectoliters of red, rosé, and white wine annually, more than
three-quarters of which is sold in bulk to merchants in Sète. Founded in
1965, the Ghisonaccia Cooperative, located south of Aleria, makes
approximately 55,000 hectoliters. Located in Aghione, west of Aleria,

Table 8.2   Vine Hectarage by Producing Region, 1960–1982

	1960		1982	
	Hectares	Percent	Hectares	Percent
New producing regions: [a]				
Côte Orientale	–	–	9,300	41.1
Marana	–	–	859	3.9
La Casinca	–	–	904	4.0
Cervione	–	–	940	4.1
Porto Vecchio	150	.9	1,800	7.9
Total	150	.9	13,803	61.0
Older producing regions: [b]				
Sartène-Figari	1,989	13.0	5,300	23.4
Calvi-Calenzana	965	6.3	1,000	4.4
Patrimonio-Cap Corse	5,779	38.0	1,200	5.3
Ajaccio	3,140	20.5	1,100	4.9
Other	3,258	21.3	222	1.0
Total	15,131	99.1	8,822	39.0
Grand total	15,281	100.0	22,625	100.0

[a] Eastern portion with extensive, well-mechanized holdings.
[b] On hillsides more than 100 m in elevation; small plots with little mechanization.

Source: French Ministry of Agriculture.

the third cooperative of note is known for a much smaller output, but higher quality wine. Of the numerous private producers, *Dne. du Tavignane* and *Ch. Pianiccia* enjoy excellent reputations.

Porto Vecchio, with 1,800 hectares, is the newest viticultural frontier of Corsica. Large holdings, new equipment, new vinification techniques, and new varieties have altered this traditional 200-hectare vineyard (1950) into one of the better red and rosé wine areas on the island, the red being by far the better of the two. The largest producer, SOPROVEC, makes a complete line, nearly all of which is bulk wine. One of the oldest and best producers is the 700-hectare Genoese estate *Dne. de Santa-Maria*, followed by *Clos Valle-Vecchia* and *Dne. de Torraccia*.

Sartène and Figari

Sartène is the largest of the old, traditional vineyards located in south-western Corsica in the valleys of Baracci, Ortolo, and Rizzanese. It has the reputation for being the finest vineyard, responsible for about half of all AOC wine, mainly from four traditional varieties: Sciacarello, Vermentino, Barbarossa, and Carcaghioulu. Although the area produces full-bodied, well-flavored, and alcoholic red, rosé, and white wines, the red is much better and rivals, or surpasses, equivalents from any other area on the island. The 5,300-hectare vineyard is widely scattered over sixteen wine-producing communes and hamlets, of which Guincheto, Granace, Sotta, Rigari, Monaccia, Pianottoli, and St.-Lucie-de-Tallano are the most important. The latter has the reputation for the best red wine on the island, the only one that can truly be described as a *vin de garde*. Two above-average producers in the Figari region are *Poggio d'Oro* and *Dne. de Canella*.

Balagne–Calvi–Calenzana

The Balagne–Calvi–Calenzana viticultural region is located on the north-western coast between L'Ile Rousse and Galeria. The widely dispersed vineyards are protected by mountains and forests which create a microclimate characterized by reduced amounts of precipitation. It is one of the oldest vineyards and one with a strong Genoese heritage. Having suffered badly during and after the *phylloxera* crisis, it has recently been rejuvenated by *pied noirs*. A red, rosé, and white region with a tremendous future, its wines are all considered to be the fruitiest of any other producing region, and therefore most appealing to the ever-increasing tourist trade. It is also the largest single concentration of estate-produced wine on the island, with the potential of making more AOC wine than any other vineyard. In addition to the usual array of the table wines, specialties include the Sciacarello-dominated red of Calvi, and the traditionally made, *rancio*-flavored white Muscat wines that have enjoyed a local reputation for nearly 2,000 years. In addition, red, rosé, and white wines can be made either by indigenous or "French" varieties, the former being darker in color and fuller on the palate, and the latter, lighter and more delicate. The biggest producer, and one of the largest cooperatives in Corsica, is *La Cave Coopérative de la Balagne,* located in Calvi. It not only has an above-average reputation, but it makes one of the best white wines. Of the many private producers, *Dne. de Lozari* is a large producer with a good reputation for reliability. *Georges Domerc* makes interesting, fresh, zesty, easily drinkable red, rosé, and white wines. *Clos Calveze, Bel Horizon, Grands Domaines de Calvi, Dne. de Vaitella, Dne. Figarella,* and *Couvent d'Alzipratu* all also enjoy a good reputation. In the Calezana area, the *Coopérative de Calenzana et de Balagne, Clos Rochebelle,* and *Dne. de Pietralba* are above average and reliable. Upslope from Lozari, *Clos Malaspina* enjoys an above-average reputation.

Patrimonio and Le Cap Corse

Two of the oldest delimited viticultural regions of the island, Patrimonio and Le Cap Corse, are located on the extreme northern section, of which the former, with 1,200 hectares, is the largest and the most important. Patrimonio is an ancient hilltop town located halfway between Bastia and the Gulf of Saint Florent. Lying in the center of the "nebbio" (foggy) reegion overlooking the Gulf of Saint Florent, it was the first area to achieve AOC status in 1958. The finest AOC vineyards exist only on hillsides containing a schistous subsoil overlain by limestone and sand. These are found mainly in the communes of Patrimonio, Barbaggio, Farinole, Poggio, d'Oletta, and portions of Oletta and St.-Florent.

Practically the entire vineyard is sited on terraces, and there are three wines of note. The white, dry, fragrant, and fresh, is quite drinkable and free of bitterness and oxidation; the rosé is "heady," full, and fragrant, with a deep color; and the red, equally alcoholic, is well scented, fruity, robust, lighter in color than most, but often dull. Their character is unique because they are the only vineyards in Corsica whose soil contains substantial amounts of limestone. The rosé is distinctive because grapes are vatted for only twelve hours and are, as a consequence, referred to as "rosé d'une nuit," the best of which is made from Grenache Noir. The traditional red wine is made from a minimum of 60 percent Nielluccio blended with various proportions of Grenache, Sciacarello, Carignan, Cinsault, and Vermentino. Lighter versions are made from Grenache, Alicante Bouschet, Cinsault, and Carignan, but they are not as good. When a wine is made entirely from Sciacarello, it is called "particolare" and considered the finest in the region. Barbaggio, located southwest of Patrimonio, has the reputation of producing the darkest, most concentrated, and longest-lived of all Patrimonio wines.

The oldest of the various Corsica cooperatives and the largest producer,

La Casinca, lies on the outskirts of the producing region in Vescovato, south of Bastia on the edge of the delimited area. *Clos de Bernardi, Clos Marfisi,* and *Dominique Gentile* all enjoy above-average reputations in the production of fresh, zesty white and red wine.

Le Cap Corse, considered by many to be the most "Italian" of the Corse vineyards, is a fingerlike peninsula located in the extreme northern tip. It is the only vineyard whose main emphasis is the production of sweet wine, the finest of which is made from the white Muscat in and around the town of Rogliano and, to a lesser extent, the towns of Cunturi, Morsiglia, and Tomino. Secondary to olive, almond, and orange production, the fewer than 600 hectares of vine are cultivated in small, inaccessible villages in highland areas. The dominant vines, various Muscats, Vermentino, and Aleatico, produce wines that are highly underrated and offer extraordinary opportunity for future expansion. More than three-quarters of output is sweet wine, locally called "Muscatillu" or "Impossitu," depending on the degree of grape dehydration prior to fermentation. The "Muscatillu" is similar to Frontignan and Lunel, but lacks the necessary technical expertise to produce lightness and delicacy. The "Impossitu" is similar to Cyprian Commandaria and, again, is not as delicate or well balanced. A third sweet wine, "Rappu," similar to Malaga, is a local specialty rarely encountered in the bottle. The best wines are always sold as "Vins de Cap Corse." Located in Rogliano is *Clos Nicrosi,* known for above-average, dry white wine and a smooth, rich, sweet, white Muscat.

Coteaux d'Ajaccio

This 1,700-hectare vineyard is named after the capital, Ajaccio, the island's second-largest city and the birthplace of Napoleon. While some vineyards lie on flat ground, the majority, and the best sites, are located on the steep hills that surround the city or are dispersed among forty villages producing red, rosé, and white wines of varying quality. The primary areas of cultivation are the slopes along the Taravo, Prunelli, Gravone, Liamore, and Sagone river valleys. The population, history, and grape varieties have always exhibited a stronger imprint of Genoese culture than any other area in Corsica.

Of the three types of wine made, the red is by far the most important in terms of reputation and production. But although it has the reputation of a VDQS wine, it rarely attains that humble quality level. Among the many producers, *Clos d'Alzetto, Dne. Peraldi, Dne. de Paviglia, Martini,* and *Clos Capitoro* enjoy above-average reputations.

9

THE WINES OF LANGUEDOC-ROUSSILLON

THE Languedoc-Roussillon vineyard, most commonly referred to as the Midi, is a vast viticultural area stretching from the Rhône River to the Spanish border. It is an area of maquis, garlic, herb, bare rock, cloudless skies, and an expansive sea of dull, hot, common wine, 80 percent of which is blended, sold in bulk, and the basis of the daily table wine purchased throughout much of France. The region, extending for nealry 200 kilometers, is arc-shaped and consists of innumerable coastal lagoons, wide and narrow coastal plains with alluvial and sandy soil, interior hills, and a mountainous hinterland. Officially, Languedoc-Roussillon encompasses all or portions of five departments: Lozère (located in the extreme north, a minor entity), Gard (shared with the southern Rhône vineyard), Hérault, Aude, and Pyrenées-Orientales. With nearly 400,000 hectares of wine grape vines, the Midi represents 40 percent of all vine hectarage and nearly 50 percent of the nation's total wine production. The Midi is thirteen times larger than Burgundy, four times larger than the Gironde, and nearly seven times larger than the entire Loire. It also accounts for nearly one-third of the nation's table grape hectarage. Within the region, viticulture employs nearly half of the entire rural population and represents a similar percentage of the agricultural product.

With an annual output of 25 to 30 million hectoliters, the Midi is also one of the largest vineyards in the world. Its hectarage represents 5 percent of the world's planted wine grapes, and its wine production varies between 8 and 10 percent of world output. If Languedoc-Roussillon were an independent country, it would rank fourth in production after Italy, France, and the U.S.S.R., and its annual consumption regularly exceeds the combined totals of the United States and Germany. Its immense productivity is highlighted by the fact that while its hectarage is but one-quarter of its immediate neighbor to the south, its wine output is about the same or slightly below that of Spain's. The reputation of the region rests on sheer volume and four types of wine: *vin ordinaire* (low in acidity, flavorless, and coarse on the palate); undrinkable wine that is distilled into alcohol (as much as 20 percent of total output); small quantities of average red, rosé, and white table wine carrying AOC labels; and significant quantities of VDN, the one distinctive specialty. Figure 9.1 shows the total wine production of Languedoc-Roussillon since 1850.

Noticeably different from areas to the north and Provence to the east, the Midi is a very distinct region in terms of climate, soils, vegetation, and social and economic characteristics. In contrast with the mist and fog of coastal Brittany, the Midi is a region of blazing sunshine, brilliant flowers, cloudless skies, dessicating aridity, and small, stunted, and widely dispersed vegetation. While Provence and Corsica are also located within a Mediterranean climatic zone, their mountainous character enables them to intercept far greater quantities of rain along their western exposures. The Midi, on the other hand, is entirely situated within the lee exposures of the Pyrenées and Cévennes mountain ranges, and as a consequence, the typical Mediterranean climate characterized by dry, hot summers and mild, rainy winters is slightly exaggerated. Compared to all other viticultural areas in the nation, the Midi enjoys the longest frost-free season, has the highest mean annual temperatures, has the longest drought season, and experiences the most erratic precipitation patterns. The area also experiences the highest incidence and diversity of wind, of which *Tramontane, Mistral, Cers, Albe, Canigounenc, Gargal, Marinade,* and *Embrum* winds are the most important.

The occurrence of a wet winter and a dry summer results in distinctive xerophytic and annual vegetation able to adapt to and withstand the summer drought, intense evaporation, and the presence of dessicating winds. As a consequence, trees such as evergreens, oak, olive, and pine are stunted, widely scattered, and do not resemble the deciduous forests of

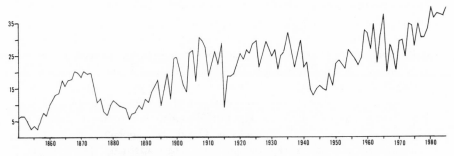

Figure 9.1   Languedoc-Roussillon: Wine Production, 1850–1985
(in millions of hectoliters)

central and northern France. On rock outcrops and on hilly terrain, maquis vegetation is found everywhere. Along a broad stretch of south-facing slopes at the foot of the Cévennes, the drier, highly porous limestone soils no longer support maquis, but scattered tufts of annual vegetation and holly bushes called "garrigue." Over significant but irregular geographical configurations is *lapies,* or bare limestone etched and pitted by the elements, supporting nothing but annual vegetation and shrubby herbs such as lavender, rosemary, and thyme.

The soils formed by the semi-desertic Mediterranean climate are skeletal, devoid of organic matter, dry, highly mineralized, complex, and not subject to simple classification. Each of the four major topographic features has developed its own distinctive soils. From the coast and proceeding inland they are sandy dunes, coastal plains, first series of coastal hills, and interior mountainous basins and hills. Sand dunes, called "hot soils" because of their ability to absorb solar radiation easily, are found throughout the region but are most prevalent from the Grand Rhône to Agde. Over the past 100 years they have become very popular because of their resistance to *phylloxera* infestation and low real estate value, but in the final analysis, they produce only average quality wine. Historically, Picpoul, Terret, and Aramon grapes have managed to adapt very well but are slowly being replaced by lower yielding, aromatic vines. The topography of the coastal plain, flat to gently rolling with a number of minor tablelands and escarpments, contains soils that are highly variable in mineral composition and character. In flat to low-lying areas, clay and deep alluvium dominates, but on upper margins there is more sand, gravel, and stone, with the very best sites lying on a limestone subsoil. Productivity on alluvial and clay soil is exceptionally high, and the vines vary from poor to just passable. The dominant grape varieties are the Aramon, Carignan Noir, and other nonaromatic grapes.

The small, irregular, and isolated character of the coastal hill zone is punctuated by limestone and calcareous rock on remnant alluvial terraces. In all cases, wine quality can be appreciably higher in quality than that from the coastal flatlands. But where the soil is of alluvial origin, as in the lower Hérault, Aude, and Orb river valleys, fertility is high and wine quality low as it is based on Aramon Noir, Carignan Noir, and Terret grapes. Where limestone is close to the surface and *terra rossa* soils prevail (red-colored soils derived from insoluble iron oxides), wine quality is appreciably better. Typical areas include Riversaltes and the exposed terraces along the Tech, Tet, Agly, and Aude valleys. The interior hills and basins of Languedoc-Roussillon are widely recognized as being the finest wine-producing regions. The hillside soils, the product of coluvial and alluvial deposition, are gravelly and stony and character, thin, dry, well drained, and low in natural fertility. They warm up quickly, but their color and chemical attributes can vary widely with the nature of the parent material or the instrument of soil deposition. The best stony soils are dark in color (from schist or slate), red or yellowish (from limestone and calcareous rock), and are able to make the finest red table wine in the Midi, especially those from the Côtes du Roussillon-Villages, Minervois, Corbières, St.-Chinian, Faguères, Collioure, and Maury appellations.

Cultural and Economic History

The cultural and economic history of Languedoc-Roussillon is just as diverse as its physical irregularity. While Catalan influences are prominent in much of Roussillon, the entire Midi, in sharp contrast to the dominant *Langue d'Oil* of the rest of France, is still the center for the explicit *Langue d'Oc* dialect. Reflecting countless military invasions, the population is of mixed Mediterranean stock with a good number still exhibiting a long tradition of quaint customs that have endured in semi-isolation for centuries.

Languedoc-Roussillon has been the most economically backward region of mainland France. Nearly devoid of industry, with poor transportation connections and recalcitrant agricultural activities, it has been a major area of outmigration. Unlike Alsace, the Loire, and other areas of northern France, the area supports no dairying, no green grass for seven months of the year, no extensive livestock save for sheep and goats, no rye or hardy winter vegetables, and no vast tracks of deciduous forest. The countryside is mainly deserted because farmers live in villages, not on their farms. The total population of less than 3 million accounts for about 5 percent of the nation's total; of the eight principal cities, Montpellier is the largest with 150,000, followed by Perpignan with 85,000, Carcassonne with 65,000, and Narbonne with 40,000.

Mixed farming agricultural activities based on animal husbandry cover most of France; a specialized type of cultivation such as viticulture, fruit trees, vegetables, wheat, citrus, and olive growing dominates the rural economy of the Midi. In terms of land, more than 50 percent is exposed rock or soil too thin for productive use; about 30 percent of the area is maquis or rough grazing land; and only 20 percent of the region is capable of sustaining commercial agriculture without benefit of irrigation. Rooted in self-sufficiency, the area experienced some semblance of change only after the introduction of the railroad; in many areas not until World War I did wooden implements give way to the steel plow and artificial fertilizer increase yield sufficiently for farmers to rise above subsistence levels.

While vinegrowing dates back to the ancient Greeks and Romans, the steady succession of barbaric northern tribes dominated the history of the region for centuries after the fall of the Roman Empire. Early in the 8th century the entire region fell to the Moors, only to be retaken in 778 when Charlemagne incorporated the area to the kingdom of Aquitaine. During the crusading period there was a short-lived renaissance when a number of religious orders established vineyards, the most important of which were the Benedictines, Carthusians, Knights Templars, and Knights Hospitalers. In the 13th century, the Albigensian heresy spread throughout the region and spilled into the southwestern portion of France, where a crusade was organized to stamp it out. During the Inquisition, the French kings gradually subdued most of the region; by 1659 the entire Midi was incorporated with France. Throughout the period of religious conflict and political subjugation, viticulture was a cottage industry, totally subsistent in nature. The first significant industrial and commercial expansion took place in the 17th century when the central government initiated an ambitious program of textile manufacturing and mining development. As the region took full advantage of its position at the crossroads between the Mediterranean and the Atlantic, economic conditions improved. Later (1666), the Canal du Midi was opened, connecting the port of Sète with the Garonne River; in 1681 the Canal du Languedoc was completed. Vinegrowing and winemaking slowly began to emerge as important industries, and by the end of the 18th century hectarage was approximately 225,000 and the annual output about 4 million hectoliters.

It is important to note that throughout this period, agriculture was dominated by the classical Mediterranean "trinity" of wheat, olive, and vine and by extensive sheep and goat grazing, all of which were confined to the hilly, mountainous interior. The small vineyards were located next to villages, while wheat and olive occupied the lower slopes. Sheep and goat herding migrated seasonally between the high pastures in summer and lowlands in winter in a pattern known as transhumance. With the eradication of malaria from selected coastal locations in the first half and the coming of the railroad in the second half of the 19th century, man and vine shifted gradually and persistently to lower elevations near the coast. This development accelerated after the *phylloxera* epidemic because American rootstocks did not take well in the hilly regions, so vines were planted in sandy soils along the entire Mediterranean coast. To this day, the largest estates and the biggest average individual vineland holdings are found here (the Midi contains more than 95 percent of all viticultural holdings larger than 100 hectares). These factors contrast sharply with the fragmented exploitations of the Loire, Burgundy, and especially Alsace. Hectarage nearly doubled during the period 1800 to 1875, recovered quickly after the *phylloxera* epidemic, and expanded slowly to reach 460,000 hectares in 1955. Wine production, due to efficient vineyard practices, exploded from 15 million hectoliters in 1875 to more than 35 million hectoliters in the 1980s.

By the first decade of the 20th century, this blissful picture of efficient, high-yielding, large-scale production of *vin ordinaire* produced mixed blessings. Poor vintages in the rest of France reduced stocks and elevated the price of *vin ordinaire* and, hence, the coffers of the Midi vigneron. Eventually, however, the boom turned to bust when prices fell precipitously in highly productive years, as in 1907, 1930, 1953 through 1955, and 1974–75. This pattern of overproduction since the formation of the European Economic Community was aggravated by three additional factors. One was the loss of Algerian *vin ordinaire,* which prompted the importation of large quantities of Italian bulk wine from Puglia and Sicily, a development that exacerbated tensions. Second, the period of overproduction after 1950 was characterized by strikes, roadblocks, bloodshed, wanton physical destruction, general confusion, and political turmoil. The balance of supply and demand, always in disequilibrium, reached serious levels in the late 1970s when it was magnified by the continuous and persistent decline in the domestic consumption of *vin ordinaire* (between 1955 and 1980, per capita consumption dropped from 120 to 80 liters). While consumption declined by 1 percent each year and hectarage dropped by more than 60,000 hectares, the annual output of Midi wine, thanks to technological advances, continued to increase, reaching 32 million hectoliters in 1983. The issue of overproduction is also complicated by existing EEC trade policies and the principle of member competition within the organization. Italy is able to undersell French *vin ordinaire* by a wide margin, and the entry of Spain and Portugal into the EEC will probably continue to weaken the price structure of basic Midi wine.

Over the years, the government, in an attempt to alleviate the ever-growing dimensions of the "wine lake," has promulgated a program of price support by buying up surplus wine and distilling it. Because it now buys as much as the entire output of the Gironde as "surplus" at a cost of more than five billion FF, the "wine lake" issue has become a political *cause célèbre.* Under the strain of overproduction, the illegal practices of chaptalization, and adding alcohol, unfermented grape juice, grape concentrate, and dried grapes to the must and wine became unbearable. By the early 1970s, a herculean effort attempted to reduce output and increase quality levels.

Post–1950 Developments

The Midi of old relied excessively on agriculture, and because it lacked coal, oil, gas and metals, it had a circumscribed industrial base. It was the largest agricultural region in the nation and an area of chronic outmigration and an aging population. Over the past thirty years, however, three important events have restructured the regional economy. A massive governmental effort, similar to the Italian experiment in the Mezzogiorno, fragmented the area into industrial growth areas. The triangular area between Montpellier, Nîmes, and Arles was identified as a region of industrial development; three areas were targeted for large-scale reforestation; the area of the middle Orb west of Bèziers, the region between the lower Orb and Hérault, and the flat area northwest of Montpellier were selected for large-scale irrigation; and six tourist development zones were delineated with a combined 75,000-bed capacity. As a result: (a) arable land has quadrupled, with new crops such as rice, cotton, sugarbeets, and vegetables expanding rapidly at the expense of traditional crops; (b) the growth of coastal cities has prompted intraregional migration, with the largest cities as magnets for people leaving interior hill villages; (c) average farm size has increased dramatically; and (d) the tourist facilities have stimulated on-site wine sales of at least 400,000 cases annually.

The second-most-important development was the arrival of nearly 250,000 French Algerian *pied noirs,* half of whom settled in the department of Hérault, one-quarter in Gard, and one-fifth in Roussillon. The *pied noirs* have enlarged farm size, reduced the percentage of nonaromatic grape varieties, planted better, low-yielding stock, and proved to be the better farmers. Further, by introducing stainless steel and carbonic maceration techniques, they have managed to control volatile acidity and to produce fruitier, more flavorful wine than indigenous vignerons. The third and most important development of the past thirty years was the effect of the "Chirac Plan" of 1973, a working plan that would eventually allow the region to compete favorably with the EEC and other major international wine producers. The plan was supposed to accelerate the uprooting of vines in marginal areas throughout France, but in particular in the Midi, the Loire, and Corsica. While more than 50,000 marginal hectares have been uprooted since 1970, the largest single area of decline within the Midi vineyard has been the department of Hérault.

In the final analysis, the economic prospects for the future appear to be bright. Government proposals to improve quality through education, better equipment, and new grape varieties have been quite successful, and although the dry, red wines of the region are unable to compete with Portuguese Dao, Italian blends, or even with California jug wine, the historic abuses have been substantially reduced. Quality wine production is on the ascent, as are varietals and estate bottling.

THE WINES OF LANGUEDOC

Languedoc, an irregularly defined region of plain, hill, and mountain, stretches in an arc from the Rhône River to Maury and represents the northern and most important area of the Midi vineyard. It includes the departments of Lozère, Aude, Hérault, and a small portion of Gard. The four collectively possess more than 325,000 hectares of vineland (one-third of the national total) that produce more than 28 million hectoliters of wine annually, or approximately 40 percent of the nation's total output. The region represents the core of *vin ordinaire* production, contains the largest viticultural exploitations in terms of size, and more than one-third of all cooperatives.

Of the 28 million hectoliters of wine produced each year, fewer than 1

Table 9.1   AOC, VDN, and VDQS Wine Production in Languedoc, 1980

Appellation	Hectoliters	Percent
AOC		
Minervois Rouge[a]	222,464	14.7
Minervois Blanc	1,726	.1
St.-Chinian Rouge[b]	101,396	6.7
Blanquette de Limoux Blanc	79,976	5.3
Fitou	64,531	4.3
Faugères Rouge[b]	46,757	3.1
Clairette du Languedoc Blanc	11,445	.8
Clairette de Bellegarde Blanc	1,754	.1
Coteaux du Languedoc Rouge[a] (all districts combined)	189,574	12.5
Total	719,623	47.7
VDN		
Muscat de Frontignan Blanc	16,096	1.1
Muscat de Lunel Blanc	5,782	.4
Muscat de Mireval Blanc	4,947	.3
Muscat de St.-Jean de Minervois Blanc	1,125	.1
Total	27,950	1.8
VDQS		
Corbières Rouge	565,499	37.4
Corbières Blanc	7,545	.5
Corbières Superieures Rouge	5,000	.3
Corbières Superieures Blanc	2,266	.1
Costières du Gard Rouge	152,992	10.1
Costières du Gard Blanc	5,129	.3
Picpoul de Pinet Blanc	9,302	.6
Cabardès Rouge	8,777	.6
Côtes de Malepère Rouge[c]	8,775	.6
Total	765,285	50.5
General Total	1,512,858	100.0

[a] AOC status granted in 1985.
[b] AOC status granted in 1982.
[c] VDQS status granted in 1983.

Source: French Ministry of Agriculture.

million are officially classified as AOC and VDQS. The remainder is *vin ordinaire,* representing more than two-thirds of the national output—a dubious distinction that accurately reflects the quality of wine produced. While Languedoc produces about 4 percent of all AOC wine, it manages to produce about two-thirds of the nation's total VDQS. Nevertheless, it is important to note that over the past thirty years, the amount of AOC wine has increased from 300,000 to more than 800,000 hectoliters, a figure that is expected to double by 1995. Of the four departments in the Languedoc vineyard, Aude is the most significant in the production of quality red AOC wine. It contains Blanquette de Limoux, Corbières (VDQS), Fitou, nearly half of the AOC Minervois district, and two emerging, soon-to-be AOC vineyards—Côtes de Malepère and Cabardès. Hérault, the largest department in terms of hectarage and production, contains some of the best portions of Minervois, St.-Chinian, Faugères, four VDN appellations, and the emerging Coteaux du Languedoc group. The extreme southern portion of Gard contains the small AOC Clairette du Languedoc and the large VDQS Costières du Gard appellations.

For centuries, the reputation of Languedoc wines rested on the production of large quantities of cheap, innocuous bulk wine, most of it *vin ordinaire* or, as the trade calls it, *vin de consommation courante*. Red dominates (more than 90 percent), followed by rosé and white. Approximately 1 percent is VDN wine, which, along with equivalents from Roussillon, appears to be enjoying a resurgence in popularity. Blanquette de Limoux, a sparkling wine with a distinctive flavor, is produced in the hilly uplands of Limoux and remains the leading appellation for quality sparkling wine.

In general, wine quality is based on location and altitude. Based on Carignan, Alicante Bouschet, and Aramon, the cheapest of all Languedoc wine originates from the coastal sections. Containing between 8 percent and 10 percent alcohol, it is considered only "cafe" wine. Farther inland, on higher ground with better grape varieties, alcohol content rises to

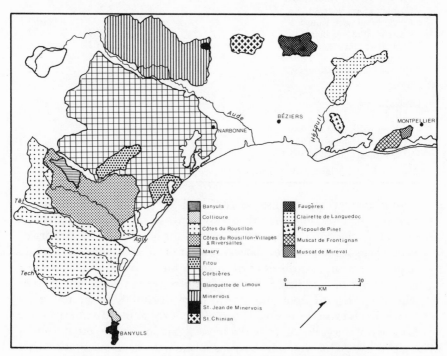

Figure 9.2   Languedoc-Roussillon: Major Appellations

higher levels and the quality improves. In the interior upper slopes, mainly in Minervois, St.-Chinian, Faugères, Muscat de St.-Jean de Minervois, and portions of Corbières, alcohol levels rise by several percentage points, and the wine is even better. The association of quality wine production with altitude is no coincidence; better wine is always associated with low yields, and the forementioned areas give the lowest yields in Languedoc—usually less than 40 hectoliters to the hectare and often as little as 25—a considerable difference from 150 or more hectoliters to the hectare in the coastal vineyards. It is also important to note that while upland areas produce only 2 percent of all the wine in the region, they are responsible for nearly all AOC wines. Finally, the historic public perception of inexpensive, unstable *vin ordinaire* is rapidly changing for the better. Vineyards have been replanted with better varieties, grapes have been subjected to new vinification techniques, and better winery management has been introduced, all contributing to the produc-

Table 9.2   Major Grape Varieties in Aude, Hérault, Gard, and Pyrenées-Orientales, 1968 and 1979

	1968		1979		1968	1979
					Percent of national total	
Grape variety	Hectares	Percent[a]	Hectares	Percent[a]		
Carignan Noir	175,700	41.0	174,900	44.2	83.2	84.5
Aramon	107,200	25.0	57,400	14.5	51.0	90.5
Cinsaut	7,900	1.8	33,200	8.4	43.6	64.3
Alicante Bouschet	11,100	2.6	15,400	3.9	54.1	70.6
Genache Noir	23,900	5.5	31,500	8.0	47.0	40.6
Grenache Blanc	13,400	3.1	15,200	3.8	95.0	94.0
Morrastel Bouschet	8,400	1.9	1,500	.4	94.4	94.0
Mauzac	900	.2	1,900	.5	9.4	30.0
Merlot Noir	300		2,700	.7	1.1	7.0
Terret Gris	13,000	3.0	8,700	2.2	98.0	98.0
Villard Blanc	10,000	2.3	5,600	1.4	47.0	97.0
Cabernet Sauvignon	100		1,900	.5	.8	8.3
Syrah	300		4,300	1.1	11.5	35.2
Grand Noir	8,500	2.0	1,100	.3	36.5	41.0
Villard Noir	3,900	.9	1,400	.3	13.0	18.0
Mourvèdre	100		600	.1	12.5	19.3
Ugni Blanc	1,700	.4	3,500	.9	1.8	2.7
Clairette Blanc	4,000	.9	2,100	.5	31.0	40.0
Auburn	400	.1	1,200	.3	12.5	21.0
Carignan Blanc	700	.2	600	.1	37.0	26.0
Couderc Noir	6,500	1.5	2,800	.7	28.0	36.4
Others	32,900	7.6	28,500	7.2		
Total	430,900	100.0	396,000	100.0		

[a]Percent of regional total.

Source: French Ministry of Agriculture.

Table 9.3 Major Grape Varieties in the Department of Hérault, 1968 and 1979

Grape variety	1968		1979		As percent of national total
	Hectares	Percent[a]	Hectares	Percent[a]	
Carignan Noir	52,900	33.0	61,000	42.6	30
Aramon	56,000	35.0	30,600	21.4	48
Cinsaut	4,600	2.9	15,600	10.9	30
Terret Gris	10,300	6.5	7,700	5.4	87
Alicante Bouschet	4,600	2.9	6,500	4.5	30
Grenache Noir	8,000	5.0	6,200	4.3	8
Villard Blanc	4,000	2.5	2,600	1.8	45
Ugni Blanc	1,200	.8	1,500	1.0	
Clairette	1,800	1.2	800	.6	15
Merlot Noir	300	.1	800	.6	
Syrah	300		700	.6	
Morrastel Bouschet	3,600	2.3	500	.3	
Grand Noir	3,500	2.2	300	.2	
Cabernet Sauvignon			300	.2	
Others	8,900	5.6	8,011	5.6	
Total	160,000	100.0	143,111	100.0	

[a]Percent of departmental total.

Source: French Ministry of Agriculture.

tion of a significantly better product. Although Languedoc continues to produce a large amount of bad and indifferent wine, the quantity is much less than before.

Carignan, the dominant grape of France, is well suited to the summer drought conditions of the Midi and is ubiquitous throughout the region. Covering 44 percent of the planted area of the Midi, it represents approximately 85 percent of all plantings in France. Taking the name from the city of Cariñena in Aragon, it was historically the most common variety from the Pyrenées to the Rhône, with more than 300,000 hectares planted on the eve of the *phylloxera* epidemic. Depending on the location, the vine yields well, resists disease, produces 12 percent alcohol, blends well, and has a nice color. Its major problems are developing a heavy deposit in the bottle, early oxidization, and a lack of distinctive flavor and aroma. It is also sensitive to frost and *oidium*. This omnipresent vine is declining in importance along the interior upland areas, holding steady in some coastal hilly locations, and increasing hectarage along the flat coastal regions. In addition to Carignan Noir, there is also Carignan Gris and minuscule amounts of Blanc. The single largest stretch of Carignan vines is found in the departments of Aude (68,000 hectares) and Héraul (61,000). While the four Midi departments have made a determined effort to reduce the absolute and percentage amount of Carignan to upgrade quality, significant reductions have been realized only in the department of Pyrenées-Orientales, where the plantings have dropped

Table 9.4   Major Grape Varieties in the Aude Department, 1968 and 1979

	1968		1979		As percent of national total
Grape variety	Hectares	Percent[a]	Hectares	Percent[a]	
Carignan Noir	70,700	59.1	68,600	59.6	33
Cinsaut	1,300	1.1	8,300	7.2	16
Aramon	17,300	14.5	8,100	7.0	13
Alicante Bouschet	3,300	2.8	5,700	5.0	26
Grenache Noir	3,100	2.6	5,400	4.7	7
Grenache Blanc	2,400	2.0	3,200	2.8	20
Mauzac	900	.8	1,900	1.7	30
Merlot			1,300	1.2	
Terret Gris	2,300	1.9	1,200	1.0	13
Morrastel Bouschet	3,900	3.3	900	.8	
Villard Blanc	2,200	1.8	700	.6	12
Cabernet Sauvignon			600	.5	
Syrah			500	.4	
Grand Noir	1,600	1.3	400	.3	15
Villard Noir	1,400	1.2	400	.3	5
Others	9,100	7.6	7,969	6.9	
Total	119,500	100.0	115,169	100.0	

[a] Percent of departmental total.
Source: French Ministry of Agriculture.

from 22 percent to 10 percent of the nation's total over the past thirty years. While the percentage of Carignan has remained almost stable in the department of Aude (34.8 to 33.1 for the period 1968 to 1979), total hectarage devoted to this variety has actually increased by 22,100 hectares, and the national percentage raised from 22.9 to 29.4. It is also interesting to note that it has increased in Hérault, Gard, Var, Vaucluse, and Haute Corse. The areas of above-average-quality wine production (particularly from old vines) are the department of Pyrenées-Orientales and the highland elevations of the Minervois and Corbières. Throughout the rest of the producing region, the vine yields an inferior, harsh product, which, although not half as bad as Aramon, is usually linked with the poor image of the "meridional" (southern) wines of the Midi.

The second most widely planted grape variety in the Midi is the Aramon, a high-yielding vine known for weak color, a flat taste, and a lack of an assertive aroma—hence, reasons why it is mixed with *teinturiers* (red juice grapes) like Alicante Bouschet to make it more marketable. Aramon is generally found along the flat coastal regions and is the major casualty in the concerted effort to abandon undesirable vineland and uproot objectionable vines. Of the approximately 58,000 hectares planted in the four major Midi departments, Hérault is the leading area of localization with 30,000 hectares, or 21 percent of department hectarage and 48 percent of all national plantings. The Gard department, with 18,000 hectares and 28 percent of all plantings, is the second-largest area of concentration, followed by Aude with 8,100 hectares. Collectively, the Midi accounts for 90 percent of all Aramon hectarage in France.

The third-most-common grape variety, the Cinsault, also the most rapidly expanding variety in the region, has increased hectarage from 8,000 in 1968 to more than 33,000 in 1979. Although not a heavy yielder like Aramon, and in sharp contrast to most other "meridional" varieties, it is early ripening and capable of producing alcohol between 11 percent and 12 percent. Considerably better than Aramon in terms of color, fruity flavor, suppleness and freshness, Cinsault is the preferred vine for quality rosé production. It has a tendency to oxidize but improves tremendously when blended with "fragrant" varieties such as Mourvèdre and Syrah. Nearly half of all national plantings in 1979 were found in the department of Hérault and Aude—15,600 and 8,300, respectively. Of all grape varieties in the Midi, the Cinsault is nearly absent in the department of Pyrenées-Orientales—a very unusual phenomenon. Grenache Noir, thr fourth most widely planted grape in the Midi, increased hectarage from 3,300 in 1958 to 23,300 in 1979. Although not ideally suited for the coastal margins, it has replaced a good deal of the Aramon, Alicante Bouschet, and Couderc Noir throughout the area. Depending on the producing district, the Grenache Blanc and Gris appear to be maintaining their hectarage.

Grape varieties that increased their hectarage at the expense of nonaromatic varieties for the period 1968 to 1979 were Mauzac, Merlot Noir, Cabernet Sauvignon, Syrah, Mourvèdre, Ugni Blanc, Aubun, and Muscat Blanc à Petits Grains. The Mourvèdre, in particular, should have an excellent future because a good portion of Languedoc contains ideal growing conditions for this fickle variety. Historically scorned for its meager yield, it has been revived as a "noble" grape capable of improving Carignan and Cinsault. Because it matures late it is capable of raising alcohol levels beyond 12 percent; it has excellent color and a superb fragrance, ages well, and has an affinity of improving "flabby," low-acid wines. The other grape with a promising future is the Muscat à Petits Grains, the only "meridional" variety that is exceptionally fragrant, yields well, matures early, and is able to grow on limestone-rich soils. It is currently enjoying a renaissance due to increased demand for Muscat-based VDN wines.

The dominant "Bordeaux" varieties—Cabernet Sauvignon and Merlot Noir—are largely confined to the highest elevations of St.-Chinian, Faugères, Minervois, Corbières, and Roussillon. The only nonaromatic variety currently increasing hectarage is Alicante Bouschet, an early ripening *teinturier* that does particularly well in fertile coastal regions. It was historically used by vignerons for its high color intensity to make fresh grape juice and to add color to the feeble Aramon when making wine. It is the only recommended variety among the many Bouschets and is rapidly replacing the inferior Morrastel Bouschet.

Other varieties in decline include all Terrets, Villard Noir and Blanc, Grand Noir, Clairette, and Couderc Noir. The Terrets are an obscure family of grapes in all three colors, with the Gris dominating hectarage. In Languedoc, Terret Gris is used to produce inexpensive wines destined for vermouth and distilled beverage production. While its decline in hectarage is substantial, its total demise will not occur in the near future. Grand Noir is a late-ripening, high-yielding variety producing a tasteless wine with low alcohol levels. Couderc Noir, a successful hybrid that maintains high yields, ripens late, and makes reasonable quality rosé, is currently in decline and is being replaced by the more popular (and superior) Cinsault. Contrary to official statistics, a considerable amount of Couderc Noir is being cultivated. Villard Noir and Blanc produce full-flavored, savory, assertive, but coarse wines; and as a result these vines are major targets for uprooting. Historically a basic vine for the production of white wine, Clairette is in full retreat, being replaced in part by Ugni Blanc.

Minervois

Named after the fortified medieval town of Minerve, Minervois is the third-largest AOC appellation in the Midi with an average annual production of more than 200,000 hectoliters. Located north of Corbières and west of St.-Chinian, Minervois comprises the area between Carcassonne and St.-Chinian. It is a land of incised river valleys, denuded hillsides, castles, medieval fortified towns, scattered forest, and vineyards. For most of the sixty-one villages (45 in the department of Aude and 16 in Hérault), vine cultivation is the most profitable agricultural activity. There are more than 33,000 hectares (8,000 officially classified for the production of AOC wine), nearly 5,000 growers, and forty-four cooperatives, or one for every major village. Three-quarters of all wine is made by cooperatives, 10 percent by negociants, and the remainder by private growers. Although the appellation produces red, rosé, and white wine, the former dominates with 96 percent of total output. White wine has increased in production and improved tremendously in recent years, while rosé is considered a local curiosity. Although the entire region produces between 2.5 and 3 million hectoliters of wine, AOC Minervois represents only 10 percent of the total.

Climatically the region suffers from spring frost, excessive aridity, and wide diurnal and seasonal extremes in temperature. Characterized by an erratic and torrential pattern, precipitation falls mainly during the winter months. Rainfall varies between 300 mm and 700 mm annually, depending on altitude and exposure, and the entire region is buffeted by the dry *Cers* wind. The natural vegetation is a combination of stunted deciduous trees, garrigue, scattered pine, evergreen oak, wild thyme, and lavender.

Sheep and goat grazing activities, although declining, still persist over large sections.

Minervois sits at the foot of the Montagne Noir, and because it is badly eroded, limestone, schist, and other rocks are exposed everywhere. The soils are a mixture of alluvial and colluvial material, stony, dry, and poor in natural fertility. The most important communes are St.-Jean-de-Minervois, Minerve, Aigues-Vives, Azillanet, Argeliers, Ginestas, Paraza, Olonzac, La Livinière, Laredorte, Badens Laure-Minervois, Rieux-Minervois, Trausse, Villeneuve-Minervois, and Caunes-Minervois.

While wine production dates back to the time of the ancient Greeks and Romans, it was not until the construction of the Canal du Midi in the 17th century and the penetration of railroads in the 19th century that vinegrowing began to expand seriously. The area was first delimited in 1980, VDQS status was awarded in 1951, and by 1960 a growing and energetic regional syndicate of growers and cooperatives was in place that advocated a rapid and strong movement to change the historic grape varieties and improve the quality of the wine. Eventually a petition was made to the INAO, and AOC status was awarded in 1985. The evolution of the region from an area of *vin ordinaire* to VDQS and to eventual AOC quality wine production was short and painful. AOC boundary lines, yields, authorized grape varieties, and other qualifying elements of the new appellation caused bitter arguments. Both Aramon and Alicante Bouschet have been virtually eliminated, Carignan has been reduced by one-third, Cinsault has been reduced by one-quarter, and all hybrids have been banned (at one time they represented more than 20 percent of the total hectarage). As a result, Syrah (for all vineyards) and the Mourvèdre (reserved for the hottest and driest soils) are mandatory and may be accompanied by Grenache Noir, Lladoner Pelut Noir, Cinsault, Picpoul Noir, and others. The finest properties have a tendency to introduce Cabernet Sauvignon, Merlot Noir, and Malbec, to increase the percentage of Mourvèdre, Syrah, and Grenache Noir, and to reduce the rest. For white wine production, the preferred grapes are Macabeo, Bourboulenc, and Malvoise, followed by Grenache Blanc, Picpoul Blanc, Terret Blanc, and Clairette. With new stainless steel and temperature-controlled fermentation tanks, wine quality has improved markedly. When well made, red wine is strong, fragrant, full-bodied, and well flavored. White wine is particularly full on the palate, alcoholic, fragrant, and robust. The long-neglected and scorned wines of Minervois have recently become a "hot item" in northern France and western Europe and offer above-average value.

Despite the fact that Minervois is one huge syncline with vineyards clinging to the schistous and limestone hillsides, the Syndicate Cru Minervois distinguishes two climatic and twelve microclimatic-pedalogic producing districts, ten of which are generalized (see Fig. 9.3). From west to east they are:

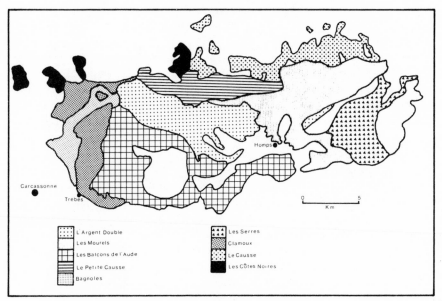

Figure 9.3   The Minervois Vineyard

Atlantic-Mediterranean Zone

1. In a northern tier of seven fragmented vineyards, called "les Cotes Noires," schist rock dominates and supports a forest of white oak. The climate is humid, the winds westerly, and the summers rainy. It is the least important of the three districts in the production of red and rosé wine, but above average in the production of sprightly, fragrant white wine.

2. A region of grey calcaire soil produces slightly better red and softer white than the above. Along with district three, below, the area is called "Calmoux" and is known for the production of soft, early maturing red wine.

3. An irregular district of brown limestone soil produces the finest red and soft, early maturing white wine. The key villages from north to south are Villeneuve-Minervois, Bagnoles, Malves, Villalier, and Trebes, all of which contain major cooperatives. Among private producers the most important are *Dne. Poudou; Ch. du Donjon; Ch. de Malves,* and *Ch. de St.-Julia.*

Mediterranean Climatic Zone

4. The large, irregular, hot, dry region called "les Balcons de l'Aude" consists of highly eroded limestone soil that is very stony and brown in color and supports Aleppo pine and aromatic herbs. The dominant red wines are soft, supple, early maturing, spicy, and very satisfying. The rosé is less good, but the white is rich, aromatic, and quaffable. In addition to the principal cooperative in Laure-Minervois, the major

growths are *Ch. de Fabas, Ch. de Baudelle, Dne. Metairie Grande, Ch. de Russol, Dne. Prat Majou, Ch. de Badens, Ch. de Blomac, Ch. Tournouzelle,* and *Dne. la Boulandière.*

5. Along both banks of the l'Argen Double River lies a small but important vineyard centered around the communes of Peyriac-Minervois, Rieux-Minervois, Trausse-Minervois, and Pepieux. The stony limestone soils produce medium-bodied, well-flavored red wines and dry, supple, white wines based on Bourboulenc, Macabeo, Terret Blanc, and Grenache Blanc. The principal producer is *Caves les Coteaux de Minervois,* and the major growths are *Dne. de Homps, Ch. de Rieux-Minervois, Dne. Domergue, Ch. de Paulignan,* and *Ch. de Floris.*

6. "Le Petite Causse," cooler and more humid than the two previous areas to the south, is a region dominated by soft calcareous rock that produces the finest *vin de garde* wines in the appellation. The principal communes are Caunes-Minervois, La Livinière, Siran, Cesseras, and Azillanet. Besides the three main cooperatives, this region contains some of the largest and finest properties in the entire appellation: *Ch. de Villerambert, Ch. de Gourgazaud, Dne. de la Senche, Dne. de Ste.-Eulalie, Dne. Maris, Ch. de Siran,* and *Dne. St.-Albert.*

7. "Le Causse" represents the northern tier of highly soluble limestone with a distinct "karst" topography and dry, brown-colored soils. The dominant red wines are known for their *vin de garde* features—dark color, rich, concentrated flavors, and aroma. White wines, based on Grenache Blanc and Macabeo, are full, powerful, and heavily scented. Along the north bank of the Cesse River within the confines of La Caunette are three outstanding properties: *Dne. le Cazal, Dne. de Babio,* and *Dne. de la*

Plate 9.1   The vineyards of Ch. Fabas

Calvez. Surrounding the rustic medieval town of Minerve are four excellent growths known for *vin de garde* red wine: *Dne. Fraisse Mayranne, Dne. le Pech, Ch. de Minerve,* and *Dne. le Boucard.*

8. "Les Mourels," a large, irregular, rugged mountainous region with exposed limestone, produces full, strong, *vin de garde* red wine very similar to "Le Causse" but with more finesse and delicacy. Principal areas of production are Olonzac, Homps, Azillanet, Aigne, and Aignes-Vives. Production is dominated by three large cooperatives and the following above-average producers: *Dne. le Pech d'André, Ch. de Cabezac,* and *Ch. d'Oupia.*

9. "Les Serres" is a region of terraced slopes with brown limestone soil that produces firm but fruity red and excellent white wine. The hot and arid climate reduces yields, but overall quality standards are high. Production, mainly confined around the communes of Poujols-Minervois and Ginestas, consists of the following estates: *Dne. Meyzonnièr, Ch. de Paraza, Dne. de Rousseau, Dne. de la Lécugne, Ch. du Vergel,* and *Dne. de l'Herbe Sainte.*

10. The St.-Jean-Minervois vineyard, located on karstic soils in a subhumid climatic region, is known for two principal growers—*Dne. de Barroubio* and *Michel Sigé.*

St.-Chinian

St.-Chinian, with an annual output of more than 100,000 hectoliters, is the largest of the communal appellations in the semi-official "Coteaux du Languedoc" appellation. A widely scattered vineyard of twenty villages, it lies along the foot of the Cévennes mountains. Along with Faugères, it attained AOC status in 1982. Here, the Grenache Noir and Cinsault dominate, although Carignan is also present. The wine is dark in color, full bodied, softer than its immediate neighbors, and highlighted by a spicy flavor. Although the appellation has more than 5,000 hectares authorized for production, less than 2,000 are currently planted in vines that produce 100,000 hectoliters. While the large cooperative at St.-Chinian dominates production, three small growers make outstanding wine: *Ch. Coujan, Dne. des Calmette,* and *Dne. des Jougla.*

Faugères

Faugères, located northeast of St.-Chinian at a much higher elevation, is the second-largest AOC vineyard (50,000 hectoliters) in the "Coteaux du Languedoc" group. Locally the wine, which is made from Cinsault, Carignan, and Grenache Noir is called the "wine of passion." It has a splendid red color and a fresh cherry-flavored sensation in the mouth, is rich in extract, is substantial and satisfying on the palate, and is significantly more assertive than St.-Chinian. The soils are derived from schist, and the individual vineyards are intermingled with maqui and scrubland. Hectarage, approximately half of St.-Chinian, is confined to seven villages, of which Faugères, Autignac, and Fos are the most important. The three major growths are *Ch. Haut-Fabreges, Dne. du Fraisse,* and *Gilbert Alquier.*

Fitou

Named after the small coastal town of the same name, Fitou is a 2,000-hectare vineyard located just north of Riversaltes in the Aude department. The appellation is divided into two distinct, geographic producing districts, one along the coast north of Fitou and the second in the hilly interior north and south of the village of Tuchan, the latter an area of gentle, rounded, and denuded hills. Although the coastal region is by far the more important in the production of wine, the vineyards in both areas form isolated clumps of greenery and are not contiguous. The principal communes are Caves, Paziols, Tuchan, Cascastel, Villeneuve, Lapalme, Treilles, Fitou, and Leucate.

The wine is red, the very best of which is full and substantial on the palate, generous, high in alcohol, and definitely mouth-filling. The *vin de garde* versions spend eighteen months in wood prior to bottling and are capable of maturing for an additional five to eight years in the bottle. Hectarage is limited to better grape varieties such as Grenache Noir, Syrah, and Mourvèdre. More than 90 percent of total output is made by seven cooperatives, all of which have done much to improve quality in recent years. As a result, the wine has become very popular and appears to be consistently well made. As a consequence, prices in recent years have escalated to the levels of medium to high-quality Côtes du Rhône, and because of its consistency has found a good home in the tourist-rich restaurants and hotels along the coast. *Dne. de Nouvelles* and *Paul Colomer* are two important producers.

Blanquette de Limoux

The Limoux vineyard is situated in the upper reaches of the Aude valley, 23 kilometers south of the medieval bastide town of Carcassonne. It is the largest AOC appellation within the department of Aude and produces one of the most unusual sparkling wines of France. This little-known wine is called Blanquette de Limoux, after the historic name of the indigenous Mauzac grape and the principal town in the appellation, Limoux.

Although the Romans introduced the commercial aspects of vine-growing to the region, winemaking was not important until a still white wine from the Mauzac grape was made early in the 10th century. Limoux rose to prominence only after the Benedictine monks of the Abbey of St.-Hilaire began experimenting and eventually produced, in the middle of the 16th century, a sparkling wine. This was a formidable achievement for a region long known for the production of red wine and a major source of controversy, since it predated Dom Perignon's achievements by more than 100 years. The novelty made the wine widely known (four dozen bottles of Blanquette de Limoux were discovered in Thomas Jefferson's cellar after his death), but because transportation costs to the more affluent urban centers of northern France proved formidable, the wine and its reputation languished under the more popular sparkling wines of Champagne and the Loire valley. By the time the *phylloxera* epidemic struck the region, production of Blanquette had become a minor cottage industry, long forgotten by the consumer, and its notoriety lapsed into a curious historical footnote.

Today the Blanquette de Limoux area is a sizable, 2,500-hectare vineyard producing 100,000 hectoliters of sparkling wine annually. The producing region encompasses forty-two settlements and more than 1,000 growers, and is the third-largest sparkling wine–producing area in the nation. Although it was historically a predominantly red wine region, the local vignerons began replanting the Mauzac grape after 1920; by 1948 there were 165 hectares of vineland producing a mere 2,100 hectoliters of sparkling wine. Since then, hectarage has doubled every nine years, and output now exceeds 100,000 hectoliters and is expected to approach 200,000 hectoliters over the next twenty years. The syndicate of local vignerons, first formed in 1929, proved so successful that the producing region was delimited soon after; AOC status was awarded in 1938. Recently, 3,200 hectares were authorized for future plantings, thereby raising the total potential hectarage to nearly 6,000.

The producing region lies midway between Atlantic and Mediterranean climatic influences. Winters are mild and rainy, while summers are sunny, dry, and hot. The soil, derived from limestone, is very porous and unproductive for most agricultural crops except the hardy vine; the two most important historic crops of the region, prunes and wheat, are slowly declining in favor of vine cultivation. The altitude of the vineyards varies between 150 and 350 meters; the north-facing slopes are wooded with vineyards mainly confined to southerly, well-exposed locations. Of the forty-one villages and hamlets in the appellation, most are located immediately to the north and south of Limoux, with Pomas, Pieusse, Cournanel, and Roquetaillade the most important.

Blanquette de Limoux, a "Blanc de Blancs," is made from three white grapes—Mauzac, Chenin Blanc, and Chardonnay—with the former dominating the blend. It is an extraordinary sparkling wine with a delicate flavor, a pronounced bouquet and a lovely pale color. Although it can be full-bodied, well flavored, and fruity with a persistent mousse, it often lacks the zest, refreshing crispness, and the "chalky-yeasty" flavor of first-rate Champagne. But since it is consistently well made and is moderately priced, it offers excellent value. The wine owes its distinctive flavor, aroma, and bouquet to the Mauzac, a grape that produces small berries and grape clusters, has high sugar levels, and ripens early. The vine does particularly well in the limestone soils of the region and produces an above-average and highly distinctive wine that has caught the imagination of the consumer. One-third of all Mauzac vines in France are planted in the Limoux vineyard, where it contributes as much as 85 percent of the final blend. The recent arrival of Chardonnay (historically Mauzac was mixed with Clairette) now accounts for approximately 5 percent of the blend; it imparts firmness, acidity, and finesse. Ten percent of the blend is Chenin Blanc for both fruit and tartness.

Appellation legislation restricts yields to 40 hectoliters per hectare and the minimum alcohol content to 9 percent; and the first 100 liters of pressed must is derived from 150 kilograms of grapes. The wine is essentially made by the same process as Champagne, with fermentation lasting up to three weeks in stainless steel and under temperature-controlled conditions. The minimum amount of aging on the lees is twelve months; luxury cuvées receive a much longer contact period. It is made only white and in Brut, Demi-Brut, Demi-Doux, and Doux styles. Within the appellation, a still and dry "Limoux Nature" is also made, but is not the equal of Blanquette. While a small but growing number of independent producers exist, more than 90 percent of all Blanquette is made by the local cooperative—*Producteurs de Blanquette de Limoux.* Founded in 1946, it has become the largest sparkling wine cooperative in the nation, and its modern, efficient, and well-organized management team has maintained high quality standards. Exports of Blanquette rose from fewer than 100,000 bottles in 1973 to 2 million in 1985; by 1995

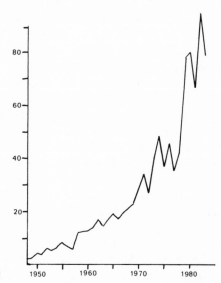

Figure 9.4   Blanquette de
Limoux: Wine Production,
1948–1982
(in thousands of hectoliters)

more than 3.5 million bottles will probably be exported. Another, smaller cooperative in Limoux produces fresh, zesty wine that offers good value.

Clairette du Languedoc

Clairette du Languedoc, a dry white wine (small quantities of semi-sweet wine also exist) made from the Clairette grape, originates from a group of fourteen villages along the middle course of the Hérault River. This comparatively small, 13,000-hectoliter appellation covers the hilly regions of the Soubergues, in particular the villages of Paulhan, Adissan, Fontès, Péret, Ceyras, Pézenas, Cabrières, Aspiran, and Brignac. Except for one small section around the village of Montagnac, the 300-hectare region, widely diffused within a much larger red wine–producing area, lies entirely along the left bank of the Hérault River north of Pézenas. Annual production fluctuates between 12,000 and 16,000 hectoliters, a figure that has doubled in the past twenty years, and because more than 1,000 additional hectares have been authorized for production, the prognosis for continued growth is optimistic. Although recently improved, the wine has a marked tendency to oxidize rapidly. It resembles Clairette-de-Bellegarde but is not quite as good. More than three-quarters of production is made by the cooperative *Les Vignerons du Ceressou.* Two private producers of note are *Ch. de la Condamine Bertrand* and *Ch. St.-André.*

Lying along the right bank of the Hérault, outside the eastern margins of the Clairette du Languedoc appellation, is the superb *Mas de Daumas-Gassac* estate. This unlikely location is the site of an expertly made red wine with unbelievable richness, concentrated flavor, and intense bouquet. The vineyard, 200 meters in elevation, is sited on well-drained soil planted in Pinot Noir, Cabernet Franc, Cabernet Sauvignon, Merlot, Malbec, Syrah, and Tannat. The vines grow without benefit of chemical fertilizers or pesticides, the grapes are hand-selected, fermentation is long and slow, eighteen months of Allier wood-aging follows. The resulting wine is absolutely stunning, reliable, dark in color, dense, and tannin-rich. Because of the estate's location, the wine is sold as a *vin de pays,* yet it offers outstanding value and is a must for the serious cellar. *Dne. de Capion* is another excellent property.

Clairette de Bellegarde

Clairette de Bellegarde is a gold-colored, full-bodied, fruity, alcoholic wine made entirely from Clairette grapes. The appellation's 60 hectares are located on a tiny outcrop of limestone located between the southern margins of the Costières-du-Gard vineyard and the Canal du Rhône a Sète. Although the wine is dry and moderately scented, it must be consumed before its second birthday because it is subject to rapid oxidation and marred by excessive bitterness. While nearly all the wine is made by the local cooperative, *Dne. de l'Amerine* and *Dne. St.-Louis-la-Perdrix* enjoy a good reputation.

Coteaux du Languedoc

Coteaux du Languedoc (recently elevated to AOC status) is a broad, loosely defined, widely dispersed red wine region of eleven appellations that stretches from the outskirts of Narbonne to the left bank of the Vidourle River near Nîmes. It occupies wind-swept coastal areas and interior denuded "moors" and hills, once known as "septimanie," easily defended points of higher elevation. As a result, they attracted ancient Greeks and Romans, and since then a host of invading armies, particularly Visigoths, Arabs, and Franks. The soils are composed either of schist or limestone, the latter producing softer, more delicate, early maturing wines. The collective hectarage for the eleven appellations approaches 7,500, and annual production varies between 300,000 and 400,000 hectoliters, or approximately 15 percent of all VDQS production. The 1,200 growers belong to cooperatives, who sell more than half of the finished wine to negociants. Less than 10 percent of all wine is made by private growers, and while very little is exported, this will probably change.

Historically the wines were made from a trinity of grapes—Carignan, Grenache Noir, and Cinsault—with small additions of Terret Noir, Clairette, Picpoul, Malvoisie, and others. To increase quality, the last four have recently decreased in hectarage while Mourvèdre and Syrah have expanded. While Grenache Noir contributes a minimum of 20 percent to the blend, no single variety is allowed to exceed 50 percent of the total; as of 1990, the 10 percent contribution of Mourvèdre and Syrah will be raised to 20 percent. In a further effort to tighten quality control, local appellation authorities have rejected as much as 30 percent of all wine submitted by growers as unsuitable and unworthy of communal appellation standards. Red wine is deeply colored, well flavored, round, and capable of bottle improvement for more than three years.

Located east of Narbonne along the coast, *La Clape* is a 30,000-hectoliter vineyard in the department of Aude. Located on a limestone plateau barely 200 meters high, the vineyard is buffeted by the *Fiera* wind. The appellation makes all three colors, and like all other appellations within the Coteaux du Languedoc designation, the dominant vine is Carignan. When mixed with Syrah and Mourvèdre, it assumes a more supple, fresher character, which despite its assertive and spicy flavor, is consumed young. Because of its excellent location along the tourist route, La Clape is enjoying a wine boom of significant proportions. Approxi-

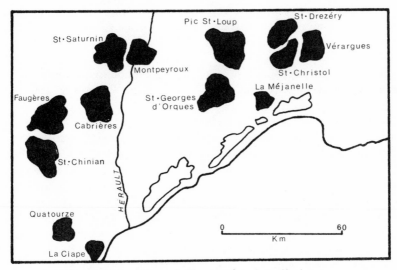

Figure 9.5   Côtes du Languedoc Appellations

mately half of production is made by private producers, all of whom have
little difficulty selling wine directly to the passing motorist. Among the
many private producers, *Dne. des Monges-Schaefer, Dne. de Rivière La Haut,
Ch. de Pech-Redon, Ch. de Pech Celeyran, Ch. de Roquette-sur-Mer, Dne, de
Vires, Ch. de Complazens, Ch. de Ricardelle de la Clape,* and *Dne. de St.-
Pierre-la-Garrigue* are considered above average.

Located north and west of La Clape, *Quatourze,* measuring 6 by 12
kilometers, is a 13,000-hectoliter appellation in the Aude department.
Bounded by a gray and white quartz soil, its wines are deeply colored,
alcoholic, full-bodied, but coarse. Historically strong enough to be
considered true *vins de medicin,* they were shipped north to improve the
feeble light-colored wines of the Rhône and Saône. Although very rustic
when young, the wine benefits greatly from two to three years bottle-
aging. A rare white wine is also made from Malvoisie, Macabeo, Grenache
Blanc, and others. Nearly all the wine of this little-known region is made
by cooperatives. *Cabrières,* a small 7,000-hectoliter appellation, is located
along the left bank of the Hérault River on soil very similar to that of
Faugères, its neighbor to the west. The wine historically had, in addition
to the usual blend of Carignan, Cinsault, and Grenache Noir, a high
percentage of Oeillade, the best of which was named "Vermeil" and had
the aroma and bouquet of ripe grape, thyme, and lavender. While Louis
XIV might have been enthusiastic about it, the wine today is less exotic
and made by *Cave Coopérative Les Coteaux de Cabrières,* a quality-oriented
firm.

Pic-St.-Loup, due north of Montpellier in typical garigue countryside, is, with 38,000 hectoliters, the largest communal appellation. Made from Carignan, Cinsault, Alicante Bouschet, and Oeillade, the wine is light colored but high in alcohol and not the equal of other districts within the Coteaux du Languedoc grouping. The appellation also produces small quantities of a dry, crisp white wine, with a pronounced mineral taste, made from Macabeo, Grenache Blanc, and Clairette. Three large cooperatives with a combined hectarage of nearly 2,000 hectares produce more than 95 percent of the entire output. A charming village with clean streets, *St.-Drézéry* has none of the usual semi-abandoned characteristics of other Midi settlements. Located along the left bank of the Vidourle River, it is contiguous to St.-Christol and Vérargues. Annual production is barely 4,000 hectoliters and often less than 2,500, which is small by Languedoc standards. The wine, made from the usual trinity of Carignan, Cinsault, and Grenache Noir, is light, consumed slightly chilled, and incapable of bottle improvement. The *St.-Christol* vineyard, located on a high bank overlooking the Vidourle River, produces 7,000 hectoliters of dark, vinuous red wine that lacks harmony and suppleness. With an annual production of 20,000 hectoliters, *Vérargues* is the largest of the three northernmost vineyards. The area exhibits some variety, with a decent rosé and a spicy red, but inconsistency unfortunately precludes the establishment of a good reputation. *Coteaux de la Méjanelle* is a 13,000-hectoliter vineyard sandwiched between Etang de Mauguio, Lunel, and Montpellier. Its pebbly red soil is alluvial in origin and similar to the wine-producing regions of the southern Rhône. The red wine, which contains above-average percentages of Mourvèdre, has an excellent aroma, is dark ruby in color, and is surprisingly smooth on the palate. Offering considerable value, the finest label is marketed as "Les Coteaux de la Méjanelles." *Dne. de la Costière, Ch. de Flaugerques* and *Mas de Calage* are three important growths.

St.-Georges-d'Orques, located to the west of Montpellier amid pine and olive trees, is one of the least known of the eleven Coteaux du Languedoc appellations. While the Cinsault-dominated red wine is fruitier than most, this 13,000-hectoliter vineyard does not appear to be growing nor competing effectively with olive production. Two-thirds of output is by the local cooperative; nearly all of it is light, fruity, quite quaffable, and a good value. *Ch. de l'Engarran* is the principal growth with a reputation. *Montpeyroux* is a 12,000-hectoliter vineyard located on friable limestone along the left bank of the Hérault River adjacent to St.-Saturnin. Made primarily (again) from Carignan, Cinsault, and Grenache Noir, it is coarse, high in alcohol, and hot on the palate. While it improves a little with bottle-aging, it does not merit the extra time. *St.-Saturnin,* located on high ground, is locally described as the land of "garlic, thyme, laurel and olive." The appellation produces 16,000 hectoliters of red and rosé wines, both of which have an unusual "truffle" scent and are made from Carignon, Grenache Noir, Syrah, Mourvèdre, and Cinsault, in that order.

Muscat de Frontignan

The Languedoc region of Midi contains four *Vins Doux Naturel* (VDN) appellations—Muscat de Frontignan, Muscat de Lunel, Muscat de Mireval, and Muscat de St.-Jean de Minervois. All four appellations are widely scattered and collectively account for less than 5 percent of all VDN production. All are white, fragrant, and flavorful, but are less fine and delicate than those of Roussillon.

The best known of the four, and one of the oldest, Muscat de Frontignan is the most important VDN appellation of Languedoc. The French satirist Rabelais mentioned it in the 16th century, and numerous French kings, particularly Louis XIV, were especially fond of it. Production today, after a 100-year history of uncertainty, fluctuates between 15,000 and 20,000 hectoliters, or double its pre–World War II output. While the large and heavily mechanized vineyards northeast of Montpellier are located on sand and alluvial pebble, Muscat de Frontignan is situated south of Montpellier on excellent limestone soil. The dominant grape, the Muscat Blanc à Petits Grains, is surrounded by a sea of inferior red grapes producing extremely high yields. The wine has a beautiful gold color and a pronounced bouquet; it is well balanced, surprisingly refreshing and, although sweet, not cloying. Fewer than 500 hectares of grapes are planted, and the entire appellation is an area of middle-sized growers, nearly all of whom belong to neighboring cooperatives. The appellation was first delimited in 1935 and includes the important commune of Vic-la-Gardiole. *Ch. de la Peyrade* is the principal private producer.

Muscat de Lunel

Lunel, midway between Nîmes and Montpellier, is a town of 1,500 people in the midst of a flat, sandy region covered with pebbles. While Grenache, Carignan, Cinsault, Aramon, and Alicante Bouschet dominate hectarage and *vin ordinaire* is the principal wine, the Muscat d'Alexendria, a veritable island in a sea of inferior grapes, produces the finest wine in the area. Output varies between 4,500 and 7,500 hectoliters, and like all other VDN–producing regions, production has been rising steadily over the past forty years. Although its quality is markedly below that of Riversaltes, Banyuls, and Muscat de Frontignan, Lunel seems to compete well. The largest producer, the *Caves Coopératives Muscat de Lunel*, is responsible for nearly the entire output.

Muscat de Mireval

The Muscat de Mireval appellation is a second cousin to its next-door neighbor, Muscat de Frontignan. It is located on soil that contains far less limestone but more sand, pebble, and alluvial material. The wine, although technically sound, offers little value outside the region and is rarely encountered in good restaurants. The largest producer, *Cave de Mireval–Cave de Rabelais,* makes 25,000 cases.

Muscat de St.-Jean-de-Minervois

The smallest of the Midi VDN wines, Muscat de St.-Jean-de-Minervois, is located in a tiny pocket of limestone soil between Minervois and St.-Chinian. The only mountain VDN wine, it is very sweet, delicate, fruity, heady, well balanced, yellow to amber in color, and above average in quality. Although fewer than 150 hectares are devoted to its production, a rise in demand could quickly increase the planting of Muscat vines to cover an area ten times the present planting. The *Caves Coopératives de St.-Jean-de-Minervois* in St.-Chinian is the largest producer, and *Dne. de Barroubio* is the most prominent growth.

Corbières

Corbières, a 40,000-hectare vineyard located in the Aube department, is bounded by Blanquette de Limoux on the west, Roussillon in the south, and along the northern margins by Minervois and the regional capital of Narbonne. Since 1977 it has been the nation's largest VDQS region, with an annual output that varies between 700,000 and 800,000 hectoliters, of which 95 percent is red. Due to governmental programs (outlined earlier), wine production and hectarage have steadily declined: as recently as thirty-five years ago, production exceeded 1.4 million hectoliters, or more than 50 percent greater than present levels of output. The area is one of gentle rolling hills with numerous interior basins that are essentially denuded, leaving only scattered, stunted pine and maquis vegetation. Corbières is very Mediterranean in character with extensive sheep and goat grazing, dispersed vineyards, a low population density, and small, unimportant villages. The western portions are more mountainous, and the numerous streams and rivers are semipermanent. Although the limestone and schistous soils are low in fertility, the very best vineland is sited on reddish-colored limestone soils.

The Corbières appellation consists of three quality producing zones. The coastal area makes the most common Carignan-dominated wine that is widely used for blending purposes. Since 1985, the Carignan grape has been limited to a maximum of 75 percent of the blend, and because the percentage of Mourvèdre and Syrah have increased, wine quality is expected to improve significantly. A better middle zone on higher ground around Lézignan produces darker, fuller wine; since 1985, Carignan has been restricted to 70 percent of its blend. A third zone, widely diffused in the hillier, more isolated interior and western regions of the department, produces the finest "mountain" wines of the appellation. Here the Carignan is restricted to 60 percent of the blend. After Carignan, the second-most-important grape is Cinsault, followed by Aramon, Alicante Bouschet, and Grenache Blanc and Noir. Grape varieties currently increasing in percentage of total hectarage and acting as prime movers in wine improvement are Syrah, Mourvèdre, Merlot, and Cabernet Sauvignon. Because grape varieties vary enormously with the producing district, the quality of the final product varies widely within the appellation. Most wines are early maturing, medium-bodied, dull, often harsh and with an unimpressive aroma. White wine, made from Grenache Blanc, Malvoisie, Macabeo, Muscat, and Picpoul, represents less than 2 percent of total output. Approximately 4 percent of total output is rosé, made primarily from Carignan and Cinsault. Although the producing district is fairly extensive, the largest and most interesting areas of production center around Lézignan, Narbonne, Largrasse, Sigean, Durban, Mouthoumet, Tuchan, Bizanet, Boutenac, Cruissan, Fabrezan, Montséret, Villeneuve, and Cascastel. A large percentage of the total output is destined for the vermouth industry.

Corbières is classic "paysan" country of nearly 5,000 small growers, 90 percent of whom belong to the ubiquitous village cooperative. Of the 134 cooperatives in the department, approximately 40 are located in the Corbières VDQS–producing region. The majority are modest in size, and the largest are located in Bizanet, Paziols, Portel, Durban, and Cascastel. Among the many growths, *Dne. de Lastours, Ch. les Palais, Dne. de Montjoie, Ch. de Bouguignan, Ch. de Quilhanet, Ch. de Beauregard, Prieuré de St.-Amans, Dne. de St.-Maurice, Ch. des Ollieux, Ch. la Tour Fabrezan, Dne. de la Voulte Gasparet, Dne. de Villemajou, Ch. le Bouis, Ch. de Nouvelles, Ch. de Montredon, Ch. de Vaugelas, Ch. de Pech Latt,* and *Ch. de Caraguilhes* are considered important.

Costières du Gard

Located just south of Nîmes, Costières-du-Gard, another VDQS appellation with more than 3,500 hectares, is second in size to Corbières. It is a 175,000-hectoliter red, rosé and white wine-producing region that makes below average to mediocre wines. The principal red grape varieties are Carignan, Terret Noir, Cinsault, Mourvèdre, and Grenache Noir. White wine is made from Picpoul, Ugni Blanc, Macabeo, Marsanne, and Roussanne. All wines are coarse, high in alcohol, and easily oxidized, and thereby offer little value. Nearly the entire output is made by five medium-sized cooperatives. Six large private properties with average to above-average reputations are *Ch. de la Tuilerie, Mas de la Tardive, Dne. St.-Louis-la-Perdrix, Dne. de l'Amarine, Ch. Belle-Coste,* and *Ch. de Campuget.*

Picpoul de Pinet

Picpoul de Pinet is a small, 10,000-hectoliter dry white wine region located between Pézenas and Bassin de Thau. This little-known white wine, made primarily from Picpoul, enjoys a well established local reputation and is in the process of hectarage expansion. But despite its lightness and delicate flavor, excessive oxidation is a constant problem. Nearly all of production is made by several cooperatives.

Other Wine-Producing Areas

As well as the AOC and VDQS appellations discussed above, Languedoc supports 62 *vin de pays* regions with an annual output of at least 20 million hectoliters. Within this large group, the three largest in terms of production are Coteaux de Peyriac, Golfe du Lion, and Collines de la Moure. Of the four, the Golfe du Lion region, located mainly in the Camargue, is perhaps the most interesting. The Camargue is a substantial, flat sand dune region largely covered with salt marsh, lagoon, and unstable beach. With nearly half of its total area protected as state land, its primary uses are the grazing of bulls, wild horses, sheep, and the production of wild lavender, thyme, mint, and flowers. The Camargue is located south and east of Arles, the first significant city west of Marseille and known for its Roman artifacts and the ghost of Van Gogh. The viticultural holdings are extensive, and well mechanized, and the yields are absolutely colossal. Of the more than thirty different vines grown, Carignan and Aramon are the leading red grapes; Ugni Blanc and Clairette are the dominant whites. With one notable exception, the wines of the region are undistinguished and below *vin de pays* quality. Despite Camargue's long neglect as a viticultural region, more than 4,000 hectares were planted during the decade of the 1880s when it was discovered that sandy soils discourage the growth of the *phylloxera* aphid. The hectarage has since risen to more than 15,000, with approximately 50 percent of all vines planted in sand being ungrafted. Thanks to desalinization techniques, vines are sited today on knolls and old marine terraces whose soil is almost pure sand. Viticulture here was first introduced by a large number of religious orders, and for a short time, the Hospitallers were the largest property owners.

The largest property owner and producer of wine in France today is the well-managed firm of *Domaines Viticoles des Salins du Midi*. The company was in the salt business in Sète in 1956, when it began purchasing sand dunes. It now cultivates more than 2,000 hectares distributed over eight large vineyards—six in Languedoc and two in Provence. The grapes are scientifically grown and mechanically harvested, and vinification techniques are the product of state-of-the-art technology. In addition to "meridional" grapes, the firm has introduced all the "noble" grapes of Burgundy, the Loire, Alsace, and Bordeaux, thus becoming the single largest owner of Cabernet Sauvignon grapes in the Midi. The principal label is "Listel," a name derived from Ile de Stel ("island of sand"). The firm makes huge quantities (more than 160,000 hectoliters) of varietal,

Plate 9.2   The "sand" vineyards of Domaines Viticoles
des Salins du Midi

blended, table, sparkling, and dessert wines whose quality is well above average for the region. The principal properties are *Dne. de Jarras, Dne. du Ch. St-Jean de la Pinede, Mas de la Petite Sylve, Mas de Soult, Mas du Daladel, Dne. du Bosquet, Dne. du Château de Villeroy,* and *Dne. de St.-Louis de la Mer.*

THE WINES OF ROUSSILLON

Southernmost in France, the ancient province of Roussillon (a name derived from the ancient Catalan region Rusilo) lies wholly within the modern department of Pyrenées-Orientales. The jewel of the Midi— hilly, picturesque, with considerable charm and character—it rivals Provence, the middle Loire, and Alsace for panache. The area, which is rich in Catalan culture and history, is filled with uncommon and whimsical towns, customs, and folklore. Salses, for example, contains a remarkable 15th-century geometric fortress; Baixas and Castelnau are two of the most romantic villages in France; and Tautavel contains significant archaeological digs. Centrally located, Perpignan was for a time the capital of the Spanish kingdom of Majorca, and since 1642 of Roussillon as well. It boasts a medieval merchant's exchange, a fair-sized Gothic cathedral, and a 14th-century royal palace. Perpignan sits in the center of the growing fruit and tourist industry and is the department's principal wine center.

The entire province, lying south and west of the Aude River, consists of an upland, hilly countryside bordered by a coastal plain enclosed on three sides by hills and mountains. To the north lies the Corbières region, an area of few cities; along the western boundary, the beautiful Canigou Mountain rises to heights greater than 2,800 meters. On the south, the Spanish Pyrenées extend into France with cork, scrub oak, maquis, and breathtaking scenery. The topography is deeply incised by three semi-permanent, east-flowing rivers: the Tech, Tet, and Agly, all important in the production of wine and deciduous fruit. About two-thirds of all vineyards are located along the eastern margins of the department, the Riveraltes producing region alone having 10,000 hectares, or nearly one-fifth of departmental total.

The distinctly Mediterranean climate is influenced by three regional winds. The *Tramontane,* the most common, is cold, dry, bitterly uncomfortable, and often violent. It accentuates the evaporation of moisture from the soil and hastens the transpiration of moisture from biotic matter,

Table 9.5   AOC Wine Production in the Department of
Pyrenées-Orientales, 1980

Appellation	Hectoliters	Percent
Côtes du Roussillon Rouge	194,060	20.1
Côtes du Roussillon Blanc	7,640	.8
Côtes du Roussillon–Villages Rouge	74,119	7.7
Collioure	2,210	.2
Vins Doux Naturels (VDN)		
Riversaltes Rouge	39,680	4.1
Riversaltes Blanc	456,672	47.4
Muscat de Riversaltes Blanc	95,490	10.0
Maury Rouge	47,316	4.9
Banyuls Grand Cru Rouge	7,701	.8
Banyuls Rouge	38,136	4.0
Grand Roussillon Rouge	140	
Grand Roussillon Blanc		
Total AOC wine production	963,164	100.0

Source: French Ministry of Agriculture.

thus increasing the incidence of aridity as measured by evaporation rates. The *Marinada,* a hot, humid air mass blowing in summer and fall, promotes disease; the *Grec* or *Gargal,* blowing from the northeast, is cold and humid. The summer drought plus the severity of the regional wind patterns creates unpredictable and extreme seasonal climatic patterns unlike in any other area in the south of France. Approximately 60 percent of the entire department is scattered forest of scrub pine, oak, and maquis, and less than 36 percent of the entire land area is cultivated. Forty percent of all arable land is planted in vines, 30 percent in fruit trees, and the remainder in wheat, olives, and vegetable truck farms. Along higher elevations, transhumance activities are still common, although not as widespread as they once were. Despite a history of chronic outmigration, the department exhibits a more prosperous picture than portions of the Midi farther north.

The evolution of vine hectarage over the past 136 years is shown in Figure 9.6, which indicates steady growth prior to 1880 and severe declines after the *phylloxera* epidemic, the first decade of the 20th century, and the world economic depression of the 1930s. The post–1950 decline in hectarage from 69,000 to the present level of 53,000 is directly attributed to the steady phasing-out of inferior vineland and the higher yields attained in the better AOC producing regions. While total hectarage over the past 100 years has been reduced by half, output has nearly doubled. It is interesting to note that the Pyrenées-Orientales department is the fourth-largest vinegrowing department of Languedoc-Roussillon: wine production is about 30 percent that of Gard, 35 percent of Aude, and about 20 percent of Hérault. The department, containing 93 cooperatives and 15,000 growers, produces about 2.5 million hectoliters annually. More than three-quarters of total output, made by cooperatives, is consistently well above average by French standards and offers good to excellent value.

Historically, Roussillon was an area of *vin de consummation courante:* wines that were light-colored, moderately alcoholic, sold to the "cafe"

Figure 9.6   Pyrenées-Orientales: Vine Hectarage, 1850–1982
(in thousands of hectares)

trade, and almost all marketed in bulk at rock-bottom prices. The second-most-important category was Vin Doux Naturel (VDN, also called Natural Sweet Wines—NSW), the only AOC wines of the region until the formation of the Côtes du Roussillon appellation in 1977. The third type of wine was *vin de medicin,* a strong red wine that was the prime ingredient for Byrrh and Dubonnet production. Two-thirds to three-quarters of today's total output of nearly 1 million hectoliters of AOC wine is VDN wine, the staple wine of the region. Although production doubled during the past fifty years, its share of AOC output is expected to double again over the next thirty. Even more impressive than VDN production in the department is the current success of red, rosé, and white Côtes du Roussillon and Côtes du Roussillon–Villages, whose combined output is expected to jump from one-quarter to about half of total AOC output by 1995. While Roussillon no longer produces VDQS wine, it does have four important *vins de pays:* Catalan, Côtes Catalanes, Val d'Agly, and Coteaux Fenouillèdes. The last two, located in the high reaches of the Tet and Agly valleys, are much the better and may become AOC districts in the near future.

Historically, the sweet and dry wines of Roussillon were characterized by excessive aging and oxidation, thus acquiring what the Spanish call a *rancio* flavor and bouquet—features that are culturally acquired and not currently in favor with the international community. The wines were often unbalanced and poorly colored, and the heavy additions of sulfur acted as a major impediment to aroma and bouquet development. During the past twenty years, however, stainless steel, controlled low-tempera-ture carbonic maceration, and quicker and better crushing methods, coupled with the technical ability to reduce both the incidence of oxidation and the necessity for high-sulfur additions, have done much to improve quallity of both dry and sweet wines. Table wines in particular are now fuller and fresher on the palate, better balanced, much fruitier, and devoid of the pronounced *rancio* flavor and odor. As a result, Roussillon is now responsible for more than three-quarters of all AOC wine in the Midi and is widely recognized as the quality wine region of Mediterranean France.

Four principal grape varieties account for 88 percent of the planted area. In descending order they are Carignan Noir, Grenache Blanc, Grenache Noir, and Macabeo. Two Muscats—the Muscat Blanc à Petits Grains and Muscat d'Alexandria—account for another 7 percent. White grapes, constituting 40 percent of the total hectarage, are used almost entirely for the production of sweet wine. Various Muscats, Grenache Noir and Blanc, Malvoisie, Macabeo, Mourvèdre (also known as Mataro, its Spanish name), and Aramon were the traditional grapes of Roussillon. But as the Mourvèdre and Aramon failed to make good dessert wine and did not graft well after the *phylloxera* epidemic, their prominence has been significantly reduced. With time, Carignan Noir became the most

Table 9.6   Major Grape Varieties in the Department of Pyrenées-Orientales,
1968 and 1979

Grape variety	1968 Hectares	Percent[a]	1969 Hectares	Percent[a]	Percent of national total
Carignan Noir	35,400	53.1	22,900	40.3	11
Grenache Blanc	11,000	16.4	12,000	21.1	75
Grenache Noir	8,800	13.2	8,200	14.4	11
Macabeo	5,200	7.7	6,200	10.9	89
Muscat d'Alexandria			2,900	5.1	94
Muscat Blanc à Petits Grains	1,000	1.6	1,200	2.1	59
Carignan Blanc	600	.9	600	1.1	
Aramon	2,400	3.6	500	.9	
Cinsault	100	.1	300	.5	
Syrah			300	.5	
Alicante Bouschet	300	.5	200	.4	
Morrastel Bouschet	900	1.3	100	.2	
Others	1,100	1.6	1,400	2.5	
Totals	66,800	100.0	56,800	100.0	

[a]Percent of departmental total.

Source: French Ministry of Agriculture.

important grape for the production of dry red wine, and the Macabeo for
the production of dry white wine. It is interesting to note the high
percentages of specific grape varieties in terms of their national distribution in the department of Pyrenées-Orientales today: 89 percent for
Macabeo, 94 percent for Muscat d'Alexandria; 75 percent for Grenache
Blanc, and 59 percent for Muscat Blanc à Petits Grains. The principal
grape, Carignan Noir, showed a dramatic drop in hectarage during the
last intercensus period, and its current share of total national plantings is
only 11 percent. Fifty years ago the Carignan Noir acccounted for nearly
four-fifths of total hectarage, but since the formation of the AOC Côtes du
Roussillon appellation, its share is expected to decline still further.
Varieties on the rise at the expense of Carignan Noir are Grenache Noir,
Cinsault, Syrah, Cabernet Sauvignon, and Merlot.

Côtes du Roussillon and Côtes du Roussillon–Villages

The Côtes du Roussillon VDQS appellation was formed in 1972 as a
union for three existing appellations: Roussillon des Aspres, Corbières du
Roussillon, and Corbières Supérieures du Roussillon. It was elevated to
AOC status in 1977 and subdivided into Côtes du Roussillon and Côtes
du Roussillon–Villages. Starting from a modest output of 20,000 hectoliters in 1978, production steadily increased to 280,000 in 1980, and by
1995 is expected to reach at least 500,000 hectoliters. The officially
delimited area includes portions of the coastal terraces, the north bank of

the Agly valley from Perpignan to St.-Paul-de-Fenouillet, both banks of the Tet, and all the Maury appellation, including the broad undulating plateau of Aspres and Thuir and the rugged foothills of the Alberes Mountains overlooking the torrential Tech River. The rocky and pebbly soils are derived from schist, limestone and slate, and are so dry they are commonly referred to as the "earth of Aspres" to emphasize the hard growing conditions. Although the upper highland areas receive more than 600 mm of rain, lowland sections receive half that amount, a good portion of which runs off the hard surface and never reaches the vine roots. Unless picked slightly "green," grapes tend to wither on the vine, which encourages the development of the peculiar *rancio* flavor of Roussillon wines. Although the appellation lacks physical homogeneity in terms of geology and climate, its raison d'être lies only in its landscape of rock, pine, and stunted oak, and in its individual winemakers who want to improve the quality of the dry red, rosé, and white wines of the region.

The two appellations account for at least 25 percent of all AOC wine— all of it dry, more than 95 percent red, 3 percent rosé, with only minor amounts of white. Red and rosé wines are made from a base of Carignan, a grape that does exceptionally well in the hilly and stony regions of the Roussillon uplands. Historically it contributed betweeen 80 and 95 percent of the total blend, and nearly 100 percent in the slate soils of Caramany, Latour de France, Montner, and Monastir. At present, it is limited to 70 percent of the blend, and by the end of the decade will be reduced to 50 percent. The second-most-immportant grape is the Grenache Noir, followed by Cinsault and Lladoner Pelut, an obscure vine related to Grenache Noir. While Mourvèdre, Syrah, and Macabeo are collectively restricted to 70 percent among the secondary grouping, Cabernet Sauvignon and Merlot (limited to 10 percent) are expected to increase in the near future.

Red wine is brilliant ruby in color, very fruity, and surprisingly round in flavor. More than half is made in the "new method," which is to say the "Beaujolais style," a wine not too dissimilar from the authentic version except that it is drier and more austere on the palate. The very best, however, contains only a small portion of wine fermented by carbonic maceration; the bulk is made by more traditional means and aged in wood for at least six months, and as a consequence is more complex, fuller in body, darker in color, tannin-rich, firm on the palate, and capable of extended bottle improvement. Markedly improved in recent years, Côtes du Roussillon rosé, made primarily from Cinsault and Carignan with small infusions of Grenache Noir, is fruity and dry. The very best comes from the "rosé town" of Rasigueres on the north bank of the Agly River. Côtes du Roussillon Blanc, made only from slightly green Macabeo grapes to assure high acid levels, is fresh, often tart, flavorful, and alcoholic.

Côtes du Roussillon–Villages, restricted to the production of red wine only, is one-third the size of the larger Côtes du Roussillon appellation and differs significantly in a number of key elements. Minimum alcohol is increased from 11 percent to 12 percent, while the yield is reduced from 50 to 45 hectoliters to the hectare. In addition, the Villages appellation regulates vine density and pruning methods, and mandates that at least 60 percent of all grapes be vinified by the carbonic maceration method. Furthermore, while the regional syndicate refuses appellation status for 15 percent of all Côtes du Roussillon wine, it rejects 20 percent of all samples submitted for Villages status. As a result, the Côtes du Roussillon–Villages appellation has generated a reputation for the production of the finest and most reliable dry red wine in the entire Midi (although there are formidable arguments in favor for Minervois and some Corbières). When compared with the regional appellation, the Villages wine is darker in color, displays greater concentration of flavor, aroma, and body, and matures between three and six years, or twice as long as the regional wine. Not only is the wine assertive, chewy, and extremely palatable, but it often offers extraordinary value.

The Côtes du Roussillon–Villages appellation is confined to the highland region between the Tet River and the northern boundary of the Roussillon department. It is limited to twenty-six villages, the most important of which are Caramany, Latour-de-France, Cassagne, Montner, Monastir, Estagel, and Planèzes. Approximately 10 percent of all Côtes du Roussillon and Villages wine is consumed within the region, 60 percent in the rest of France, and the remainder, in ever-increasing quantities, in Belgium, Holland, West Germany, the United Kingdom, and the United States.

More than forty cooperatives produce Côtes du Roussillon and Villages wine, nearly all of which have special arrangements with larger firms engaged in national and overseas distribution. The Latour-de-France cooperative, for example, has had a very profitable and progressive relationship with the Nicolas firm to supply above-average wine at modest prices. While cooperative quality standards appear to be above average, those of Baixas, Tautavel, Maury, Estagel, Montner, St.-Paul-de-Fenouillet, Cassagnes, Latour-de-France, and Caramany are particularly good. The largest producer is *Groupement Intercoopératif Aspres Roussillon,* a powerful syndicate of vignerons and cooperatives encompassing 4,271 growers and fourteen cooperatives controlling more than 7,500 hectares in 32 communes. Of the more than 150 major private producers, the following are the most important: *Ch. Cap de Fouste, Dne. St.-Luc, Chais de l'Oratoire, Dne. de Montcalm, Société Cazes Frères, Ch. d'Avallrich, Calvet-Marty, Bella Vista, Dne. de la Canterrane, Dne. de la Casenove, Dne. de la Clos St.-Georges, Cave Cremadeils, Mouilin de Breuil, Ch. de Valmy, Ch. Fontes, Dne. de Canterrane, Ch. l'Esparrou, Illiberis, Jaubert-Noury, Boudau, Henry Limouzy, Dne. Sarda-Malet,* and *Dne. St.-Luc.*

Collioure

North of Port-Vendres the coastal village of Collioure is part of the Banyuls vineyard. It is famous for its unique church, anchovies and, since 1970, its fashionable tourist clientèle. It also produces a dry red wine that is the complete antithesis of sweet Banyuls and the other VDN wines that dominate Roussillon. Despite having acquired its AOC status in 1949, only 60 hectares of vineland produce 2,000 hectoliters of full-bodied, well-flavored, tannin-rich wine that ages well but unfortunately has yet to captivate the attention of the outside world. Made from a variable mixture of Mourvèdre, Grenache Noir, Carignan Noir, and Syrah, it contains between 12 percent and 13 percent alcohol and is aged in oak for at least nine months. Not only is the wine distinctive, but it offers excellent value and has the potential for considerable growth. *Celliers des Templiers* and *Dne. du Mas Blanc* both produce excellent wine.

The Vins Doux Naturels (VDN) Wines of Roussillon

France produces a large quantity of Vin Doux Naturel—700,000 to 800,000 hectoliters annually, of which 95 percent is produced in the department of Pyrenées-Orientales. Approximately 82 percent is white, the remainder red and rosé, with the latter the least important of the three. VDN wine is made from overripe grapes and the addition of 196-proof ethyl alcohol to amplify overall alcohol levels to as much as 22 percent, the objective being the maintenance of high unfermented sugar levels and wine preservation. Depending on the desired character of the final product, the wine can be made sec (dry and very rare), demi-sec (semi-dry and equally rare), semi-doux (semi-sweet and more common), or doux (sweet and the most common). VDN wine differs from Vins de Liqueur (VDL), which is nothing more than sweet grape must with added alcohol (also called *mistelle*) without the benefit of fermentation, used in the making of aperitifs. With its output amounting to less than 20,000 hectoliters, VDL is not up to the quality levels of VDN and does not enjoy the benefit of classified status.

Historically, the important wines of Roussillon were all VDN, and like many others emanating from the Mediterranean, high in alcohol and very popular in central and northern Europe. For a short time they imitated the wines of Oporto, but eventually declined in the international marketplace either because of politics, fraudulent practices, and/or changing consumer preferences. The *rancio*-flavored wines, widely admired in the region and throughout southern France, are particularly disliked in foreign markets, hence their limited appeal abroad. The export apex for this wine occurred from 1890 to 1917, when more than 400,000 hectoliters of VDN wine were exported, mostly to Russia as a less expensive alternative to Sauternes. Today, more than 90 percent of production is consumed within France. Despite the apparent demise of sweet wine (with the possible exceptions of Oporto and Sherry), production of VDN wine has doubled within the past fifty years, and its growth momentum is expected to continue in the near future. Chilled, it makes an excellent aperitif, and when well made and aged it offers considerable value compared to other sweet and/or fortified wines. More than 90 percent of all VDN is made by the ten leading cooperatives in Roussillon. The largest-selling VDN in foreign markets is white Rivesaltes, particularly the Muscat, followed by Banyuls.

For more than three centuries four main grape varieties have dominated the production of sweet Roussillon wine: Grenache, several Muscats, Macabeo, and Malvoisie, all of which constitute at least 90 percent of the planted hectarage. Secondary grapes, primarily Carignan Noir and Blanc, are grown in Banyuls and Maury; while Mauzac, well adapted in limestone soils, blends very well with Grenache, Macabeo, and Alicante Bouschet. The dominant grapes in the production of red and rosé VDN are Grenache Noir, Gris, and Blanc. Considered the oldest, Grenache Noir is most evident in Maury and Banyuls, where it yields wine with an excellent bouquet. Grenache Gris, well adapted in Maury, Banyuls, and the hillier portions of the department, enjoys high yields, but the quality of the wine is less than ideal. Grenache Blanc, a very vigorous vine, has adapted well to the dry, arid climate of the Agly valley and the Rivesaltes region. Of the many Muscats grown, the Muscat d'Alexandria, with the highest concentration on the limestone soils of Rivesaltes, is widely considered the finest for the production of white VDN. Perhaps the oldest of all the four primary grapes, it dates back to the time of the early Greeks. While it is very fragrant, sweet, and flavorful, it oxidizes easily and hence is subject to heavy sulfuring. In Rivesaltes, the intensely scented wine leaves a clean, fresh taste on the palate. It ages well for five years, but beyond that it turns brown and its aroma diminishes rapidly. If the winemaker can preserve freshness and aroma, the finished product is delicate and quite memorable.

The Malvoisie, along with the Muscat, came from Greece 2,000 years ago. It is found in the Côte d'Agly but does not appear to be well distributed in the rest of Roussillon. Although there are many types, the best is the early ripening white berry that resists fungus diseases and has adapted well on limestone and sandy soils. It ages well and has a pronounced aroma but tends to develop strong *rancio* flavors, and hence is less important now than in the past. Like the Grenache and a host of other grapes, the Macabeo, also of Spanish origin, was once limited only to the Côtes d'Agly region. It is the same grape that is used in the production of the famed "cooked" wine of Malaga, but in Roussillon it is responsible for a good deal of the best dry, white wine. There are two major types, both of which yield well: large and small berry, the former considered better in the production of VDN and the latter in the production of table wine very similar to Ugni Blanc. Because both types resist dry, dessicating winds, their alcohol levels are often quite high. When judiciously mixed with Mauzac, the Macabeo adds finesse, softness, and balance to all VDN wines.

The color of VDN wine can be white, rosé, or red, the latter usually slightly less sweet than the white but fuller and heavier on the palate. White VDN, especially when made from 100 percent Muscat, has a beautiful color and is more delicate. For all three colors, in the absence of a prescribed formula the final product varies with the producer and local tradition. At their best, they are all rich, with multiple layers of fruity aroma and flavor superimposed on varying degrees of *rancio* flavor and bouquet, the latter more common in red than white VDN wine. The key to quality production today rests on the ability of the winemaker to limit the amount of oxidation and maintain sufficiently high acid levels to balance sweetness. Finally, the proper timing of spirit application appears to have a decided effect on the preservation of the delicate bouquet, primarily in the production of Muscat-dominated VDN.

Rivesaltes

Although the wine is named after the important and imposing medieval fortified town of Rivesaltes, it can originate from a wide area on both sides of the Agly and Tet rivers (see Fig. 9.7). The producing region and its 11,000 hectares consist of 86 villages within the department of Pyrenées-Orientales and nine others in the department of Aude. The producing region is essentially limited to non-schistous and slate soils containing limestone and quartz, which are reddish in color, rich in potassium, but low in phosphorous—pedologic features decidedly different from Banyuls and Maury.

The huge, 500,000-hectoliter output, representing more than 72 percent of all VDN hectarage and production, is the product of rather low yields. Despite its large production and long, varied history, the wine is mainly consumed in France and has long been forgotten in foreign markets. Red Rivesaltes, with a beautiful red-gold color that changes to an equally engaging tawny color with age, is a light-weight imitation of Banyuls and nothing more. It is based on Grenache Noir and contains small amounts of Macabeo; unlike Banyuls, it is also laced with Muscat. The rosé has an enticing color but is not as sweet as the red and white. White Rivesaltes, by far the most important, is made from a more limited number of grape varieties than the red or rosé. Although the Grenache Blanc and Macabeo dominate, the wine is a weak sister to, and less expensive than, the superior Muscat de Rivesaltes.

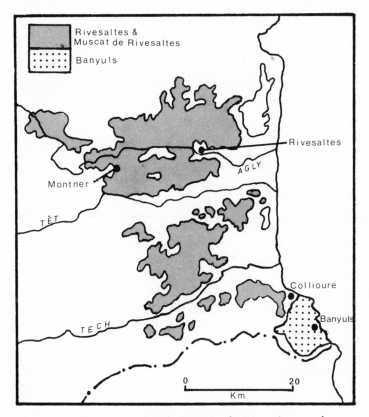

Figure 9.7   Rivesaltes, Muscat de Rivesaltes, and
Banyuls Apellations

Muscat de Rivesaltes

Muscat de Rivesaltes is the second-largest VDN appellation. Although
the name "Rivesaltes" is used, the appellation encompasses superior
limestone sites and the vines are limited to white Muscats. The appellation contains 5,000 hectares and produces 100,000 hectoliters of excellent wine. Although the producing region is widespread, the two areas
with an established reputation for above-average wine are Rivesaltes and
Baixas.

The color of the very best bottles is always a beautiful golden yellow,
the bouquet is penetrating, and the taste is rich, full, and satisfying. It is
the only VDN that can be sold during the year of its production, because
it is at its best when aroma and acid levels are fresh. Contrary to
prevailing opinion about the demise of sweet wines, the output of Muscat
de Rivesaltes has tripled since 1945, and although it is widely considered
a "lesser" wine than Banyuls and Muscat de Frontignan, it remains the

most popular Muscat in France. The most popular brand, "Aphroditis," is a wine with a superb gold color that is well scented, not overly sweet, and rich and luscious on the palate. It is aged in oak for 18 months and offers excellent value. Of the private producers, *Boudau, Ch. de Caladroy, Dne. de Garria, Cazes Frères, Mas de la Garrigue, Ch. de Jau,* and *Ch. de Rey* all make excellent VDN.

Banyuls and Grand Cru Banyuls

Located on the Spanish border and bounded by the Mediterranean Sea, two rivers, and the Pyrenées, the 2,600-hectare Banyuls vineyard is the southernmost viticultural region in France. The appellation takes its name from the quaint red-tiled village of 2,000 inhabitants perched on a hillside overlooking the Mediterranean Sea. Although the modern vineyard was first delimited in 1909 and AOC status awarded only in 1936, wine has been produced along a 25-kilometer stretch of the Mediterranean coast since early Carthaginian times. The production of sweet wine in the Cyprian manner first occurred in the 13th century with the arrival of the Templars from the eastern Mediterranean. The appellation includes only four communes with the right to produce grapes used to make Banyuls: Cerbère, Port-Vendres, Banyuls, and Collioure. Although hectarage is substantially higher than that in the Maury vineyard, low yields restrict production in most years to levels below Maury's, thus placing the Banyul appellation fourth in the hierarchy of production (Banyuls has 9 percent of VDN hectarage but produces only 6 percent of its output).

The dark schistous rock, heavily fissured to allow excellent root penetration, allows only a thin layer of soil to accumulate on the surface. Assembled into narrow terraces facing the Mediterranean and sheltered from westerly and northerly winds, the amphitheater-shaped hillsides accentuate hot and dry climatic conditions that increase grape berry sugar levels. The yields per hectare are rarely more than 20 and often as low as 8 hectoliters to the hectare.

Its small size notwithstanding, Banyuls is the best-known of all VDN Roussillon wines and the one most likely to be encountered in smart restaurants through southern France. It is made primarily from Grenache Noir, with varying additions of Grenache Blanc, Malvoisie, and Macabeo (the aromatic Mauzac is now disallowed). Because the blend is not standardized, the color of the finished product varies significantly by producer. The very best is dark, extremely fragrant, highly concentrated in extract and flavor, and with age assumes a *rancio* flavor that is the hallmark of a good Banyuls, although its intensity in recent years has been reduced. One last feature that sets it apart from its neighbors to the north is its propensity to maintain higher-than-normal acid levels, a characteristic that adds immense balance and durability. The unfortified version of the wine was widely known to the popes of Avignon in the 14th century and was very popular throughout France during the 18th and 19th centuries.

The designation "Banyuls Grand Cru" indicates an appellation superior to plain Banyuls: it is made from at least 75 percent (and sometimes 100 percent) Grenache Noir grapes that contain a much larger percentage of dehydrated grape berries from the lowest yielding sites, and only in selected vintages. Moreover, it is aged for a minimum of thirty months instead of the conventional twelve, contains at least 18 percent alcohol, and is always vintage-dated. As a consequence, it is the VDN wine in Roussillon with the highest concentration of aroma, bouquet, flavor, and balance, and the most expensive to produce. Banyuls also produces a dry red and rosé, principally from Grenache Noir, but these are inferior to the solid table wine made within the commune borders of Collioure.

The serene, magnificently landscaped countryside of Banyuls, with its pine, olive, scrub oak, lavender, and rosemary hills, is a vineyard of small growers. Of the 1,200 growers, only 18 exploit more than 10 hectares, and the largest 250 produce more than 50 percent of all grapes. This is easy to understand, since the entire vineyard is terraced and the more inaccessible sites are apt to be abandoned. There are nine cooperatives in the region, five of which have joined together to form the "Templars" brand, responsible for 95 percent of all Banyuls Grand Cru and 55 percent of all plain Banyuls. Banyuls Templars Vieux, the top-of-the-line label, is a wine aged longer in wood (in the open air) and in bottle prior to release. It is made from 50 percent Grenache Noir, 45 percent Grenache Blanc and Gris, and 5 percent Carignan Noir. The firm also produces 85 percent of all AOC Collioure. Among private producers, *Robert Doutres, Parcé Frères,* and *Dne. du Mas Blanc* all make excellent Banyuls.

Maury

The Maury VDN appellation, located in an isolated area along the north bank of the Agly River, contains between 1,200 and 1,500 hectares of vineland and produces about 45,000 hectoliters of above-average-quality sweet wine annually. Production, like in so many other VDN appellations, has doubled since 1940, and because half of the allocated hectarage is currently in production, the potential to reach the production levels of Muscat de Rivesaltes is within striking range. Its current output, the third highest among VDN–producing regions, represents about 7 percent of all VDN production and 5 percent of total VDN hectarage. Although above average in quality, the wines of this little-known vineyard are rarely encountered in export markets.

The barren countryside, devoid of extensive forest and productive agricultural pursuits, embraces about twelve villages, of which Maury, St.-Paul-de-Fenouillet, and Lesquerde are the most important. The wine that they produce is sweet, dark in color, very similar to Port, and made almost entirely from Grenache Noir. The deep ruby-colored wine, harsh and alcoholic when young, ages well after several years in wood or bottle-aging into a mild, smooth, easily drinkable, mahogany-colored libation that offers excellent value. The schistous soils, skeletal in character and dark in color, contain high potassium and phosphorous levels but rarely yield more than 25 hectoliters to the hectare. In addition to *Les Vignerons de Maury,* the largest producer, *Mas Amiel* and *Jean-Louis Lafage* are two excellent private growers.

Grand Roussillon

Grand Roussillon is a general regional appellation for the lesser VDN wines of Banyuls, Rivesaltes, Maury, and other appellations. Wine quality is below average, output is small and highly variable, and the alcohol level varies between 15 and 21.5 percent.

INDEX

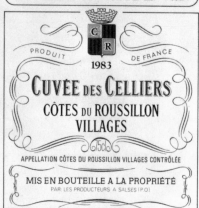

PRODUIT DE FRANCE

1983

CUVÉE DES CELLIERS
CÔTES DU ROUSSILLON
VILLAGES

75cl

APPELLATION CÔTES DU ROUSSILLON VILLAGES CONTRÔLÉE

MIS EN BOUTEILLE A LA PROPRIÉTÉ
PAR LES PRODUCTEURS A SALSES (P.O)

WURMSER

Château de Saint Jean

CÔTES DU RHÔNE
APPELLATION CÔTES DU RHÔNE CONTRÔLÉE

Gabriel Meffre, Propriétaire - Le Plan de Dieu - Travaillan (Vaucluse)

SPÉCIMEN **Château-Chalon**
APPELLATION CONTRÔLÉE

PRODUIT DU CÉLÈBRE VIGNOBLE DE GRAND CRÛ CONSTITUÉ A L'ENTOURS
DE L'ABBAYE DE CHÂTEAU-CHALON au QUATORZIÈME SIÈCLE

62 cl

MIS EN BOUTEILLES PAR
JEAN BOURDY - ARLAY - JURA

N° 16 Modèle Déposé   PRODUCE OF FRANCE

CHATEAU DES BACHELARDS
FLEURIE
APPELLATION FLEURIE CONTROLÉE
Mr. Roger LOMBARD-PLATET · Propriétaire

MIS EN BOUTEILLE PAR **THORIN** F 71570 PONTANEVAUX
Produce of France

LA MOULINE

E.GUIGAL

CÔTE-RÔTIE
APPELLATION "CÔTE-RÔTIE" CONTROLÉE
Elevé et mis en bouteille par
E.GUIGAL. Propriétaire Négociant. Eleveur à AMPUIS (Rhône)

75cl

PRODUCE OF FRANCE   Imp Vacher 69 Caluire